T0333299

THE STRUGGLE FOR INDIA'S SOUL

SHASHI THAROOR

The Struggle for India's Soul

Nationalism and the Fate of Democracy

HURST & COMPANY, LONDON

First published in the United Kingdom in 2021 by
C. Hurst & Co. (Publishers) Ltd.,
83 Torbay Road, London NW6 7DT
© Shashi Tharoor, 2021
All rights reserved.
Printed and bound in Great Britain by Bell and Bain Ltd, Glasgow

The right of Shashi Tharoor to be identified as the author of
this publication is asserted by him in accordance with the
Copyright, Designs and Patents Act, 1988.

Distributed in the United States, Canada and Latin America by
Oxford University Press, 198 Madison Avenue, New York, NY 10016,
United States of America.

A Cataloguing-in-Publication data record for this book
is available from the British Library.

ISBN: 9781787385597

This book is printed using paper from registered sustainable
and managed sources.

www.hurstpublishers.com

For my sons
Ishaan and Kanishk
who have grappled with issues of nationalism
in their lives and work

CONTENTS

CONTENTS

PROLOGUE

A CONGENITAL INDIAN NATIONALIST

The question of nationality and nationhood is not, for me, a purely theoretical issue, the stuff of political philosophy or intellectual argument. It is an intensely personal matter. I was born in London, in 1956, to Indian parents who carried the passports of their newly independent country, just six years after the establishment of the Republic of India. Thanks to the laws prevalent in the United Kingdom, I was eligible from birth for a British passport, an option I have never exercised. The choice remains available: not to make that choice is, therefore, a decision I have consciously taken.

The issue has arisen at various stages of my life. When I won a scholarship to go to graduate school in the United States, at the age of ninteeen, in 1975, I planned to stop in London to visit relatives and friends on the way over. I duly applied for what, in those days, was known as an "entry permit," and settled down in the waiting-room of the British deputy high commission in Calcutta (as it then was) for my turn to pay the requisite fee and collect it. Instead, to my surprise and consternation, I was singled out and summoned to the office of the deputy high commissioner. Wondering what I had done to merit this, I nervously entered the dignitary's enormous office, only to be told, "I'm afraid we can't give you an entry permit."

"What have I done wrong?" I stuttered. "Was there any mistake on my application form?"

"No, not at all," he said with a smile. "You see, your birth certificate means that you are entitled to a British passport."

"But I don't want a British passport!" I expostulated. "I just want an entry permit."

"I understand that," said the deputy high commissioner. "But you see, we can't give an entry permit to someone who is entitled to a passport. That's against our rules."

I was stumped by this unexpected development. "Are you saying to me that I can't visit London? Unless I take a British passport?"

"No, I'm not saying that," he hastened to assure me. "We can't issue you an entry permit, but they cannot deny you entry into London when you have the absolute right to live there. Just go to London and show the immigration officer that you were born there, and they will let you in. They won't even stamp your passport."

I nodded somewhat dubiously at this assurance, but since he refused to accede to my pleas to issue me a permit anyway, went off clutching my Indian passport and hoping for the best. It worked exactly as he had said it would: I landed at London Heathrow and was waved in without any trouble, the immigration officer even helpfully telling me that in future I could use the much shorter lines for British nationals, since, as far as they were concerned, I was one.

This happened a few more times until, in 1979, Margaret Thatcher became prime minister and decided that the entry permit system for Commonwealth citizens was too lax and that we would all require visas. When I checked with the British consulate in Geneva, the city I was based in at the time, I was told there was no provision for exceptions. So, I applied for a visa, paying the extortionate fees the British were charging in order to discourage potential immigration from the Commonwealth.

But the attractions of theatre, cricket, books, and family friends—all of whom were just an eight-hour drive and a Channel-ferry ride away from Geneva—meant that my wife and I kept going rather often to Britain, and repeated applications for a visa became a rather expensive proposition. I returned to the charge, raising with the friendly British consul in Geneva the paradox of my being eligible for a passport but having to pay through my nose for a visa every time I wanted to set foot in a country in which I was legally entitled to live.

She admitted this was irrational, and a flaw in the rules—but there was a possible way out. While tightening entry policy, Mrs Thatcher's government had also created something called a "Certification of the Right of Abode," intended principally for people of British descent, whose parents and grandparents had been born in the colonies, and who would therefore not be eligible under the new law for automatic entry to, or residence in Britain, even though they were plainly of British stock. Though I was not of British stock, she thought perhaps the same certificate on my passport would eliminate my problem.

A couple of head-scratching weeks later, the call came from her office: her proposal had been rejected by London. "The problem," she said apologetically, "is that under British law, we cannot certify an entitlement that is yours by right."

I threw up my hands at that wonderfully British statement of principle, affirming a status while preventing its practical fulfilment. (I was all too aware that Indians have inherited this wonderful bureaucratic talent too, thanks to British colonialism!) But the consul, a woman of great empathy as well as creativity, was not deterred. In a few days, she asked me to come back to her office. "I have a solution for you," she said cheerfully. She stuck the certificate in my passport, pulled out her pen and crossed out the word "Certification". Then, in her own hand, she wrote the word "Confirmation".

"There," she beamed brightly, handing me my passport. "I cannot certify your birthright, but there's no rule telling me I can't confirm it. You can use that instead of a visa."

It worked: for a couple of decades afterwards, I was able to breeze in and out past British immigration with the Confirmation of the Right of Abode certificate in my passport, testifying to the fact that I was entitled to more than I was willing to claim. Then computerization and standardization came in, the rules once again had to be applied with no ambiguity, and I was once again required to pay visa rates for a printed certificate (with no handwritten emendation), this time needing to be renewed every five years at an ever-stiffer fee. At one renewal a British consular officer in New York helpfully reminded me that (at that time) it only cost 15 pounds for a passport whereas my certificate cost 65 pounds. I replied: "I'm happy to pay for the privilege of remaining Indian. I may have been born in Britain, but when I look in the mirror, I see an Indian."

It's difficult to explain this nativism in one who has spent a lifetime acquiring and embodying a cosmopolitan, even globalist, sensibility, so unfashionable today in a world of growing hyper-nationalism. But from a young age, when some of my classmates at school in Bombay teased me about my foreign birth, I have found myself consciously interrogating myself on the question of who I was. My father was an idealist of the generation that had won freedom—though, at not-yet-eighteen when Independence came, he had not personally fought for it, he had supported the nationalist movement, and, heeding Mahatma Gandhi's call, had dropped his caste-derived surname. In 1948 he had gone to London straight from his Kerala village, with his elder brother's sponsorship, in much the same spirit as other Keralites starting out in life might have tried their luck in Bombay or Calcutta. Arriving as a student not yet aged nineteen, he had soon begun his working life there, representing Indian newspapers that still maintained offices in the old metropolitan capital. But, after a happy decade in London, he and my mother chose to return to India, because they believed that was where they belonged. Ironically, as India descended into an increasingly corrupt and poorly functioning state, where highly-taxed salaried professionals like himself found it increasingly hard to make ends meet, my father sometimes regretted that decision. But, having come back to India, he imparted to me, his first-born son, a passionate sense of belonging, not just to a physical country called India, but to the idea that it represented in the world.

That idea—of a magnificent experiment in pulling a vast, multi-lingual, multi-ethnic population out of poverty and misery through democracy and pluralism—was one that engaged and captivated me, and which I have, in one way or another, explored in over twenty books, both fiction and non-fiction. I did so even while living abroad and working for the United Nations for twenty-nine years, which further complicated the issue for me. For nearly three decades I was that rare animal, an "international civil servant," meant to serve not my own country's national interests but the collective interests of humanity; but I had joined an organization where my nationality defined and limited the very prospects of entry, since the recruitment of the central United Nations staff was subject to "geographical distribution," and national quotas determined whether you could be recruited to a vacancy for which you were qualified. (Indeed, it was because Indians were considered "over-represented" in the UN proper that I joined the UN system in the Office of the UN High Commissioner for Refugees, an agency or "programme" of the parent body where no nationality quotas applied.)

If this were not contradictory enough, I found myself serving refugees who had fled their own nation-states, negotiating with governments to permit other countries' nationals entry into their territories, and later, as a peace-keeping official, interceding in wars between and within nations. At UN Headquarters I worked with teams of colleagues whom I knew by their skills, talents, specializations, and peccadilloes, rather than their passports. They were "the field guy," "the admin whiz," "the brilliant draftswoman", "the legal eagle," and so on, never the Brazilian, the Japanese, the German, or the Kenyan—in the service of the blue flag, their nationalities simply did not matter.

When that career ended, after an unsuccessful though close run for the top job of Secretary-General, I had the option of staying on abroad, and acquiring permanent residence in one of three possible countries. I did not. I could not. I came home, to plunge myself into the maelstrom of Indian politics, thereby making my own modest contribution to the evolution of that great Indian experiment. Leaving the world of the UN to enter Indian politics, where public figures wore their patriotism on their sleeves, I swapped my UN lapel pin for the Indian tricolour and learned to stop saying "we" when I meant the international community. I was a full-fledged nationalist again.

But what did that mean? Today, as I write these words during the second term of the Bharatiya Janata Party government of Prime Minister Narendra Modi, I see much of that noble national experiment gravely threatened by a fundamental challenge to the very essence of Indian nationalism—the "idea of India" that was built up in the course of a seven-decade struggle for independence from Britain, and another seven decades of post-colonial governance that consolidated the nature and character of Independent India. Mr Modi's BJP has spent its years in government contesting this remarkable and irreplaceable embodiment of the country's essence by arguing that there can be an alternative idea of India, promoting an assortment of political, social, and cultural elements that would convert a pluralist, multi-religious democracy into a "Hindu rashtra", and delegitimizing dissent through labelling disagreement with its actions and statements as "anti-national." The frequent use of that term has raised the corollary—if my disagreement is anti-national, what then is pro-national?

While I am constantly engaged in the minutiae of the immediate political contestations around these debates, as a Member of Parliament, as well as a guest columnist in a variety of Indian publications, I found it necessary to seize the opportunity to step back from the daily fray and reflect somewhat more broadly on the issues involved. My objective was to situate the passions currently swirling in Indian politics in the wider context of the very concepts of nationalism and patriotism, then apply those to the Indian experience and contemporary Indian reality. The result is this book.

I seek neither to write a textbook of political science nor presume to offer definitive answers to the issues this book attempts to raise. *The Struggle for India's Soul* seeks to offer one observer's notes towards an understanding of nationalism in the world, and specifically in India today. The various forms of ethnic nationalism in the world (including religious, linguistic, cultural, and other nationalisms based on immutable factors); India's own anti-colonial nationalism that converted itself into a civic nationalism anchored in a democratic Constitution; and the conflict over contemporary attempts to convert that into a religio-cultural nationalism today, are the principal themes of this book. If it provokes further debate and reflection on these very important questions, it will have served its purpose.

Shashi Tharoor   *New Delhi, June 2021*

PART ONE

THE IDEA OF NATIONALISM

I grew up in an India in which one took a few things for granted: "Nationalism" was A Good Thing, the nationalist movement was heroic, the nationalist struggle against the British had been led by great figures of extraordinary qualities—Mahatma Gandhi, Jawaharlal Nehru, and the rest—and the historic legacy of Indian nationalism was one of which every Indian should be proud. My own nationalism, as I have explained in the Prologue, came from a sense of belonging that was both derived from my birth to Indian parents, and a conscious act of allegiance to the post-colonial state of India that had emerged from the ruins of the British Raj. The values I imbibed at home and were instilled in me in school were the values of the nationalist movement (which we knew of as "the Freedom Struggle"): inclusivity, acceptance of difference, celebration of diversity, respect for all religions, equality and fraternity, concern for the poor. If anyone asked me in high school or college what I understood by Indian nationalism, these are the elements I would probably have identified.

But there were really no ideological contestations over nationalism in my childhood; it was just assumed, a state of being, an indissoluble part of the prevailing ethos. We were all nationalists, proud of the fluttering tricolour on the school's flagpole, suitably boastful about having ended nearly two centuries of British rule. (That we spoke of this nationalist triumph in the language bequeathed to us by the colonists did not trouble us schoolchildren unduly.) The state embodied this nationalism and made it real. It was built and run by the Indian National Congress, which had had epitomized Indian nationalism, but which accepted that the right to disagree with and to oppose the government was a vital element of Indian democracy, and that its critics were no less nationalist than the Congress itself.

1

1

THE EMERGENCE OF NATIONALISM

Few concepts have gone through as many transformations of connotation as nationalism. The word itself, in English, goes back in common usage only to 1844, though it is argued that the proposition that "the English people were a nation" dawned with the Tudors in the late 15th century. In ancient Rome, the word "nation"—natio—actually meant "litter", as in a cat's progeny, and referred to foreigners and migrants who were deemed sub-human by Roman citizens, but the term gradually lost its implications of contempt and began to refer to a community of shared opinion.[1] The Latin roots 'natio' and 'natus' (both come from 'nascor' or 'I am born', whose perfect form is 'natus sum', I have been born) point to the fact that to the ancient Romans, 'natio' was merely a group of people who were associated by birth conditions—typically of a larger tribe, or a confederacy bestowed by blood, but of those who were not worthy of being deemed Roman citizens. Interestingly, a 'natio' had a specific size dimension to it. 'Natio' was larger than a family, but smaller than a clan ('stirps') and smaller than a people ('gens'). Cicero talks of Jews and Syrians as 'nationes natae servituti' ("people born to servitude").[2]

"Nation" began to be used in the mid-19th century as a synonym for devotion to one's country, for advocating its national spirit or aspirations, but in the days of vast empires—the British, the French, the Ottoman, the Austro-Hungarian—this was not necessarily a reputable sentiment, since to be a nationalist was to be against the empire of which one's nation was a part. Nationalism rested on an expressed desire for national unity and independence, and this could only be achieved by extracting one's nation from the imperium; not surprisingly, nationalism was looked askance at by the prevailing orthodoxy of the age. There were important differences, though, between the Ottoman and Austro-Hungarian Empires, on the one hand, that were consciously multi-ethnic, and the British and the French, who were explicitly developing nationalist models and ideologies at home while imposing their imperiums abroad. Little African and Asian children in Senegal or Vietnam were taught by the French Empire to dutifully recite "Nos ancêtres les Gaulois," "Our ancestors the Gauls". Assimilation was the name of the imperial game, and it worked both ways; Queen Victoria was, after all, Empress of India. But these were for public consumption; the reality, for a colonial subject, was of racial separation and racial hierarchy.

Historically, the French and American revolutions in the late 18th century were the first to challenge the nation-eroding sweep of the mighty empires that had hitherto been imagined to be the acme of political organization. (The Haitian revolution followed soon after, at the start of the nineteenth century.) While the Americans unseated the British empire that was still in the process of establishing itself around the world, the French defenestrated their own king, challenging the very notion of divine right that had legitimized monarchy and its territorial ambitions. After a few years of floundering as a collection of colonies united only by their determination to be rid of British rule, the Americans inaugurated a new idea of nationhood born of a unified people with common political and economic interests, under a system combining democracy with capitalism. Modern-day nationalism was born.

Both these revolutions inspired the emergence of nationalism as a worldwide phenomenon in the mid-19th century, starting with the ideas of German Romanticism, the ferment of the revolutions of 1848, the reunification of Italy by Garibaldi, Cavour and Mazzini, and of Germany by Bismarck, and taking in the new countries of Latin America along the way. These featured the familiar elements of people's attachment to their native land and soil, the traditional cultural heritage inherited from their parents, and allegiance to the established authorities ruling their homelands, and converted them into a newly-defined loyalty to a nation-state. (Interestingly enough, the attempts by arch-conservatives like Metternich to suppress nationalisms where they arose point to an important historical irony: that modern liberalism was unthinkable without nationalism.)

It was only with the First World War, and the collapse of two large empires in Europe, the Ottoman and the Austro-Hungarian, that nationalism became seen as a broadly admirable concept, standing heroically for the freedom, self-determination, independence, unity and prosperity of subject peoples. A number of newly-free nations were spawned in Europe in this heady burst of nationalist fervour. The idea of nationalism was given a renewed fillip and universal applicability after the Second World War, with the freedom of a large number of hitherto colonized countries in the so-called Third World, whose liberation from subjugation under the imperialist yoke marked the second heyday of nationalism, this time of the anti-colonial variety.

But the failures and limitations of many of the nation-states born in the twentieth century, and the descent of several into chaos, corruption and dictatorship (and in a few cases, their own internal conflicts over nationality and nationalistic disputes over territory with neighbouring countries, leading to violence, civil war and even fragmentation), made nationalism less heroic in many eyes by the last quarter of the century. The concept seemed a veneer, a cloak to mask venality, tyranny and exploitation under the garb of self-determination. And the emergence of globalization after 1980 created a world in which nationalism also seemed less necessary, an impediment even, in the march of prosperity made possible by the satellite communications revolution, jet travel, the ease of moving millions across the world with the pulse of a cursor or the click of a mouse. In the globalized world, nationalism seemed somehow less important at a time when nations were giving up more and more of their sovereignty to achieve greater prosperity.

The profound disillusionment with nationalism—the doctrine, after all, of the likes of Hitler and Mussolini—at the end of the Second World War may have helped created the great age of globalism that reached its apogee in the three decades after 1980. Certainly nationalism, after ripping apart Europe for half a century, lost some of its appeal, and prompted the establishment of international economic, military, and political organizations such as NATO, the European Coal and Steel Community (1952–2002), Euratom, the Common Market, later known as the European Economic Community, and finally the European Union, which began to acquire some of the trappings of a supranational entity. Writers like Francis Fukuyama advanced the idea at the end of the Cold War that conflict would no longer be driven by the competition of great powers and nations: the "end of history" meant that the fundamental issues had been settled. It was possible to speak of subsuming nationalism in a larger internationalist project: even the reunification of Germany in 1990 was welcomed by those who had previously feared German unity, because German nationalism had been tamed by its subordination to the European project. The dissolution of the nation-state may not have seemed in prospect, but its dilution certainly was.

The setbacks endured by the globalization experiment with the recession of 2008–09, followed by the rise of ethno-nationalist populism in a startling number of countries in the second decade of the 21st century, has given nationalism another burst of relevance. There were two precursors to this development: the advent and spread of neo-liberalism, and the backlash in developed countries to globalization. The former saw the dominance, in the world's macro-economic thinking, of what became known as the "Washington Consensus", whose custodians were not just the governments of the US and its allies but also international organizations such as the World Bank, the International Monetary Fund, and the World Trade Organization. The latter, the backlash against globalization, reflected the crumbling of that consensus at its very source.

The doctrine of neoliberalism is commonly attributed to the economist Friedrich von Hayek, hailed by Margaret Thatcher and Ronald Reagan as their inspiration, whose impact on economic policy in the era of globalization, thanks also to the dissemination of his ideas by acolytes like Milton Friedman, was immense. Hayek's was a philosophy that went beyond economics, for he conceived of society itself, in the British writer Stephen Metcalf's brilliant summary, "as a kind of universal market (and not, for example, a *polis*, a civil sphere or a kind of family) and of human beings as profit-and-loss calculators (and not bearers of grace, or of inalienable rights and duties).... [Hayek's neoliberalism] was a way of reordering social reality, and of rethinking our status as individuals."[3] Hayek constructed neoliberalism as sufficient unto itself: the deregulated market would function as the over-arching "mind" that would govern and direct all human affairs, protecting individuals against the excesses of governments, whose only job was to keep the market free. Individuals would of course act in their economic self-interest, but the product of their choices would lead to better results than governments could craft through policy interventions.

Rampant economic growth and what was dubbed (by Alan Greenspan) as the "irrational exuberance" of the 1990s, especially after the fall of the Soviet Union and the collapse of the Berlin Wall, led the world into a period of widespread financial deregulation and privatization, expanding free trade, the creation of businesses whose supply-chains cut across many countries, and a worldwide illusion of rising prosperity. Neoliberalism came into its own, privileging a heady cocktail of free-market policies, including deregulating capital markets, lowering trade barriers, eliminating price controls, establishing global supply chains, rampant privatization, and the reduction or abandonment of state welfare for the poor, often accompanied by austerity measures to bring fiscal policies in line with what Western ratings agencies wanted to see.

But the seeming success of economic globalization also facilitated the illusion of the "end of history" (seen as the ultimate triumph of liberal democracy and capitalism), the heedless and hubristic military adventurism of the "global war on terror", including disastrously unsuccessful wars in Afghanistan, Iraq and Syria, which displaced nearly 20 million people (among the largest refugee crises in modern history), all of which in turn led to the market crash, and an unprecedented level of inequality and suffering among the working-class of the developed world. The top 1% of the global population came to own half the world's wealth, while the bottom 70% had less than 3%. With the Great Recession that began in 2008–09 and political convulsions in a number of countries, what Metcalf calls "the militant parochialism of Brexit Britain and Trumpist America"[4] was the result, as was rising ethno-nationalism, populist authoritarianism, and illiberal democracy in a slew of countries. As Metcalf puts it, "There was, from the beginning, an inevitable relationship between the utopian ideal of the free market and the dystopian present in which we find ourselves; between the market as unique discloser of value and guardian of liberty, and our current descent into post-truth and illiberalism."[5]

As the writer Tyler Stiem explains, the problem was that neoliberalism's pretensions of universalism and over-idealization of the market ignored the deep inequality that existed between and within nations: "Applied as a broad, one-size-fits-all solution to the challenges facing impoverished and traumatised post-Soviet and postcolonial nations (as well as increasingly multicultural countries in the west, with complicated histories of their own), neoliberalism couldn't help but be disastrous for many people".[6] In June 2016, three economists in the IMF's Research Department officially and openly questioned neo-liberalism in a prominent paper. While praising aspects of the neoliberal agenda—the poverty alleviation made possible by the expansion of global trade, the transfer of technology to developing economies and the "more efficient provision of services" resulting from the privatization of state-owned enterprises—the authors concluded that the benefits of increased growth "seem fairly difficult to establish", that inequality increased as a result of neoliberal policies, and that this in turn hurt the level and sustainability of growth.[7]

Interesting recent research by Quinn Slobodian argues that neoliberals used states and global institutions—the United Nations, the European Court of Justice, the World Trade Organization, and international investment law—to insulate financial markets against sovereign states, resist political change, and stave off turbulent democratic demands for greater equality and social justice.[8] Far from discarding the regulatory state, Slobodian says, neoliberals wanted to harness it to their grand project of protecting capitalism on a global scale. It was a project, he suggests, that changed the world, but that was also undermined time and again by the inequality, unrelenting change, and social injustice that accompanied it. A backlash was inevitable.

Much of 21st century nationalism, it can be argued, is shaped by the current crisis of globalism. Kenichi Ohmae's classic bestseller *The Borderless World* argued persuasively in 1990 that national borders are less relevant than ever before in the new globally interlinked world economy.[9] His certitudes did not survive three decades. Globalization was seen by much of the Western public as the ultimate project of the neo-liberals, conceived by people in fancy boardrooms who made money out of trading in money and shamelessly exploiting the privations of the poor. The predictable backlash took two forms: economic and cultural. The economic backlash was straightforward. The poor and the unemployed in the developed world began to feel that they had no stake in the globalized system, and demanded to know why their governments' policies benefited people in faraway lands like China and India with what used to be *their* jobs. They wanted to reduce the growing inequality in every "developed" economy and go back to the security of older, more familiar economic ways, in which each generation assumed they would earn more and live better than their parents did. The cultural backlash derived from the same resentment but expressed itself in a different arena: the political denunciation of global trade led to hostility towards foreigners, as more and more people sought the comforts of traditional identity and ways of life. Rage was expressed against the "alchemical brew served up in the name of progress—liberal politics, theologies of social emancipation, technocrats, trade agreements, multiculturalism".[10] Animated often by bitter working-class and lower-middle class resentment of global elites—in Ece Temelkuran's words, "the masses easily adapt to the new narratives of their victimhood"—this translated into a rejection of the entire brew—cosmopolitanism, multiculturalism, and secularism in the name of cultural rootedness, religious or ethnic identity and nationalist authenticity.[11]

Political leaders were quick to seize the opportunity to tap into both kinds of backlash against globalization. The scholars Yascha Mounk and Jordan Kyle suggest the rise of populism goes back to 1990,[12] but there is no doubt that it accelerated with the increasing resentment against globalization. Leaders like Donald Trump, who rose to the presidency of the United States on slogans of "America First" and "Make America Great Again"; Boris Johnson, who took his nation out of the European Union on a wave of xenophobic populism; Russia's Vladimir Putin, who has presided over the resurgence of Russian nationalism after the shambolic collapse of the Soviet Union; Recep Tayyip

Erdogan of Turkey and Narendra Modi of India, who successfully persuaded their voters that they were more authentic embodiments of their nations than the allegedly rootless secular cosmopolitans they sought to displace; and a host of others—from Jair Bolsonaro of Brazil to Viktor Orbán of Hungary—who combined nationalist fervour with a determined articulation of popular prejudices, all restored nationalism to its place as the default model of national self-definition. (Collectively, they constitute what may oxymoronically be called a "National International".) To be sure, they were challenged by liberal intellectuals who lamented their defiance of the recent consensus that the world was moving ineluctably towards greater integration, where borders were becoming less relevant and sovereignty could be pooled for the benefit of humanity as a whole. But, given the emotional appeal of nationalism to most voters, these internationalists could not win elections; nationalists could.

The British writer David Goodhart has interestingly argued that in the global battle between the "anywheres" (cosmopolitans comfortable anywhere in the world, flitting between business-class lounges and five-star hotels, the votaries of globalization who thought of themselves as citizens of the world) and the "somewheres" (those rooted in a place, a land, an ethnicity, a religion, and local assumptions and traditional prejudices), the "somewheres" had won.[13] Their leaders could claim an authenticity that legitimized their right to represent their peoples, in all their true essence—their hopes, their dreams, their fears and hatreds. Their language echoed that of their forebears in the agrarian movement in the US in the 1890s (which failed to seize power) who had memorably called themselves "populists" from the Latin "populus", or people, and pledged to "get rid of 'the plutocrats, the aristocrats, and all the other rats', install the people in power, and all would be well".[14] In more recent years, populism was seen as a reaction to modernization, and the yearning for a simpler, rural life. Today's populism is arguably an updated form of the same yearning for simplicity (and simplistic answers) on the part of "the people" threatened by the complexities of globalization. This explained both nationalism and xenophobia, both Brexit and the Hungarians sealing their borders, both Hindutva in India and the rise of Alternative für Deutschland in Germany.

There is something to be said for Goodhart's thesis, though it is challenged on various grounds: first, because the somewhere/anywhere binary overlooks the fact you can be rooted in your community and still "travel" elsewhere, that is, you can be a citizen of your neighbourhood, your city, your country, and of the entire world; and second, because ethnic minorities and other non-native groups have proven themselves capable of forming meaningful, rooted communities and local belongings in western countries. Worse, it is

9

startlingly reminiscent of what Adolf Hitler said in 1933, condemning "[the] clique … people who are at home both nowhere and everywhere, who do not have anywhere a soil on which they have grown up, but who live in Berlin today, in Brussels tomorrow, Paris the day after that, and then again in Prague or Vienna or London, and who feel at home everywhere".[15] The German right-wing leader Alexander Gauland, of the Alternative für Deutschland, speaking in 2018, seemed to echo Hitler: "The globalised class … [live] … almost exclusively in big cities, speak fluent English, and when they move from Berlin to London or Singapore for jobs, they find similar flats, houses, restaurants, shops and private schools".[16] This is presumably not the company Goodhart wishes to keep.

There is also the argument that in public culture (especially in the UK, but US, too) supposedly "authentic" attitudes have been very much in the mainstream, far more so than liberal internationalism. Interestingly, some recent scholarship questions such facile binaries altogether, notably the anthropologist Aihwa Ong's much-discussed work on "flexible citizenship". Prof Ong suggests that intensified travel, communications, and mass media have created a transnational Chinese public, who symbolize both the fluidity of capital and the tension between national and personal identities in an era of globalization.[17] The argument could be extended to other national groups, expatriate Indians in particular.

Both sets of arguments have their merits, and prompt me to explore the subtle and unsubtle differences between citizenship, nationality and patriotism in great detail later in this volume. In essence, however, citizenship is a status granted by a state, to which appertain certain rights, such as the right to vote, to own property, to seek consular protection abroad, and so on. Citizenship usually comes with entitlement to a passport. Nationality is a fact of being; one can consider oneself the national of a country on ethnic, linguistic or other grounds without having legally been accorded its citizenship. Patriotism, as we shall see, is the love of one's homeland; it is an emotional feeling, conveying a sense of belonging rather than a legal status or a political identity. But on understandings of citizenship, there is little doubt which case is found more persuasive by recent political leaders around the world. Former British Prime Minister Theresa May famously pooh-poohed the "anywheres" and the "flexibles" when she said, ""Today, too many people in positions of power behave as though they have more in common with international elites than with the people down the road, the people they employ, the people they pass on the street … but if you believe you are a citizen of the world, you are a citizen of nowhere. You don't understand what citizenship means."[18]

2

A VERY RECENT IDEA

I remember reading once the somewhat bemused account of a British writer who had encountered a black African, impeccably attired, on an aircraft in the 1940s. The writer, curious about his fellow passenger, wanted to know where he was from, and ventured to ask the stranger his nationality. The African drew himself up to his fullest height in his seat and replied with great pride, "Moi? Je suis francais." ("Me? I am French".)

The Briton was nonplussed. He could not imagine a brown-skinned subject of Britain's colonial empire in India feeling able to say "I am British"; even if the Indian carried a British colonial passport, he would have said he was Indian, not least because British rule did not empower him to feel British. But the notion of nationhood was clearly experienced differently by the African in the next seat. He had no doubt that he was French.

Almost eight decades later, in mid-2018, a popular joke went around that France was the last African country to remain in the football World Cup, because so many of the French players had sub-Saharan ancestry. To passionate French supporters of the national team, their nationality was unrelated to their visible ethnicity—but to the racialist right wing, it was a betrayal. The philosopher Alain Finkielkraut even wrote that the French soccer team "has become black, black, black and [France] the laughingstock of Europe".[1] To people like him, being French required participation in a certain type of national homogeneity, one of whose unavoidable markers was white skin.

As we have seen in the previous chapter, the consciousness of "the nation" as *the* social unit is, in historical terms, a very recent idea, emerging in a specific (and rather limited) historical period. Before the 19th century, people did not see themselves as constituents of a nation, let alone a nation-state: their sense of belonging was related to a locality, a much smaller territory than most nations, and their allegiance was to an individual (a baron, a duke, a prince, a feudal lord, or their equivalents in various societies), a city-state, or at most a king who controlled that territory. As Thomas Hobbes had theorized, the fact was that the lives of most people had been "nasty, brutish and short" before a strong ruler, a Leviathan, arose to impose order;[2] allegiance was therefore inevitably to that ruler, who ensured the security and prosperity of his subjects. Larger loyalties were extremely difficult to parse: for example, in the land of Malabar, where my ancestors lived, as late as the second half of the 18th century, local chiefs, rajahs, and tribal lords were linked through tributary relationships (much of it ceremonial) to a more powerful overlord far away, such as the Zamorin of Calicut, who in turn had to negotiate with multi-ethnic, multi-cultural empires (the Vijayanagara empire once, the advancing British later) and trade and form military alliances with the Deccan sultanates, against other aggressors like the Portuguese and the Dutch. It would have been very difficult for my ancestors in Palakkad to have explained which "nation" they belonged to.

Of course, group and community sentiments are as old as human civilization; families, clans and tribes have constituted meaningful units since time immemorial. Larger communities were defined in various ways. In the Islamic world, for example, Ibn Khaldun drew an important distinction between loyalty to the *ummah* (a nominally universal category covering all Muslims everywhere) and to the *asabiyyah*—a group or clan.[3] As modern communications and weaponry permitted those small territories to expand, the domain of the individual they swore loyalty to extended much farther afield, but here too it was not confined by any ideas of nationhood—rather the kingdom was a reflection of the king's power, the material resources (in men and treasure) that he could command, and the limitations imposed by geography as well as by the countervailing power of other kings. The classic ancient Indian treatise on statecraft, the *Arthashastra* of Kautilya, brilliantly analyses the duties, role and responsibilities of the king; but there is no reference to the idea of a nation.[4] Statecraft is predicated on both *artha* (material well-being) and *dharma* (righteousness and spiritual good), which Kautilya cleverly weaves together to argue that the King should pursue a state policy aiming at material progress in order to ensure success. The loyalty of the subjects is mentioned and has to be earned and maintained, but of loyalty to a national idea, there is no conception. For Kautilya, the state (coeval with 'raja' or 'swami') was more important than the 'nation'. Implicit in his writing is the assumption that people of different nations or languages can be subsumed in a state but the state mechanisms must be permanently guarded. Kautilya's theory of the state is usually called the 'saptanga' doctrine—the seven limbs that constitute the state: swami (king), amatya (ministers), janapada (land), durga (forts), kosha (treasury), danda (internal security), mitra (allies). But, anticipating a favourite approach of nationalists two millennia later, Kautilya added an eighth characteristic: shatru (enemy)—which includes sahaja shatru (enemies from within), krtrima shatru (enemies by design), and prakrita shatru (enemies by fate, e.g., neighbouring states). In all of this, the idea of 'people' is taken for granted, but there is no concept of "nation".

Individuals, therefore, belonged to principalities, kingdoms, and empires delimited by the power of their rulers and nothing more. One might imagine, in the heyday of the Mughal empire, an Indian in the far-flung south imagining himself a Mughal subject; but Indian kings and emperors were linked through tributary relationships, which meant the writ of the Mughal emperor did not always apply universally within his own empire, and the emperor had to negotiate support from the provincial governors he had himself appointed, some of whom, like Nizam-ul-Mulk in Hyderabad, reigned no differently from the sovereign ruler to whom he nominally owed allegiance. (Interestingly enough, new scholarship exploring the relationship between the Mughal emperor and his subjects has overturned the assumption that the urban masses were merely passive objects of rule and remained unable to express collective political aspirations until the coming of colonialism. They could be actors in their own right, but always in a space demarcated by the emperor, not by any conception of the nation).[5]

This meant that for people in most of the world, well into the middle of the 19th century, their allegiance was to individuals, groups and rulers, rather than around anything resembling the idea of a "nation". You were the subject of Her Majesty Queen Elizabeth or paid tribute to Emperor Akbar—you were not the citizen of a state or the member of a defined nation. The concept of nationalism arose when the absolute power of the ruler became untenable in more complex societies, and power began to be diffused; at that stage, people began to relate to each other by identifiable and unchanging common features that could be considered the attributes of a nation—a political entity broadly understood to be united by a defined geography, ethnicity, language, religion, and culture, common (and idealized) heroes, and a shared identity and sense of community for all its constituent people. In the mid-18th century, French Foreign Minister René-Louis de Voyer de Paulmy, Marquis d'Argenson, remarked that "the word nation and state have never been used as much as they are today... Under Louis XIV the two words were never spoken, and one did not have so much as an idea of them."[6] Nationalism, for the first time, identified the state or nation with the people, determining the nature and boundaries of the state on ethnographic lines. The nationalist idea was that each "nationality" so defined should form a state of its own to include, ideally, all members of that nationality. The emergence of the ideas of popular sovereignty and self-determination, involving a common citizenship in which all could partake, enabled the rise of a collective consciousness that expressed itself as nationalism.

What I have been discussing thus far is my own basic rendering of the key elements of nationalism. As the scholar Dusan Kecmanovic has averred, "there are no two authors, whether sociologists, historians, political scientists, or psychologists, who define nationalism in the same way."[7] The British social anthropologist Ernest Gellner, the (somewhat Eurocentric and urban) high priest of nationalism studies, for instance, has argued that nationalism is not the awakening of nations to self-consciousness but rather the invention of nations where they did not exist (or, at least, did not previously exist).[8] The Indian historian Partha Chatterjee succinctly wrote that "a nation is a historically constituted, stable community of people, formed on the basis of a common language, territory, economic life, and psychological make-up manifested in a common culture".[9] The Indian-American scholar Homi Bhabha further elaborated "nation-ness" as people imagining themselves as "we" but in an ambivalent, indeterminate way. In Bhabha's account, the nation emerges through narration, and as a narrative; it is "a system of cultural signification" that must be understood "*as it is written*," or narrated.[10] Importantly, the national narrative is not singular, and key to Bhabha's account is the idea that the nation itself "opens up the possibility of other narratives of the people and their difference."[11]

Scholars warn of the perils of conflating nation and state. Since many nations have not been able to establish states and exist within larger "multinational" states, like the Tibetan nation, and other nations are divided among multiple states, like the Kurdish nation, the nation is specifically *not* always the state. Citizenship is accorded by the state; nationality inheres in the nation. That is why—though nationhood, the national principle or national consciousness may be (sometimes violently) incarnated in the state—the "nation" is not the same as the "nation-state" for rigorous theorists, unlike for many nationalists, for whom the synonymousness of nation and state has often been an article of faith. ("Tutto nello Stato, niente al di fuori dello Stato, nulla contro lo Stato" said Benito Mussolini: "Everything in the State, nothing outside the State, nothing against the State".)[12]

Benedict Anderson, whose *Imagined Communities* transformed the way we discuss and understand nationalism, has argued that nationalism is more like religion and kinship than a set of ideas. Its political appeal stands in stark contrast, Anderson says, to its "philosophical poverty and even incoherence." "Unlike most other isms, nationalism has never produced its own grand thinker: no Hobbeses, Toquevilles, Marxes or Webers."[13] On the inadequacies of philosophy I am not qualified to comment; but incoherence is evident from a wide reading of the extensive literature on nationalism. There is so much out there on the subject that one would be hard pressed to categorize the various types of nationalism in coherent terms. The novelist Salman Rushdie's formulation of "a dream we all agreed to dream"[14] seems just as apposite as any rigorous scholar's theory.

I am concerned principally in this book with essentially two forms of nationalism: ethnic nationalism and all its subsets and variants—linguistic, cultural, territorial, religious, revolutionary—and civic nationalism. The idea of nationalism, to my mind, is essentially divisible into those forms of nationalism that are changeless (like ethnicity and the rest) and those where the sense of nationhood inheres in institutions, practices, and systems enshrined in a constitution and reaffirmed regularly through a democratic vote. Whereas ethnic nationhood inheres in the body, civic nationalism appeals to the mind; it is a nationalism of constitutions and institutions you respect, rather than identities you are born into.

Civic nationalism, a form of nationalism which I will discuss in some detail in this volume, is a concept that drives those states that derive their political legitimacy not from ethnicity, religion, language, culture, or any of the immutable trappings that people acquire from birth, but from the consent and active participation of their citizens, as free members of a democratic polity. Ideas of civic nationalism are said to have originated from the writings of philosophers like Locke and Rousseau, and especially with the latter's 1762 book *The Social Contract*, which describes the legitimacy of government being derived from the "general will" of the people. Membership of the civic nation is voluntary and can be acquired not only by birth but by immigration and usually (except in a handful of countries) renunciation of other allegiances. Civic nationalism requires liberal democratic institutions, constitutionalism that guarantees freedom of speech and association, and representative democracy, and is therefore the form of nationalism most closely associated with the modern state. Since these essential attributes are not totally inconsistent with the majoritarian impulse prevalent in ethno-nationalist "illiberal democracies", civic nationalism rests on liberal constitutionalism to prevent such distortions. While the United States of America and France are often described as prototypes of civic nationalism, anti-colonial nationalism like India's evolved into civic nationalism, and, arguably, a once ethnic nationalism like Germany's has been transformed into the same variant of nationalism today.

In using "ethnic nationalism" as shorthand for what most people traditionally understand by the idea of nationalism, I admit, of course, that nationalism always goes a step farther than mere ethnocentrism, in that it seeks and demands loyalty to a politically distinct entity, requires membership in an organized mass social group or community, insists on fealty to a formalized ideology, and requires of its adherents the performance of certain actions or behaviours to confirm their allegiance to the nation, such as saluting the flag, singing the anthem, or swearing loyalty to the state. Still, if its basis is the unchanging qualities one largely acquires by the accidental circumstance of birth, it falls into the category that one tends to call "classic" ethnic nationalism. Civic nationalism, while still nationalist, is distinguished from ethnic nationalism by the very fact that ethnicity and its trappings are irrelevant to a nationalist's sense of allegiance to his country.

The German philosopher Friederich Meinecke had argued for a similar dichotomous treatment: kultur-nation versus staats-nation. He had Germany and France in mind for the two archetypes. What I propose to discuss in this volume, though, goes beyond Meinecke; I seek to examine ways of belonging. One, that is linked to some immutable or at least seemingly ineradicable form of belonging—tribe, caste, language—and the other, what might be considered a subscription model of belonging, a form of membership that is about agreeing on certain norms of behaviour. The former has a biological and physical basis; the latter is a mental and social construct. It is through the prism of these two broad categories, and the conflict that arises when one is sought to be transformed into the other, that I discuss nationalism and its anxieties in India in the Parts that follow.

3

THE SIGNIFICANCE OF CULTURE

When a unified Italian nation was born in 1861 out of the union of a mosaic of principalities and statelets, a nationalist leader, painter, and author, Massimo Taparelli, Marquis d'Azeglio, was moved to remark: "We have created Italy. Now all we need to do is to create Italians." The role of a common culture in cementing national identity is almost matched by the role of nationalism in promoting a common culture. It took the existence of Italy to create an Italian people, as opposed to Piedmontese, Venetians, Sicilians, and the like. The two forces are often mutually self-reinforcing.

If we delve a little deeper into the history of nationalism, it is clear that the rise of nationalist feelings was attributable to a number of developments. The success of the old monarchs was itself an unwitting contributor: by creating large centralized states, kings and emperors destroyed the old feudal allegiances and led people to think of themselves as belonging to a larger entity than just their local unit. But that entity was symbolized only by one man, the king. The yearning for other features and common factors to tie oneself to one's fellow men began to manifest itself in the idea of the nation as the repository of those commonalities. As we have seen, the influence of new theories of the sovereignty of the people and of individual rights began to undermine the old absolute monarchs, first in the English civil war of the mid-17th century, and then most strikingly in France and America in the late 18th, in both of which "the people" replaced "the king" as the locus and nucleus of the nation. No longer was the king the head of state, the embodiment of the nation; if the nation belonged to the people, the state had to be the people's state, a national state—a nation-state. The very idea of the king's domain became replaced in people's minds by the idea of the people's fatherland or motherland, *their* nation by birth and allegiance, not the king's by virtue of conquest. War was no longer the king's men fighting against his enemies, but the nation at arms, in defence of the nation-state.

The civilizational dimension of nation creation also came into play. Earlier, just as political organization was not structured around the idea of a nation, so too civilization was not thought of as a national phenomenon. Traditionally, in Europe, civilization was seen as emerging from religious practice; despite all the different nationalities professing Christianity, there was but one Christendom. Within the Catholic Church, the authority of the church at first superseded that of the temporal ruler: in the famous clash between Pope Gregory VII and King Henry IV of the Holy Roman Empire over who got to appoint church officials in the Empire, the pope used the awful power of excommunication to bring the emperor to heel. (Henry had to wait three days in the bitter cold in Canossa in the winter of 1077, then walk barefoot through the snow to kneel before the pope and beg forgiveness before his excommunication was revoked.) The fear of God prevailed over the might of Caesar.

True, half a millennium later, Henry VIII in England engineered a different outcome to a similar clash when he disaffiliated himself from the Pope and created the Church of England as what one might call a "national church", but he remains an exception to the general rule of spiritual authority dominating the temporal throughout this period of Christianity. Similarly, Islam was spread over, and therefore divided among, a number of different states and kingdoms, but there was a common Islamic civilization to which all Muslims belonged. However, one difference between the two monotheisms was that there was no Muslim equivalent of the pope—a spiritual authority whose power transcended the monarch's. When the idea of the caliph emerged, he was both a powerful ruler and the spiritual symbol of the faith. Recent scholarship has demonstrated how Muslim sovereigns began to imitate the exalted nature of Sufi saints: the charismatic pull of sainthood (wilayat)—rather than the draw of religious law (sharia) or holy war (jihad)—inspired a new style of sovereignty in Islam.[1] An exception evolved in the Shia sect of Islam, especially in Iran and Iraq, where, over time, in the last few centuries, religious leaders did separate themselves as a force within the state, with an identifiable city and space of their own, creating its own complications in the 19th and 20th centuries. But that was also an exception.

In both the Christian and Islamic traditions, the idea that civilization and what one might refer to as national loyalty was determined by religion persisted till the Middle Ages. True, the Greek and Russian Orthodox churches were subservient to the state (Byzantine emperors appointed the patriarchs and metropolitans), but it is largely correct to say that religious affiliations and loyalties substituted for any notions of "'citizenship'" in pre-modern times; people's rights and duties—other than those accruing from residence, profession, or servitude—were primarily determined by religious law and religious authority, which held sway over them as a result of their membership of that specific religious community.

Though religion retained its influence well into the age of empire and into the early 20th century—"muscular Christianity" was an important part of imperial British nationalism, and equally, there was no anti-colonial Irish nationalism without the Catholic church—religion's dominance inevitably declined from the era of Canossa. Religion was gradually replaced, initially not by nationality, but in elite culture (in the periods of the Renaissance, from the 15th to the 17th centuries, and Classicism, 1750–1825) by a reverence for the even older ancient Greek and Roman tradition as the fount of European civilization (and thereby, in those Eurocentric times, of all human civilization). As late as the beginning of the 19th century, this was considered the universal norm, valid for all peoples, just as, within it, French civilization, language, and cuisine was admired as the highest manifestation of European culture, meant to be studied and emulated as the ideal civilization for educated people of all nationalities. (People were taught to believe, as US President John F. Kennedy was to say centuries later: "Every man has two countries: his own and France.")[2]

The increasing secularization of life, and spread of education in Europe, further weakened the dominance of the church. The church had promoted ancient languages and rituals (though local languages began to emerge after the Reformation), but secular society strengthened the growth and importance of vernacular languages. Poets, historians, and scholars began to emphasize cultural nationalism, composing odes to the glories of the motherland, evoking a "cultural consciousness" of national heritage, bolstered by symbols and myths, ideally derived from the mists of antiquity. An important objective of the development of a national language—and the linguistic chauvinism that accompanied it—was to draw a linguistic boundary between the language of the nationalist and the language of the enemy. Reviving a vernacular national culture was a vital part of nationalism: in a Prussia where the official language of the court and its aesthetic ideals were French, and even the king, Frederick the Great, notoriously described German as a semi-barbarous tongue, it became indispensable for nationalist thinkers like Johann Gottlieb Fichte to write in German. Poets seized upon their native idiom to express their longings. Poetry, the scholar Nazneen Ahmed observes, "is a powerful national form due to its capacity as a vehicle for the performance of collective expression ("nation-language") and the ritualized remembrance of collective trauma."[3] Anyone opposing the nationalists' assertion of linguistic identity was accused of opposing the struggle for national identity and autonomy itself.

Linguistic chauvinism arose hand-in-hand with the growth of a national consciousness in education. The "nationalization" of political loyalties, and the rise of the nation-state, was accompanied by the conviction that national-ism itself possessed a civilizational component. By the beginning of the 20th century, civilization became coterminous with nationalism: the image of the Nazis listening to Wagner and performing the *Gotterdammerung* while building autobahns and grandiose buildings is the epitome of the idea of the "national civilization". As the scholar J. R. Llobera observes, modern national identity appeared in Western Europe at a time "when all the intermediary bonds were collapsing, and religion itself was losing its grip on the masses."[4] Nationalism can be said to have offered itself as a ready substitute for religion, standing on the same all-encompassing framework—a doctrine that, in its more extreme manifestations as in Germany and Italy, guided all major aspects of a person's life in society, regulated his duties and obligations, and offered him both intangible rewards and painful punishments.

Even as the world has come to admit of far greater respect for diverse manifestations of human civilization, many ethno-nationalist leaders have taken to patronizing various manifestations of their native cultures—these are seen as proof of their unique national civilizations. Gellner has observed: "Cultural diversity is our manifest destiny and men reach fulfilment through their distinctive national cultures, not through some bloodless universality."[5] Culture is, in many ways, essential to the nationalist project: without cul-tural differences, after all, how could 'nations' identify and define them-selves, and how could they distinguish themselves from their enemies? Sometimes culture trumps other drivers of nationalism, such as religion: Pakistan was created in 1947 as a state embodying the "national" aspirations of India's Muslims, but within twenty-four years of its establishment, as has been mentioned, it was broken into two as its largest province, East Bengal, asserted a separate nationalism based on the assertion of its own ethnicity, culture and language.

Max Weber stressed that, in the eyes of its nationals, "the significance of the 'nation' is usually anchored in the superiority, or at least irreplaceability, of the cultural values that are to be preserved and developed only through the cultivation of the group."[6] The politicization of the native culture, Anthony

Smith observes, often goes hand in hand with the purification of the community. This means, "first of all, jettisoning all 'alien' cultural traits—words, customs, dress, food, artistic styles—and reappropriating vernacular traits for a renewed indigenous culture."[7] Thus, in India's anti-colonial nationalist movement, the Swadeshi leader Bipin Chandra Pal declared as early as 1910: "The movement of social and religious revival which preceded the present Nationalist Movement, represented really the return of the national consciousness to itself. It was not really a conflict between the progressive and conservative elements of Indian society, as superficial observers have tried to make it out, but a conflict between aggressive European and progressive Indian culture. It was India's mental and moral protest against the intellectual and ethical domination of Europe."[8]

From this process emerged a distinct national culture, which soon sought to be coterminous with a state. Many nation-states have developed distinctive cultures of their own, so that people have an instinctive understanding of an "American accent", "French cuisine", "German efficiency", "Italian design", and so on. The stereotypes that accompany such notions of "national culture" are best captured in the old joke that describes Heaven as a place where the police are British, the cooks are French, the engineers are German, the administrators are Swiss, and the lovers are Italian; whereas in Hell, the police are German, the cooks are British, the engineers are Italian, the administrators are French, and the lovers are Swiss! But when (to use a facile example) a Chinese official in a Western suit and tie exalts his nation's heritage at the opening ceremony of the Beijing Olympics, can he meaningfully speak of a purely national civilization anymore? Doesn't every civilization in the globalized world partake of influences well beyond its own borders? Is there, anywhere, any longer, any such thing as a "pure" national civilization? This is an issue to which we will return later in this volume when we discuss India's debates over nationalism.

The growth of capitalism and commerce was another factor that helped shape nationalism. As trade expanded across the world, with the constant invention of newer and faster means of communication, transport, and ever-improving logistics, it led to the rise of entrepreneurial and trading middle classes who had a major impact on nationalism. It is no accident, for instance, that the rise of the very idea of English nationalism coincided with the rise of the English trading middle classes. The onset of the Industrial Revolution led to the emergence of an integrated, nationwide economy with global reach, along with a national public sphere, and the creation of a national myth whereby the success of British capitalism was projected as a civilizing force for the world at large. This was also when the British people began to identify with the "nation" of "Great Britain", rather than with the local units of their family, town, county, or region, or by reverence to their monarchy.

This drive was initially entirely compatible with empires: indeed, Marxists have long argued that imperialism was merely the highest form of capitalism, using conquest to drive the creation of ever-larger markets, and consolidating dominance abroad in order to extract resources through the plunder of the colonies for the benefit of capitalists in metropolitan capitals. But when nationalism rose, capital was quick to see the advantages of allying its commercial interests with the political interests of nation-states. The advent of national pride could also be extended, in the process, to pride in the commercial success of the nation's commercial flag-bearers, its corporations. The British East India Company, though a private enterprise, had a royal charter, the power to raise armies and use military force, and the active support of the monarchy, Parliament, and the British establishment. Its victories and conquests were hailed at home as national achievements of the British people; its profits, repatriated to the home country, occasioned national rejoicing, and the Indian revolt against it in 1857 provoked bloodcurdlingly racist nationalist passion in Britain.

Paradoxically, therefore, the same capitalism that extended around the globe under imperial domination has also given birth to the idea of economic nationalism. However, nationalists tend to think that economic problems essentially originate abroad and can only be fixed by economic-nationalist responses. Their preference thus tends to be for tariffs, subsidies, import quotas, or other restrictions and barriers placed on foreign commerce in order to protect domestic industries and businesses against competitors from other nations, and the promotion of economic self-reliance at home.

This happened in India for several decades after it gained independence, which is why post-colonial nationalism is often identified with what I have dubbed "the economics of nationalism". It started with the work of late 19th century nationalists such as Dadabhai Naoroji (*Poverty and UnBritish Rule in India*) and R. C. Dutt, who demonstrated in detail their "drain theory", substantiating how India had been drained of its resources by British rule. As the historian Bipan Chandra has documented in his work, Indian nationalism arose in objection to the practice of British colonial administrators—which I have detailed in my book *Inglorious Empire*—siphoning off the revenues of the country for the benefit of the faraway island to which they owed their allegiance. The result was that the success of the nationalist movement brought with it a fear and rejection of foreign economic relations. Whereas in America

most people axiomatically associate capitalism with freedom, India's nationalists associated capitalism with slavery—because the East India Company came
to trade and stayed on to rule. Our nationalist leaders were suspicious of
every foreigner with a briefcase, seeing him as the thin end of a neo-imperial
wedge. Instead of integrating India into the global capitalist system, as a few
post-colonial countries like Singapore so effectively were to do, India's leaders were convinced that the political independence they had fought for could
only be guaranteed through economic independence. So self-reliance became
the slogan, protectionist barriers went up, and India frittered away 45 years
of development and prosperity with bureaucrats rather than businessmen on
the "commanding heights" of the economy, spending an unconscionable
length of time subsidizing unproductivity, regulating stagnation, and trying
to alleviate poverty through a system that only seemed to distribute it more
widely. (Which only goes to prove that one of the lessons you learn from
history is that history sometimes teaches the wrong lessons.)

It took a crippling financial crisis in 1991 to prompt India to abandon the
economics of nationalism and change course, and now that seems truly irre-
versible, even if the economics of nationalism continued to have passionate
adherents well into the 21st century in the fellow-travellers of the ruling BJP
government (the Swadeshi Jagran Manch, an offshoot of the RSS, still calls
for economic self-reliance, and a strong rupee—both protectionist measures—as a matter of national pride). That said, by the turn of the century,
Indian businessmen became happy to boast that theirs was among the most
globally integrated economies in the world. (Once again, though, in the aftermath of the coronavirus disaster, the "economics of nationalism" arose in
India, with Prime Minister Modi calling for "atma-nirbharta" or self-reliance
to permit India to emerge from the economic wreckage of the crisis.)

Interestingly, the emergence of the nationalist principle in politics, culture, and commerce contradicted an earlier ideal that had dominated the
thinking of large parts of the world for at least a millennium and a half—that
of the ultimate objective of political organization being the establishment of
a universal world-state. Christian political thinking, exemplified in the doctrines that sustained the Holy Roman Empire, had this ideal; the ancient
Roman Empire itself had professed the same yearning, just as Alexander the
Great and Genghis Khan had sought to achieve it in practice by the conquest
of the known world of their times. Doctrinally, the very concept of the Res
Publica Christiana ("Christian republic" or community) presupposed the ideal
of a world-state. Islam, in turn, envisaged itself prevailing over the entire
world and so making it a Dar-ul-Islam (Abode of Peace). And before them

both, Hinduism, with its philosophy based on the unity of all creation, had propounded the idea of Vasudhaiva Kutumbakam, the whole world is one family. Nationalism ran counter to these forms of political thought across the world, which stressed universal ideals, and sought the unity of all mankind as the ultimate desirable objective of political organization. It emphasized the particular rather than the general, the parochial rather than the universal, the differences rather than the commonalities.

4

THE PRISM OF IDENTITY

My former United Nations colleague Omar Bakhet was born and brought up in Eritrea in the early 1950s and was trained as a teenage guerrilla freedom-fighter during the 1960s. His "liberation movement" put him in charge of foreign relations, but he was soon thoroughly disillusioned with guerrilla life, and focused on his own foreign relations instead, fleeing Eritrea as a refugee, and studying abroad in Munich and Prague before becoming a researcher at Lund University in Sweden. Settling down in Swedish academia, he became a Swedish citizen in his 20s, and it was as a Swedish national that he joined the staff of the UN High Commissioner for Refugees in Geneva, a couple of years after I did. We became good friends.

Aside from Omar's impressive knowledge of development economics, and the politics of development, I was fascinated by the incongruity of his life story—this refugee working for refugees, a black man from the Horn of Africa, who spoke Swedish and English with the fluency of a native, and was soon amongst the most senior Swedes in the organization, around whose gregariousness many fellow-Swedes congregated.

One day, he received a call from a close friend requesting him to play host to a Swedish colleague who was coming to Geneva for the first time. Omar agreed instantly, but in those pre-mobile phone days there remained the question of how host and guest would connect. It was agreed that Omar would stand under the main clock at the Gare Cornavin, on the platform of the train from which the visitor would alight. The plan was confirmed by the two of them on the telephone.

With Scandinavian punctuality, Omar took up position under the huge clock at two minutes before the train's arrival. It disgorged its passengers, and soon enough Omar found a tall, blue-eyed Nordic man approaching him. But the man walked past, looked up at the clock, looked again at Omar, shook his head slightly, and walked on, presumably searching for another clock. A few minutes later he was back, again walking up to the clock and walking past as Omar stood there impassively. This happened a few more times, the hapless blond looking desperately around the platform as it slowly emptied, approaching a few individuals standing at other spots who might plausibly have been Swedish, shaking his head, looking at his watch. Finally, the visitor himself took up station under the clock, alongside Omar, without saying a word to him. Clearly, he had assumed his host was delayed and would come and look for him under the clock.

After fifteen minutes of this, Omar decided to put him out of his misery. In idiomatic Swedish, he asked the man: "Are you by any chance looking for me?"

The visitor was embarrassed and apologetic. "Sorry, I was told to look for a Swede", he explained, "and I didn't think it could be..."

"I'm Swedish", Omar responded bluntly, picking up the man's bags and taking him to his parked car.

When Omar told me the story I asked him whether he hadn't been unnecessarily cruel, and why he hadn't spoken up earlier. "I was offended", he replied. "The guy had been told to meet me under the clock. There I was, standing under the clock at the appointed time. Why didn't he ask me if I was Omar, whom he had come to meet? Swedes pride themselves on not being racist. Why did he assume that because I look the way I do, I couldn't be a Swede, just like him, and yet not like him?"

The story has stayed in my mind for decades and came back to me when I was thinking about issues of national identity. What made Omar Swedish? He had lived in Sweden, studied there, spoke the language, carried the passport. But was there something about his appearance, the colour of his skin, the texture of his hair, that to another Swede instinctively seemed to exclude him from the enveloping embrace of Swedish identity? To what degree was the immutability of racial ethnic identity basic to most people's conceptions of nationality?

Benedict Anderson famously defined the nation as an imagined political community—and one imagined as both inherently limited and sovereign. "It is imagined," Anderson explained, "because the members of even the smallest nation will never know most of their fellow-members, meet them, or even hear of them, yet in the minds of each lives the image of their communion.... Communities are to be distinguished, not by their falsity/genuineness, but by the style in which they are imagined.... Finally, [the nation] is imagined as a community, because, regardless of the actual inequality and exploitation that may prevail in each, the nation is conceived as a deep, horizontal comradeship. Ultimately, it is this fraternity that makes it possible, over the past two centuries for so many millions of people, not so much to kill, as willing to die for such limited imaginings."[1] The Israeli writer Yuval Harari even sees nationalism as one of those great "fictions" of human creation that help form societies and integrate large numbers of people.

But once that imagination has reified a community, the community-as-nation inevitably pursues the supposedly noble aim of gaining and maintaining sovereignty and self-governance over its own homeland, free from foreign interference. A people's conviction that its national identity reflects an ideal of self-determination, that it is the natural and ideal basis for the political organization of its people, and that its sovereignty rests on popular will, makes the nation the only rightful and legitimate source of political power in the state. Nationalism cements individual identity with collective identity, making them inseparable. Karl Popper had observed that nationalism "appeals to our tribal instincts, to passion and to prejudice, and to our nostalgic desire to be relieved from the strain of individual responsibility which it attempts to replace by a collective or group responsibility."[2] But it still involves that element of imagining. As Yuval Noah Harari puts it, "nationalism works extra hours to make us imagine that millions of strangers belong to the same community as ourselves, that we have a common past, common interests and a common future. This isn't a lie. It's imagination. Like money, limited liability companies and human rights, nations and consumer tribes are inter-subjective realities. They exist only in our collective imagination, yet their power is immense."[3]

This imagined political community reflects a single national identity, built upon shared social characteristics such as culture, language, religion, ethnicity, and a common history. It is usually accompanied by an evocation of ancient memories that provides nationals with a sense of rootedness—the sense of belonging to a venerable and even timeless community—in turn evoking both a sense of belonging to a common endeavour and a reassuring sense of predictability.

In my years at the UN dealing with the civil war in the former Yugoslavia, I was struck by how often my interlocutors on all sides referred to events from the distant past: there were two Battles of Kosovo, in 1389 and 1448, but Serbs spoke of them as if they had happened yesterday, and that they justified their resentments today, and their belligerence tomorrow. To take an example closer to home, when V. D. Savarkar (later the father of "Hindutva") was, in his youthful phase, an advocate for Hindu-Muslim unity, he declared the rebellion of 1857 to have been "India's First War of Independence", featuring as it did Indians across divides of religion, region, caste, and language, fighting under the flag of the Mughal sovereign. The appeal to a positive historical memory can play a significant role in constructing the nationalism of the present.

That timeless national community so constructed is linked to a specific territory, resulting in a certain sanctification of geography, in the worship of the "motherland" as the natural home of the nation. Next, this sanctified geography is married to a holy history. The 19th century Italian nationalist Giuseppe Mazzini, who sought to unify the peninsula's many warring principalities that had never served a common state, regarded patriotism as a duty, and love for the Fatherland as a divine mission, saying that the Fatherland was "the home wherein God has placed us, among brothers and sisters linked to us by the family ties of a common religion, history, and language." The history of a nation is marked by a shared recollection of the nation's victories and defeats in asserting itself as a national community—as well as, quite often, resentment and rejection of other nations or communities, especially foreign powers that have conquered or dominated them. In the process nationalism involves an act of purification: "purifying the people themselves", in Anthony Smith's words, "forging the "new man" and the 'new woman,' in the image of a pristine ideal found only in an idealized past of heroic splendour."[4]

"The past is an essential element, perhaps the essential element in [nationalistic] ideologies," Eric Hobsbawm has argued. "If there is no suitable past, it can always be invented. The past legitimizes. The past gives a more glorious background to a present that does not have much to show for itself".[5] Hobsbawm compares the role of history to nationalism with that of the poppy to the heroin addict. Since the project of national unity which is indispensable to the expression of nationalism requires both a shared sense of cohesion, ethnicity or brotherhood, and an identifiable, secure, recognized territory, all nationalisms seek both such fraternity, and such a homeland. At the same time, to justify nationalistic zeal, both are required to be constructed on a long history—real or imagined—of collective experience. This is what makes history so important to the very idea of nationalism and so crucial to nation-building. The construction or even invention of history is, in Smith's words, "no longer a scholarly pastime; it is a matter of national honour and collective endeavour".[6]

We will return in this book to the uses and abuses of history in Indian nationalism. But the issue is a larger one. Hans Kohn, for instance, argued that German cultural nationalism set a bad example for Asian and African nationalists: "German nationalism, with its anti-Western, anti-Enlighten-ment, and Germanophile attitude, became the model for many similar con-servative nationalist trends, from Russia to India, from Spain to Latin America—an overcompensation for political backwardness in the modern world by claims to "spiritual" superiority based upon the legendary glories of pre-modern traditions."[7]

Since history is so indispensable to nationalism, it can (and often must) be reconstructed and reinterpreted to serve the nationalist project. As the Turkish scholar Umut Özkirimli[8] asks: "To what extent is a reconstructed and reinterpreted past the same past? When we speak of the collective memories of the people, which people and whose memories are we talking about?" In Turkish nationalism, for instance, in what place (if any) do Kurdish memories figure? Özkirimli points out that, in any case, "it is not the memories themselves, but the ways in which they are used by nationalist ideologues that lead to atrocities. Serbs and Croats lived together, in fact married each other, for decades, until the rise of the likes of Tudjman and Milosevic. It is true that the present cannot alter what happened in the past, but [nationalist interpretations of] it can ignore certain elements and empha-sise others, exaggerate the relevance of some, trivialise that of others, and it can certainly distort realities."[9]

Along with a sacred geography and a reconstructed history, there was also the notion that arose from time to time in various parts of the world that the state should include all members of the dominant ethnicity that was particular to it. The German nationalism of Otto von Bismarck, for instance, unified Germany on the basis of the principle of creating a nation for all the Germanic people—the German nation. Since the nation-state was identified with the people, its legitimacy, its nature, and its extent had to be determined accord-ing to ethnographic principles. If you were a German anywhere, you belonged to the German nation embodied in the German state. This then led to the German annexation of Alsace-Lorraine against the will of its inhabitants—since the authorities in Berlin deemed them to be German on "objective" grounds of ethnicity, whatever be their own objections, or those of the coun-try to which they previously bore allegiance, France. Half a century later, Hitler extended the Bismarckian principle to Austria, another German-speaking nation, through his "Anschluss" or union with that country.

Gellner famously defined nationalism as "a political doctrine which holds that the political and national unit should be congruent."[10] This, in turn, prompts the proposition that nationalism is, and requires, a form of homog-enization, something that poses a specific challenge, as we shall see, to a

29

diverse society like India. Nationalist discourses and ideologies are used to ensure a homogeneous population, and to keep this population together, unified and sharing a common narrative, myths and symbols. Many nation-states embody a homogenization resulting from either absorption into a dominant national narrative, as with most European nations, or the elimination of discordant (and often pre-existing) narratives, like the massacres of indigenous people in the Americas, which became a precondition for the creation of viable modern nation-states in that continent. In today's China, the ruthless incarceration of over a million Uighur Muslims in concentration camps in Xinjiang province, where they are stripped of their Islamic faith, and Turkic language, made to shave beards and eat pork, and ruthlessly indoctrinated into the language, culture, and values of the majority Han Chinese, is a project of homogenization justified entirely in the name of Chinese nationalism and the integrity of the nation-state.[11]

The logic of homogenization can embody contradictions within itself. Thus, Yugoslavia was created at the end of the first World War as the result of a nationalist movement against the empires of the day, which sought to unite the South Slavic peoples of the Balkans—all descendants of Caucasian tribes that had settled the area in the 7th and 8th centuries—into one political unit. (Initially the "Kingdom of the Serbs, Croats and Slovenes" as of 1918, it acquired the name Yugoslavia in 1929.) But pan-Slavic unity proved inadequate to hold the country together once sub-nationalisms began to assert themselves on the basis of greater ethnic specificities, religious, linguistic, and historical: the Slovenes seceded in 1991, the Croats the year after, and the Yugoslav Federation broke up into six member states of the United Nations by the end of the 20th century, with a putative seventh, Kosovo, waiting in the queue.

The basis for these secessions points to the challenges of defining nationalism, even ethnic nationalism. The Slovenes considered themselves a distinct people, with a separate language. (Yet the chief in 1991 of the Yugoslav Navy, which joined the Federal Republic's efforts to put down Slovene secession, was himself Slovene.) The Serbs and Croats, however, spoke essentially the same language, known globally as Serbo-Croatian, except that the former was written in the Cyrillic script and the latter in the Roman; but the Serbs were Orthodox, and the Croats Catholic, and some on both sides considered that was enough reason to be separate nations. I recall, as a United Nations official travelling in the former Yugoslavia soon after the outbreak of war between the two "nations", meeting a Croatian commander who showed me a gruesome picture of a row of dead babies, their throats slit. "Look what these monstrous Serbs are doing to our children!" he exclaimed. Two days later, at the headquarters of a Serbian commander, I was shown the identical picture of the very same dead babies, and this time the passionate words were: "Look what these monstrous Croats are doing to our children!"

It was impossible to tell to which group these babies belonged as they were descended from the same ethnic stock. Yet both sides were divided by such intense feelings of difference, it was enough to give any advocate of ethnic nationalism a rude wake-up call. The Serbian writer Aleksandar Hemon has described his horror at watching his childhood friend and companion turn into a Serbian nationalist full of racist and fascist fantasies; Hemon writes that his friend was beyond the reach of any rational appeal, and that, despite all the shared assumptions of their youth, he himself stopped trying to reason with him, so primordial was the man's ethno-nationalism.[12]

The contradictions among the Balkan antagonists continued to multiply. When they, too, went to war, the Bosnian Muslims ended up being shelled by both warring sides; large swathes of their supposedly sovereign national territory were, in fact, controlled by the Croats and Serbs who lived in their respective zones within Bosnia-Herzegovina. The Montenegrins were once proud of describing themselves as a better sort of Serb—"mountain Serbs", or Serbs who had taken to Black Mountain redoubts to fight the Ottomans when Serbia proper surrendered to the Turkish invaders. But that common ethnic descent, common religion (Christian Orthodox), and common language did not prove enough to keep Montenegro federated to Serbia after the break-up of Yugoslavia.

Freudians speak of the psychoanalytical concept of "the narcissism of minor differences"; the phrase applies perfectly to the nationalisms of the former Yugoslavia. In writing about the Yugoslav conflicts, politician and thinker Michael Ignatieff observed[13] that closely related (often inter-related) group identities became segregated along the rigid boundaries that Sigmund Freud described in that phrase. Freud showed that small differences between people were heightened, magnified, and weaponized, particularly when these people are actually quite similar or inhabit spaces close to one another; he argued that the more similar or closely related groups of people were, the more likely they would be to amplify their small differences. Freud concluded that this was likely to be reflected in one group's pathological self-love (narcissism) for itself and its dislike and loathing of "the other" group that was similar but different from one's own, leading often to violence against the other.

All said and done, besides everything I have discussed in this chapter, the modern nation—no matter what any nation might claim, and actually believe in (such as its own timeless existence in an ancient ethnic past)—is essentially a new idea, even an imagined or invented one. As has been stated, the reason for this is simple: most nation-states today are relatively recent political units, territorially more clearly defined (whether larger or smaller) than the extent of their past manifestations, more economically integrated and unified, and more culturally homogeneous than any earlier incarnations. As the German philosopher and sociologist Jürgen Habermas has observed, the success of the nation-state was derived from its establishing relations of solidarity between the citizens as its basis, rather than the old feudal or monarchical allegiances. But, Habermas goes on to point out, "this republican achievement is endangered when, conversely, the integrative force of the nation of citizens is traced back to the pre-political fact of a quasi-natural people, that is, to something independent of and prior to the political opinion—and will-formation—of the citizens themselves."[14] The evocation of the past can thus be both a cementing factor in nationalism and one that undermines it—an important insight, as we shall see, in the context of contemporary India.

A century before Benedict Anderson's seminal work about nationalism, the French political theorist Ernest Renan, in his classic "What Is a Nation?", had called a nation "a soul, a spiritual principle. Two things, which in truth are but one, constitute this soul or spiritual principle. One lies in the past, one in the present. One is the possession in common of a rich legacy of memories; the other is present-day consent, the desire to live together, the will to perpetuate the value of the heritage that one has received in an undivided form." Renan saw the nation as "a large-scale solidarity, constituted by the feeling of the sacrifices that one has made in the past and of those one is prepared to make in the future." He quoted a Spartan song to gloss his idea of nation as soul: "We are what you were; we will be what you are." To be a "we", we must have had a shared history. To continue to be a "we", we must together inherit the future.[15]

Memory and consent, to Renan, were the essential ingredients that fed nationalism. Memory and forgetting were key to the forging of nationhood: what a nation chose to remember, and what it chose to forget, had to be collectively agreed upon in order to make nationalism possible. Memory alone could be a danger for the viability of nationalism, since "historical enquiry brings to light deeds of violence which took place at the origin of all political formations, even those whose consequences have been altogether beneficial. Unity is always effected by means of violence...."[16] Some things had to be collectively forgotten, to be erased from memory, if a nation was to be built on its ashes. In the case of the United States of America, for instance, national homogenization required both a series of massacres of Native American peoples, and then the absorption of the survivors and later arrivals (immigrants) into the dominant ethos, the national "melting-pot".

If I might be permitted a personal digression into the importance of historical forgetting, I should mention here a minor controversy that arose when I tweeted about the birth anniversary of Tipu Sultan, the late 18th-century Muslim ruler of Mysore, scourge of the expansionist British, then consolidating their Raj, but also reviled by Hindu nationalists today. The author of a Facebook post attacking me asked, "Who invited Tipu Sultan to invade Kerala?" and pointedly replied, "Well, it was the Palghat Raja, Raman Kombi Achan of the Tharoor Swaroopam!" In other words, the author alleged, I was merely carrying on a tradition of disloyalty that had run in my family for generations.

This took me aback. It is true that Palakkad was ruled by a Nair raja of the Tharoor Swaroopam for a few centuries before Tipu. It is also presumed that we belonged to a collateral branch of the Palakkad raja's original tharavad, and are descended from them. The Tharoor branches dispersed and at some point, my father's ancestors settled in Chittilamchery village where they essentially became farmers and landlords. Consequently, it is possible my critic may be right—but it is not a connection that has played a major part in family lore, and I have never heard a family member speaking of Raman Kombi Achan.

I am, therefore, reluctant to accept that my anti-colonial regard for Tipu Sultan (as a great nationalist hero who challenged the British, sent emissaries to Napoleon, and remained unconquerable in battle until ultimately betrayed) is really some sort of genetic predisposition derived from being a Tharoor. But it also complicated by the fact that the mother's side of my family—and in matrilineal Nair households, that may actually be more important than the paternal line—had a very different attitude to Tipu.

For my mother's family, the Mundaraths of Elavanchery (also in Palakkad district), suffered a different fate with Tipu. The Mundaraths were the zamindars and rulers of Elavanchery and a large part of the surrounding countryside. When news came of the imminent invasion of Tipu into Malabar, the then Mundarath karanavar loaded all the family treasures—vessels, jewels, the gold ornaments of the women—onto several carts and took them deep into the countryside to bury them for safekeeping. (Some versions say the workers who did the job were blindfolded till they got to the spot, others claim worse, that they were killed to preserve the secret.)

The Mundaraths showed great prudence and foresight, including sending off two Mundarath women to some far-flung place in the hills so that if the

33

family was massacred by Tipu's troops, the Mundarath bloodline would continue. Unfortunately for the Mundaraths, things did not go according to plan. By the time Tipu withdrew from Malabar (and was then defeated by the British), the karanavar had breathed his last, without confiding the secret of the location of his treasure trove to anyone. A frantic search was launched the moment it was safe to do so, but the family could not recover a single item.

This was a cataclysmic trauma for the Mundarath tharavad, which overnight lost vast wealth and riches—all that remained were 11th-century copper-plate inscriptions giving them title to their lands. I saw these inscriptions in the attic of the ancestral home in my childhood, but in a mishap, they were junked along with metal scrap and are lost to the family forever. And, the buried treasure remained just that, the memory of its loss a potent source of family pride and regret.

Historical memory and family memory—how curiously they cross! In Palakkad, where the ruins of one of his forts still stands, the memory of Tipu's depredations against the Nairs is still as sore as an old wound that never healed for many members of the community. For the two sides of my family, Tipu is not just a figure from the history books. It is entirely possible that I am descended from two Palakkad families, one of whom invited Tipu Sultan to attack Palakkad and the other who lost their fortune out of fear of his attack.

So, it is best that some things are forgotten, but equally some things need to be affirmed, none more important than consent. To Renan, consent, a sharing of allegiance, was indispensable to nation-building, since a "nation's existence is…a daily plebiscite, just as an individual's existence is a perpetual affirmation of life." Nations, Renan argued in his canonical lecture, were constituted by a constantly-renewed act of self-determination of their citizens. Citing the example of Switzerland and its four languages, which I have already mentioned, Renan sagely observed that "In man there is something superior to language—will. The will of Switzerland to be united, in spite of the variety of her languages, is a much more important fact than a similarity of language."

Self-determination was an alluring idea in theory, granting as it did the power of agency to citizens. But it was also an odd principle, in that it too often imparted morality to geography, justified it by history, and steered it towards destiny. This moralization of geography rested on an unholy trinity sanctified by nationalists—the people, the state, and the territory. But if this theory worked for Renan's France or Gladstone's Britain, how could it withstand the obvious question of its relevance to the British and French empires straddling the globe at the very time that Renan was speaking and writing? If self-determination gave the power of agency to citizens, why could it not do the same for these imperiums' subject peoples?

Applying such an idea to colonized India under the British Raj—Renan was writing and speaking in 1882—was, of course, impossible. But to the Indian philosopher, poet, composer, and polymath Rabindranath Tagore, it was not relevant either, since the true Indian philosophic ideal was humanism. "India has never had a real sense of nationalism", he argued. "Even though from childhood I had been taught that the idolatry of Nation is almost better than reverence for God and humanity, I believe I have outgrown that teaching, and it is my conviction that my countrymen will gain truly their India by fighting against that education which teaches them that a country is greater than the ideals of humanity."[17] Tagore was an idealist, but his feelings were grounded: he once observed that there really was no word for "nation" in any Indian language.

In a similar vein, Tagore's fellow Bengali humanist, novelist, and short story writer Sarat Chandra Chattopadhyay, asked: "Why must I cling to the customs and practices of a particular country forever, just because I happened to be born there? What does it matter if its distinctiveness is lost? Need we be so attached to it? What's the harm if everyone on earth shares the same thoughts and feelings, if they stand under a single banner of laws and regulations? What if we can't be recognized as Indians any more? Where's the harm in that? No one can object if we declare ourselves to be citizens of the world. Is that any less glorious?"[18] He may not have realized that he was echoing the musings of Epictetus, the Greek philosopher, circa 108 CE: "If the things which are said by the philosophers about the kinship between God and man are true, what else remains for men to do than what Socrates did, namely, never reply to the question: "to what country you belong?" to say that you are an Athenian or a Corinthian, but that you are a citizen of the world. For why do you say that you are an Athenian, and why do you not say that you belong to the small nook only into which your poor body was cast at birth? Is it not plain that you call yourself an Athenian or Corinthian from the place which has a greater authority and comprises not only that small nook itself and all your family, but even the whole country from which the stock of your progenitors is derived down to you."[19] (Neither Epictetus nor Sarat Chandra were likely to have featured, it would seem, on Theresa May's reading list!)

To continue with Tagore, and his take on what constituted a nation: "It is the aspect of a whole people as an organized power. This organization incessantly keeps up the insistence of the population on becoming strong and efficient. But this strenuous effort after strength and efficiency drains man's

energy from his higher nature where he is self-sacrificing and creative....
political freedom does not give us freedom when our mind is not free. The
idea of the Nation is one of the most powerful anaesthetics that man has
invented. Under the influence of its fumes the whole people can carry out its
systematic programme of the most virulent self-seeking without being in the
least aware of its moral perversion."

That moral perversion, to Tagore, was the immoral idea that one set of
people, constituted as a nation in one place, were somehow more significant,
more important, more powerful than, and therefore superior to, another set
of people constituted as a separate nation somewhere else. Such ideas
emerged from the very basic idea of a "national purpose". The German scholar
Otto Bauer had memorably suggested: "The nation is a community of character that grows out of a community of destiny rather than from a mere similarity of destiny."[20] While his ideas of character and culture might have had
merit, such notions of destiny would have alarmed Tagore, for whom the
only destiny that mattered, apart from that of the individual, was of humanity
as a whole. Tagore argued that "there is only one history—the history of man.
All national histories are merely chapters in a larger one."

Tagore's belief in the indivisibility of humankind, and the commonality of
human aims and aspirations, would not allow him to view the nation or
nationalism as in any way desirable or admirable ideas. Tagore believed that
the nation exercised a hypnotic effect on its citizenry, leading individuals to
the false belief that they are in control of their actions, whereas, in fact, they
were enslaved to the idea of the nation, in other words to an idea controlled
and manipulated by those in power. It was this sort of thing that led to the
persecution of Jews, Huguenots, Muslims, Gypsies, and others in Europe, in
quest of an ethnic homogenization that would facilitate the nationalist project
at the expense of "mere" humanity.

"A nation, in the sense of the political and economic union of a people, is
that aspect which a whole population assumes when organized for a mechani-
cal purpose", Tagore argued. "...When this organization of politics and commerce, whose other name is the Nation, becomes all powerful at the cost of
the harmony of the higher social life, then it is an evil day for humanity". In
Tagore's eyes, therefore, the nationalism inspired by a warped love of one's
nation became an ideology that sought to promote the well-being and superiority of the nation in question over the well-being of all other nations.
Alongside the sense of national pride stood the more dangerous ideas of racial
and national superiority.

According to the scholar Frederick Hertz, writing in 1943 at the peak of the Second World War, national aspirations are composed of four elements: a striving for national unity, a striving for national freedom, a striving for separateness, distinctiveness, individuality, originality, or peculiarity, and a striving for distinction among nations. Hertz considered this last element, the striving for distinction among nations, to be the strongest of all four aspirations and to underlie them all—but as he concedes, "the striving for distinction among nations, for honour, dignity, prestige and influence easily becomes a striving for domination."[21] This is a concern that recurs repeatedly in the study of nationalism.

Tagore epitomized the "humanitarian internationalists", in Gellner's phrase, "who deplore the particularism, exclusiveness, intolerance, narrowness and brutality of nationalism", but who were forced to acknowledge "that these traits are deeply and perhaps universally rooted in the human heart or mind". To Gellner, idealist thinkers like Tagore were waging a futile battle; they were "engaged in a painful, arduous struggle with the atavistic, but therefore all the more powerful, tendencies of the human heart."[22]

5

WHAT MAKES PATRIOTISM DIFFERENT

The human heart was, in fact, familiar territory to Tagore, a lyric poet ahead of being a political philosopher. As an earnest of that respect for the sentiments of the heart, Tagore would probably not have disowned the label of "patriot". His work is deeply rooted in the land, culture, and sensibility of his native Bengal, even while he was an indefatigable traveller who celebrated the whole world as his patrimony. Tagore, who had advanced the proposition that a nation can be both mrinmaya (territorial) as well as chinmaya (ideational), wrote songs of patriotism that defined the Bengali renaissance. He believed in Bengal as a torchbearer for the freedom movement—most deeply and fervently expressed by his patriotic songs *"Banglaar Mati Banglar Jaul"*, *"Aji Bangladesh e Hridoy Hothe"*and *"Moru Bijoyer Ketauno Urao"*. So it was not entirely surprising that this ardent critic of nationalism ended up as the author of two countries' national anthems—India's and Bangladesh's—and that a translation of one of his verses, perhaps even sung to one of his compositions, and attributed to a student of his, serves as a third, Sri Lanka's.

Patriotism is, after all, merely the fondness one feels for his own place or country, a love for the motherland akin to the love an individual feels for his mother. The scholar William Galston draws a distinction between patriotism and nationalism: "Patriotism denotes a special attachment to a particular political community, although not necessarily to its existing form of government. Nationalism, with which patriotism is often confused, stands for a very different phenomenon—the fusion, actual or aspirational, between shared ethnicity and state sovereignty."[1] In many Indian languages the distinction is expressed through terms derived from Sanskrit; in both Hindi and Malayalam, nationalism is 'rashtrabhakti', devotion to the state or polity, whereas patriotism is 'deshbhakti', connoting love of homeland. A patriot celebrates what he is born to, not as something inherently superior to other places or forms of being, but as right for him *because it is his*.

Patriotism can be seen in things like the pang of nostalgia for one's own patch of land, the space closest to one's own sense of being, singing of the national anthem at international sporting events, the pride in your country's athletes winning medals at the Olympic Games, the celebration of a country's Independence Day, or similar national occasions, growing misty-eyed as a familiar old song is sung, a garment worn, or a typical dish served, and in the admiration expressed for servicemen and women for their courage, dedication, and heroism in keeping a country and its residents safe. Indian Prime Minister Jawaharlal Nehru was said to have been moved to tears by Lata Mangeshkar's powerful rendition of the song, "*Ai mere watan ke logon/ zara ankh mein bhar lo pani/ Jo shahid hue hein/ unki zara yad karo qurbani* (oh people of my nation, fill your eyes with tears/remember the martyrs, their sacrifices)." Patriotism is far less ideologically-driven than nationalism, takes the successes of others in its stride (since patriots don't define their love on the basis of the failures of others) and does not involve the same destructive devotion that nationalism does. Nor does it require to be consummated in the state. Indeed, as the Indian writer Badri Raina puts it: "Patriotism, or our love of our given clime, leaves us free to value a like sentiment among peoples in other climes and countries, and free to find fault with what we may be lacking without letting bravado or false claims distort those realities. Nationalism, like religious faith, permits no such room. It asks of us that we propagate that we outshine all other peoples, cultures, climes, countries in every sphere of life because of some divine origin or exclusive right to perfection... Patriotism accepts the great reality of diversity; nationalism seeks to obliterate diversity and aims to create the world in its own abstract theology of supremacy."[2]

Patriotism is the older of the two words and dates back to the 17th century. Patriotism has long impelled passionate behaviour in defence of national ideas, which has led some to confuse it with nationalism; after all, patriotism has prompted tens of thousands of people to accept untold sacrifices, even give up their lives, for their country. In the Indian context, the historian C. A. Bayly has dated the origins of Indian nationalism much earlier than most, and links it to the development of a sense of 'traditional patriotism' in pre-colonial times, which was 'a socially active sentiment of attachment to land, language and cult' that developed long before the process of westernization had begun. This sentiment manifested itself in various ways during Company rule and finally culminated in the revolt of 1857. Early patriotism,

Bayly suggests, originated in service to a local lord broadening into "service in defence of a particular *watan* or homeland which, as in the Maratha case, was transformed by sentiment and mutual bonds of loyalty into a *desh* or [national] homeland".[3] This 'traditional patriotism' was vigorously evoked and debated during the freedom struggle, and evolved into Indian national-ism, with the participation of diverse groups of people across languages, religions, regions, castes and communities.

Oscar Wilde described patriotism as "the virtue of the vicious", but he was hardly being fair. Whereas nationalists believe that their nation and what it represents is unchallengeable, patriots love their country not out of misplaced vanity but out of love, not just *because* of its attractiveness but *in spite of* its flaws. Patriots can acknowledge their countries' failings and strive to correct them; nationalists believe there are none, and refuse to accept any that are laid out before them. Such nationalism, in the Scottish philosopher Alasdair MacIntyre's words, is 'a mindless loyalty to one's own particular nation'.[4] Whereas, as Raina writes, "Patriotism acknowledges that where I live is my beloved space, warts and all. ....It recognises that our streets are shabby, our lanes full of clutter, our habits shoddy, our resistance to rationality often grossly debilitating, our defiance of law a routine habit of mind, our male chauvinism shameful and violent, our casteism or racism or communalism deleterious to the most desirable ideals of human rights and human oneness. Patriotism recognizes that things may be better in other countries" and yet, patriots love their land with all its imperfections and work to remedy them.[5]

Patriotism, as the political theorist John H. Schaar writes, "means" love of one's homeplace, and of the familiar things and scenes associated with the homeplace. In this sense, patriotism is one of the basic human sentiments. If not a natural tendency in the species, it is at least a proclivity produced by realities basic to human life, for territoriality, along with family, has always been a primary associative bond. We become devoted to the people, places, and ways that nurture us, and what is familiar and nurturing also seems natu-ral and right. This is the root of patriotism.".[6] Schaar distinguishes between different kinds of patriotism, specifically "natural" or land-based or territo-rial patriotism, involving "a sense of indebtedness to the land itself, such as was felt by ancient Greeks or the Navaho but which is unavailable to us [Americans], since we are a rootless, restless people indifferent to the land", and the alternative, "covenanted patriotism", an idea emerging from Abraham Lincoln, who thought there was a patriotism unique to America. Americans, who were of various races and cultures, were bonded together by a political idea.

Carl Schurz (1829–1906) was an idealistic young German and soldier of fortune who was active in the failed 1848 revolution in his country. After the hopes of the revolutionaries were dashed, Schurz decided to flee to the United States, where he enlisted in the armed forces of the Union government. When the US Civil War began, he was promoted to General, won an impressive public reputation, and then became a U.S. senator after the war. Once he was attacked on the floor of the Senate by one of his colleagues, a Senator from Wisconsin, for being too willing to criticize his adopted country. Schurz responded quietly, "My country, right or wrong: if right, to be kept right; if wrong, to be set right."[7]

Patriotism of this nature is unrelated to the present circumstances of a country's politics: one can be both a true patriot and a strong critic of one's national government. As Mark Twain once put it, "Patriotism is supporting your country all the time, and your government when it deserves it."[8] To the nationalist, his government is beyond questioning: it is always right. Patriots harbour no such illusions. Patriotism, as Carlo Ginzburg noted, is not for the nation you love but the nation you are ashamed of.[9] The nationalist would consider such a statement blasphemous: his nationalism admits of no possibility of shame. "Every miserable fool who has nothing at all of which he can be proud, adopts as a last resource pride in the nation to which he belongs," wrote Schopenhauer, "he is ready and happy to defend all its faults and follies tooth and nail, thus reimbursing himself for his own inferiority."[10]

The patriot is no less devoted than the nationalist to admiring the qualities and achievements of her country, both because they are, in her view, admirable qualities and achievements, but also because they are her country's. The American poet and writer James Baldwin famously said in exile, "I love America more than any other country in the world and, exactly for this reason, I insist on the right to criticize her perpetually."[11] At the same time the patriot readily grants the same privilege to others. She takes pride in her country's achievements while recognizing and accepting that people of other countries can take pride in theirs. (In Raina's words: "Patriots understand and honour patriots in other nations. Nationalism constructs them as potential enemies.")[12] Nor does she exclude others from her love of country; she positively welcomes it. The nationalist's love for his country, on the other hand, is exclusive; it is only for his own kind, and he demonizes those outside his nationalist frame.

Lord Acton, best known for the aphorism that power corrupts and absolute power corrupts absolutely, also drew a value distinction between nationality ("our connection with the race" that is "merely natural or physical") and patriotism, which is the awareness of our moral duties to the political community.[13] Gellner has theorized that nationalism is "a distinctive species of patriotism, and one which becomes pervasive and dominant only under certain social conditions, which in fact prevail in the modern world, and nowhere else"[14] George Orwell articulated the difference between patriotism and nationalism most effectively in his celebrated 1945 essay on nationalism: "By 'patriotism' I mean devotion to a particular place and a particular way of life, which one believes to be the best in the world but has no wish to force on other people. Patriotism is of its nature defensive, both militarily and culturally. Nationalism, on the other hand, is inseparable from the desire for power. The abiding purpose of every nationalist is to secure more power and more prestige, not for himself but for the nation or other unit in which he has chosen to sink his own individuality."[15]

This is key: where patriotism can celebrate the individual as a constituent of the country whose love the patriot expresses, nationalism tends to suppress the individual by exalting the nation above any of its constituents. It rests on the premise that the individual is subordinate to the nation and that his loyalty and devotion to the nation-state must surpass any other interests he has, either as an individual or as a member of a group within the nation. Indeed, terms like "national integrity" and "national power" reflected both the totalizing tendency of nationalism and its irresistible desire to increase its power and strength in perpetuity through the mechanism of the state, as in Mussolini's statement quoted earlier.

In the 1920s to the 1940s, nationalism expressed itself at its most malign in the Fascism of Mussolini in Italy and the Nazism of Hitler in Germany, who used the economic and political turmoil of post-War Europe in the early 20th century to subjugate individual citizens to the needs of the nation. They drummed up an idea of allegiance to themselves justified by national identity and tradition; the overriding interests of the nation meant absolute obedience to its leader—"Il Duce" and "der Fuhrer" respectively—as the embodiment of the nation. The nation itself stood for the interests of the volk, the people, in a manner that subsumed the rights and interests of any individual within it. The Dutch historian Frank Dikötter's analysis of 20th century dictatorships offers an instructive guide to the cult of personality, and a template of the lies dictators tell to build and maintain their regimes.[16] In worshipping the Leader who claims to be the embodiment of the people, the people could enjoy the delusion that they were worshipping themselves through their exaltation of him.

This was most clearly typified in the nationalism exhibited during World War II by the Nazi party in Germany, whose name was a compound of "national" and "socialist", though arguably "statist" would have been a more accurate term than "socialist" for their ruling philosophy. (The full name of the Nazi party was in fact the National Socialist German Workers' Party, the first four words combining all possible political virtues of right and left and claiming to transcend both.) Hitler's Nazism was built on the idea of the superiority of the "Aryan race", of which members of the German nation were the supposed archetypes, superior to all other nations in every respect, military, cultural, intellectual, and political. (The Nazis' use of violence as an instrument of nationalism recalled the bloodthirsty fervour of the French revolutionary nationalists, which had given rise to the term "Jacobin Nationalism".)

To sum up the essential differences between the two, whereas patriotism is about acceptance, co-existence, human values and love of a country for its own sake, nationalism is about unity, power, prestige, pride and strength in relation to others. It combines both tribal notions of group loyalty and a nativist xenophobia that rejects those who are deemed inferior and inadmissible into the primordial group. As the scholar of nationalism Elie Kedourie explains, "patriotism, affection for one's own country, or one's group, loyalty to its institution, and zeal for its defence, is a sentiment known among all kinds of men; so is xenophobia, which is dislike of the stranger, the outsider, and reluctance to admit him into one's own group. Neither sentiment depends on a particular anthropology and neither asserts a particular doctrine of the state or of the individual's relation to it. Nationalism does both; it is a comprehensive doctrine which leads to a distinctive style of politics."[17] Charles de Gaulle said memorably: "Patriotism is when love of your country comes first; nationalism, when hate for people other than your own comes first".[18] Albert Einstein considered it more akin to a sickness: "Nationalism is an infantile thing. It is the measles of mankind."[19]

Part of the sickness is the compulsion of nationalism to dissolve one's individuality within it, and to reject those who do not belong. According to one scholar, nationalism constitutes a "bimodal alienation: engulfment within the group, isolation outside of it."[20] The individual is subordinated to the collective and the individual who is outside the collective is despised for not belonging.

I think back about my friend and former UN colleague Ansar Husain Khan, author of the polemical *The Rediscovery of India*, which received excellent reviews when Orient Longman published it in 1996. Ansarbhai's was an exceptional story: born to a Muslim family in 1926 in Calcutta—in undivided India—of Punjabi and "Mughal" stock, he was a star debater at Lahore

University before passing, as a 22 year-old, the examinations newly conducted by the fledgling state in 1948 to identify promising young Pakistanis for service in the United Nations.

Despite being one of the first Pakistani officials of the United Nations, Ansar-bhai discovered, with his exposure to the world at UN Headquarters, that it was India he really identified with. The positions taken by Indian diplomats at the United Nations, their leadership in challenging apartheid, Nehru's role on the Suez crisis, and the policy of non-alignment, all struck him as speaking to his own sensibilities, articulating his own soul. Pakistan, with its growing Islamization and bigotry, its collapsing governments and military coups, its craven adherence to Western-led alliances like SEATO and CENTO, did not seem to him the country he had grown up in. That country, he averred, was India; why did he now have to be Pakistani when every fibre of his moral and intellectual being rejected the two-nation theory and abhorred what had become of his land?

He then shocked everyone at the UN by applying for Indian citizenship. At first no one took him seriously; a Pakistani UN official, and a Punjabi Muslim at that, wanting to be Indian? The very idea was laughable. But he persisted, writing to the Government of India, pestering Indian diplomats he met at the UN. Meanwhile, his peers and contemporaries from Lahore University were rising up the ranks of the Pakistan civil service, becoming powerful figures in the government; while some were prepared to regard his views as an eccentricity, others began to disapprove strongly, even accusing him of treason. Relations with friends and classmates became strained; one, a house-guest of his old batchmate in Geneva, said, "If you don't like being Pakistani, take a Swiss passport, an American one. No one in Pakistan will care. But Indian? That would be unforgivable."

He stubbornly persisted; and after fighting for years—almost two decades to obtain an Indian passport, because of his convictions, Ansar Husain Khan finally received his wish. He surrendered his Pakistani passport and became an Indian.

When he finally obtained his Indian citizenship, it was at a high price in human terms; he was ostracized by his former compatriots, who refused him a visa even to visit his parents' graves. His connections with classmates, long-standing personal relationships, all proved unavailing. He could never bow his head to his interred parents again, and that was a grief he took with him to his own grave.

A man of wide reading and great erudition, this secular Muslim offered me one of the best definitions I know of the Hindu concept of dharma: "'That by which we should live"'. But the strains and stresses of his conflicted identity were too much for him to bear. Ansar-bhai was living in retirement in Geneva, Switzerland, with his gentle Swiss wife Anita, when he snapped. He pulled out a gun one morning and shot her dead. He called the police, turned himself in, and succumbed himself to a heart attack in the police lockup on the very same day.

It would be facile to suggest that it was his nationalism that killed Ansar Husain Khan. But the question of his nationality exercised his complex mind daily; it came up in almost every conversation we had. Indians were quick to embrace him; he was one of the "prominent citizens" invited by the Indian Permanent Mission in Geneva to meet prime ministers and other prominent dignitaries when they came visiting from India. I would see him there, in his long formal achkan and his shining bald head, looking for all the world like an avuncular pro-consul. But to most Indian officials it was his astonishing choice that defined him; he was always the Pakistani who switched sides, just as he would always remain, in Pakistani eyes, the traitor who crossed over to the enemy.

Ansar-bhai's story is more than that of an individual. It tells us something of what happens when nationalism divides, when its weight becomes too oppressive or when border-lines are drawn through people's hearts and minds.

Nationalism puts the blame for whatever is painful in one's own society squarely on an easily identified group: outsiders, a foreign enemy. Using the ethnic yardstick to identify and define an enemy was most notoriously practised by the United States with the internment of Japanese-Americans during World War Two, the assumption being that their ethnicity made them suspect fifth columnists for Japan, a country with which the US was at war. But India, too, had an episode that was just as disgraceful: *The Deoliwallahs*, a 2020 book by Joy Ma and Dilip D'Souza, is the story of Chinese-Indians, most born in this country, who were incarcerated in detention camps shortly after the 1962 Sino-Indian war as potential fifth columnists, and only released more than four years later, in 1967.[21] This marked the first time since the adoption of the Indian Constitution that neither birth nor belonging, nor roots or livelihood, were deemed sufficient to accord nationality in India: these thousands of innocents were detained for no other reason than that their ethnicity made them suspect—just as today, to some unsavoury nationalists, Muslim Indians' religion is deemed to raise questions about their entitlement to be regarded as citizens of India on a par with others.

At its most extreme, as with the Nazis, nationalism requires not just "enmification" (making the Other an enemy, whether the Other sees himself as an enemy or not) but the defeat and domination of those excluded from its ambit. The 'us-them' syndrome is cultivated, of which the first step is "de-individualization", in which people of a different ethno-national background are no longer seen as individuals, but rather as members of a broader, undifferentiated stereotype. If a society is lucky the syndrome stops there, as it has so far in India; if not, it descends to the second step, of de-humanization, reducing the other to non-human status and no longer entitled to basic human considerations of decency, respect or even (as with Hitler and the Jews) life. Francis Fukuyama dubs as megalothymia ("a new word with ancient Greek roots") this desire to be recognized as superior to other people, and adds that nationalism represents a transmutation of the megalothymia of earlier ages into a more modern and democratic form.[22]

George Orwell saw this clearly: "A nationalist is one who thinks solely, or mainly, in terms of competitive prestige. …. his thoughts always turn on victories, defeats, triumphs and humiliations. … every event that happens seems to him a demonstration that his own side is on the upgrade and some hated rival is on the downgrade."[23] According to Orwell, "While nationalism can unite people, it must be noted that it unites people against other people."

Orwell, writing just after the savagery of the Second World War, seared by the horrors of the Holocaust and Hiroshima and the evils of Fascism, was no kinder to the very idea of nationalism than Tagore. "Nationalism," he cuttingly wrote, "is power-hunger tempered by self-deception. Every nationalist is capable of the most flagrant dishonesty, but he is also—since he is conscious of serving something bigger than himself—unshakeably certain of being in the right." Tagore was moved to poetic passion by the sight of the world gearing itself up for the First World War—a war in which 1.3 million Indian troops fought, of whom as many as 74,187 were killed and another 67,000 were wounded. He wrote presciently at the dawn of the 20th century: "The last sun of the century sets amidst the blood-red clouds of the West and the whirlwind of hatred. The naked passion of self-love of Nations, in its drunken delirium of greed, is dancing to the clash of steel and the howling verses of vengeance."

Both Tagore and Orwell saw nationalism as essentially immoral. This was why Tagore could bluntly assert, 'I am not against this nation or that nation, but against the idea of the nation itself'. Whereas Tagore's ideal of morality was a somewhat dreamy and spiritual globalism, Orwell's moral objections to nationalism were, at bottom, ethical ones: nationalists lived by double standards, condemning outrages by others but excusing them when committed by 'our' side. What Tagore and Orwell saw as nationalism's moral failing is, of course, what has produced its darker side. The nationalist sees his own as the ultimate nation. Any who disagree, whether because of ideology, religion, ethnicity or simply because they belong to another nation, are opposed and have to be put down. In Tagore's words, "Whether through falsehood or error, we have to prove our own superiority to ourselves, and in the process, denigrate other nations." Nationalism, in its extreme forms, has led to warfare, genocide, racial extermination, the mass expulsion of populations and the "ethnic cleansing" that has blighted the world in recent years, in places like Bosnia, Rwanda and Georgia.

And yet for all that, nationalism continues to be a powerful force in the shaping of modern consciousness and for most people, mediates the way in which the meaning of the world is constituted for them.

6

JANUS-FACED NATIONALISM

On the morning of 12 September 1919, Gabriele D'Annunzio (1863–1938), an Italian author, poet, novelist, journalist, politician, parliamentarian, and hero of the First World War, marched into the Adriatic port city of Fiume at the head of a ragtag bunch of nationalists, including dozens of renegade Italian officers and soldiers. They were joyfully welcomed and hailed as liberators by the large local Italian population, who wanted their city to become part of Italy, in contrast to the Italian government, which, like other Allied governments at the end of the War, intended to allot Fiume to the newly-founded kingdom of Serbs, Croats and Slovenes (later known as Yugoslavia). D'Annunzio and his colleagues, Italian nationalists who planned the takeover of Fiume in order to make the city's incorporation into Italy a fait accompli, ruled the port city for about a year, running a somewhat eccentric regime. It didn't last: though many Italians saw their enterprise as a patriotic uprising, they were defeated by Italian regular forces in December 1920 and forced to leave. D'Annunzio survived the setback; Fiume, ceded to the Yugoslavs, was later annexed by Mussolini's government, and D'Annunzio was hailed as the national poet of Italy by the Fascist regime of Mussolini. But what was undertaken as a nationalist endeavour can be said to have failed, both in the short and the long terms: today, as Rijeka, the former Fiume is a city in the Republic of Croatia.[1]

The Italians of Fiume considered the city to be an intrinsic part of the Italian nation, and D'Annunzio, a poet and a warrior, enthusiastically sought to make this conviction reality. They believed that there was something almost mystical in the spirit of Italian nationhood that would either subsume or overwhelm the Croats and other non-Italians of the city. Each nation always represents more than the sum total of its citizens: it has a personality of its own. Marx and Engels understood this appeal of the nation, but drew a distinction between nationalities and nations. Nationalities only became nations when they acquired a state of their own. Otherwise, to Marx, they would remain 'historyless people." (Geschistchslosen Volker). Joseph Stalin, in his seminal 1913 work, *Marxism and the National Question*, argued that "A nation is a historically constituted, stable community of people, formed on the basis of a common language, territory, economic life, and psychological make-up manifested in a common culture." To him, a nation rested on these elements, plus a shared tradition, and geographical and historical homogeneity—the very elements that Marx and Engels had deemed insufficient to constitute a nation. But, in the final analysis, he ended up in the same place as the ideologues his exegesis sought to explain, for Stalin advocated the unification of various nationalities into a unified state, thereby preserving the Marxian distinction between nation-state and nationality.

The impetus for Stalin was his and Lenin's concern about the possible fragmentation of the revolutionary movement in the Russian Empire on nationalist lines. Denouncing national culture and nationalist sentiment, both Lenin and Stalin exalted the international nature of the Communist Revolution. Stalin was able to put his theory into practice in constituting the Soviet Union as a state made of several distinct nationalities, who were recognized as such but did not axiomatically become nations or states. This Marxist idea of nation as an organizing principle, rather than a source of statehood, was finally repudiated only upon the collapse of the USSR in 1991, when national identities long suppressed under the Soviet straitjacket reasserted themselves to constitute independent nation-states. Each has been busy resurrecting and cultivating its own nationalisms, reviving ancient epics, rewriting history and treating the eight decades of subsuming their nationality under the Soviet Union as an aberration in their long and glorious "national" past.

The question arises whether nationalism, then, is wholly negative, in contrast to largely positive patriotism. The answer is that, in the scholar Tom Nairn's words, "all nationalism is both healthy and morbid. Both progress and regress are inscribed in its genetic code from the start."[2] Some scholars have called nationalism a "Janus" concept, two-faced in its capacity to be both good and bad.[3] "There is one [face]," in the words of the philosopher Etienne Balibar, "which tends to construct a state or a community and the one which tends to subjugate, to destroy; the one which refers to right and the one which refers to might; the one which tolerates other nationalisms and may even argue in their defence and include them in a single historical perspective… and the one which radically excludes them in an imperialist and racist perspective."[4] The legal scholar Lea Brilmayer makes a case for the moral significance of nationalism, arguing that "nationalism, itself, is morally transparent, and that this fact accounts for its ability to coexist equally well with good and evil."[5]

This "moral transparency" is apparent in "The American's Creed" written by William Tyler Page in 1917, later passed as a resolution by the US House of Representatives on April 3, 1918, that reads:

> I believe in the United States of America, as a government of the people, by the people, for the people; whose just powers are derived from the consent of the governed; a democracy in a republic; a sovereign Nation of many sovereign States; a perfect union, one and inseparable; established upon those principles of freedom, equality, justice, and humanity for which American patriots sacrificed their lives and fortunes. I therefore believe it is my duty to my country to love it, to support its Constitution, to obey its laws, to respect its flag, and to defend it against all enemies.[6]

Nothing there that, once applied to one's own nation, any nationalist anywhere could reasonably object to. Personally, I am somewhat sympathetic to the Tagore-Orwell consensus that nationalism essentially lends itself to negative outcomes; but I must admit the more nuanced view, well expressed by scholars like Hans Kohn, who distinguished between "good" and "evil" nationalism, German nationalism typifying the latter.[7] The positive view of nationalism is that it is a constructive force, an ideology that builds a state (the nation-state) and so organizes a community of people more efficiently and purposefully, promoting the cohesion of democratic institutions and values; the negative view sees it as a malign, chauvinist, hostile, and power-hungry ideology that tends to subjugate and destroy. The positive view is predicated on the acknowledgement that nationalism has driven many successful independence movements, including the Greek and Irish revolutions (both against imperial powers that denied them their nationhood), the Zionist movement that created modern Israel, and the dissolution of the Soviet Union (which permitted the reassertion of earlier nationalisms long stifled in the collective enterprise of Soviet Communism). The negative viewpoints to the Nazis, the Italian Fascists, and the half-century of nationalist conflict that twice tore the world apart in the first half of the 20th century. "Nationalist conflict has caused enormous suffering, both directly and indirectly", Gellner wrote. "Nationalism is not just a phenomenon, it is also a problem."[8]

Of course, a cynical interpretation of such examples is that nationalism is "good" when it succeeds and "bad" when it fails, since history is written by the winners and the losers can be dismissed as rebels, secessionists or worse. The verdict on Kurdish nationalism, for instance, is yet to be written, since it has succeeded only partly with the achievement of autonomy but not sovereignty in Iraq, with control of territory but not recognition in Syria, and been somewhat suppressed in Iran and Turkey—the countries over whose territories the Kurdish people, and therefore a putative Kurdish nation, would extend.

As for myself, I am inclined to associate what some call "good nationalism" with civic nationalism and patriotism, and leave the bald term "nationalism" to what is seen by most as "bad nationalism". "At its core", writes the American scholar Amitai Etzioni, "patriotism points to passionate concern for one's fellow citizens and the community they share, a resolve to love one's nation despite its defects and to work for its flourishing. This is what I mean by "good" nationalism".[9] While 'good nationalism' and 'patriotism' have a lot in common, there are still differences between the two—what we understand by "good nationalism" is really civic nationalism with liberal democracy stirred in, whereas patriotism is largely a positive emotional and sentimental love of homeland. Speaking for myself, when I refer to my own nationalism, spurn any non-Indian allegiance, and proudly wear a tricolour lapel-pin every day, I am really subscribing to a hybrid of good nationalism and patriotism that rests on the institutional and constitutional pillars of civic nationalism. Between patriotism and nationalism, though, I would argue that patriotism is about what is right and nationalism is about might. Both involve love of country and a willingness to make the ultimate sacrifice for it, but while the patriot is prepared to die for his homeland, the nationalist is prepared to kill for his state.

Scholars across a vast literature have identified five major elements in nationalism: the yearning for national unity (and even uniformity), the requirement of exclusive loyalty, the striving for national (rather than individual) freedom, the aspiration for exclusiveness and distinctiveness, and the quest for honour and prestige among nations. This last is where the biggest problem lies, for this quest for honour and prestige easily becomes an urge for domination. When a nation's dignity requires the defeat of others, when your honour is seen through the need to assert your superiority to others, nationalism can easily degenerate into chauvinism, belligerence and the rejection of co-existence.

As Jawaharlal Nehru wrote in the American periodical *Asia* in 1938, as war clouds gathered above Europe:

> Nationalism is in ill odour today in the West and has become the parent of aggressiveness, intolerance and brutal violence. All that is reactionary seeks shelter under that name—fascism, imperialism, race bigotry, and the crushing of that free spirit of enquiry which gave the semblance of greatness to Europe

in the nineteenth century. Culture succumbs before its onslaught and civilization decays. Democracy and freedom are its pet aversions, and in its name innocent men and women and children in Spain are bombed to death, and fierce race persecution takes place.

Yet it was nationalism that built up the nations of Europe a hundred years ago and provided the background for that civilization whose end seems to be drawing near. And it is nationalism which is the driving force today in the countries of the East which suffer under foreign domination and seek freedom. To them it brings unity and vitality and a lifting of the burdens of the spirit which subjection entails. There is virtue in it up to a certain stage—till then it is a progressive force adding to human freedom. But even then it is a narrowing creed and a nation seeking freedom, like a person who is sick, can think of little besides its own struggle and its own misery.

India has been no exception to this rule and often, in the intensity of her struggle, she has forgotten the world and thought only in terms of herself. But as strength came to her and confidence born of success, she began to look beyond her frontiers....[10]

It is ironic that, in its earliest expressions, nationalism breathed a certain spirit of universalism. When the French overthrew their king with shouts of "Liberty, equality, fraternity" and proclaimed their Declaration of the Rights of Man and of the Citizen, they were asserting a slogan and a set of principles that they believed to be valid not only for themselves, the French people, but for all people everywhere. There was a quasi-religious fervour to the enterprise. As the sociologist Mark Jurgensmeyer observes, religion and nationalism both provide an overarching framework of moral order, a carapace that commands ultimate loyalty from those who shelter under it. "Nowhere is this common form of loyalty more evident than in the ability of nationalism and religion, alone among all forms of allegiance, to give moral sanction to martyrdom and violence."[11] The scholar Llobera attributes the success of nationalism in modernity largely to "the sacred character that the nation has inherited from religion. In its essence the nation is the secularized god of our times".[12]

However, for all certitudes and positives associated with nationalism, side by side there have always been negatives and ambiguities as well. In a report on nationalism in 1939, as the dark clouds of World War II were gathering in the skies above, the Royal Institute of International Affairs at Chatham House, London, referred to the ambiguity in understanding nationalism. Its report observed that the term nationalism "is used in such a sense that Mazzini, Gladstone, and Woodrow Wilson can be described as exponents of nationalism, as well as Herr Hitler."[13]

7

THE ERA OF GLOBALIZATION

The British historian Arnold Toynbee prophesied in a 1970 dialogue with Japanese professor Kei Wakaizumi, the end of nationalism and the creation of a world-state.[1] Nationalism, Toynbee argued, was the "real religion today of a majority of people," and "has been the ruin of one civilization after another." The only effective counter to nationalism, he felt, was the political unification of the world, preceded by a "world-wide spiritual revolution." He looked forward "to a time when every human being will belong to" a world society, a world state, and a world city".

Toynbee was an eminent historian—his twelve-volume *A Study of History* continues to be regarded as a magisterial classic—but an awareness of the past does not necessarily guarantee accuracy about the future, and his prediction has not worn well. It is true enough that for a short while it seemed likely to be borne out, as the ideology of nationalism, rampant and universal in 1939 (and indeed in 1979), seemed unlikely to survive the era of globalization. During the heady three decades (roughly 1980–2010) when that phenomenon appeared to have swept the world, Toynbee seemed prescient indeed. Globalization—accompanied not just by dramatic increases in capital flows across borders, and the frequency and ease of jet travel and international migration, but also by a revolution in satellite communications, and the birth and spread of the internet—intensified the interconnectedness between nations and the peoples of the world. It was reasonable to question whether in a world in which ever-speedier technology, and ever-faster transport and communication, were eroding geography and distance, the territorially-defined classic idea of nationalism made any sense as the principal organizing principle of human activity. The dominance of neo-liberalism and free-market ideology, whose success and prosperity depended on its ability to transcend borders, seemed to underscore the increasing irrelevance of national, let alone ethnic, boundaries.

But today the trend has been reversed, and the coronavirus pandemic appears to have reinforced the increasing preference for isolationism and protectionism in preference to globalization. The question of whether nationalism could survive in today's world was already being asked less and less in the last decade, when the political backlash against globalization, especially in the developed world, resulted in the resurgence of various varieties of indignant nationalism and other particularisms. A world government looks a far more unlikely prospect today than it did in 1945, when US President Harry S. Truman carried in his wallet Tennyson's poem "Locksley Hall," with its idealistic lines:

> For I dipt into the future, far as human eye could see,
> Saw the Vision of the world, and all the wonder that would be;
> Saw the heavens fill with commerce, argosies of magic sails,
> Pilots of the purple twilight dropping down with costly bales;...
> Till the war-drum throbb'd no longer, and the battle-flags were furl'd
> In the Parliament of man, the Federation of the world.
> There the common sense of most shall hold a fretful realm in awe,
> And the kindly earth shall slumber, lapt in universal law.

Neither Tennyson nor Truman could have foreseen the era of Trump, whose "America First" nationalism has been expressed in contempt for the "Parliament of man", where commerce has been reduced to minatory trade wars, and where "universal law", to the extent it exists, frays at the edges in such "federations of the world" as the World Trade Organization and the World Health Organization, both reeling in different ways from Trumpist assaults on their procedures, rules and resources.

Some would argue that nationalist sentiment had never faded even in the heyday of globalization, and that is why it became the natural vehicle for the crystallization and articulation of the backlash. As far back as 1968 the thinker and scholar Stanley Hoffmann took issue with the then-rising view that national states would eventually become obsolete—that ideas of national sovereignty, in an increasingly functionalist world characterized by the emergence and strengthening of institutions like the European Community, could be chewed up leaf by leaf like an artichoke. Hoffmann's riposte was classic: that while this argument was all very well, even an artichoke has a heart, which remains intact after the leaves have been eaten. In other words, people will transfer their loyalty away from the nation-state to something else (like the EU) for purposes of specific advantage, up to a point, but only so far—that is, until it reaches their heart. For, Hoffman argued, the nation is, among other things, 'a daily routine, a community based on habit'.[2]

This habit—these habits—were reflected in much of ordinary political and cultural life even during the era of globalization. As the scholar of nationalism Liah Greenfeld put it, "A European identity could not add dignity to the masses of ordinary British, French, Italian or Dutch citizens because it was Britain, France, Italy and the Netherlands that made Europe dignified in the first place."[3] They were visible in people's pride in their national traditions of food and drink, art and music, cinema and literature, the idiosyncrasies of their monarchs. Even sport. I used to joke for years that as a lifelong UN official I was a convinced internationalist, but every time India played a cricket Test match or entered a World Cup, I rediscovered my inner Indian nationalist! Nationalism, in the relatively benign sense of a patriotic attachment to a particular homeland, and yearning for its success, is inescapable.

This came home to me when watching, on television in New York, the 1996 cricket World Cup final with a friend and colleague from the United Nations. The match was between Sri Lanka and Australia, so I was a relatively neutral spectator, albeit with a bias in favour of my homeland's subcontinental neighbours. My companion on the occasion, Palitha Kohona, had an unusual history. A Sinhalese born in Sri Lanka, he had migrated to Australia, studied law there, worked for the Australian government, and had been seconded to the UN as an Australian official. As the match began he was entirely politically correct, expressing the hope that the country of his formal legal allegiance, Australia, would win. But as the game progressed, it became impossible for him to hide his true feelings, becoming visibly (and soon enough, audibly) elated at every Sri Lankan success—and, towards the end, cheering the underdog Lankans on to their famous victory. I told him after the match that whatever his passport said, he had proven that day that blood mattered more than citizenship, and that he was clearly a Sri Lankan at heart and not the Australian he was officially supposed to be. It did not surprise me, in the end, when he reverse-migrated to the country of his birth, rising to senior governmental office in Colombo as Foreign Secretary, and ending as Sri Lanka's Permanent Representative to the very United Nations he had served as an Australian.

Nationalism of this kind partakes of some of the ethno-chauvinist elements of the more aggressive version, but at bottom is little more than the expression of solidarity with others with whom one shares a common home, or a common cultural history. Scholars might draw careful distinctions among blood, passport, residence, citizenship, patriotism, and nationalism; to me, as I have said earlier, this kind of nationalism is just a form of patriotism, of love for something beyond oneself that one identifies as "MINE"—something you belong to and that belongs to you. It need not threaten others: "I do not want that our loyalty as Indians should be in the slightest way affected by any competitive loyalty," said the great Indian constitutionalist Bhimrao Ramji Ambedkar, "whether that loyalty arises out of our religion, out of our culture or out of our language. I want all people to be Indians first, Indian last and nothing else but Indians."[4]

It is in their denial of this basic human phenomenon, in favour of the "bloodless universality" that Gellner mentions, that many internationalist-minded cosmopolitans falter. They sometimes offer their own globalized worldly sophistication as a 'third way' between reactionary traditionalism or fanatic nationalism, on the one hand, and totally rootless corporatized global capitalism, on the other. There is a certain appeal to the middle path between these extremes, famously characterized by Benjamin Barber as "Jihad versus McWorld".[5] But the essential problem remains that globalized cosmopolitanism fails to come to terms with the elements of tradition, community, ethnicity, religion, and love of homeland that it associates with nationalism. Why is that convinced Europeanists like the Scots, for instance, clamour for independence from a much smaller geographical entity, the United Kingdom? The advocates of the Third Way would be quick to respond that the answer lies in multilateralism—that the Scots, like the Catalans and the Basques, want an independent Scotland within a "United" (but loosely united) Europe.

In such a world people would have two citizenships, one of their immediate political community (in this case Scotland) and one of a wider regional community (in this case the European Union). Through much of the second half of the 20th century, European thinkers, in a Kantian way, had argued that national self-preservation required the subordination of nationalism and state sovereignty to something larger—an international sovereignty expressed regionally among countries with compatible traditions. With globalization, the argument was extended farther, to make the point that national self-preservation even required the integration of national economic and trade interests with those of the globalized world economy. As a typical enthusiast of this idea, writing just after the Second World War, argued, "The true nationalist must therefore become a true internationalist in order to avoid the peril of the impoverishment and destruction of his nation."[6] In Europe, the EU offered an ideal model; NATO—conceived, in Lord Ismay's memorable words, "to keep the Russians out, the Americans in, and the Germans down"[7]—was a necessary precondition, creating the conditions of security that allowed open borders, a customs union and internal free trade. This in turn allowed Germany, blamed for igniting two World Wars, to at last abandon its territorially-aggrandizing nationalism in favour of economic prosperity.

Recent polls suggest that patriotism is waning in appeal in some European countries: asked the question "how patriotic are you?" by a YouGov poll in 2015, only 9% of Germans answered "very", as opposed to 49% of Americans and 48% of Chinese. Of course, the way patriotism slipped into nationalism, and then into Nazism, in their country will have been in the back of the minds of many Germans and explains their anxiety to show themselves as good Europeans. A further 37% said they were "slightly patriotic," 34% said they were "not very patriotic," and 11% averred they were "not at all patriotic".[8] This is partly a reflection of the modern German education system, which after a couple of decades of denial about the horrors of the past, decided to confront them head on and teach schoolchildren what was done by the Nazis in the name of nationalism. Children sobered by being bused to the sites of Nazi-era concentration camps like Dachau or Bergen-Belsen for instruction are understandably less susceptible to the heady emotional appeal of nationalism. Such sentiments may have been diluted by the more recent rise of nativist movements like Pegida (now eclipsed) and Alternative für Deutschland, and the current strains within the EU, but they point to a certain strand of belief in Europe that has few parallels elsewhere. A 2020 survey asked people in 19 countries whether they thought they live "in the best country in the world," and their answers were taken to determine which were the most patriotic. In no country did the majority choose to say "yes"; the most patriotic country in the world by this measure was the US, with 41%. India was second with 35%, and the UK ninth, with just 13%.[9]

In parts of the world other than Europe, especially the newly-independent former colonies jealously seeking to safeguard their hard-won independence and sovereignty, the non-patriotic kind of multilateralism has scant appeal. As one Indian diplomat said to me, "For two hundred years we lost our freedom to a bunch of foreigners claiming they had a 'civilizing mission' in our homeland. Why would we want to be at the receiving end of a late-20th century version of somebody else's civilizing mission' today?" But the multilateralists would argue that in most developing countries—making an honourable exception for India—the relative failure in state-building, that had led to talk of 'failed states' in Africa, meant that the peoples of those states would find greater security and prosperity if they subsumed their sovereignty in a benevolent and undoubtedly more efficient regional or global governance. This argument did not appeal to the leaders of developing countries. And they were able, not unreasonably, to point to the undeniable fact that in the foundational Charter of the United Nations itself, self-determination had been deemed to be the basis of global peace and security. They were in no rush to give it up.

8

THE BETTER NATIONALISM

When my son Ishaan—a half-Malayali, part-Bengali, part-Kashmiri, Indian born in Singapore, who had grown up since the age of six in the United States, studied there, married an American-born woman, and spent his adult life working for a pair of prominent American media houses—announced in 2020 that he had obtained American citizenship, it was America's "civic nationalism" that he celebrated, taking pains to distinguish it from the "blood and soil nationalism" of other countries. As a father who had made the opposite choice in returning to the land of my forebears, I was deeply conflicted about his decision: relinquishing his Indian passport seemed almost a betrayal, an abandonment of his own kind. And yet even as that thought occurred to me, I realized how laughable it would seem to those of Ishaan's generation, who, even as they are connected atavistically from the heart to the land of their ancestors, are far more concerned about identifying the right environment in which they can thrive than on mystical notions of nationalism within old-fashioned territorial boundaries.

Ishaan reacted to my *angst* by saying pointedly that he would have been happy to retain his Indian passport, too, if only India permitted dual nationality. But India does not, insisting, unlike the US, that national allegiance is indivisible, and that every individual can only truly be loyal to one nation. Instead, it grants its non-citizen diaspora a certificate fraudulently called an Overseas Citizenship of India, which it is not: it is merely a lifetime visa, which can (as happened during the 2020 pandemic) be suspended or revoked in exactly the same way as other visas. In fact, the Indian policy towards its diaspora reeks of bad faith, placing its expatriates in the invidious position of either retaining their Indian passport, and so seeming to exploit their host countries, or depriving themselves of their motherland if they choose a different passport. But as I know from my efforts to raise the issue, there is no traction in the Indian establishment for the idea of offering dual citizenship to diaspora Indians. And so many who would have loved to remain Indian, too, while affirming their commitment to new lives elsewhere by claiming those nationalities, have no choice but to forego their instinctively patriotic first option.

Though I have dealt so far principally with the political expression of ethnographically-conceived nationalism, it is important to acknowledge that there has emerged in recent years this other concept of nationalism whose dimensions are not defined principally in terms of shared ethnicity, language or religion, though it does accept the importance of a common heritage and culture. In "civic nationalism", ethnicity cedes primacy to shared citizenship, values, institutions, and constitutional rights and obligations. The patriotism of a civic nationalist is no less than that of a "blood-and-soil" nationalist, but it emerges from a sense of belonging to a nation defined by such constitutional elements, rather than by mystical allegiance to an atavistic fatherland. The United States is the country most commonly portrayed as the epitome of civic nationalism, a "melting pot" of diverse ethnicities united by their allegiance to the US Constitution and the values and practices developed under it over two and a half centuries.

Civic nationalism acknowledges that belonging and citizenship involve multiple and layered affiliations. Rather than ethnicity, religion, language, or even fear of an Other serving as a unifying force, the nation is held together by a sense of mutual commitment among citizens to a common set of ideals, values and rules. This would include the acceptance of differences among them on subsidiary principles and convictions, a respect for diversity, and the co-existence of multiple identities, all rendered secure by sheltering under the common national identity. As the philosopher Theodore Adorno wrote: "An emancipated society…would not be a unitary state, but the realization of universality in the reconciliation of differences." He conceived of "the better state" as "one in which people could be different without fear."[1] Such a benign and tolerant idea of nationhood re-conceives nationalism as a concept applicable to modern, inclusive, multi-ethnic, multi-lingual, and multi-faith societies, as opposed to the conventional understanding of the nation as a cultural and historic entity to which all nationals belonged by blood, and from birth.

Civic nationalism usually requires liberal democracy in order to evolve. Ethnic nationalism seems to require of its adherents that they should literally not think beyond their genes. While a basic building-block of any nation is bound to be ethnic, it can evolve into something more noble, egalitarian, civilized, equal, and respectful and welcoming of all those who constitute it, through a process of creating a civic nationalism. This kind of nationalism relies less on instruments of power and domination than on a network of institutions that constitute checks and balances on the government's power, formally limit the executive's authority, and prevent democracy from descending into crass majoritarianism by collectively protecting the rights of religious, linguistic, sexual, cultural, and other minorities. The formal mechanisms include the rule of law and law courts, parliamentary accountability to prevent governmental overreach, devolved institutions at local levels to offer alternative sources of power and authority, a vibrant civil society and a free press, independent think tanks and universities, and (arguably, above all) a strong Opposition, supporting the system but opposing the government of the day. In civic nationalism, opposition or criticism is never dismissed as treasonous, but recognized as an intrinsic part of the governance structure. Equal access is provided to education, citizenship, and community activities; language policies take into account minority and migrant interests; national symbols eschew the divisive for the unifying; legal structures buttress the primacy of such civic institutions over religious or ethnic ones. The economy is free and allows entry to all (and in socialist or social democratic variants, takes care to distribute the revenues deriving from that free economy to those on its margins). Books, magazines, films, poetry, and theatre offer not just entertainment but critique and resistance to the prevailing orthodoxy. Key to civic nationalism is the celebration of diversity, ethnic, linguistic, religious, and political.

Interestingly enough, the civic nationalism that Ishaan hailed in the US, rather than the ethnic nationalism of many other countries, is not only suited for the advanced liberal democracies of the West, but to many developing nations. Many of these, as a result of the way in which political boundaries were drawn by erstwhile colonial masters, lack a single dominant ethnicity and so do not lend themselves easily to ethnic nationalism. Since most postcolonial states, especially in Africa, are constituted by a collection of smaller political fragments with no clear ethnic majority, ethnicity or language alone cannot constitute the basis for nationhood. This is where civic nationalism could come in to save the state, by creating national institutions and practices that acknowledge and accommodate ethno-national heterogeneity. Civic nationalism could create bonds of nationhood inclusive enough to tie together disparate clans and tribes in mutual commitment and loyalty, but also loose enough not to seek to impose its own moral system on these disparate entities within the state.

Of course, civic nationalism is not necessarily a panacea for all heteroge-nous nations, since it elides the question Stalin acknowledged, of there being "nations" within the state, whose existence is not reflected in statehood—the "Ashanti nation" in Ghana, for instance, or the "Bugandan nation" in Uganda. There is a perpetual question of accommodating two loyalties within a single state—loyalty to the "nation", ethnically-conceived, and loyalty to the state established by law. Whereas in the two examples mentioned it has proved possible to invent a form of civic nationalism in both states, which has suc-ceeded in integrating multiple nations in one state, there have been violent separatist movements in others, some of which have resulted in the creation of separate states altogether—such as Eritrea and South Sudan. Those exam-ples suggest that when the two loyalties are seen as being in irreconcilable conflict, loyalty to the state often loses out in favour of the "nation". Civic nationalism, in principle, offers them a way of ensuring that the two loyalties need not be incompatible, by recognizing diversity, providing a viable basis for citizenship and building common institutions that can permit these states to achieve the good governance indispensable to development (which in turn could, ideally, make separatism unnecessary). When that works, the state flourishes; when it does not, and conflict cannot be contained, civic national-ism fails to hold a multi-national state together.

Of course, many post-colonial countries face the challenge of creating viable national political units out of the remnants of former colonies that are a patchwork of ethnicities, tribes, and linguistic groups united only by the common experience of shared foreign rule. Nationalism becomes essential to create the trust, solidarity, and mutual understanding needed for the coun-try's survival, but in many developing countries it only succeeds if it is an inclusive, liberal, democratic nationalism. The civic nationalism I have described does not seek so much "to homogenise the population as to unify them around certain shared values by allowing minorities among them to retain their own symbols [and] memories".[2]

There are other important differences. The constitutive act of traditional nationalism sees the national community as an organic whole, defined by blood and geography, into which individuals are born, and to which they are required to subordinate their private identities and interests. Civic national-ism, on the other hand, presupposes a voluntary association of individuals who, secure in their own private identities and while pursuing their private interests, join the community by free choice in a spirit of cooperation to defend their common values. At least in theory, civic nationalism would per-mit those who have joined to leave as well, but while Canada and Britain may have accorded referenda granting this privilege to Quebec and Scotland, respectively, many other nations, including the US, Spain, and India, have acted harshly against secessionism. Still, it is true that civic nationalism does not merely extol the nation's ancient glories; it admits to its imperfections, failures, and atrocities. But it finds a sense of purpose and justification in the continuing collective moral struggles for equality, dignity, and progress that help define and shape the nation as a community.

Yet, as one perceptive observer, who happens to be my other son Kanishk, has argued, "The problem with liberal nationalism of this kind—including the pluralist variety in India—is that it can be rather lofty and abstract. Its values of inclusion and equality are universal, to a fault. With reason, the borders of its moral commitment tremble and fade. Why not extend your sense of attachment and loyalty well beyond the closed circle of the nation, especially as globalization enmeshes our lives with those far away? Why shouldn't a New Yorker be as committed to a Nebraskan as to somebody in New Delhi? For a lot of us, there is nothing fuzzy about that universal sense of connection and belonging, but it does inevitably dull the strength of the particular claim of the nation."[3]

This raises an interesting conundrum. Is civic nationalism, then, too "civil" to be "nationalism" at all? If one is bound together with others because of a shared attachment to certain values and practices, why should that attachment stop at the borders of one's own nation? The answer lies in the undeniable fact that constitutions and institutions tend to be established, and extend their jurisdiction within territorially-bounded states. Loyalty to the specific form of civic nationalism practised in the USA need not be incompatible with that practised in, say, France or India, but for obvious reasons it cannot be identical. That does not prevent a shared solidarity across civic nationalisms, as liberals or socialists in one country might unite in support and defence of liberals and socialists everywhere else, if they saw their rights being endangered within their own states. But that solidarity does not necessarily undermine the specific realities of each country's own civic nationalism.

Still, the reality of my own family offers evidence in favour of Kanishk's position. My parents returned to India, but their children all joined the diaspora. After three years abroad as a student, twenty-nine as a UN official, and two more as an itinerant consultant, all while remaining an Indian citizen, I emulated my father in returning to India for good. But both my sisters settled abroad and acquired foreign passports. My sister Shobha is an American citizen, the proud mother of two Indian-American children, and grandmother to two grandchildren in whose veins flow blood from three continents and several countries. My sister Smita is British, and the mother to three brown Britons, one of whom is currently working in the United States. So, there are three different passports (and eleven addresses) among my siblings and my parents' seven grandchildren, but we are still a family, closely connected to one another and conscious, to a greater or lesser degree, of our Indian heritage. Our cultural practices are still anchored in those we learned from our parents and imparted to our children; we are in daily contact, share thoughts and photographs, holiday together, and have often reunited in our 200-year-old ancestral home in rural Palakkad, sharing memories of meals cooked by our grandmother, local lore, and family gossip, hearing stories of our history and mythology. The foreign-born members of the family all regularly visit India, the land of their parents' roots. All this may reflect little more than the miracle of modern trans-global communications, but the very fact that our different nationalities pose no impediment accentuates the question: does nationality really matter that much today? As we know, it does and it doesn't.

In parts of the world we have entered an age of increasingly benign and inclusive ideas of nationalism, reconceived as redefining states into tolerant, multi-ethnic, and multi-religious communities. A passport, a residence, even a citizenship, define less than they used to; you can be a proud Turk with homes in both Istanbul and Bremen while carrying a German passport and playing soccer for Germany as a citizen of that nation. However, challenges to this warm and fuzzy faith in the near-magical powers of reconciliation and accommodation that civic nationalism promotes have already arisen in the resurgent triumph of majoritarian nationalism preached by a long list of current world leaders—of whom the most prominent are, as we have seen, the US's Donald Trump, Britain's Boris Johnson, Brazil's Jair Bolsonaro, Hungary's Viktor Orban, Russia's Vladimir Putin, Turkey's Recep Tayyip Erdogan, Israel's Benjamin Netanyahu, and India's Narendra Modi. They are not alone either: their emulators exist in every democracy, and where they are not in power, in many cases constitute the principal Opposition to liberal governments in several European states. The American political scientist Francis Fukuyama has raised the alarm about these developments, writing that such "competing and angry nationalisms" have made populist democracy "an active threat to individual liberty".[4]

On the other side of the argument, an intellectual challenge has been mounted to civic nationalism in the work of contemporary writers like the Israeli scholar Yoram Hazony, who argues in *The Virtue of Nationalism* that the nation-state offers indispensable protection for a people against the depredations of modern liberalism, which he calls an "empire", an imperial endeavour spreading its tentacles across the globe and threatening human dignity and the freedom of people to be themselves.[5] Though Hazony, a former aide to Israel's Prime Minister Benjamin Netanyahu, evidently bases his view of nationalism on the experience of the ethno-nationalist state of Israel, he finds an echo in the work of the conservative American magazine editor Rich Lowry, author of *The Case for Nationalism*. Lowry sees nations as organic entities, built around shared identities and values, but rather than celebrating the American "civic nationalist" experience of integrating cultural and racial diversity in the national melting-pot, Lowry anchors his American nationalism in the hallowed trinity of the English language, the Christian religion, and European ancestry, canonizing in the process a pantheon of white male national icons as the only authentic American national heroes.[6] Hazony and Lowry are merely among the first intellectual exegetes of a reversion to ethno-nationalism in the contemporary world: this is not a development that is going to disappear in a hurry.

The writer and historian Jill Lepore has been paying attention, regretting that the project of thinking and writing about American nationhood has been left by liberal democrats to the ethno-nationalist chauvinists. "Who," she asked in an essay in the magazine *Foreign Affairs*, "was doing the work of providing a legible past and a plausible future—a nation—to the people who lived in the United States? Charlatans, stooges, and tyrants...When historians abandon the study of the nation, when scholars stop trying to write a common history for a people, nationalism doesn't die. Instead, it eats liberalism."[7] This is not an entirely new insight. As the British philosopher Brian Barry remarked in the 1980s, Anglo-American academia and liberal intellectual circles have found it difficult to embrace nationalism, regarding it as 'inimical to civilised values', and this has left a gap that has been exploited by the cynical opportunism of the ethno-nationalists.[8]

Britain was to see the truth of Barry's words in the mendacious xenophobia of the 2016 Brexit vote. The Leave campaign claimed a monopoly on British values, redefined to include elements that were openly racist and hostile to immigrants and residents of foreign origin speaking languages other than English. The Brexit campaign, with its stark evocation of images of 'swarms' or 'floods' of refugees and low-paid workers pouring into Britain, was a crude affirmation of the ethnic nationalism of the "Little Englanders", a far cry from the cosmopolitan multiculturalism propounded by that nation's civic nationalists. Both in the US and in Britain, contemporary nationalism is suffused with nostalgia for a purer, less mongrelized past, although much of this is imaginary and time-bound, with inconvenient details edited out: "Make

America Great Again" implies "Make America White Again", not "Make America Native American Again". Just as the Brexiteers exhorted "Leave" voters not just to take control, but to "take *back* control," Trump promised not merely to make America great, but to "make America great *again*." Sotto voce, Trumpists really meant, in the bargain, "we were great once, and we can be great once more only if we roll back the tides of foreigners and minorities who have engulfed us". In Tyler Stiem's words, "The nostalgia of Brexit and Make America Great Again is exactly an appeal to the consoling idea (for some white people) that the moral failures of the past are, in fact, the triumphs we once thought they were."[9]

9

A SENSE OF BELONGING

In the 1980s and 1990s, Britain had been grappling with the question of how to integrate minorities that were not white, Anglo-Saxon, or Christian. The challenge lay in something civic nationalists did not pay enough attention to, the emotional aspects of national culture, what scholars tend to call the "affective dimension" of belonging to a nation. An example of how collective narratives of belonging clashed with the instincts of minorities arose when British politician Norman Tebbit posited a yardstick that became infamously known as the 'Tebbit Test'. According to him, all those citizens of the UK who, in international cricket matches, cheered the England team's opponents, were not 'truly' British. The allusion was clearly to Indians, Pakistanis, and West Indians in the UK who thronged cricket grounds to cheer the teams representing their ancestral homelands when they took on the English.

The Tebbit Test raised a fair question to which civic nationalism could not provide a convincing answer: is nationalism more than the convenience of a passport or the right of residence in a particular country? Does it not involve a certain assumption of loyalty to the nation whose state one is a citizen of, in all its endeavours, whether warfare or sport? If it does, then it is reasonable to demand of racial and ethnic minorities that they should truly belong to their new country in emotive terms as well. Civic nationalists rather loftily suggest that such tests don't matter, and that in a liberal democracy, citizens should be free to support whomever they like, but this is hardly the popular majority view. (Of course, the ethno-nationalists tend to go even farther, arguing that ethnic minorities can never truly belong, and indeed do not belong at all.)

Still, the affective dimensions of belonging to a nation clearly transcend the formal convenience of citizenship rights and presuppose some willingness to abandon ancestral loyalties for new ones. This is not something that liberal democrats and civic nationalists are prepared to demand explicitly; rather, they seem to hope it will come with time, maybe over a couple of generations, as the minorities are immersed in the habits of belonging to the culture of their new nations. Others would suggest that this is not possible without overt coercive action, however. In both the US and Europe, problems have arisen over the integration of Muslim minorities, increasingly viewed by the ethno-nationalists as indigestible ingredients in the national melting-pot because of the totalizing demands of their Islamic faith and the political hostility of much of global Muslim opinion to the past and present politics of the West.

Whereas Muslim migrants were largely welcomed into many of these societies by civic nationalists who saw their presence as contributing to a creative hybridization of national identity, today there is an evident backlash from newly-assertive religio-racial nationalists in Western countries. The rejection of classic liberal multiculturalism in the West has not only come from the political right: in the Netherlands, for instance, the movement led by a gay liberal, Pym Fortuin, against Muslim immigrants actually sought to integrate them better into the host community by obliging them to abandon their traditional values and accept sexual freedom, homosexuality, and other practices in Dutch society that the immigrants recoiled from. Fortuin and his sympathizers were not seeking the expulsion of immigrants, but rather to 'nationalize' immigrant minorities by teaching them the values of Dutch citizenship, defined in terms of the dominant ethnic culture. Such thinking has found broad resonance in such decisions as France's ban of the "burqini" on beaches and in swimming-pools, a swimming costume worn by conservative Muslim women to cover them from head to toe while entering or emerging from the water.

These developments partly explain the ethno-nationalist surge in many nations, buttressed by a resurrection of religious revivalism and directed at the incompatibility with the "national heritage" of practices and behaviours of minorities, whose right to be different is upheld by secular civic nationalists. India, ironically, has had its own version of the Tebbit Test, with Hindutva chauvinists arguing that Muslims' disloyalty to India was demonstrated whenever India played Pakistan at cricket—Muslims allegedly set off celebratory firecrackers whenever their co-religionists won. Though such charges are, to a great extent, urban legends, representing extreme generalizations from a handful of isolated incidents (which have been periodically trotted out since the 1980s to serve assorted political agendas), the issue of whether national loyalty always trumps religious allegiance or other extra-national affinities has become something of an acid test of nationalist virtue, whether in India or in the West. Those civic nationalists who say that a free citizen should be free to support whichever team he likes get short shrift from the outraged, who are inflamed by tolerance for such "anti-national" conduct.

But there is an unspoken difference between two forms of belonging—citizenship and identification. Citizenship is about the conferral of rights of participation in the national collective; identification relates to the emotive dimensions of belonging. A sense of belonging to a community, a social category, or a collective, is arguably not identical to the sense of belonging to a political community, which confers certain rights of participation and concomitant responsibilities with it. Civic nationalists can argue they are only concerned with the latter, and that the former may be desirable but is not necessary; ethno-nationalists would argue that the former is a necessary precondition to the latter, and that citizenship should not be granted to those who do not belong.

It is easy enough to deplore the deniers of minority rights by rightly decrying racism, bigotry, and xenophobia as undesirable traits. But it continues to beg the question the ethno-nationalists ask: if there are no common ethnic memories and primordial loyalties which all citizens can hark back to, if there are no cementing values anchored in religion and language to concretize a sense of community allegiance, if there is no moral creed or historic heritage on which the government is anchored, and if people merely see the state as a convenient platform granting them an address and a passport to pursue their personal interests, what becomes of the nation? Is the dominant ethnicity in a nation claiming its own authenticity as a virtue axiomatically reprehensible, when so much that is said, done and believed in by minorities or immigrants is evidently "inauthentic" when posited against the nation's past history?

But conversely, who are the arbiters of authenticity anyway? In India, the passionate defenders of "Bharatiya sanskriti"—"traditional" Indian culture—have portrayed it in terms that exclude a long history of sexual permissiveness, erotic poetry, and explicit statuary (even in temples) delineating behaviours that these advocates of authenticity would deny is "truly" Indian. Would the Hindu-chauvinist rioters disrupting Valentine's Day, vandalizing shops selling Valentine's Day cards, and harassing couples on 14 February, suddenly change their behaviour if told the day was actually consecrated to the Hindu god of love, Kamadeva? What entitles the self-appointed custodians of authenticity to impose their version of nationalism on other citizens who, for one reason or another, cannot or will not conform?

It does no good to deny the legitimacy of such questions, as advocates of civic nationalism too easily tend to do. In addition to that, there is the challenge of defining what constitutes loyalty to the nation: is it loyalty to an idea, to a constitution, to the actions of the government of the day, to the dominant faith, to the cultural practices of the majority? When American citizens of Indian origin gather in a large stadium in Houston (as they did in Wembley and similar locations overseas) to see, hear and enthusiastically applaud a foreign political leader, Narendra Modi, while holding American passports and enjoying the conveniences and privilege of another land—often, as in both Houston and Wembley, in the presence of somewhat bemused national leaders to whom they owe their formal allegiance—are they somehow betraying the greater obligations of their current citizenship?

In most, perhaps all, countries that I am aware of, loyalty is defined in law only negatively. All constitutional provisions and statute-books define disloyalty: treason, sedition, espionage, sabotage, and related crimes are proscribed and punishable by law. But loyalty *to* the nation is not itself defined, and the failure to adhere to some invisible, and indivisible, code of nationalism is not illegal. For the ethno-nationalists to suggest it is illegitimate gives rise to new sources of tension that militate against the classic nationalist project of national integration.

The clash between rival communities and their contending narratives can lead to internal conflict, and in the worst cases—not yet experienced by the developed world's liberal democracies but hardly unknown in developing countries and post-colonial states—to long-term instability, administrative paralysis and even state collapse. It is not a prospect that the most idealistic civic nationalist would wish to contemplate.

PART TWO

THE IDEA OF INDIA

How do the ideas of nationalism we have described relate specifically to India? India's struggle for freedom from the British Raj had all the trappings of anti-colonial nationalism, evoking a glorious pre-colonial past, a hoary history, and a vigorous cultural heritage, including the evocation of different versions of religious faith and practice. "India," wrote the British historian E.P. Thompson, "is perhaps the most important country for the future of the world. All the convergent influences of the world run through this society.... There is not a thought that is being thought in the West or East that is not active in some Indian mind."[1]

This part discusses how Indian nationalism was reified in the Constitution adopted after three years of debate, the "idea of India" that emerged from both the nationalist movement and its institutionalization in the Republic of India, and the way in which that idea was implemented and evolved in a spirit of civic nationalism through the first seven decades of India's independence. The challenges to that idea will be discussed in subsequent parts of this book.

10

THE BASICS

"In a world where nationality and nationalism were deemed to be special virtues in a people," Dr B. R. Ambedkar observed somewhat tartly in 1940, "it was quite natural for the Hindus to feel, to use the language of Mr H. G. Wells, that it would be as improper for India to be without a nationality as it would be for a man to be without his clothes in a crowded assembly."[2] That sardonic comment by the man who would chair the Drafting Committee of India's Constitution, and be known in the West as India's James Madison (the principal draftsman of his Constitution), was not intended to be taken as a dismissal of the idea of Indian nationalism. Rather it was his way of questioning the existing underpinnings of that idea, especially in the context of the challenge that had arisen to it with the demand of the Muslim League for the partition of the country.

The 'Idea of India'—a phrase, even a cliché that I evoked in the preface to this book—has become a highly contested concept these days. But I cited it secure in the conviction that the idea of India, though the phrase is Tagore's, and so hardly recent, is, in some form or another, an even older aspiration for cultural unity that appears throughout the history of our civilization, and is arguably as old as antiquity itself. When, in explaining my choice of nationality, I had said to that British consular official, "I look in the mirror and I see an Indian," I seemed to be implying an ethnic basis for my nationhood. But that was never the whole story: while I had studied the anti-colonial nationalism that had catalysed and driven the Indian freedom struggle, and written about the civic nationalism enshrined in its Constitution, I was reflecting a far deeper sense of what being Indian meant.

At midnight on 15 August 1947, independent India was born as its first prime minister, Jawaharlal Nehru, proclaimed "a tryst with destiny…a moment…which comes but rarely in history, when we step out from the old to the new, when an age ends, and when the soul of a nation, long suppressed, finds utterance." With those words he launched India on a remarkable journey—remarkable because it was happening at all. "India," Winston Churchill once snarled, "is merely a geographical expression. It is no more a single country than the Equator." Although Churchill was often wrong about many things, it is true that no other country in the world embraces the extraordinary mixture of ethnic groups, profusion of mutually incomprehensible languages, varieties of topography and climate, diversity of religions and cultural practices, and range of levels of economic development that India does.

And yet India, as I have repeatedly said, is more than the sum of its contradictions. Those contradictions were repeatedly stressed by British rulers in self-justification for their rule. Thus Benjamin Disraeli (who memorably said that "a nation is a work of art and a work of time," gradually created by a variety of influences, including climate, soil, religion, customs, manners, historical incidents and accidents, and so on, which "form the national mind"), argued that India was not a nation: it lacked a common language, a common religion, a shared tradition, a historical experience, a cohesive majority, and a defined territory, all of which he regarded as the essential ingredients of a nation.[3] But Indian nationalists had an effective riposte. India is a country held together, in the words of Nehru, "by strong but invisible threads ... a myth and an idea, a dream and a vision, and yet very real and present and pervasive."[4]

Whichever way you think about it, the challenge of defining India is immense. It is a land of snow peaks and tropical jungles, with twenty-three major languages (listed in the Constitution) and 22,000 distinct 'dialects' (including some spoken by more people than speak Swedish, Maori, or Estonian), inhabited at the start of the third decade of the twenty-first century by 1.3 billion individuals of almost every ethnic extraction known to humanity. It has given birth to four major religions and offers a home to many more; it preaches doctrines of spirituality and wisdom, anchored in universalism and inclusivity, while still being afflicted by a caste system that visits grave disabilities upon millions of its people. It has two major classical musical traditions (Carnatic and Hindustani) to go with innumerable folk disciplines; multiple classical dance forms (Kathakali, Kuchipudi, Bharata Natyam, Kathak, Manipuri, Odissi and so on) that create a rich jambalaya of diverse cultures transmitted through gurus directly mentoring select students; and by far the largest film industry in the world. In Whitman's phrase, it is vast; it contains multitudes. Is there even, one might well ask, an unchallengeable idea of the Indian nation?

And yet I have written in my book *Inglorious Empire* about how the notion of Bharatvarsha in the Rig Veda, of a land stretching from the Himalayas to the seas, contained the original territorial notion of India; for the bounds imposed by the mountains and the oceans created common bonds as well, making the conception of India as one civilization inhabiting a coherent territorial space and a shared history truly timeless. There are deep continuities, therefore, in the imagining of Indian nationhood, that transcend centuries of internal division.

Even if "nationalism" as a concept arose in Europe in the 19th century, as I have observed, people everywhere had a sense of belonging to communities larger than themselves: after all, the notion of the Muslim umma, or Sankaracharya's conception of Hinduism's sacred geography, both imply large communities that people could identify with. In this sense it is not contradictory to argue that India is an "old" nation, even though "nation" is a new concept. But the nation became a salient *political* category in India only with the anti-colonial struggle, the case for collective self-government, and the dawn of democracy. So long as India was governed by monarchs or empires, Indians were subjects, and the question of identification was often more cultural than political. As Indians became citizens, the story changed.

I will return to this theme. For now, let me stress that the idea of India as a modern nation based on a certain conception of human rights and citizenship, vigorously backed by due process of law, and equality before law, is a relatively recent and strikingly modern idea. Earlier conceptions of India drew their inspiration from mythology and theology. The modern idea of India, despite the mystical influence of Tagore, and the spiritual and moral influences of Gandhiji, is a robustly secular and legal construct based upon the vision and intellect of our founding fathers, notably (in alphabetical order!) Ambedkar, Nehru, and Patel. The Preamble of the Constitution itself is the most eloquent enumeration of this vision. In its description of the defining traits of the Indian republic, and its conception of justice, liberty, equality and fraternity, it firmly proclaims that the law will be the bedrock of the national project.

To my mind, the role of liberal constitutionalism in shaping and undergirding the civic nationalism of India is the dominant strand in the broader story of the evolution and modernization of Indian society, especially over the last century. The principal task of any Constitution is to constitute: that is, to define the rules, the shared norms, values and systems under which the state will function and the nation will evolve. Every society has an interdependent relationship with the legal systems that govern it, which is both complex and, especially in our turbulent times, continuously and vociferously contested. It is through this interplay that communities become societies, societies become civilizations, and civilizations acquire a sense of national and historical character.

The Chairman of the Drafting Committee of the Constituent Assembly, Dr B. R. Ambedkar, would no doubt have argued that the constitutional roots of Indian republicanism ran deep. He remarked that some ancient Indian states were republics, notably those of the Lichhavis who ruled northern Bihar and lower Nepal in the 6th and 5th centuries BCE (around the Buddha's time), the Mallas, centred in the city of Kusinagara, and the Vajji (or Vriji) confederation, based in the city of Vaishali. Early Indian republicanism can be traced back to the independent gana sanghas, which appear to have existed between the 6th and 4th centuries BCE. The Greek historian Diodorus, describing India at the time of Alexander the Great's invasion in 326 BCE (though he was writing two centuries later), recorded that independent and democratic republics existed in India.[5] They seemed, however, to include a monarch or raja, and a deliberative assembly that met regularly and discussed all major state decisions. The gana sanghas had full financial, administrative, and judicial authority and elected the raja, who therefore was not a hereditary monarch. The raja reported to the assembly and in some states, was assisted by a council of other nobles.

The oldest Indian republics varied in their constitutional arrangements. The Licchavis had a primary governing body of 7,077 heads of the most important families in the republic, while the Shakyas, Koliyas, and Mallas opened their assembly to the participation of all men, rich and poor. Villages had their own assemblies, under local chiefs called gramakas. But despite the assemblies, it is not entirely clear whether the composition and participation were truly popular, and the unequal caste duties and privileges of the members might well have affected their roles in the state, whatever be the formal importance of the institutions. Still, in the absence of hereditary monarchs with absolute powers, these states allow India to claim a standing equal to that of ancient Greece or Rome in the evolutionary history of the republic. It is no surprise, then, that while the ancient and medieval worlds largely celebrated kings and conquerors, India, while generally observing the same traditions, had other inspirations to hark back to before it entered the era of monarchs and emperors. The early Indian polities had systems, edicts, and policies, but not legislation in the sense we would understand the term today.

The British interlude was undoubtedly transformative, and it helped introduce the idea of "the law" as the guiding principle of government, and therefore, implicitly (when one came into being) of the state. With the advent of the law, lawyers naturally rose to prominence in affairs of state. Since the Age of Enlightenment, many of the great people who changed the course of their nations, and the world, for good, and sometimes for the worse, have been lawyers. India was no exception: in the Constituent Assembly, Ambedkar, Nehru, and Patel were all lawyers (as were the principal progenitors of the subcontinent's two nationalisms before Independence, Mahatma Gandhi and Mohamed Ali Jinnah). These men, and increasingly women—the Founding Fathers and Mothers of the Indian Republic—had the vision and the intellect to anticipate the problems and challenges that all civilizations in the modern era have had to confront. Though elected by the limited franchise permitted by the British in their rationing of democratic freedoms to Indians, the members of the Constituent Assembly, across all political lines and backgrounds, enjoyed great legitimacy, particularly those whose leadership of the freedom struggle had entailed great personal commitment and sacrifice. In the process, these distinguished lawyers found the best check-and-balance mechanism in the political and legal system created by and reflected in the book of law, the Constitution, to combat these challenges and to protect the interests of all Indians in equal measure.

In dealing with the vast and complex realities of a subcontinent of 330 million people, politically administered in a dozen different administrative units, while seeking to integrate over 600 "princely states" into the new Republic, and in devising systems and rules to embrace all of them, the founders had to acknowledge the need to produce political unity out of ethnic, religious, cultural, linguistic, and communal diversity. As I argued nearly a quarter of a century ago in *India: From Midnight to the Millennium*, the most viable approach to India lies in a simple insight: the singular thing about India is that you can only speak of it in the plural. There are, in the hackneyed phrase, many Indias. Everything exists in countless variants. There is no single standard, no fixed stereotype, no "one way". Throughout the first seven decades of independence, India's pluralism was acknowledged in its constitutional and political arrangements, which encouraged a bewildering variety of social groups, religious communities, sectional interests, and far-fetched ideologies to flourish and contend. Even though India was partitioned when the British carved chunks out of it to create a homeland for its Muslims, it embraced the Muslims who remained (for decades there were more Muslims in India than in Pakistan), and sustained them through an official policy of secularism that is now bitterly challenged by its current ruling party. In an era when most developing countries chose authoritarian models of government, claiming these were needed to promote nation-building and to steer economic development, India chose to be a multi-party democracy. And despite many ups and downs, and moments of greater or lesser stress on its democratic institutions (of which more later in this volume), India has remained a democracy—flawed, perhaps, but flourishing. Many observers abroad have been astonished by India's survival as a pluralist state. But India could hardly have survived as anything else. Pluralism is a reality that emerges from the very nature of the country; it is a choice made inevitable by India's geography and reaffirmed by its history.

Pluralism and inclusiveness have long marked the essence of India. India's is a civilization that, over millennia, has offered refuge and, more importantly, religious and cultural freedom, to Jews, Parsis, several varieties of Christians, and, of course, Muslims. Jews came to Kerala centuries before Christ, with the destruction by the Babylonians of their First Temple, and they knew no persecution on Indian soil until the Portuguese arrived in the sixteenth century to inflict it. Christianity arrived on Indian soil with St Thomas the Apostle (the Doubting Thomas of Biblical lore), who came to the Kerala coast some time before 52 CE and was welcomed on shore, if legend is to be believed, by a flute-playing Jewish girl. He made many converts, so there are Indians today whose ancestors were Christian well before any Europeans discovered Christianity. Islam is portrayed by some in the north as a religion of invaders who pillaged and conquered, but in Kerala, where Islam came through traders, travellers and missionaries rather than by the sword, a south Indian king was so impressed by the message of the Prophet that he travelled to Arabia to meet the great teacher himself. The king, Cheruman Perumal, perished in the attempt, but the Kerala coconuts he took with him have sprouted trees that flourish to this day on the southern coast of Oman. Indeed, the Zamorin of Calicut was so impressed by the seafaring skills of the Muslim community (epitomized in the famed and fearless Kunjali Maricars) that he issued a decree obliging each fisherman's family to bring up one son as a Muslim to man his all-Muslim navy!

India's heritage of diversity means that in the Kolkata neighbourhood where I lived during my high school years, the wail of the muezzin calling the Islamic faithful to prayer routinely blended with the chant of mantras and the tinkling of bells at the local Shiva temple, accompanied by the Sikh gurudwara's reading of verses from the Guru Granth Sahib, with St Paul's Cathedral just round the corner. Today, I represent in the national Parliament the constituency of Thiruvananthapuram, the capital of Kerala, where the gleaming white dome of the Palayam Juma Masjid stands diagonally across from the lofty spires of St Joseph's Cathedral, and just around the corner from both, abutting the mosque, is one of the city's oldest temples, consecrated to Lord Ganesha. My experiences and encounters in my constituency remind me daily that India is home to more Christians than Australia and nearly as many Muslims as Pakistan.

That is the India I lay claim to.

11

THE CHALLENGE OF DEFINITION

The first challenge, then, is that we cannot define India by generalization. One of the few generalizations that can safely be made about India is that nothing can be taken for granted about the country. Not even its name: for the word India comes from the River Indus, which flows in Pakistan. And India clung on to the label despite a large section of nativists wanting to change its constitutional name to Bharat, the term by which it is called in most Indian languages.

Given all this, how does one define the Indian idea?

The British like to point out, in moments of self-justifying exculpation, that India is *their* achievement, that they deserve credit for the political unity of India—indeed, that the very idea of 'India' as one entity (now three, but one during the British Raj, and even larger in 1914 than when the British left in 1947) instead of multiple warring principalities and statelets is the unchallengeable contribution of British imperial rule. I have gone at length into this claim in *Inglorious Empire*. But one should remember that this is an ex post facto argument: the conventional British view, during the heyday of the Empire, was that of Sir John Strachey, who argued in a speech at Cambridge University in 1880 that India did not have a distinct political or social identity, and was not a nation. This, Strachey told his Cambridge audience, 'is the first and most essential thing to learn about India—that there is not, and never was an India, or even any country of India possessing, according to any European ideas, any sort of unity, physical, political, social or religious'. There was no Indian nation or country in the past; nor would there be one in the future. 'Scotland is more like Spain than Bengal is like the Punjab.' Strachey thought it 'conceivable that national sympathies may arise in particular Indian countries', but 'that they should ever extend to India generally, that "men of the Punjab, Bengal, the North-western Provinces, and Madras, should ever feel that they belong to one Indian nation, is impossible. You might with as much reason and probability look forward to a time when a single nation will have taken the place of the various nations of Europe."[1]

It is a far cry from the smug certitudes of this late Victorian chauvinist to the claim that India's political unity was created by the British. But as I wrote in *Inglorious Empire*, it is difficult to refute that latter proposition except with a provable hypothesis: that throughout the history of the subcontinent, there has existed an impulsion for unity. This was manifest in the several kingdoms throughout Indian history that sought to extend their reach across all of the subcontinent: the Maurya (322–185 BCE), Gupta (at its peak, 320–550 CE), and Mughal (1526–1857 CE) empires, and to a lesser extent, the Vijayanagara kingdom in the Deccan (at its peak 1136–1565 CE) and the Maratha confederacy (1674–1818 CE). Every period of disorder throughout Indian history has been followed by a centralizing impulse, and had the British not been the first to take advantage of India's disorder with superior weaponry, it is entirely possible that an Indian ruler, most likely a Maratha warrior, would have accomplished what the British did, and consolidated his rule over most of the subcontinent.

The same impulse is also manifest in some of the imaginative visions of our nation, such as in the ancient epics the Mahabharata and the Ramayana, which reflect a conception of India that twentieth-century nationalists would have recognized. These epics have an unparalleled place in the Indian national consciousness: their stories are familiar to Indians of various castes, languages and regions across the subcontinent, uniting them in celebration of the same larger-than-life heroes and heroines, whose stories have been told in dozens of translations and variations. Allusions to the epics, though part of the Hindu tradition, are ever-present in daily conversation; since many non-Hindu Indians are almost as familiar with the epic characters and stories, it is not incorrect to postulate that the ancient concept of India they conjure up is well-known to the majority of Indians in a non-sectarian way. When gaudy Bollywood versions of the epics were telecast as serials, first in 1988 and then again during the coronavirus lockdown in 2020, they attracted record audiences of every stripe. (The script and dialogues for the TV serial version of the Mahabharata were written by a Muslim poet, Dr Rahi Masoom Raza). This was why, when I decided to reinvent the epic form in my satirical fiction about the shaping of 20th century India, I chose to transform the characters, episodes and ideas of the Mahabharata as the framework narrative for my *The Great Indian Novel*. The landscape the Pandavas saw in the Mahabharata (composed approximately in the period 400 BCE to 400 CE) was a pan-Indian landscape, as their travels throughout it demonstrated, and through their tale, Indians speaking hundreds of languages and thousands of dialects in all the places named in the epic, enjoyed a civilizational unity. Lord Rama's journey through India and his epic battle against the demon-king of Lanka, retold in the Ramayana, reflect the same national idea.

After all, India has enjoyed cultural and geographical unity throughout the ages, going back at least to Emperor Ashoka in the third century BCE. The vision of Indian unity was physically embodied by the Hindu sage Adi Shankara, whose travels at the cusp of the 10th century, establishing his mutths in Srinagar, Dwarka, Puri and Sringeri, helped knit together the spiritual ethos of India within what the Harvard scholar Diana Eck has dubbed its "sacred geography". Eck's writings on India's sacred geography extensively delineate ancient ideas of a political unity mediated through ideas of sacredness. As Eck explains: "Considering its long history, India has had but a few hours of political and administrative unity. Its unity as a nation, however, has been firmly constituted by the sacred geography it has held in common and revered: its mountains, forests, rivers, hilltop shrines...linked with the tracks of pilgrimage."[2]

Nor was this oneness to be found only in the 'Hindu' epics I have mentioned. The rest of the world saw India as one: the Buddhist Chinese travellers Hsuen Tsang and Faxian did, for instance, And Marco Polo wrote of India as the country he stopped in en route to China. Arabs, Turks and Persians regarded the entire subcontinent as 'al-Hind' and all Indians as 'Hindi', whether they hailed from Punjab, Bengal or Kerala. The great nationalist Maulana Azad, a Muslim divine himself, once remarked upon how, at the Haj, all Indians, whether they were Pathans or Tamizhs, were considered by other Muslims to be from one land—all 'Hindis'—and regarded themselves as such. Surely such impulses, fulfilled in those distant times by emperors and sages, would with modern transport, communications and far-sighted leaders, have translated themselves into political unity?

Counterfactuals are, of course, impossible to prove. One cannot assert, for instance, with any degree of certitude, events that did not occur, nor name that centralizing figure who might have been India's Bismarck, Mazzini, Atatürk, or Garibaldi in the absence of the British. But historical events find their own dramatis personae, and it is unreasonable to suggest that what happened everywhere else would not have happened in India. Counterfactuals are theoretical but facts are what they are. The facts point clearly to the dismantling of the pre-existing political institutions of India by the British, the fomenting of communal division, and systematic political discrimination with a view to maintaining and extending British domination.

In the years after their victory at the Battle of Plassey in 1757, the British astutely fomented cleavages among the Indian princes, and steadily consolidated their dominion through a policy that came to be dubbed, after 1858, 'divide and rule'. The sight of Hindu and Muslim soldiers rebelling together in 1857, and fighting side by side, willing to rally under the command of each other and pledge joint allegiance to the enfeebled Mughal monarch, alarmed the British, who did not take long to conclude that dividing the two groups and pitting them against one another was the most effective way to ensure the unchallenged continuance of Empire. As early as 1859, the then British governor of Bombay, Lord Elphinstone, advised London that "*divide et impera* was the old Roman maxim, and it should be ours." The creation and perpetuation of Hindu–Muslim antagonism was the most significant accomplishment of British imperial policy: the project of divide et impera would reach its culmination in the horrors of Partition that eventually accompanied the collapse of British authority in 1947. It is difficult, therefore, to buy the self-serving imperial argument that Britain bequeathed to India its political unity and democracy.

I would argue, as Nehru did, that the idea of India, epitomized in another Tagore phrase that has become a cliché—"The sole effort of India has always been to establish unity in diversity, to direct many paths to the same end, and to perceive the one in the many, profoundly and unambiguously."—rested on the acknowledgement of a deep-rooted, underlying desire for harmony despite India's vast heterogeneity, heterodoxy, and plurality. This was true well before Independence, and crystallized in opposition to the foreign imperium. Under British rule, early Indian nationalist self-assertion occurred in various episodes—the great revolt of 1857, which some nationalist historians dubbed "the First War of Indian Independence", the popular resistance to the Partition of Bengal in 1905 (the first major British administrative action explicitly taken for communally divisive reasons), the Swadeshi movement for self-reliance and rejection of British goods around the same time, the absorption of ideas of liberty and self-determination through the influence of western education and the transfusion of western ideals. The socialist leader Jayaprakash Narayan explained that this resistance created Indian nationalism: "It was only when British rule was established over the entire length and breadth of the country that India was united politically under one government. That political unity was however imposed from above and did not in itself constitute nationhood. It was in the process of *opposition* to this imposed rule that Indian nationalism took its birth."[3]

In all of these, as also in overcoming the challenges of the integration of the 565 "princely states", and the reorganization of the Indian Union following the exit of the British, the principles of our national movement were upheld, most notably that of communal amity and harmony. This is why when Jinnah argued that religion was a valid basis for separate nationhood and demanded a country be carved out for India's Muslims, Gandhi and Nehru never accepted his logic. The nationalist movement split, not on ideology (Marxists versus free-marketeers, for instance) nor on region (northerners versus southerners, perhaps) but on this one question of principle alone: should religion be the determinant of nationhood? Nehru and his fellow nationalists (other than the Muslim League and the Hindu Mahasabha) answered with an emphatic "no". To say "yes" would have been to reduce the multi-layered palimpsest of India to a country of and for Hindus, and this, Nehru saw, would do violence to the conception of India that he cherished, valued so greatly and articulated so powerfully.

Tagore defined "the idea of India" evocatively in his 1917 book, *Nationalism*: "In India, our difficulties being internal, our history has been the history of continual social adjustment and not that of organized power for defence and aggression. Neither the colourless vagueness of cosmopolitanism, nor the fierce self-idolatry of nation-worship is the goal of human history. And India has been trying to accomplish her task through social regulation of differ-ences, on the one hand, and the spiritual recognition of unity, on the other." [Tagore here seems to be recalling Swami Vivekananda's distinction between tolerance, a patronizing idea, and acceptance, which is predicated on respect for others.]

"She has made grave errors in setting up the boundary walls too rigidly between races," Tagore went on [arguably he meant to include "religions" in this then-popular term "races"], "in perpetuating the results of inferiority in her classifications [caste]; often she has crippled her children's minds and narrowed their lives in order to fit them into her social forms; but for centu-ries new experiments have been made and adjustments carried out. Her mis-sion has been like that of a hostess to provide proper accommodation to her numerous guests whose habits and requirements are different from one another. It is giving rise to infinite complexities whose solution depends not merely upon tactfulness but sympathy and true realization of the unity of man."[4] As Jayaprakash Narayan explained, "that sense of unity so eloquently spoken by Rabindranath [Tagore] was not a nationalistic sentiment but a spiri-tual and cultural sentiment that was based upon a common outlook on life, 'unity of spirit' as Tagore called it, and a common pattern of social living."[5]

Dealing with these complexities was no small challenge, but it helped solidify the sense of shared nationhood as part of the lived reality of the people. And this was done in conscious repudiation of the European idea of the nation-state as the political embodiment of a homogenous community: India's was a non-European nationalism, embracing, indeed celebrating and guaranteeing, its own diversity. As the eminent Indian historian Romila Thapar put it in describing the Indian nation: "A nation referred to the people that inhabited a territory who saw themselves as an evolved community created by drawing upon the range of communities that existed prior to the nation. It was based on a shared history, interests and aspirations frequently expressed in a common culture that in turn drew from multiple cultures."[6]

Khan Abdul Ghaffar Khan, the "Frontier Gandhi," was an embodiment of Indian nationalism who found his country taken away from him despite himself. Born and raised a Muslim in the overwhelmingly Muslim North-West Frontier Province (NWFP) of British India, bordering Afghanistan, "Badshah" (Emperor) Khan, as he was known, was an early and passionate advocate of the Indian nationalist cause articulated by Mahatma Gandhi. A tall, gaunt, imposing man, he organized his warlike people into a nationalist force for peace, the Khudai Khidmatgars (Servants of God), and became an unyielding voice for Indian unity and composite, as opposed to religious or communal, nationalism. Though, like Gandhi, he shunned political office himself, he supported his brother, Dr Khan Saheb, who led the Congress Party in his province. When the Muslim League, campaigning on a separatist platform, swept a majority of the Muslim seats in the 1946 elections, Badshah Khan's NWFP alone held out as the only Muslim-majority province to elect a Congress government. But it was to no avail: when Partition came and the Muslims of Muslim-majority provinces were accorded a state of their own, NWFP went to Pakistan. Badshah Khan, who resisted the idea of Partition till the end, was a broken man. He found himself in a religio-nationalist state whose very existence he abhorred, constantly persecuted and jailed by its government for objecting to its policies, accused of nameless crimes and hounded till the end.

In turn, the country in which he was revered, India, was showing worrying signs even in his own lifetime of succumbing to the same malady as his own new nation-state. In a 1969 address to a joint session of the Indian Parliament at a time when the state of Gujarat was burning with communal violence, he made a passionate appeal to Indian nationalists to uphold peace and amity. His words were addressed to people of both rioting communities:

> Country alone can be the basis for nationality, not religion. Unfortunately in India religion has been identified with nationality. That is how the country came to be partitioned. The question now is whether you will try to eradicate

this mentality or by your actions foster and lend support to the very mentality of which the 'two-nation' theory was the fruit?[7]

It was a question to which most Indian parliamentarians that day would not have hesitated to answer with a ringing affirmation of the secularism and pluralism for which Badshah Khan was renowned. His words haunt us today, when it is no longer possible to predict with confidence the same response.

The violence, indeed, brings to mind the dismissal of the very 'possibility of self-government in India' by the Victorian poet (and author of the imperial-ist anthem *The White Man's Burden*), Rudyard Kipling. Visiting Australia in 1891, Kipling said bluntly: 'They (Indians) are 4,000 years old out there, much too old to learn that business [self-rule]. Law and order is what they want and we are there to give it to them and we give it to them straight.'[8] The achievement of self-government in India, and the maintenance of "law and order" by democratic means, remains a core repudiation of the racism that animated much British contempt for Indian nationalism. An analysis of how it was affirmed, given constitutional shape, and implemented, will help us understand what it is that was disparaged then, and on very different grounds, is currently being challenged today.

12

WE ARE ALL MINORITIES IN INDIA

How did India preserve and protect a viable idea of itself in the course of the last seventy-plus years, while it grew from 370 million people to 1.3 billion, re-organized its state structures, and sought to defend itself from internal and external dangers, all the while remaining democratic? I have tried to answer this question at length in several of my books and will do so here briefly as well. Certainly, the accomplishment is extraordinary, and worthy of celebration.

Amid India's myriad problems, it is democracy that has given Indians of every imaginable caste, creed, culture, and cause the chance to break free of their age-old subsistence-level existence. There is social oppression and caste tyranny, particularly in rural India, but democracy offers the victims a means of escape, and often—thanks to the determination with which the poor and oppressed exercise their franchise—of triumph. The various schemes established by successive governments from Independence onwards for the betterment of the rural poor are a result of this connection between India's citizens and the State.

And yet, in the more than seven decades since we became free, democracy has failed to unify us as a people or create an undivided political community. Instead, we have become more conscious than ever of what divides us: religion, region, caste, language, ethnicity. The political system has become looser and more fragmented. Politicians mobilize support along ever-narrower lines of political identity. It has become more important to be a 'backward caste', a 'tribal', or a religious chauvinist, than to be an Indian; and to some it is more important to be a 'proud' Hindu than to be an Indian. This is particularly ironic because one of the early strengths of Nehruvian India—the resilience of the nationalist movement, principally by means of the Congress Party serving as an all-embracing, all-inclusive agglomeration of the major political tendencies in the country—stifled the normal process of political contention, as differing ideas about the future direction of the country were all accommodated within one capacious political party rather than divided among several competing ones advocating distinct policies. With the emergence and growth of other political forces, politicians have been tempted to organize themselves around identities (or to create parties to reflect a specific identity). Caste and religion have been the most potent—some would say the most pernicious—of these identities.

Caste, which Nehru and his ilk abhorred and believed would disappear from the social matrix of modern India, has not merely survived and thrived, but has become an instrument for highly effective political mobilization. Candidates are picked by their parties with an eye towards the caste loyalties they can call upon; often their appeal is overtly to voters of their own caste or sub-caste, urging them to elect one of their own. The result has been the growth of caste-consciousness and casteism throughout society. In many states, caste determines educational opportunities, job prospects, and governmental promotions; all too often, people say you cannot go forward unless you're a 'backward'. In 2008, Supreme Court Justice R. V. Raveendran observed that "when more and more people aspire for backwardness instead of 'forwardness', the country itself stagnates."[1] Yet there is no political appetite to review in Parliament, let alone roll back, any of the reservation provisions. Justice Raveendran's fear in the same judgement that "perpetuating caste-based reservation would divide the country permanently on caste lines" appears to be borne out by the extent to which caste-consciousness has become even more politically entrenched since his judgement.

As I have remarked elsewhere, a distinctive feature of the Nehruvian legacy was its visionary rejection of India's assorted bigotries and particularisms. All four generations of Nehrus in public life have been secular in outlook and conduct, whether personal or professional. Their appeal transcends caste, region, language, and religion, something virtually impossible to say of most other leading Indian politicians. But whether through elections or quotas, political mobilization in contemporary India has asserted the power of old identities, habits, faiths, and prejudices. Transcending them will be a major challenge for the Indian polity in the twenty-first century.

One does, therefore, inevitably ask the question: What makes India a nation? When an Indian advertises his nationalism, what is the national identity of which he speaks? Tagore had written, in his 1917 essay on 'Nationalism in India', of the challenges India faced in "developing a national self-consciousness as well as the need for that consciousness to be grounded in Indian cultural sensibilities."[2] A century later, where do we stand?

It is striking that, less than a century after d'Azeglio's remark about creating Italians, no Indian nationalist succumbed to the temptation to express a similar thought. The prime exponent of modern Indian nationalism, Nehru, would never have spoken of 'creating Indians,' because he believed that India and Indians had existed for millennia before he articulated their political aspirations in the twentieth century.

Nonetheless, the India that was born in 1947 was in a very real sense a new creation: a state that made fellow citizens of the Ladakhi and the Laccadivian for the first time, divided Punjabi from Punjabi for the first time, and asked a Keralite peasant to feel allegiance to a Kashmiri Pandit ruling in Delhi, also for the first time. This is why I felt emboldened to subtitle my 2003 biography of Nehru *The Invention of India*.

In *India from Midnight to the Millennium*, I illustrated what this meant with a simple story. When India celebrated the forty-ninth anniversary of its independence from British rule in 1996, our then prime minister, H. D. Deve Gowda, stood on the ramparts of Delhi's seventeenth-century Red Fort and delivered the traditional Independence Day address to the nation in Hindi, one of India's official languages, and its most widely spoken one. Ten other prime ministers had done exactly the same thing forty-eight times before him, but what was unusual this time was that Deve Gowda, a southerner from the state of Karnataka, spoke to the country in a language of which he did not know a word. Tradition and politics required a speech in Hindi, so he gave one—the words having been written out for him in his native Kannada script, in which they, of course, made no sense.

Such an episode is almost inconceivable elsewhere, but it represents the best of the oddities that help make India what it is. It is impossible to conceive of a Frenchman who does not speak French, but India has no equivalent assumption: half the country does not speak or understand Hindi. Only in India could a nation be ruled by a man who did not understand its dominant language; only in India, for that matter, is the principal language one that half the population does not understand; and only in India could this particular solution have been found to enable the prime minister to address his people. Nor was the phenomenon exclusive to one prime minister. I have sat in the row behind the podium in the Red Fort as a junior colleague of Prime Minister Manmohan Singh and observed him turning the pages of his text from right to left, since—born as he was in what is today Pakistan—he had learned Hindustani in the Urdu script. Deve Gowda reading Hindi in Kannada, Manmohan Singh in Urdu—seeing these practices during the prime ministerial address on Independence Day was a startling affirmation of Indian pluralism.

For, as I have often argued, we are all minorities in India. A typical Indian stepping off a train, say, a Hindi-speaking Hindu male from the Gangetic plain state of Uttar Pradesh (UP), might cherish the illusion that he represents the 'majority community', to use an expression much favoured by the less industrious of our journalists. But he, literally, does not. As a Hindi-speaking Hindu he belongs to the faith adhered to by some 80 per cent of the population, but a majority of the country does not speak Hindi; a majority does not hail from Uttar Pradesh; and if he were visiting, say, Kerala, he would discover that a majority there is not even male. Even more tellingly, our archetypal UP Hindi-speaking Hindu has only to mingle with the polyglot, multi-hued crowds thronging any of India's major railway stations to realize how much of a minority he really is. Even his Hinduism is no guarantee of majority-hood, because his caste automatically places him in a minority as well: if he is a Brahmin, 90 per cent of his fellow Indians are not; if he is a Yadav, a 'backward class', 85 per cent of Indians are not, and so on.

Or take language. The Constitution of India recognizes twenty-three today—our rupee notes proclaim their value in fifteen languages—but, in fact, as I have stated earlier, there are twenty-three major Indian languages, and thirty-five which are spoken by more than a million people (and these are languages, with their own scripts, grammatical structures, and cultural assumptions, not just dialects—if we were to count dialects, there are more than 22,000). Each of the native speakers of these languages is in a linguistic minority, for none enjoys majority status in India. Thanks in part to the popularity of Bombay's Hindi cinema, Hindi is understood, if not always well spoken, by about half the population of India, but it is in no sense the language of the majority; indeed, its locutions, gender rules, and script are unfamiliar to most Indians in the south or north-east.

Ethnicity further complicates the notion of a majority community. Most of the time, an Indian's name immediately reveals where he is from, and what his mother tongue is; when we introduce ourselves, we are advertising our origins. Despite some intermarriage at the elite levels in the cities, Indians still largely remain endogamous, and a Bengali is easily distinguished from a Punjabi. The difference this reflects is often more apparent than the elements of commonality. A Karnataka Brahmin shares his Hindu faith with a Bihari Kurmi, but feels little identity with him in respect of appearance, dress, customs, tastes, language, or political objectives. At the same time a Tamil Hindu would feel that he has far more in common with a Tamil Christian or Muslim than with, say, a Haryanvi Jat with whom he formally shares a religion.

Why do I harp on these differences? Only to make the point that Indian nationalism is a rare animal indeed. This land imposes no narrow conformities on its citizens: you can be many things and one thing. You can be a good Muslim, a good Keralite, and a good Indian all at once. As I mentioned in the previous section, when Yugoslavia was tearing itself apart in a civil war among peoples all descended from the same Slavic tribes that had settled in the Balkan peninsula a millennium earlier, learned Freudians pointed to the disagreements that arise out of 'the narcissism of minor differences'. The phrase was apposite, and one I came to appreciate as a UN official dealing with the crisis, when people speaking near-identical languages and bearing the same family names, descended from the same Slavic settlers, butchered each other in their desire for domination or separation. Against the narcissism of minor differences, in India we celebrate the commonality of major differences. To stand Michael Ignatieff's memorable phrase on its head, we are a land of belonging rather than of blood.

This means that the basis of Indian nationhood is unusual in today's world. Talking about Indian nationalism reminds me of the probably apocryphal story of two law professors arguing about a problem. When one suggests a practical solution to the dilemma, the other counters: "It may work in practice, but will it work in theory?" Indian nationalism has worked in practice, but it does not stand up very well in theory. It is not based on language, since we have multiple Indian languages. It is not based on geography (the "natural" geography of the subcontinent—framed by the mountains and the sea—was mutilated by the partition of 1947); and if anything, geography only accustoms Indians to the idea of difference. It is not based on ethnicity (the "Indian" accommodates a diversity of racial types in which many Indians have more in common with foreigners than with other Indians—Indian Punjabis and Bengalis, for instance, have more in common with Pakistanis and Bangladeshis, respectively, than they do with Poonawallas or Bangaloreans). And it is not based on religion—as I have stressed repeatedly, we are home to every faith known to mankind, and Hinduism, the majority religion,—a faith without a national organization, no established church or ecclesiastical hierarchy, no Hindu Pope, no Hindu Mecca, no Sabbath day, no uniform beliefs or modes of worship—exemplifies the diversity within that majority. So Indian nationalism is the nationalism of an idea, the idea of what I have dubbed an ever land—emerging from an ancient civilization, united by a shared history, sustained by pluralist democracy under the rule of law.

As I never tire of pointing out, the fundamental DNA of India, then, is of one land embracing many. It is the idea that a nation may incorporate differences of caste, creed, colour, culture, cuisine, conviction, consonant, costume, and custom, and still rally around a democratic consensus. That consensus is around the simple principle that in a democracy under the rule of law, you don't really need to agree all the time—except on the ground rules of how you will disagree. The reason India has survived all the stresses and strains that have beset it for over seventy years, and that led so many to predict its imminent disintegration, is that it maintained consensus on how to manage without consensus. Today, some in positions of power in India seem to be questioning those ground rules, and that sadly is why it is all the more essential to reaffirm them now. What knits this entire concept of Indian nationhood together is, of course, the rule of law, enshrined in our Constitution.

13

THE CONSTITUTION AND INDIAN NATIONHOOD

Jawaharlal Nehru's opening remarks when he moved the motion at the newly established Constituent Assembly on 13 December 1946 gives us a sense of the immense pressure and responsibility on the lawmakers to ensure that they responded fittingly to the situation and did justice to the task of Constitution-making. They were conscious they had to preserve the essential past while marching towards the future. Nehru said, "We are at the end of an era and possibly very soon we shall embark upon a new age; and my mind goes back to the great past of India, to the 5,000 years of India's history, from the very dawn of that history which might be considered almost the dawn of human history, till today. All that past crowds around me and exhilarates me and, at the same time, somewhat oppresses me. Am I worthy of that past? When I think also of the future, the greater future I hope, standing on this sword's edge of the present between this mighty past and the mightier future, I tremble a little and feel overwhelmed by this mighty task. We have come here at a strange moment in India's history. I do not know but I do feel that there is some magic in this moment of transition from the old to the new, something of that magic which one sees when the night turns into day and even though the day may be a cloudy one, it is day after all, for when the clouds move away we can see the sun later on."[1]

We should also recall Dr Ambedkar's concluding remarks to the Constituent Assembly in the 'The Grammar of Anarchy' speech he gave on 25 November 1949. He informed us of the maladies of India and its ideal state, to be ensured by the rule of law. In a magisterial expression of India through the prism of politics, law, and social hierarchies, he said: "In politics we will be recognizing the principle of one man one vote and one vote one value. In our social and economic life, we shall, by reason of our social and economic structure, continue to deny the principle of one man one value.

How long shall we continue to live this life of contradictions?"[2] Ambedkar's eloquent assault on discrimination and untouchability for the first time cogently expanded the reach of the Indian idea to incorporate the nation's vast, neglected underclass.

Ambedkar—a product of Columbia University and the London School of Economics, and the first Indian principal of the prestigious Government Law College in Bombay—was deeply troubled by the iniquities of the caste system and the fear of many Dalits that national independence would merely lead to the social and political dominance of the upper castes. As an opponent of caste, and a nationalist, he believed that the Dalits must support India's freedom from British rule but they must pursue their struggle for equal rights within the framework of the new constitution that he had a major hand in drafting. In a controversial radio address in 1942, he had expressed the view, on behalf of his fledgling Labour Party, that nationalism "is only a means to an end. It is not an end in itself to which Labour can agree to sacrifice the essential principles of life."[3] National belonging, in other words, had no moral significance in itself; nationalism could unite Indians, but only to serve the fulfilment of "essential principles".

As Ambedkar stressed eight years later in the Constituent Assembly, the working instrument of our democracy is the Constitution of India. It is the basic framework of our democracy. Under the scheme of our Constitution, the three main organs of the State are the legislature, the executive, and the judiciary. The Constitution defines their powers, delimits their jurisdictions, demarcates their responsibilities, and regulates their relationships with one another, and with the people. But the most important contribution of the Constitution to Indian civic nationalism was that of representation centred on individuals. As Madhav Khosla explains in his impressive book of legal history, *India's Founding Moment*, the political apparatus of establishing a constitutional democracy in postcolonial India—a land that was 'poor and literate; divided by caste, religion, and languages; and burdened by centuries of tradition',[4] involved an attempt to free Indians from prevailing types of knowledge and understanding, to place citizens in a realm of individual agency and deliberation that was appropriate to self-rule and to alter the relationship that they shared with one another.

The founders of the republic chose—as the chairman of the Constitution's Drafting Committee, Dr Ambedkar, recognized—to impose a liberal Constitution upon a society which was not liberal, hidebound as it was by traditional customs and entrenched prejudices relating to caste, religion, and social hierarchies. They saw the principles of liberal constitutionalism—the centrality of the state, noncommunal political representation, and so on—as responsive to the challenges posed by the burden of democracy. In keeping with contemporary liberal thought, they committed India to a common language of the rule of law, constructed a centralized state, and rejected localism, and instituted a model of representation whose units were individuals rather than groups. The key objective, according to Khosla, was to 'allow Indians to arrive at outcomes agreeable to free and equal individuals'. That was not easy.

Constitutions are (and Ambedkar explicitly made this point) tools to control and restrain state power. The challenge lies in reconciling restrictions on state power with popular rule—to prevent temporary majorities (since in a democracy, a majority is temporary, though some people forget that) from completely undoing what the Constitution has provided. Khosla suggests that the founders of the Indian republic held a conception of democracy that went beyond majority rule and rejected, in Ronald Dworkin's notable phrase, 'the majoritarian premise'.[5] They subordinated politics to law. As Dr Ambedkar put it, the rights of Indian citizens could not 'be taken away by any legislature merely because it happens to have a majority'.

The struggle for Indian independence was after all not simply a struggle for freedom from alien rule. It was a shift away from an administration of law and order centred on imperial despotism. Thus was born the idea of 'constitutional morality', meaning 'the commitment to constitutional means, to its processes and structures, alongside a commitment to free speech, scrutiny of public action [and] legal limitations on the exercise of power.' This was how freedom was intended to flourish in India. Of course, Dr. Ambedkar realized it is perfectly possible to pervert the Constitution, without changing its form, by merely changing the form of the administration to make it inconsistent and opposed to the spirit of the Constitution. Ambedkar argued that constitutional morality 'is not a natural sentiment. It has to be cultivated. We must realize that our people have yet to learn it. Democracy in India is only a top dressing on an Indian soil which is essentially undemocratic'. He insisted that the Directive Principles—an unusual feature of the Indian Constitution not found elsewhere—were necessary because although the rules of democracy mandated that the people must elect those who will hold power, the principles confirmed that 'whoever captures power will not be free to do what he likes with it'.

It is sometimes said that Dr Ambedkar publicly disowned his own Constitution. This makes too much of an emotional speech in Parliament in 1953, when in a testy exchange with other MPs in the Rajya Sabha, he declared: "We lawyers defend many things. People always keep on saying to me, "Oh! you are the maker of the Constitution." My answer is I was a hack. What I was asked to do, I did much against my will."[6] The fact is that in the last years of his life Ambedkar was troubled about the majoritarianism inherent in the Constitution. "It was clear," he had said before becoming chairman of the Drafting Committee, "that if the British system was copied it would result in permanently vesting executive power in a communal majority."[7] As a member of the Constituent Assembly, he went along with its majority view, but in a 1953 interview to the BBC, he reiterated in more negative terms something he had already warned against in that Assembly: "Democracy will not work," he declared gloomily, "for the simple reason we have got a social structure which is totally incompatible with parliamentary democracy."[8]

In the Constitution, Ambedkar, despite the public and private misgivings that I have touched upon, took a more optimistic view of the prospects of democracy in India by asking Indians to have a new understanding of authority. They would be liberated through submission to an impersonal force that saw them as equal agents, and that liberated spirit would make possible socioeconomic transformation. Both were equally important. India's Independence Day was not meant to be just a ritual of song and dance, the hoisting of the flag and the singing of the anthem. The real significance of Independence lay in the freedom of the mind. Indians were meant to be able to recognize and overcome, in Tagore's immortal phrase, a world that had been "been broken up into fragments by narrow domestic walls."[9] The multifaceted philosopher and thinker explained further, "My countrymen will gain truly their India by fighting against that education which teaches them that a country is greater than the ideals of humanity."[10]

This was an unusual kind of nationalist idea. But it led to the second overriding objective, less Tagore's than that of leaders like Jawaharlal Nehru— that democracy in India would need to necessarily entail equality and a decent standard of living for all. For Nehru, the establishment of a free and democratic India required the substitution of the economic power of a few rich individuals by a form of state control that could end poverty, reduce unemployment and improve material conditions. After all, the egregious Winston Churchill had predicted that after the departure of the British, "India will fall back quite rapidly through the centuries into the barbarism and privations of the Middle Ages".[11] Nehru knew that Independence would be justified only by giving the lie to such prophecies through development and progress.

It is also striking that the Constituent Assembly rejected separate electorates, weighted representation, and reservations on the basis of religion. Only days before Indian independence, and the Partition of British India, Sardar Vallabhbhai Patel, in his capacity as Chairman of the Advisory Committee on Minorities and Fundamental Rights, wrote to the President of the Assembly, Rajendra Prasad, to explain why separate electorates had been rejected. Differentiated citizenship on the basis of religion, Patel argued, had already been tried in the colonial era and had led to Partition. The answer lay in moving away from a representative framework that recognized identities that were regarded as stable and fixed, and towards a model of citizenship centred on the political participation of individuals. Such a model would allow the categories of majority and minority to be constantly defined and redefined within the fluid domain of politics and it would thereby offer the greatest form of security to all citizens.[12]

The key intellectual division among the Constitution-makers was not between those who wanted a united territorial India and those who did not; that issue was settled by Partition, which occurred soon after the Assembly began its work. The key debate in the Constituent Assembly was between those who wanted to assert a conception of individual citizenship in India that went beyond immutable identities (like religion or caste) and those who insisted on Indian nationhood being defined as a confederation of such inescapable identities. Many nationalists who argued passionately outside the Constituent Assembly for a united India (including, many would argue, both Azad and Gandhi), nonetheless thought that India was indeed a collection of distinct communities, who could flourish together in amicable co-existence. But the Constituent Assembly, led by Nehru and Ambedkar, went in the opposite direction, consciously opting for individual citizenship as the root of nationhood, transcending the limitations that India's communities imposed on their members.

Ambedkar made this clear in a speech from which I have already quoted a sentence in the previous chapter. "I do not believe there is any place in this country for any particular culture, whether it is a Hindu culture, or a Muhammadan culture or a Kanarese culture or a Gujarati culture. There are things we cannot deny, but they are not to be cultivated as advantages, they are to be treated as disadvantages, as something which divides our loyalty and takes away from us our common goal," he argued. "That common goal is the building up of the feeling that we are all Indians. I do not like what some people say, that we are Indians first and Hindus afterwards or Muslims afterwards. I am not satisfied with that... I do not want that our loyalty as Indians should be in the slightest way affected by any competitive loyalty, whether that loyalty arises out of our religion, out of our culture

101

or out of our language. I want all people to be Indians first, Indians last and nothing else but Indians..."[13]

This fundamental difference of opinion—whether people are Hindus or Muslims first, or Indians first—continues to haunt our politics today. The nationalist movement was divided between two sets of ideas, that held by those who saw religious identity as the determinant of their nationhood, and those who believed in an inclusive India for everyone, irrespective of faith, where rights were guaranteed to individuals rather than to religious communities. The former became the idea of Pakistan, the latter the idea of India. Pakistan was created as a state with a dominant religion, a state that discriminates against its minorities and denies them equal rights. But India never accepted the logic that had partitioned the country: our freedom struggle was for all, and the newly independent India would also be for all.

After the country gained its freedom, the view that was relegated to the fringes throughout the nationalist struggle, and the first four decades of independence, began to grow in strength and popular appeal in the last three decades—the notion of India as a state identified with the religion professed by the majority—a Hindu rashtra. We will discuss that, and the philosophy of Hindutva that advocates it, in more detail in the next part of the book.

14

A LIVING DOCUMENT

It is particularly striking, when examined in today's context, that India's Constitution makers explicitly rejected the notion of religion playing any role in citizenship, arguing that each individual voter exercised agency in the democratic project and should not be reduced to the pre-existing loyalties of religious affiliation. 'For India's founders', Khosla observes, 'one could not be a political agent unless one's political identity was self-created.' The Constitution granted representation not to one's pre-determined identity (religion) but to one's individual expression of agency. That was why the individual vote was so important. Democratic politics could not be reduced to the advocacy of pre-set interests; interests instead had to be expressed through politics. 'The very constitution of one's identity as a citizen', Khosla explains, 'was itself a form of freedom'.

At the same time, the Indian Constitution acknowledged group rights, such as the right of religious denominations to establish and maintain institutions for religious and charitable purposes (Article 26(a)), or the right of a 'section of the citizens' to conserve a distinct language, script or culture (Article 29(1)). There were also provisions to protect the interests of Scheduled Tribes (Article 19(5)) and a specific provision in Article 25 stating that a "heavy responsibility" would be cast on the majority to see that minorities feel secure. But though the Constitution recognized groups as bearing constitutional rights—thus departing from departure from the 'singular unification' model—Justice Dhananjaya Chandrachud of the Supreme Court has argued that this "was nested in the understanding that membership of groups had a unique role of crafting and determining individual identity....In elevating groups as distinct rights holders as well as empowering state intervention to address historical injustice and inequality perpetrated by group membership, the framers located liberalism within the pluralist reality of India and conceptualized every individual as located at an intersection between liberal individualism and plural belonging....At the time of its birth, the nation was conceptualized as incorporating its vast diversity and not eliminating it."[1]

This ability to recognize groups and yet adjudicate the rights of their individual members, and the adaptability of the Constitution to the ever-changing realities of national life, have effectively made it a vehicle of social change. Equally important, this process has been substantially facilitated by Parliament, the institution conceived for that very purpose by the Constitution. The Constitution created itself as a self-generating and self-correcting entity, a living document that allowed for its own amendment to meet the changes of the times, subject to the Doctrine of Basic Structure, again an invention of the judiciary.

The Constitution, which came into force on 26 January 1950, has been amended over a hundred times by Parliament, a creature created inter alia for that very purpose by the Constitution. The small-minded may consider the high number of amendments as one of the weaknesses of India's Constitution, but those with a broader vision would understand that it is actually a sign of its inherent strength—a strength that derives from its ability to be flexible without the risk of self-destruction. It has the exemplary in-built ability to adjust to the needs of the times and the fact that this is enabled through a thoroughly democratic and representative process has been key to its effectiveness in moving our society forward in a more broadly inclusive manner.

During the journey of the Constitution, there have been innumerable instances which have either corroded or nurtured this central idea. As I have maintained, much progress took place under the purview of Pandit Jawaharlal Nehru. The first amendment in 1951 abolished zamindari or feudal landlordism (though this went against the right to property), and placed "reasonable" restrictions on free speech, much to the dismay of libertarians, while the seventh amendment in 1956 laid the foundation for the establishment of states on linguistic lines. The creation of states, union territories, and their autonomy, brought many of the north-eastern states and new territories to the Indian union, and provided legitimacy to extending the embrace of India to these territories. But it also asserted the primacy of the union, the Centre: India was not, unlike the US, a collection of states coming together to constitute a nation, but a nation through the ages that had the power to create states as sub-units of itself.

During the Emergency, the forty-second amendment, involving various articles, brought two key principles of the Indian idea, hitherto implicit rather than explicit, formally into the Constitution—"Socialist and Secular". The idea of India is inseparable from these ideas, the dark period of their insertion notwithstanding, which is why no subsequent government has undone them so far, even if the original constitution-makers had considered it unnecessary to insert these words into the document. Various other amendments to the Constitution (the twenty-third, forty-fifth, fifty-first amendments, among others) have tried to make the basic nature of India more inclusive as they tried to protect the interests of vulnerable sections of Indian society. Activist judges have taken the constitution beyond strict legislation to promote human rights and welfare in a series of landmark judgements. As one of the world's largest democracies, India has struggled to provide education to all its children; the landmark eighty-sixth amendment was passed in 2009 conferring on all children in the age group of 6 to 14 years the right to free and compulsory education. The Right to Information Act, passed in June 2005, is another hallmark of how the law guides and derives value from the principles of civic nationalism and of governmental accountability to the Indian people. By ensuring the disclosure of information on demand to the Indian public, the law enshrined in the Constitution of our land emphatically acknowledges their right to accountability. The Right to Life under Article 21 was interpreted to include "the Right to Know". A landmark 2018 judgement affirming the Right to Privacy has bolstered this indispensable element of the citizen's freedom. This framework of rights—to knowledge, information, education, and privacy—have asserted a new infrastructure of empowered citizenship that is indispensable in a participatory democracy.

Although amendments to the Constitution have often been timely and necessary, it must be said here that there are other aspects of the country's legal framework that need, but have been denied, a thorough overhaul. For example, the Victorian-era Penal Code, drafted by Macaulay without consulting any Indians in 1837, and enacted by the British colonial administration in 1861, is full of iniquities that undermine the quality of the rule of law in our country and make the Code ripe for amendment, if not total rewriting. Many of the provisions of the Code have ceased to apply in Britain, but we carry on that country's unfortunate colonial legacy in India. These include the pernicious sedition law, Section 124A, which is misused daily by state governments, and the lower courts, despite decades of Supreme Court rulings that sedition should only apply to incitement to violence; the notorious Section 377, discriminating against a section of our society for their sexual orientation, which stayed on the statute books till the Supreme Court finally read it down two years ago; and a host of examples of gender bias against women. The latter have been to a great extent remedied by a series of progressive judgements by the Supreme Court. Whatever the arguments over individual provisions, I fully support former Indian President Pranab Mukherjee's appeal in 2016 to scrap the Penal Code and write a new one reflecting our experience and needs as an independent nation. Starting from scratch, building on national experience, and moving from an ethos of imperial oppression to one of democratic community-building, would give the country a penal code more in tune with the principles of civic nationalism.

In the recent past, the Anna Hazare movement, by clamouring for legislation to install an all-powerful national ombudsman, raised the question of the role of civil society in determining legislative priorities in our democracy. A Lokpal Bill was introduced by the government in Parliament in response to the strength of numbers in the streets. Members of Parliament felt they had no choice but to go along with this, though some who had serious misgivings about the Bill privately wondered what their role was supposed to be, with Parliament's law-making functions being encroached upon by civil society on the one hand and the judiciary (through its innovative but intrusive Public Interest Litigations) on the other.

There is no doubt that today's lawmakers face new and tougher challenges than ever before. The rapid advancement and penetration of information technology, improving social indicators, the change in demography, the growing economic prowess of our nation, the rise of new global threats, and our ever-greater international integration, all impose new constraints on the sovereign function of law-making, even as they also allow new opportunities. The techniques for surveillance being developed by the government—and whose use received a boost with the imperative need to track those who might have been exposed to carriers of the coronavirus in 2020—could, in a post-COVID-19 world, be used to trace the movements and contacts of citizens, the Right to Privacy notwithstanding. The suspension for months of any pretence of parliamentary oversight of executive actions during the government's handling of the COVID-19 crisis, and the acquiescence of the entire political class in this process, raised serious doubts about whether Indian democracy would survive the virus unscathed.

The civil society protests of recent years add another challenge. In a democracy, there are specific rights accorded to citizens by the state to help them exercise their political freedoms: freedom of speech and political association and related rights allow citizens—in other words, members of civil society—to get together, argue and discuss, debate and criticize, protest and strike (and in Kerala—only in Kerala!—to declare enforced shutdowns inconveniencing the general public), and even go on fasts and hunger-strikes, in order to support or challenge their governments. This is an essential part of promoting governmental accountability between elections: no one can seriously argue that a citizen's democratic rights begin and end with the right to choose his government through voting alone.

Indeed, as Amartya Sen so brilliantly asserted with reference to India in his *The Argumentative Indian*, it is through perpetual discussions and engagement with "the reach of reason" that a deliberative citizen democracy is created.[2] Amartya Sen's emphasis on robust discourse in India is derided by his critics as upper caste, male, classist, and academic. After all, they ask, who gets to speak in India, to whom, and how? Speech is deeply imbued with class, caste, gender, and educational bias. This is hardly unique to India: the U.S. did not reserve a place at the high table for Africans, Native Americans, the Irish, and the Chinese at various times, and the Dred Scott decision in 1857 even declared that free blacks, as the descendants of slaves, were not citizens. As opposed to that India had a constitutionally-based, far-reaching affirmative action programme for its Dalits at a time when many US states were still denying large numbers of blacks the vote. Democracy takes time to evolve and deepen; its imperfections are not cause to dismiss it, but rather to affirm the vital importance of improving and strengthening it.

There is often a useful distinction to be made between law and legitimacy: law is passed by legislatures at the behest of the executive, but legitimacy inheres in the representative character of those proposing and enacting the law, and in the extent to which they are seen as embodying, and acting upon, the best interests of the people as a whole. The greater the extent to which ordinary people are engaged with, concerned by, and empowered to determine their own political destiny, the more they accept the decisions of the state institutions, and the more legitimate the law becomes to the people. One is reminded of the famous formulation of Rousseau:

> It is to law alone that men owe justice and liberty. It is this salutary organ of the will of all which establishes in civil rights the natural equality between men. It is this celestial voice which dictates to each citizen the precepts of public reason, and teaches him to act according to the rules of his own judgment and not to behave inconsistently with himself. It is with this voice alone that political leaders should speak when they command.[3]

So, to that extent, civil society does and should have an influence on lawmaking. But that is not the same thing as saying it should have a direct role. In Switzerland, for example, ordinary citizens can actually bypass the elected legislature and write laws by proposing and then voting for these propositions in referenda that are organized by the State and whose outcomes are recognized by the government as having the full binding force of law. That is not the case, however, in most other democracies, where civil society's impact is confined to the influence it is able to bring to bear on the elected lawmakers, through the shaping of public opinion, effective lobbying, media campaigns and mass movements.

In India, we preserve the national idea by enabling these key aspects of the democratic process. This could be said to suit the democratic temper of our people. In ancient times, as we have noted in an earlier Part, our civilization had sabhas and samitis where kingdoms and even empires were ruled on the principle of democratic functioning, extending right from the grass-roots level in the form of panchayats and councils, which represented the broad as well as specific segments of the populace, to the royal courts where maharajahs took advice from learned and wise elders. This tradition is important to recall, since it confirms that both majority as well as minority opinion were given due importance in the formulation of public policy. This was no mean achievement in a nation and society as diverse and heterogeneous as India, with its innumerable groups and socio-religious identities. The law has the responsibility to preserve this diversity, allow each individual component to feel secure within it, and yet guide the nation's progressive evolution.

The importance of disagreement and debate to the evolution of Indian nationalism was understood well before independence by Lala Lajpat Rai, a doughty Congressman who also served a stint as President of the Hindu Mahasabha. In an article on "Hindu nationalism" in 1902, responding to a screed on Hindu disunity by Pandit Madho Ram (who labelled himself a "Hindu Nationalist") Lala Lajpat Rai declared:

> the idea of nationality does not necessarily imply a complete union amongst all its members on all matters, social, religious or political; nor does it suggest the existence of a state of perfect concord and harmony among its members or leaders, or the freedom of the latter from all human weaknesses such as to personalities or indulgences in strong or even abusive language amongst, and towards each other.... The truth is that honest differences, controversial discussions, and criticisms of public men by public men, are absolutely necessary for the healthy growth and progress of nationality.... It is wrong to suppose that the idea of nationalism or nationality requires a complete union in all details of religious, social, economical, or political life or that it requires a complete freedom from sectarian quarrels or disputes or jealousies.[4]

This healthy spirit of acceptance of difference, of constitutional encouragement of debate and discussion, fuelled by a thriving free media, contentious civil society forums, energetic human rights groups, assorted autonomous institutions and the repeated spectacle of our remarkable general elections, are all assets for India's civic nationalism. Together with a fractious and competitive political culture, sustained by the protective framework of the Constitution, they have made of India a rare example of the successful management of diversity in the developing world.

15

"INDIC CIVILIZATION" AND INDIANNESS

I have been musing about the nature of Indian nationhood for at least the last four decades, ever since a distinguished foreigner said to me: "You Indians have allowed yourself to forget that there is such a thing as Indic civilization. And we are its last outpost."

The words were spoken to me in 1982, when I headed the UN office in Singapore, by the Khmer nationalist politician and one-time prime minister, Son Sann, lamenting India's support for Vietnam in its conquest of Cambodia in 1979. To Son Sann, a venerable figure already in his late 70s, Cambodia was an "Indic civilization" being overrun by the forces of a Sinic state, and he was bewildered that India, the fount of his country's heritage, should sympathize with a people as distinctly un-Indian as the Vietnamese. Given that Vietnam's invasion had put an end to the blood-soaked terror of the rule of the Khmer Rouges, I was more inclined to see the choice politically than in terms of civilizational heritage. But Son Sann's words stayed with me.

They came back to mind during a visit to Angkor Wat, perhaps the greatest Hindu temple ever built anywhere in the world—and in Cambodia, not in India. To walk past those exquisite sculptures recounting tales from the Ramayana and the Mahabharata, to have my Cambodian guide tell me about the significance of the symbols protecting the shrine—the naga, the simha, and the garuda, corresponding, he said earnestly, to today's navy, army, and air force—and to marvel at the epic scale of a Hindu temple as impressive as the finest cathedral or mosque anywhere in the world, was also to marvel at the extraordinary reach of a major strand of our culture beyond our own shores. Hinduism was brought to Cambodia by merchants and travellers more than a millennium ago. It has long since disappeared, supplanted by Buddhism, also an Indian export. But at its peak Hinduism profoundly influenced the culture, music, dance and mythology of the Cambodian people. My

Cambodian guide at Bayon, a few minutes' drive from Angkor Wat, spoke with admiration of a sensibility which, in the 16th century, saw Hindus and Buddhists worship side by side in adjoining shrines within the same temple complex. That seems inconceivable today in India, where contestations over places of worship have been reduced to winner-takes-all.

Perhaps Son Sann was right, and Cambodia is indeed the last outpost of Indic civilization in a world increasingly Sinified. But what exactly does that mean? At a time when the north of India was reeling under waves of conquest and cultural stagnation, our forefathers in the South and East were exporting aspects of Indianness to South-east Asia. It was an anonymous task, carried out not, for the most part, by warriors blazing across the land bearing swords of conquest, but by individuals who had come in peace, to trade, to teach, and to persuade. Their impact was profound. To this day, the kings of Thailand are crowned in the presence of Brahmin priests; the Muslims of Java still bear Sanskritized names, despite their conversion to Islam, a faith whose adherents normally bear names originating in Arabia; Garuda is Indonesia's national airline, and Ramayana its best-selling brand of clove cigars; even the Philippines has produced a pop-dance ballet about Rama's quest for his kidnapped queen. Many Southeast Asian countries also mirror the idea of a "sacred geography": the old Thai kingdom of Ayyuthaya derived its name from the Indian Ayodhya, and places in Thailand are associated with events in the Ramayana epic, such as a hill where Hanuman was sent to find the Sanjeevani. Since 1782, Thai kings are still named Rama in continuation of the Ramayana tradition; the current monarch is Rama X. The Javanese city of Yogyakarta in Indonesia is also a transliteration of Ayodhya.

Indeed the pioneering French Indologist Sylvain Levi spoke and wrote of "le monde Indien" or "greater India", a concept echoed in the American Sanskrit scholar Sheldon Pollock's "the Sanskrit cosmopolis". Both terms refer to countries whose cultures were Indic in the sense of having been strongly influenced by Sanskrit language and literature. For such scholars, the geographical idea of India (the subcontinent bordered by the Arabian Sea, the Bay of Bengal and the Himalayan mountains) and the geopolitical idea of India (today the Republic of India; at its biggest extent, the British Raj as it was in 1914, or more pragmatically, the British India of 1947) are inadequate—for the civilizational idea of India is much broader. In a perverse way, it is also narrower, for Indic civilization was often not as well-entrenched in some parts of today's Republic of India as it was in countries that were never part of any Indian polity, like Burma, Thailand, Cambodia, Sri Lanka, Java, Bali, or Sumatra. These countries, at least during large parts of the first millennium

CE, were "culturally as much Indian as Andhra Pradesh or Bangladesh during that very period", argues Gerard Fussman. "In these countries, non-Sanskritic languages were spoken and local gods were worshipped. But the language of culture and politics was Sanskrit as in India proper, or Pali; the upper strata's cults were Hindu or Buddhist, as in India proper; artists and architects followed the precepts of Sanskrit technical treatises".[1]

But contemporary international politics has rendered all this much less significant than the modern indices of strategic thinking, economic interests, and geopolitical affinities. India is far less important to the countries that still bear any "Indic" influence than, say, China, whose significance is contemporary, rather than civilizational.

Should we care, and what, if anything, does this have to do with the idea of India? Of course, we should care: no great civilization can afford to be indifferent to the way in which it is perceived by others. But what, today, is Indic civilization? Can we afford to anchor ourselves in a purely atavistic view of ourselves, hailing the religious and cultural heritage of our forebears without recognizing the extent to which we ourselves have changed? The examples I have cited so far are, after all, all from the Hindu tradition. But isn't Indian civilization today an evolved hybrid, that draws as much from the influence of Islam, Buddhism, Christianity and Sikhism, not to mention two centuries of British colonial rule? Can we speak of Indian culture today without qawwali, the poetry of Ghalib, or for that matter the game of cricket, our de facto national sport? When an Indian dons "national dress" for a formal event, he wears a variant of the sherwani, which did not exist before the Muslim invasions of India. When Indian Hindus voted a few years ago, in a cynical and contrived competition on the Internet, to select the "new seven wonders" of the modern world, they voted for the Taj Mahal constructed by a Mughal king, not for Angkor Wat, the most magnificent architectural product of their religion. So, doesn't Indianness today—composed of elements influenced by various civilizations that have made their homes on Indian soil—subsume the classical Indic civilization that Son Sann was referring to? It does, and we are all much the better for it.

A different aspect of the question arose in 1999 when a crisis erupted in the Indian National Congress party over the issue of its President Sonia Gandhi's eligibility to lead the country. This brought to the forefront a vital question that has, in different ways, engaged this writer—the question, "Who is an Indian?" Or, to put it differently: "What does it mean to be mean to be 'an Indian' today?"

Three powerful Congress politicians, Sharad Pawar, Purno Sangma, and Tariq Anwar—with classic Congress secularism, a Hindu, a Christian, and a Muslim—essentially answered that question by averring that Mrs Gandhi was unfit to be prime minister because she was born in Italy of non-Indian stock. In the extraordinary letter they delivered to her, and leaked to the newspapers, the three party leaders declared: "It is not possible that a country of 980 million, with a wealth of education, competence and ability, can have anyone other than an Indian, born of Indian soil, to head its government."[2] They went so far as to ask her to propose a constitutional amendment requiring that the offices of president and prime minister be held only by natural-born Indian citizens.

This territorial and ethnic notion of Indian nationhood was a curious one on many counts, and particularly so coming from long-standing members of the Indian National Congress, a party whose first president was the Scottish-born Allan Octavian Hume in 1885, and amongst whose most redoubtable leaders (and elected presidents) were the Irish Annie Besant (1917) and the English Nellie Sengupta (1933), who both had no difficulty being accepted as authentic Indian nationalists. Even more curious was the implicit repudiation of the views of the Congress' greatest-ever leader, Mahatma Gandhi, who tried to make the party a representative microcosm of an India he saw as eclectic, agglomerative, and diverse; and even of an earlier nationalist leader associated with Hindu revivalism, Bal Gangadhar Tilak, who had memorably declared almost a century before:

> 'Alienness' has to do with interests. Alienness is certainly not concerned with white or black skin. Alienness is not concerned with religion. Alienness is not concerned with trade or profession. I do not consider him an alien who wishes to make an arrangement whereby that country in which he has to live, his children have to live and his future generations have to live, may see good days and be benefitted. He may not perhaps go with me to the same temple to pray to God, perhaps there may be no intermarriage and inter-dining between him and me. All these are minor questions. But, if a man is exerting himself for the good of India, and takes measures in that direction, I do not consider him an alien.[3]

The three musketeers of the nativist revolt did, of course, anticipate the criticism of betraying Gandhi. Consequently, they went out of their way to reinvent the Mahatma on their side. "India has always lived in the spirit of the Mahatma's words, 'Let the winds from all over sweep into my room,'" they wrote with fealty if not accuracy. "But again he said, "I will not be swept off my feet." We accept with interest and humility the best which we can gather from the north, south, east or west and we absorb them into our soil. But our inspiration, our soul, our honour, our pride, our dignity, is rooted in our soil. It has to be of this earth." The contradiction between their paraphrase of the Mahatma's views (absorbing the best from all directions) and their emotive "rooting" of "honour, pride and dignity" in the "soil" of "this earth" was so blatant it hardly needed pointing out. Yet, it suffered a further inaccuracy: by law, even a "natural-born Indian" is one who has just one grandparent born in undivided India, as defined by the Government of India Act, 1935. You do not have to be "of this soil" to be an Indian by birth.

But Sonia Gandhi is, of course, an Indian by marriage and naturalization, not birth. So, the usual chauvinists and xenophobes were quick to jump on the bandwagon started by the soil-sprung triumvirate. So did political opportunists of other stripes. The Samata Party's spokesperson, Jaya Jaitly, in clamouring for an amendment to the Citizenship Act, declared that it was "an insult to the self-respect of a nation of 100 crores to have a foreigner at the helm."[4] Her reasoning was that Mrs Gandhi "will never be able to fully understand the intricacies of our culture" because "cultural impulses are gained in the early stages of life". This argument is preposterous, since some of the greatest experts on Indian culture, who have forgotten more than most Indians will ever know about Bharatiya sanskriti—from A. L. Basham to Richard Lannoy to R. C. Zaehner to Sylvain Levi—were foreigners. Worse, by this logic no South Indian should be able to marry a North Indian, since her "cultural impulses" for uthappams and ottamthullal would have been set before she entered the world of chhole bhature and karva chauth. This was a slippery path for Jaya Jaitly, a South Indian married to a northerner, to tread.

Throughout its history, the Congress Party has articulated and defended the idea that Indian nationalism is inclusive, tolerant, and pluralist, and that there are no acid tests of birth, religion, ethnicity, or even territory that disqualify one who wants to claim Indianness. As the political scientist Ashutosh Varshney maintained, Sonia Gandhi "is an Indian—by her citizenship, by her act of living in India, and by the way she has adopted a new home. [A]n Indian is one who accepts the ethos of India."[5] And Congress politician Mani Shankar Aiyar turned the absurd "cultural" argument on its head by pointing out that "it is a disrespect to the millennial traditions of India to question the credentials of a daughter-in-law."[6]

Sonia Gandhi herself made her own nationalist case: "Though born in a foreign land, I chose India as my country," she declared. "I am Indian and shall remain so till my last breath. India is my motherland, dearer to me than my own life."[7](A Biblical reference comes to mind here, from the Book of Ruth, who accepts the Israelite people as her own. In Ruth 1:16–17, Ruth tells Naomi, her Israelite mother-in-law, "Where you go I will go, and where you stay I will stay. Your people will be my people and your God my God. Where you die I will die, and there I will be buried. May the Lord deal with me, be it ever so severely, if even death separates you and me.") But Sonia Gandhi was actually not the issue. Her personal fate was for her party, herself, and, above all, the electorate to decide. (And when her party won the election in 2004, and anointed her as its choice for Prime Minister, she gracefully relinquished that role to Dr Manmohan Singh, rendering the controversy academic, even as the late BJP politician Sushma Swaraj threatened to shave her head in mourning and sit on vigil outside Parliament.) The real issue was, and remains, whether Indians should let intolerant politicians, convinced of their own righteousness, decide who is qualified to be an authentic Indian.

I have often argued—and have done so in this book as well—that the assertion of "us" and "them" is the worst kind of thinking that can poison the national mind. This land imposes no narrow conformities on its citizens: you can be many things *and* one thing. You can be fair-skinned, sari-wearing, and Italian-speaking, and you would not be more foreign to my grandmother in Kerala than someone who is "wheatish-complexioned", wears a salwar-kameez, and speaks Punjabi. Our nation absorbs both these types of people; both are equally "foreign" to some of us, equally Indian to us all. Our founding fathers wrote a constitution for their dreams; we have given passports to their ideals. To start disqualifying Indian citizens from the privileges of Indianness is not just pernicious: it is an affront to the very premise of Indian nationalism. As I have said before, and will say again: *An India that denies itself to some of us could end up being denied to all of us.*

The answer to the civilizational question is that today we celebrate an Indian culture that is truly pluralistic in its inspirations and its manifestations, a culture that is fully representative of the 21st century India that is making such remarkable progress in the eyes of the world. My generation was brought up to take pluralism for granted, and to reject the communalism that had partitioned the nation when the British left. In rejecting the case for Pakistan, Indian nationalism also rejected the very idea that religion should be a determinant of nationhood. We never fell into the insidious trap of agreeing that, since Partition had established a state for Muslims, what remained was a state for Hindus. To accept the premise of Indian nationhood, you had to spurn the logic that had divided the country.

This was what that much-abused term "secularism", inserted into the Constitution only in 1976 but implicit in its provisions from the very start, meant for most of us. Western dictionaries defined secularism as the absence of religion, but Indian secularism meant a profusion of religions; the state engaged with all of them but privileged none. Secularism in India did not mean irreligiousness, which even atheist parties such as the communists or the southern Dravida Munnetra Kazhagam (DMK) party found unpopular amongst their voters; indeed, as I wrote in *Why I Am A Hindu*, during Kolkata's annual Durga Puja, the communist parties compete with each other to put up the most lavish Puja pandals, pavilions to the goddess Durga. Rather, secularism meant, in the Indian tradition, multi-religiousness. This had ancient historical roots in the Indian tradition of secular tolerance practiced by such rulers as the Buddhist Emperor Ashoka and the Muslim Emperor Akbar 1800 years apart. Amartya Sen has shown that Ashoka's edicts promoted the human rights of all in the 3rd century before Christ, a time when Aristotle's writings on freedom explicitly excluded women and slaves, an exception the Indian monarch did not make.[8] It was at a time when the Catholics of Europe were tyrannizing each other (and persecuting Jews) with their Inquisition, while burning heretics at the stake, that the Mughal Emperor Akbar was proclaiming in Delhi that "no man should be interfered with on account of religion, and anyone is to be allowed to go over to a religion that pleases him."[9]

Throughout the decades after Independence, the political culture of the country reflected these secular assumptions and attitudes. As I have relished pointing out, though the Indian population is nearly 80 per cent Hindu, and the country was partitioned as a result of a demand for a separate Muslim homeland, three of India's fourteen presidents (and four of its vice-presidents) have been Muslims; so were innumerable governors, cabinet ministers, chief ministers of states, ambassadors, generals, and Supreme Court justices (and chief justices). One of my favourite examples of our secularism, and without a doubt one of the most striking, has to do with the war with Pakistan in 1971: the Indian Air Force in the northern sector was commanded by a Muslim (Idris Hasan Latif); the Indian Army commander was a Parsi (Sam Manekshaw); the General Officer Commanding-in-Chief of the forces that marched into Bangladesh was a Sikh (Jagjit Singh Aurora), and the general flown in to negotiate the surrender of the Pakistani forces in East Bengal was Jewish (J.F.R. Jacob). That was the idea of India, effortlessly being played out on the battlefront.

But in the 1940 book from which I quoted at the beginning of this chapter, Dr Ambedkar conceded the case for Pakistan, arguing that, though their religion did not necessarily justify the argument for a separate nationality, if "the Musalmans" wanted separation there was not much that the others could do about it. Ambedkar, discussing the differences between Hindus and Muslims in pre-Partition India, wrote: "The things that divide are far more vital than the things which unite. In depending upon certain common features of Hindu and Mohamedan social life, in relying upon common language, common race and common country, the Hindu is mistaking what is accidental and superficial for what is essential and fundamental. The political and religious antagonisms divide the Hindus and the Musalmans far more deeply than the so-called common things are able to bind them together."[10]

He was being realistic in the circumstances of that time, and, in light of the Partition that did occur seven years later, prescient. He did concede, "The prospects might perhaps be different if the past of the two communities can be forgotten by both," though his book argued that such forgetting was unlikely.[11] But in that same year of 1940, a different speech was made by a devout Indian Muslim leader, Maulana Abul Kalam Azad, in Ramgarh, that articulated a very different Muslim perspective—a speech all the more remarkable for being made (as we know in hindsight) in a losing cause. Because of the circumstances, and because it actively evoked memory rather than forgetting, it is all the more worth quoting from extensively:

> I am a Musalman and am proud of that fact. Islam's splendid traditions of thirteen hundred years are my inheritance. I am unwilling to lose even the smallest part of this inheritance. The teaching and history of Islam, its arts and letters and civilization are my wealth and my fortune. It is my duty to protect them.

> As a Musalman I have a special interest in Islamic religion and culture and I cannot tolerate any interference with them. But in addition to these sentiments, I have others also which the realities and conditions of my life have forced upon me. The spirit of Islam does not come in the way of these sentiments; it guides and helps me forward. I am proud of being an Indian. I am a part of the indivisible unity that is Indian nationality. I am indispensable to this noble edifice and without me this splendid structure of India is incomplete. I am an essential element which has gone to build India. I can never surrender this claim.

> It was India's historic destiny that many human races and cultures and religions should flow to her, finding a home in her hospitable soil, and that many a caravan should find rest here. Even before the dawn of history, these caravans trekked into India and wave after wave of new-comers followed. This vast and fertile land gave welcome to all and took them to her bosom. One of the last of these caravans, following the footsteps of its predecessors, was that of the followers of Islam. This came here and settled here for good. This led to a

meeting of the culture-currents of two different races. Like Ganga and Jamuna, they flowed for a while through separate courses, but nature's immutable law brought them together and joined them in a *sangam*. This fusion was a notable event in history. Since then, destiny, in her own hidden way, began to fashion a new India in place of the old. We brought our treasures with us, and India too was full of the riches of her own precious heritage. We gave our wealth to her and she unlocked the doors of her own treasures to us. We gave her, what she needed most, the most precious of gifts from Islam's treasury, the message of democracy and human equality.

Full eleven centuries have passed by since then. Islam has now as great a claim on the soil of India as Hinduism. If Hinduism has been the religion of the people here for several thousands of years, Islam also has been their religion for a thousand years. Just as a Hindu can say with pride that he is an Indian and follows Hinduism, so also we can say with equal pride that we are Indians and follow Islam. I shall enlarge this orbit still further. The Indian Christian is equally entitled to say with pride that he is an Indian and is following a religion of India, namely Christianity.

… These thousand years of our joint life has moulded us into a common nationality. This cannot be done artificially. Nature does her fashioning through her hidden processes in the course of centuries. The cast has now been moulded and destiny has set her seal upon it. Whether we like it or not, we have become an Indian nation, united and indivisible. No fantasy or artificial scheming to separate and divide can break this unity. We must accept the logic of fact and history….

Azad's stirring words failed to prevent Partition and the departure of a substantial percentage of India's Muslims from the national fold. But others remained, and some even came back—in March 1948, for instance, no fewer than 22,000 Muslims returned from West Pakistan to India, to the consternation of the authorities who had listed their abandoned homes as "evacuee property", and who slowed down the flow by introducing a permit system for these returning migrants, reducing the number to some 2,000 returnees by July. Till the cusp of the 21st century, Indian Muslims outnumbered Pakistan's.

Partition divided hearts and families. The wars of 1948 and 1965 between the two countries featured stories of siblings—children of the same parents—firing on each other. In 1948, pitted on opposite sides in the same military engagement in the mountains of Kashmir, were Major Sahibzada Yunus Khan of India and his younger brother Major Sahibzada Yaqub Khan of Pakistan. Both brothers had served together in the British Army as young officers in the

THE STRUGGLE FOR INDIA'S SOUL

European theatre during the Second World War, but Partition led each to opt for different armies. It is said that a shot fired by the elder brother in 1948 wounded the younger, and Yunus cried out, "*Chhote* [young one]—don't be upset. We're soldiers and we must do our duty." Yunus retired as a colonel but his younger brother rose to be a general, and later an ambassador and foreign minister of Pakistan.

Major Maroof Raza, who abandoned a stellar career in the Indian Army to become a defence strategist and commentator on military affairs, recounted this story[12] about the 1965 war that he heard from a retired Indian officer, who, in turn, had heard it from a visiting Pakistani brigadier, Brig. Beg. In September 1965, at the peak of the tank battles between the two armies, Beg, then a young Pakistani lieutenant, was asked to undertake a commando raid before dawn to eliminate an Indian tank commander. Under cover of darkness, he climbed aboard an Indian tank, and spotted, through the open cupola, a major poring over maps, planning for the next day's battle. Shooting the Indian officer in the head, he removed the cloth epaulets from his victim's shoulders as proof of his deed, along with a holy pendant from the officer's pocket. Returning to his own lines, he handed his trophies over to his commander, a brigadier, remarking that he was quite surprised that India's army also had Muslim officers who were fighting with such commitment and valour against Pakistan. Let the story continue in Raza's words: "At that point his Brigade Commander's hands began to shake and he couldn't control his emotions any more. His voice became heavy and his eyes filled with tears as he slumped into a chair. Lieutenant Beg asked the [Commander], with due respect, what the problem was. In a voice choked with emotion, he replied: 'Young man, I have just realised from the evidence you have provided that I had tasked you to kill my younger brother... I hadn't the foggiest idea that the 16 Cavalry was pitted against us. Major M.A.R. Sheikh, whom you have killed, was my younger brother.'"

The Indian officer narrating the story to Raza then revealed the clincher: he himself was the youngest brother of three in that family: "And as the [visiting] Brigadier stared at him in disbelief, the narrator of this tale requested Brigadier Beg to visit his family home—which was only a few hours' drive from where they were—to meet his aged mother, who had always wanted to meet someone who had fought against her son. When the Pakistani Brigadier [Beg] met the old begum the next day (who didn't know that her son had died of wounds inflicted by Beg) she seemed pleased that the enemy thought well of him.

"Records show that Major Sheikh died of wounds in his head sustained in battle near Sialkot on 10 September 1965. He was posthumously awarded the gallantry award of a Vir Chakra. His brother, the Brigade Commander, rose on to become a General in Pakistan."

The story is poignant at many levels: the officer unknowingly ordering the killing of his own brother (though he might well have accomplished the same on the battlefield); and the killer visiting the mother of his victim who was also the mother of his commander, in the company of his victim's younger brother. It is almost impossible to imagine the welter of emotions that must have swirled through the minds of each of the personages in this story. One people, divided into two nations, is bad enough; one family, divided between two nations at war with each other, is unbearably tragic.

But the India Azad spoke of, in which he remained after Partition and which he ably served as a cabinet minister until his death in 1958, chose to continue to incarnate his faith. The idea of India celebrates the various elements that comprise it: if the USA is a melting pot, as I have long argued, then to me India is a thali, a selection of sumptuous dishes in different bowls. Each tastes different, and does not necessarily mix with the next, but they belong together on the same plate, and they complement each other in making the meal a satisfying repast.

Each Indian is free to nurture multiple identities: regional, religious, caste, linguistic, ethnic. Indians love to ask each other where they are from, and this simple question usually stumps me. When people ask me where I was born, I have to confess it was London, though I do not consider myself to be "from" there. I could say I am from Thiruvananthapuram, which I represent in Parliament; but to many in Thiruvananthapuram, I am really from Palakkad, my ancestral district, where my parents' families hail from, and which would be described as my "native place" in our distinctive and quite accurate way of phrasing it. In Delhi, I would say I am from Kerala; in Kerala, people would notice my caste, Nair, or my religion, Hindu; outside Kerala, I would be called a Malayali, a reference to my mother tongue. But for all my sentimental attachment to each of these identities, they all co-exist within me; village, constituency, religion, language, state, and nation (and, for that matter, the world) are all mine to claim—and all exert their claim on me. But I am secure in each of these identities because of the sheltering carapace of one overall identity: that of being Indian.

PART THREE

THE HINDUTVA IDEA OF INDIA

It must have been a slow news day.

The hysteria on our television channels in late 2018 over a remark I had made many times before (and tweeted in 2013)—that the BJP's agenda of a "Hindu rashtra", if it succeeded in capturing both Houses of Parliament as well as a majority of the states, would reduce India to, in Nehru's words, a "Hindu Pakistan"—was bizarre. It stretched credulity to see so many hours devoted to distorting two words and accusing their author of everything from being anti-Hindu to anti-national.

The idea of India I have described, embodied in the Constitution, is that of civic nationalism sanctified by Indic civilization and suffused by an ethos of pluralism. This was the Indian nationalists' answer to the challenge posed by Partition. On the other hand, the alternative was the Hindutva idea of a Hindu country, espoused today by the BJP/RSS, the mirror image of the Idea of Pakistan—a state with a dominant majority religion that seeks to put its minorities in a subordinate place. Its ethnic (religious, cultural, and linguistic) nationalism is often summarized in the slogan "Hindi-Hindu-Hindustan." This is the principal alternative to the civic nationalist conception of India, and it is worth examining in detail here.

16

THE DOCTRINE OF HINDUTVA

The man largely credited with the invention of the concept of Hindutva—literally 'Hinduness'—is Vinayak Damodar Savarkar (1883–1966), whose *Essentials of Hindutva*[1] laid out the concept in 1923. Republished in 1928 as *Hindutva: Who is a Hindu?* it is the foundational text of the Hindu nationalist creed. I have discussed Savarkar's ideas at length in my book *Why I Am A Hindu*, but I will briefly revisit them, and the formulations of other Hindutva ideologues, in this chapter and elsewhere in the book, as they relate to the concepts of nationhood I am exploring.

Savarkar is particularly interesting, not just because of his stature as an icon of Hindu nationalism—his portrait was installed in parliament by a BJP government, directly opposite a likeness of Mahatma Gandhi whom he sought to repudiate—but because of his own intellectual journey in that direction. In his early book on the Indian revolt of 1857, he wrote with approbation of Hindu-Muslim unity and stated that both were brothers from the same mother. (For Savarkar, of all people—a man who went on, as President of the Hindu Mahasabha in 1937, to argue that Hindus and Muslims were two distinct nations—to speak of Muslims as brothers, reminds me of the old saw attributed to a cynic at the end of the French revolution: "When I saw what men did in the name of fraternity, I resolved if I had a brother to call him cousin.")[2] After eleven years' rigorous imprisonment and penal servitude in the Andamans (I have visited his cell in the Cellular Jail, now a museum), and on the basis of multiple craven letters to the British begging for forgiveness and pleading undying loyalty to the King-Emperor, Savarkar was released, a changed man. Henceforward, he turned into a proponent of ethno-religious nationalism, despite being, as a young revolutionary, very much in favour of an all-encompassing understanding of India. (Another who made the same journey from being hailed as an "Ambassador of Hindu-

Muslim unity" to becoming a proponent of religious nationalism was, ironically, Mohamed Ali Jinnah.)

Savarkar chose the term 'Hindutva' to describe the 'quality of being a Hindu' in ethnic, cultural, and political terms. He argued that a Hindu is one who considers India to be his motherland (matrbhumi), the land of his ancestors (pitrbhumi), and his holy land (punyabhumi). India is the land of the Hindus since their ethnicity is Indian and since the Hindu faith originated in India. (Other faiths that were born in India, like Sikhism, Buddhism, and Jainism also qualified, in Savarkar's terms, as variants of Hinduism since they fulfilled the same three criteria; but Islam and Christianity, born outside India, did not). Thus, a Hindu is someone born of Hindu parents, who regards India—'this land of Bharatvarsha, from the Indus to the Seas'—as his motherland as well as his holy land, 'that is the cradle-land of his religion.'[3]

In keeping with the race doctrines of the times, Savarkar conceived Hindutva as an indefinable quality inherent in the Hindu 'race', which could not be identified directly with the specific tenets of Hinduism. To him, the religion was therefore a subset of the political idea, rather than synonymous with it—something many of its proponents today would be surprised to hear. Despite this distinction, Hindutva would help achieve the political consolidation of the Hindu people, since Savarkar also argued that a Muslim or a Christian, even if born in India, could not claim allegiance to the three essentials of Hindutva: 'a common nation (rashtra), a common race (jati) and a common civilization (sanskriti), as represented in a common history, common heroes, a common literature, a common art, a common law and a common jurisprudence, common fairs and festivals, rites and rituals, ceremonies and sacraments.'[4] Hindus, defined as possessing these common values and practices, constituted the Indian nation—a nation that had existed since antiquity, since Savarkar was explicitly rejecting the British view that India was, in Churchill's notorious phrase, which I have quoted earlier, 'a geographical expression.... No more a single country than the Equator.'

Savarkar's vision of Hindutva saw it as the underlying principle of a 'Hindu Rashtra' that extended across the Indian subcontinent, and was rooted in an undivided India bounded by the mountains and the seas ('Akhand Bharat') corresponding to the territorial aspirations of ancient dynasties like the Mauryas (320 BCE–180 BCE), who under Chandragupta and Ashoka, had managed to knit most of the subcontinent under their control. In the words of a later RSS publication, *Sri Guruji, the Man and his Mission*, 'It became evident that Hindus were the nation in Bharat and that Hindutva was Rashtriyatva [nationalism].'[5]

For Savarkar, Hindu-ness was synonymous with Indianness, properly understood. Savarkar's idea of Hindutva was expansive: 'Hindutva is not a word but a history. Not only the spiritual or religious history of our people as at times it is mistaken to be by being confounded with the other cognate term Hinduism, but a history in full... Hindutva embraces all the departments of thought and activity of the whole Being of our Hindu race.'[6] In turn, the Hindu 'race' was inextricably bound to the idea of the nation. As Savarkar put it, 'We Hindus are bound together not only by the tie of the love we bear to a common fatherland and by the common blood that courses through our veins and keeps our hearts throbbing and our affections warm, but also by the tie of the common homage we pay to our great civilization— our Hindu culture'.

As noted, however, his idea of Hindutva excluded those whose ancestors came from elsewhere or whose lands lay outside India—thereby eliminating Muslim and Christians, India's two most significant minorities, from his frame of reference. What their place would be in Savarkar's construction of the nation was not made explicitly clear, but the best they could hope for was a sort of second-class citizenship in which they could live in India only on sufferance.

This logic was taken even farther by M. S. Golwalkar (1906–1973), the sarsangchalak or head of the Rashtriya Swayamsevak Sangh (RSS) for three decades (1940–1973), who supplanted Savarkar as the principal ideologue of Hindu nationalism, notably in his 1939 screed *We, or Our Nationhood Defined*[7] and in the anthology of his writings and speeches, *Bunch of Thoughts*.[8] Golwalkar made it clear in his writings that India was the holy land of the Hindus. He writes: 'Hindusthan is the land of the Hindus and is the terra firma for the Hindu nation alone to flourish upon....' According to him, India was a pristine Hindu country in ancient times, a place of unparalleled glory destroyed in successive assaults by foreign invaders. He felt that a 'national regeneration' was necessary.[9]

Savarkar did not react very kindly to the takeover of his ideology by the more religion-minded Golwalkar; for instance, he opposed cow worship, which Golwalkar exalted, declared that people should eat what they liked and what they could afford, showed little patience for Hindu holy men, advocated an end to the caste-system, sought rapid social transformation, avowed personal atheism and staunch rationalism, and once commented caustically about RSS volunteers that apart from joining the RSS, they seemed to have accomplished little in life. New books by Vaibhav Purandare[10] and Vikram Sampath[11] portray Savarkar as far more of a social reformer than a Hindu revivalist; it was Golwalkar and the RSS that took Hindutva in a more explicitly "fundamentalist" direction.

Throughout his writings, Golwalkar expressed the view that the national regeneration of this 'Hindu nation' (the 'motherland' for which the 'Hindu people' shed their blood) could only come about through the revival of its Hindu-ness. Golwalkar rejected the concept of what he called 'territorial nationalism', the modern variant of nationalism which identified a state with its territory and bestowed equal rights of citizenship on all those who lived within it. That, to Golwalkar, made no sense: a territory was not a nation, a people constituted a nation. Who were these people? In the Indian case, Hindus. Golwalkar and the RSS became passionate advocates of 'cultural nationalism'. This, of course, is directly opposed to the civic nationalism enshrined in the Constitution of India.

India's independence from colonial rule in 1947, Golwalkar argued, did not constitute real freedom because the new leaders held on to the 'perverted concept of nationalism' that located all who lived on India's territory as equal constituents of the nation. 'The concept of territorial nationalism,' he wrote, 'has verily emasculated our nation and what more can we expect of a body deprived of its vital energy? ...[and] so it is that we see today the germs of corruption, disintegration and dissipation eating into the vitals of our nation for having given up the natural living nationalism in the pursuit of an unnatural, unscientific and lifeless hybrid concept of territorial nationalism.'[12]

Golwalkar's *Bunch of Thoughts* goes on to argue that territorial nationalism is a barbarism, since a nation is 'not a mere bundle of political and economic rights' but an embodiment of national culture—in India, 'ancient and sublime' Hinduism. In the book, Golwalkar sneers at democracy—which he sees as alien to Hindu culture. As I demonstrate in my book *Why I Am a Hindu*, Golwalkar intended traditional Hindu practices to prevail in his dystopia, including caste discrimination.

The alternative to territorial nationalism, to Golwalkar, was a nationalism based on race. In *We, or Our Nationhood Defined*, at the height of Hitler's rise, Golwalkar wrote: 'To keep up the purity of the Race and its culture, Germany shocked the world by her purging the country of the Semitic Races—the Jews. Race pride at its highest has been manifested here. Germany has also shown how well-nigh impossible it is for Races and cultures, having differences going to the root, to be assimilated into one united whole, a good lesson for us in Hindustan to learn and profit by.'[13]

This marked an evolution from Savarkar's notion that saw Hindutva as principally a cultural identity and the Hindu religion as a part of a national

Hindu culture. In an important respect, Golwalkar reversed Savarkar's logic: 'With us,' he wrote, 'culture is but a product of our all-comprehensive religion, a part of its body and not distinguishable from it.' From Golwalkar onwards, Hindutva was seen as an ideology seeking to establish the hegemony of Hindus, Hindu values and the Hindu way of life in the political arrangements of India. In this he was building on Savarkar's derisive rejection of Gandhian 'universalism' and 'non-violence' which he considered delusionary opiates; instead of Gandhi's moral lessons in favour of peace, Savarkar advocated the 'political virility' of Hindutva, an idea which found full flower in Golwalkar.

Golwalkar made no bones about the principal targets of his race-hatred: 'Ever since that evil day, when Moslems first landed in Hindustan, right up to the present moment, the Hindu Nation has been gallantly fighting on to shake off the despoilers. The Race Spirit has been awakening'.[14] The association of Hindutva with an explicitly anti-Muslim agenda can be traced to its unambiguous avowal by Golwalkar. But 'race'—fashionable though the term was when Golwalkar wrote in the 1930s, especially in the context of Nazi ideology—was not a totally accurate word for what he meant, not least since many, indeed most, of India's Muslims were descended from Hindu ancestors themselves and therefore were of the same race or ethnicity as the Hindus for whom Golwalkar was speaking.

According to the proponents of Hindutva, despite that common descent, Muslims had cut themselves off from Hindu culture: they prayed in Arabic, rather than the Sanskrit born on Indian soil, turned to a foreign city (Mecca) as their holiest of holies, and owed allegiance to a holy book, and beliefs spawned by it, that had no roots in the sacred land of India. V. S. Naipaul echoes this thought in his *Among the Believers*: 'It turns out now that the Arabs were the most successful imperialists of all time; since to be conquered by them (and then to be like them) is still, in the minds of the faithful, to be saved.'[15]

Golwalkar's answer was to seek the assimilation of Muslims and other minorities into the Hindu nationalist mainstream by forcing them to abandon these external allegiances (rather as the Jews were forced to adopt outward signs of adherence to Christianity during the Spanish Inquisition four and a half centuries earlier). The German notion of a Volksgeist, a 'race spirit' to which everyone would have to conform, appealed strongly to Golwalkar. To remain in India, Muslims would have to submit themselves to Hindus. Recalling the parable of Prophet Muhammad going to the mountain, Golwalkar wrote: 'In the Indian situation, the Hindu is the mountain, and the

Muslim population, Mohammed. I need not elaborate.' A few paragraphs earlier, I have quoted his approving words about Nazi theories of race. There is more in his writing that is even more chilling. Golwalkar's hatred for non-Hindus was especially virulent when it came to Muslims and Christians; he regarded Parsis and Jews in India as model minorities who knew their place and did not ruffle any Hindu feathers. In his pungent view: '[H]ere was already a full-fledged ancient nation of the Hindus and the various communities which were living in the country were here either as guests, the Jews and Parsis, or as invaders, the Muslims and Christians.' He added: 'They never faced the question how all such heterogenous groups could be called as children of the soil merely because, by an accident, they happened to reside in a common territory under the rule of a common enemy.'

Golwalkar strongly opposed any talk of a secular Indian state. As he wrote in *We, or Our Nationhood Defined*: 'There are only two courses open to these foreign elements', Golwalkar went on, 'either to merge themselves in the national race and adopt its culture, or to live at its mercy so long as the national race may allow them to do so and quit the country at the sweet will of the national race.... In Hindustan, land of the Hindus, lives and should live the Hindu Nation....All others are traitors and enemies to the National Cause.... [The] foreign races in Hindusthan must...lose their separate existence to merge in the Hindu race, or may stay in the country, wholly subordinated to the Hindu Nation, claiming nothing, deserving no privileges, far less any preferential treatment—not even citizen's rights.' In a December 1947 speech, four months after Partition, Golwalkar, referring to Muslims, said that 'no power on earth' could keep Muslims in Hindustan. 'They should have to quit this country....'[16]

The RSS's official understanding of Hindutva embraced this Golwalkar idea till very recently. In their reply to the tribunal constituted under the Unlawful Activities (Prevention) Act 1967 to hear a case on the RSS in 1993, the RSS made an official statement arguing that "the cultural nationality of India, in the conviction of the RSS, is Hindu and it was inclusive of all who are born and who have adopted Bharat as their Motherland."

This statement, of course, elides the 'holy land' problem in Savarkar's famous tripartite formula: if you are a Muslim, Christian or Parsi, however 'Hindu' you may be culturally, India is not your holy land. Hindutva acolytes gloss over this contradiction by suggesting that the key lies in these minorities acknowledging their foundational Hindu-ness: if they see themselves as 'Muhammadan Hindus', 'Christian Hindus' and 'Parsi Hindus', India can accept them. Since few, if any, of the believers in these faiths are ready to see themselves in such terms, of course, it is logical to assume they remain unwelcome in Hindutva-led India.

It is striking that the proponents of Hindutva share so much with twenti-eth-century Muslim modernists in South Asia and West Asia—their concep-tion of a glorious past, their imagining of a fall from that past (blamed on internal cultural failings and rapacious outsiders), their stilted conception of culture and cultural difference, their negative appraisal of 'Western' values and 'Westernization', and their fervent desire for the political unity of a religious community as the essential requirement for the attainment or re-establishment of national glory. This emerged from a major chip on the col-lective shoulder, born from a historical memory of humiliation, and sustained by a continuing sense of insecurity that seems irrational in a majority popula-tion. Colonization meant that even as Indians resisted it, some colonial con-cepts and categories were deeply internalized—including that of the nation-state as the ideal vehicle for collective aspirations. But while some nationalists had the imagination to move beyond its limitations and not require one lan-guage, one religion, and a uniform identity, others, out of insecurity and fear that this would open us up to weakness again, insisted upon the opposite. There is a constant paranoia and fear behind Hindutva, which is also why so much of it revolves around fear-mongering. There is always need to define itself against an "Other". More confident civic nationalists and patriots do not feel that need. Golwalkar's views of nationalism continue to inspire his politi-cal followers nearly half a century after his death—except that, unlike when he expressed them, those who believe such things are actually in power now and in a position to do something about them.

Inspired by the example of Nazi Germany, Golwalkar had appalling ideas on how "foreigners" should be dealt with. As he regarded Muslims, Christians, and communists as "hostile elements within the country" who posed "a far greater menace to national security than aggressors from outside," if they refused to convert or submit, he intimated, they would have to be purged—forced to "quit the country at the sweet will of the national race."[17]

It is difficult to translate this kind of language in contemporary terms, except to draw invidious parallels—such as some have drawn between the Citizenship (Amendment) Act (CAA) of 2019 and the proposed National Register of Citizens, on the one hand, and Germany's 1935 Nuremberg Laws, on the other. The Nazis restricted German citizenship only to those who had been granted citizenship papers by the Third Reich; the BJP govern-ment of Narendra Modi proposed to do something similar. That, in many ways, sums up the alternative idea of India on offer.

17

HINDU RASHTRA UPDATED

A more moderate and indeed sophisticated advocate of Hindu rashtra was Pandit Deen Dayal Upadhyaya (1916–68), who was a principal leader, and briefly president, of the BJP's forerunner, the Bharatiya Jana Sangh. Much of Upadhyaya's philosophical thinking focused on what constituted the Indian nation, and why, in his view, it had failed to become strong and unified. Upadhyaya saw this failure in moral terms—political corruption, the general public's lack of any urge to make India strong and prosperous, a 'degeneration' of society and the fading away of the idealism that had inspired the struggle for freedom. Indians had misled themselves into equating freedom with the mere overthrow of foreign rule; this negative view overlooked the need for something far more positive, a genuine and patriotic love for the motherland.

Interestingly, the early anti-colonial nationalists had seen a revival of interest in Hinduism as entirely compatible with, indeed necessary for, their cause. This was especially true of Madan Mohan Malaviya and the "Lal-Bal-Pal" trio of Lala Lajpat Rai, Bal Gangadhar Tilak and Bipin Chandra Pal, who saw in the mobilization of Hindus an opportunity for forging a new Indian nationalism against the British. The Swadeshi leader Bipin Chandra Pal argued as early as 1910 that: "In India, among the Hindus, civic religion is growing through an easy and natural process, out of the old symbolism and ritualism of the people. Hinduism has, indeed, like all ethnic systems, this advantage over credal religions, that its symbols and rituals, its sacraments and mysteries, are all partly religious and partly civic, partly social and partly spiritual. In fact, in Hinduism, the social and the spiritual are strangely blended together. Consequently, the new national spirit has found apt vehicles for expressing itself in the current religious rites and formulas of the people."[1]

Pal, as a prominent Indian nationalist, had argued that such a reawakening was in fact a nationalist reassertion in the face of European colonization. "The movement of social and religious revival which preceded the present Nationalist Movement, represented really the return of the national consciousness to itself. It was not really a conflict between the progressive and conservative elements of Indian society, as superficial observers have tried to make it out, but a conflict between aggressive European and progressive Indian culture. It was India's mental and moral protest against the intellectual and ethical domination of Europe."[2]

Deen Dayal Upadhyaya would have concurred, but would have gone farther. Like Savarkar and Golwalkar, Upadhyaya too deplored the concept of territorial nationalism, which saw the Indian nation as being formed of all the peoples who reside in this land. In his view reducing India to a territory and everyone who lived on it elided fundamental questions that needed to be answered: Whose nation is this? What is freedom for? What kind of life do we want to develop here? What set of values are we going to accept? What does the concept of nationhood really signify?

A territory and its inhabitants, Westernized Indians seemed to believe, would embrace Hindus, Muslims, Christians and others under a common nationhood to resist British rule. This was a fallacy, according to Upadhyaya. 'A nation is not a mere geographical unit. The primary need of nationalism is the feeling of boundless dedication in the hearts of the people for their land. Our feeling for the motherland has a basis: our long, continuous habitation in the same land creates, by association, a sense of "my-ness".'[3]

The disappearance of the foreign power, Upadhyaya believed, had left a vacuum before a people accustomed to the 'negative patriotism' of anti-colonialism. Nationalism had to consist of far more than the mere rejection of foreign rule. Upadhyaya spurned the Western idea of nationalism as a political force spawned by the French Revolution and its values; he abjured the notion that a nation is made up of various constituent elements that can be itemized, such as a common race, religion, land, traditions, shared experience of calamities, means of transport, common political administration and so on. Such ideas, he believed, missed the essential ethos of nationalism—love for the motherland.

Since love for the motherland had never been inculcated in its inhabitants, their lives in independent India were now centred on money and lust or greed—artha and kama in the classic quartet of human aspirations enumerated in the *Purusharthas*, at the expense of dharma and moksha, faith and salvation. This modern materialism Upadhyaya saw as a major societal flaw.

As he wrote in his book, *Rashtra Jeevan Ki Disha* (The Direction of National Life):[4] "All our ailments in today's political life have their origin in our avarice. A race for rights has banished the noble idea of service.... [A] transformation in our attitude can be brought about only on the basis of the ideals of Indian culture."

Dazzled by the material advances made by the so-called developed countries, Upadhyaya argued, India, too, had taken to aping the foreigners under the rubric of 'Five-Year Plans' and development projects. India had written a Constitution imitative of the West, divorced from any real connection to our mode of life and from authentically Indian ideas about the relationship between the individual and society. (In this he was echoing Golwalkar, who had lamented that our 'cumbersome' Constitution was all the more deficient for incorporating 'absolutely nothing' from the *Manusmriti).*

Upadhyaya thus felt the need for a Hindu political philosophy befitting an ancient nation like Bharat. This would have to be based on a positive concept of patriotism and a comprehensive vision of the nation as a complete entity— its security, its unity, its growth and development, the welfare of its entire populace and the full development of every individual—based on its inherent character, culture, spiritual underpinnings, and permanent values that have, as he saw them, stood the test of time.

For Upadhyaya, our ancient country had a special personality distinct from that of other nations; it had an ethos of its own. Only a national philosophy that reflected this could be successful; only an authentic Indian approach would ensure happiness for Indians. Upadhyaya was convinced that independent India could not rely upon Western concepts like individualism, democracy, socialism, communism or capitalism; it had to reject these formulae and find its own approach. Unfortunately, in his view, India's polity after Independence had been built upon these superficial and feeble Western foundations rather than authentic Hindu ones. India's polity had to be anchored in the traditions and ethos of India's own ancient Hindu culture.

As we have seen, Upadhyaya was clear, like Savarkar and Golwalkar, that reducing the Indian national idea to a territory and all the people on it was fallacious. The rejection of "territorial nationalism" is fundamental to all the principal thinkers of the Hindutva project. It was this sort of thinking, he argued sternly, that had led the nationalist movement, from the Khilafat agitation onwards, to turn towards a policy of appeasement of the Muslim community, a policy in turn sought to be justified by the need to forge a united front against the British. The RSS's founder leader, Dr K. B. Hedgewar (whose Marathi biography Upadhyaya translated) had pointed to the 'ideological confusion' this approach created. Muslim communalism, in his and Upadhyaya's view, had become more prominent and aggressive, while Congress leaders bent over backwards more and more to accommodate them.

The Partition of 1947 was undoubtedly a defeat for those who had wanted to preserve a united India, but it was not a failure of India's unity as much as it was the defeat of misconceived utopian efforts to embrace non-Hindus in the name of national unity. It was not that the objective was wrong, in Upadhyaya's view, but the methods to achieve the preservation of our unity through minority appeasement were flawed and so the battle was lost. 'Every nation,' Upadhyaya said, 'wants to live a happy and prosperous life according to its own nature and that is the motive behind its intense desire for freedom. The nation that tries to follow a path of thought and action discordant with its own nature, meets with disaster. This is why our nation has been caught up in a whirlpool of difficulties.' India could and should contribute to the world 'in consonance with our culture and traditions.'

That culture was, of course, Hindu. In India, 'there exists only one culture…. There are no separate cultures here for Muslims and Christians.' Every community, therefore, including Muslims and Christians, 'must identify themselves with the age-long national cultural stream that was Hindu culture in this country.' His logic was that 'unless all people become part of the same cultural stream, national unity or integration is impossible. If we want to preserve Indian nationalism, this is the only way.' To him, 'the national cultural stream would continue to remain one and those who cannot identify themselves with it would not be considered nationals.'

To Upadhyaya, the national culture to which he was referring had to be Hindu; it explicitly could not be Muslim. 'Mecca, Medina, Hassan and Hussain, Sohrab and Rustom and Bulbul may be very significant in their own ways but they do not form a part of Indian national life and stream of Indian culture. How can those who are emotionally associated with these and look upon [the] Rama and Krishna tradition as alien be described as nationals? We see that the moment anybody embraces Islam, an effort is made to cut him off from the entire tradition of this country and connect him to the alien tradition.'

Muslims, said Upadhyaya, even related differently to India's past: 'Some events involve triumph, some our humiliation. The memories of our glorious deeds make us proud; ignominies make us hang our heads in shame.' But Hindus saw such historical events differently from Muslims. 'Aggressions by Mohammed Ghori or Mahmood Ghazni naturally fill us with agony. We develop a feeling of attachment to Prithviraj [Chauhan] and other patriots. If instead, any person feels pride for the aggressors and no love for the

Motherland, he can lay no claim to patriotism. The memory of Rana Pratap, Chhatrapati Shivaji or Guru Gobind Singh makes us bow down our heads with respect and devotion. On the other hand, the names of Aurangzeb, Alauddin, Clive or Dalhousie, fill us with anger that is natural towards foreign aggressors.' Only Hindu society, Upadhyaya underscored, felt this way about its heroes, supporting Rana Pratap over Akbar; therefore there was really no ground for doubt that Indian nationalism is Hindu nationalism.

Upadhyaya's conclusion was blunt: the Muslims sought 'to destroy the values of Indian culture, its ideals, national heroes, traditions, places of devotion and worship', and therefore 'can never become an indivisible part of this country.' In Upadhayaya's vision, the inherent consciousness of unity, identical ties of history and tradition, relations of affinity between the land and the people and shared aspirations and hopes, made Hindustan a nation of Hindus. 'We shall have to concede that our nationality is none other than Hindu nationality. If any outsider comes into this country he shall have to move in step and adjust himself with Hindu nationality.'

But Upadhyaya did not adopt his mentor Golwalkar's ideas about dealing with India's Muslims as Hitler had dealt with the Jews. 'No sensible man will say that six crores of Muslims should be eradicated or thrown out of India,' he admitted in an article titled 'Akhand Bharat: Objectives and Means'. '[B]ut then they will have to identify themselves completely with Indian life.' Muslims had to be accommodated within the Indian reality, but on what basis? 'This unity...can be established only among homogeneous cultures, not among the contrary ones. A preparation of various cereals and pulses mixed together can be prepared: but if sand particles find their way into it, the whole food is spoilt', he explained. The way to eliminate these 'sand particles' was to 'purify' or 'nationalize Muslims'—to 'make Muslims proper Indians'. The Congress-led nationalist movement had wrongly tried to forge Hindu-Muslim unity against the British, but 'unless all people become part of the same cultural stream, national unity or integration is impossible.... A situation will have to be created in which political aspirations of Islam in India will be rooted out. Then and then alone can a longing for cultural unity take root.'

In demanding of Muslims and other minorities this subordination to, and total identification with, a Hindu state, Upadhyaya—while his reasons differed in both premise and approach—arrived at the same place as Savarkar and Golwalkar. But Upadhyaya went a few steps beyond them in developing the concept more fully.

In building a case for his formulation, Upadhyaya specifically disavowed the existing Constitution of India (which makes all the more curious the enthusiastic zeal with which his devotees today, from Prime Minister Modi on down, swear by it and celebrate every milestone in its adoption). As Upadhyaya put it in *Rashtra Jeevan Ki Disha*: 'We became free in 1947. The English quit India. We felt what was considered to be the greatest obstacle in the path of our effort of nation building was removed" But Indian leaders... failed to see that our inherent national ideals and traditions should be reflected in our Constitution.... The result was that our national culture and traditions were never reflected in these ideologies borrowed from elsewhere and so they utterly failed to touch the chords of our national being.'[5]

Having rejected its premise, Upadhyaya was scathing about the Constitution's drafting and adoption: a nation, he argued, 'is not like a club which can be started or dissolved. A nation is not created by some crores of people passing a resolution and defining a common code of behaviour binding on all its members. A certain mass of people emerges with an inherent motivation. It is,' he added, using a Hindu analogy, 'like the soul adopting the medium of the body.'

In the classic Hindu formula, a king must function according to his raj dharma, or code of governance, which is not defined by him, but is laid down for him by selfless unattached rishis. In contemporary language, Upadhyaya saw a Hindu king almost as one might a chief executive receiving his authority from the shareholders (in this case, the people), mediated through the vision of the board (in this case, the wisdom of the sages). But, he argued, the founding fathers of the Republic of India were largely Anglophile Indians schooled in Western systems of thought; their work revealed no Indianness, no Bharatiyata. The Constitution, therefore, was to him a flawed document, one incapable of guiding India towards the path of raj dharma. In fact, it condemned Hindus to slavery: 'Self-rule and independence are considered to be synonyms. A deeper thinking will bring home to us the fact that even in a free country, the nation can remain in slavery.' The Hindu nation had been enslaved by inappropriate Westernization. Even the language in which the Constitution had been drafted betrayed this reality: 'If the original draft of the Constitution had been in Hindi or in any other Indian language', he felt, the 'un-Indian element' would not have been as dominant. But his concerns, of course, went well beyond language. The Constitution's core conception of the nation, in his view, was fundamentally not Indian at all.

Upadhyaya thus questioned the very legitimacy of the Constitution and not just the process by which it was created. For Upadhyaya, the absence of the Hindu rashtra idea in the Constitution was unacceptable. For him dharma had to be the central idea behind governance and nation building. In keeping with his distaste for foreign concepts and terms, Upadhyaya explicated his beliefs through the use of Sanskrit terms to which he ascribed specific contemporary meanings. A favourite word of Upadhyaya's is chiti, which he labels the 'soul power' of a nation. He describes this soul power through a homely analogy: a barber told his customer that his razor was sixty years old, and had been used by his father. Upon further scrutiny, the customer noticed that over the years the handle and blade had been replaced many times, but the barber still claimed that the razor was the same as used by his father. It was a point of pride and prestige for him: the essence of the razor was unchanged even if its physical trappings had been altered over the years. Every nation also had such an identity that did not change with circumstances and temporal alterations. Sadly, modern India—the democratic republic that had emerged under the Constitution—had no sense of its chiti.

One example of this was in the country's constitutional structure. Upadhyaya saw the seeds of division, for instance, even in the Constitution's decision to rename the provinces as 'states' as the Americans did; this reduced India to a federation of states, a dangerously divisive concept in his view. Upadhyaya acknowledged that, unlike the US, every Indian state did not have its own constitution and that there was only one citizenship for the entire country, but he felt the formulation envisaged in the Constitution diluted the sacred idea of a unified Bharatvarsha. The Constitution should have spoken of a unitary state rather than a union of states; the chiti of Bharat was missing. He seemed unconscious of the argument that it was precisely because of these states and their linguistic basis that unity was achieved, for India was able to accommodate all its diversities and give them political expression without losing the bigger cause of united nationhood. But to him diversity was not a positive. A unitary nation imbued with the spirit of chiti creates virat shakti, the organized and unified fighting strength that protects the nation from aggression and dissension. While chiti is the soul of a nation, virat shakti is its life force. Of course, neither idea is even implicitly present in India's Constitution, underscoring, for Upadhyaya, its deeply flawed nature.

Upadhyaya worried that India's constitutional system had been created in negation of its true inherent national spirit and that if the modern Indian nation continued in this way, Hindu civilization would perish. This is what had happened, after all, to Greece and Egypt, whose modern incarnations bore no relationship to the ancient civilizations from which they claimed descent. The same stock of people might be living in those countries, but they bore no resemblance to their glorious past civilizations or forebears. Indeed, the essence of their society, its identity, had changed. This was the fate that

139

Upadhyaya feared would befall India if it continued down the secular Westernized path charted for it in its Constitution: it would lose its core identity (which lay in the form of its chiti) and in effect become something other than the continuing Bharatiya civilization that could trace its origins back to the mists of time.

The critics of Hindu Rashtra, Upadhyaya argued, found that the term was inexpedient for them in the country's competitive politics: they were afraid of losing millions of Christian and Muslim voters. Their misconception was that the use of the term excluded Muslim and Christian communities. If both these communities became one with the national cultural mainstream—without any change in their modes of worship—they would be welcome in the new India. All they had to do was to own up to the ancient traditions of India, to look upon Hindu national heroes as their national heroes, and to develop devotion for Bharat Mata. Then they would be fully accepted as nationals of the Hindu India that he envisioned.

18

A "HINDU PAKISTAN"

The previous two chapters provide the context to the "Hindu Pakistan" controversy with which I began this Part. I had inveighed against the ruling party's attempts to create a Hindutva version of Pakistan, since that was not what our freedom movement fought for, nor was it the idea of India enshrined in our Constitution.

This is not just about the minorities, as the BJP would have us believe. Many proud Hindus like myself cherish the inclusive nature of our faith and have no desire to live, as our Pakistani neighbours are forced to, in an intolerant mono-religious state. Hinduism, as Swami Vivekananda asserted, teaches the acceptance of difference as a basic credo. Hindutva is not Hinduism; it is a political doctrine, not a religious one. A "Hindu India" would not be Hindu at all, but a Sanghi Hindutva state, which is a different country altogether. People like me want to preserve the India we love, and not turn our beloved nation into the kind of religious state we were brought up to detest.

What is bizarre about the media drama over my remarks is that no one who was giving air time to multiple BJP voices, frothing at the mouth about my words, actually asked them one simple question: "Is the BJP giving up its dream of a Hindu rashtra?" Instead, pro-government voices were allowed to get away with reaffirming the PM's famous statement that the Constitution is his holy book, eliding the fact that many senior BJP leaders—from Governor Tathagatha Roy to then-Union Minister of State Anantkumar Hegde—have openly affirmed that, in the latter's words, "the BJP had come to power to change the Constitution" and that it would "do so in the near future".[1] RSS ideologue Govindacharya has declared that he is already at work on a new Hindutva Constitution for India.[2]

As we have seen, the Hindutva lobby's critique of the Constitution is a fundamental one; their idea of its flaws lies in their core belief in the Hindu

141

nation of their dreams, as opposed to the civic nationalism enshrined in the Constitution of India. Deen Dayal Upadhyaya, who rejected the Constitution of India in conception, form and substance, would be astonished to find his supposed acolytes extolling its every line and holding special commemorations in Parliament with grandiloquent speeches to mark the anniversary not just of its adoption—which, after all, is Republic Day—but even of its passage by the Constituent Assembly in a newly anointed 'Constitution Day.' But we have never heard Prime Minister Modi say, "though I admire Deen Dayal Upadhyaya, I disagree with him about the Constitution".

BJP apologists point out that the Government has done nothing to amend the constitution, and others have suggested that the Supreme Court's ruling that secularism is part of the "basic structure" of the Constitution makes the idea of a Hindutva Pakistan impossible. But the fact is that both have only been held at bay by the simple fact that the BJP has not had the numbers required to achieve their goal—two-thirds of both Houses of Parliament and half the states. By the end of 2018 they controlled 20 state assemblies and led coalitions in two more, which meant that it would not be long before the Rajya Sabha would inevitably be theirs. Their overwhelming victory in the Lok Sabha elections in 2019 and winning a plurality of seats in the Rajya Sabha in June 2020 ensured that they finally have all the elements needed to fulfil their project. The nation has been warned.

19

THE FABRICATION OF HISTORY

George Orwell had famously postulated that, "Every nationalist is haunted by the belief that the past can be altered. He spends part of his time in a fantasy world in which things happen as they should—in which, for example, the Spanish Armada was a success or the Russian Revolution was crushed in 1918—and he will transfer fragments of this world to the history books whenever possible. Much of the propagandist writing of our time amounts to plain forgery. Material facts are suppressed, dates altered, quotations removed from their context and doctored so as to change their meaning. Events which it is felt ought not to have happened are left unmentioned and ultimately denied.... Since nothing is ever quite proved or disproved, the most unmistakable fact can be impudently denied. Moreover, although endlessly brooding on power, victory, defeat, revenge, the nationalist is often somewhat uninterested in what happens in the real world. What he wants is to feel that his own unit is getting the better of some other unit, and he can more easily do this by scoring off an adversary than by examining the facts to see whether they support him...."[1]

Nearly eight decades after he wrote these words, Orwell's prescience has been borne out in India, where the rewriting of the past in the service of nationalism is well advanced. The BJP under Modi has devoted itself for years to reinventing history to suit its bleak narrative of India's past, in which the villains are all Muslims or liberals and heroic Hindus are victorious on the revised pages of history books even where they were not on the battlefield. One of the particular obsessions of the BJP in this respect is to promote the notion of an ineluctable Hindu-Muslim divide as a key enabler of the idea of Hindu nationalism.

If much of what ails our present can be traced to our past, it is important to ask to what extent the differences that have bedevilled us were real or imagined. Of those problems that trace their origins to the colonial period, the identity cleavage between Hindus and Muslims was, as several scholars have documented, defined, highlighted and fomented by the British as a deliberate strategy. In this, ironically, the arch-nationalists have become complicit in what was essentially a British imperial project.

Religion, after all, was a useful means of divide and rule. The "Hindu–Muslim divide" started with the way the British taught us to regard our own history. I have explored this at length in *Inglorious Empire*, and will touch upon it briefly here. Foundational to the colonial interpretation of Indian history was the British division of Indian history into 'periods' labelled in accordance with the religion of the rulers: thus the 'Hindu', 'Muslim' and 'British' periods formulated by James Mill in *The History of British India* (published between 1817 and 1826). Implicit in such periodization was the assumption that India was always composed of monolithic, and mutually hostile, religious communities, primarily Hindu and Muslim.

By the mid-nineteenth century, the trio of Mill, Macaulay and the England-based German Max Müller had effectively established a colonial construction of the Indian past which even Indians were taught to internalize. In their reading, Indian civilization was seen as essentially Hindu, as defined by the upper castes, and descended from the Aryan race, which invaded around 1500 BCE from the Central Asian steppes in the north, displaced and merged with indigenous populations, evolved a settled agrarian civilization, spoke Sanskrit and composed the Vedas. The Muslims came as the next wave of invaders and conquerors, in turn supplanted by the British. This history in turn became the received wisdom for late-nineteenth century Indian nationalists, whether Hindu or Muslim revivalists alike. But it suited the Hindutva view of India the most.

Romila Thapar has convincingly demonstrated that the very conception of India as a Hindu Aryan civilization, tracing a line of descent from the most ancient days to the present, is a colonial construction, perpetrated by the 3-M trio of imperial Orientalists.[2] Recent research shows that there was no "Aryan invasion" but a gradual immigration from the north and north-west over many centuries—a natural development, given that previous immigrations like this had also occurred—and that the Indians the incoming migrants found were descendants of a fading urban culture we call the Indus Valley Civilization (itself a mix of "early Indians" with tribes from the Persian plateau).[3] The Vedas were written after this interaction took place, the Rig Veda in its earliest stages; and all of Hinduism emerges from the intermingling of these groups. For Thapar, the truly nationalist historian is the one who challenges the colonial Mill-Macaulay-Mueller construction, not the one who propagates it. She points to the irony of the self-proclaimed nationalists of the Hindutva movement uncritically parroting a colonial idea in the service of their political agenda.[4] By excluding Muslims from the essential national narrative, the nineteenth-century colonial interpretation of Indian history helped give birth in the twentieth to the two-nation theory that eventually divided the country. It also legitimized, with a veneer of scholarship, the British strategic policy of 'divide and rule' in which every effort was made by the imperialists to highlight differences between Hindus and Muslims to persuade the latter that their interests were incompatible with the advancement of the former.

So, though this had no basis in pre-colonial history, the colonialists' efforts to catalogue, classify and categorize the Indians they ruled directly led to a consciousness of religious difference between Hindus and Muslims. The colonial authorities often asked representatives of the two communities to self-consciously construct an 'established' custom, such as by asking them what the prevailing beliefs and practices were around caste, or Muharram, or cow-slaughter, which prompted both groups to give an exaggeratedly rigid version of what they believed the beliefs and practices should be! In other words, colonial policies led to the hardening of these communal identities.

In fact, stories abound of the two communities habitually working together in precolonial times: for instance, Hindus helping Muslims to rebuild a shrine, or Muslims doing the same when a Hindu temple had to be reconstructed. Devout Hindus were sometimes given Muslim names and were often fluent scholars in Persian; Muslims served in the army of the Maratha warrior king, Shivaji, as did Hindu Rajputs in the forces of the fiercely proud Muslim Emperor, Aurangzeb. The Vijayanagara army included Muslim horseback contingents. At the village level, many historians argue that Hindus and Muslims shared a wide spectrum of customs and beliefs, at times even jointly worshipping the same saint or holy spot. In Kerala's famous pilgrimage site of Sabarimala, after an arduous climb to the hilltop shrine of Lord Ayyappa, the devotee first encounters a shrine to his Muslim friend and ally, Vavar Swami. In another amazing example, amazing since it is both anachronistic and syncretistic, a temple in South Arcot, Tamil Nadu, hosts a deity of Muttaal Raavuttan, a Muslim chieftain—complete with beard, kum-kum and toddy pot—who protects Draupadi in the *Mahabharata*. Note, of course, that Islam did not exist when the *Mahabharata* was composed, but in post-Islamic retellings, a Muslim chieftain has entered the plot!

As Romila Thapar explains:

Intensely devotional poetry was written by poets, some of whom were born Muslim but worshipped Hindu deities. One of the best known among them was Sayyad Ibrahim, popularly referred to as Raskhan, whose dohas and bhajans dedicated to the deity Krishna were widely recited in the sixteenth century and are still remembered by devotees of Krishna and others. The intermingling of cultures is also evident in the new kinds of classical music that was composed and sung at the courts of this period. Best known among these was the creation and evolution of Dhrupad, regarded by many as the finest form of Hindustani classical music. The Mughal court became the most impressive patron of the translation of many Sanskrit religious texts into Persian. Among these the Mahabharata (translated as the Razmnamah) and the Bhagavad Gita hold pride of place. Brahmana priests worked together with Persian scholars on these translations encouraged by Hindu and Muslim noblemen at the courts.[5]

As these examples attest, Indians of all religious communities had long lived intertwined lives, and even religious practices were rarely exclusionary: Muslim musicians played and sang Hindu devotional songs, Hindus thronged Sufi shrines and worshipped Muslim saints there, and Muslim artisans in Benares made the traditional masks for the Hindu Ram-Leela performances. Northern India celebrated what was called a 'Ganga-Jamuni *tehzeeb*', a syncretic culture that melded the cultural practices of both faiths.

The facts are clear: large-scale conflicts between Hindus and Muslims (religiously defined), only began under colonial rule; many other kinds of social strife were labelled as religious due to the colonists' Orientalist assumption that religion was the fundamental division in Indian society. Yet today too many believe in the divisive notion of Hindu or Muslim identity—even though this didn't exist in India before the nineteenth century. As Ambedkar had stated: 'If nationalism means the worship of the ancient past—the discarding of everything that is not local in origin and colour—then [we] cannot accept nationalism as [our] creed. [We] cannot allow the living faith of the dead to become the dead faith of the living.'[6]

The idea of Hindu nationalism conflates ideas of religion and culture with those of nation and state. Nationhood is by definition indivisible, whereas religion and culture take on multiple manifestations; an Indian national can be a Christian from Kerala or a Buddhist from Arunachal Pradesh, with distinct religious and cultural practices from those of a Hindu from Madhya Pradesh or a Sikh from Punjab. All these cultures of course contribute to national identity; yet no singular understanding of culture can define the nationalism of a plural land like India. In India during colonial rule, the reassertion of "Indian culture" was a nationalist project, which witnessed the revival of dance forms like Bharata Natyam and traditional classical music, as well as modern literature in Indian languages and what disappointingly evolved into the gaudy cinema of Bollywood.

But an India confident in its own cultural diversity could celebrate multiple expressions of its culture. Hindutva sees culture differently; as Golwalkar wrote, culture "is but a product of our all-comprehensive religion, a part of its body and not distinguishable from it". For the advocates of Hindutva, India's national culture is Hindu religious culture, and cultural nationalism cloaks plural India in a mantle of Hindu identity. Since Hindutva's conception of nationalism is rooted in the primacy of culture over politics, as the historian K. N. Panikkar has commented, the Hindutva effort is to create an idea of the Indian nation in which the Hindu religious identity coincides with the cultural. Worse still, as Amartya Sen points out, "Hindutva's nationalism ignores the rationalist traditions of India, a country in which some of the earliest steps in algebra, geometry, and astronomy were taken, where the decimal system emerged, where early philosophy—secular as well as religious—achieved exceptional sophistication, where people invented games like chess, pioneered sex education, and began the first systematic study of political economy. The Hindu militant chooses instead to present India—explicitly or implicitly—as a country of unquestioning idolaters, delirious fanatics, belligerent devotees, and religious murderers."[7] In this process, Indian history, following the Muslim conquests of north India, has become "ground zero" in the battle of narratives between the Hindutva lobby and the pluralists.

When, with the publication of my book *Inglorious Empire: What the British did to India*, I spoke critically of 200 years of foreign rule, the Hindutva brigade, led by Prime Minister Modi himself, consistently condemned 1200 years of foreign rule.[8] To them, the Muslim rulers of India, whether the Delhi Sultans, the Deccani Sultans or the Mughals (or the hundreds of other Muslims who occupied thrones of greater or lesser importance for several hundred years across the country) were all foreigners. I responded that while the founder of a Muslim dynasty may well have come to India from abroad, he and his descendants stayed and assimilated in this country, married Hindu women, and immersed themselves in the fortunes of this land; each Mughal Emperor after Babur had less and less connection of blood or allegiance to a foreign country. If they looted or exploited India and Indians, they spent the proceeds of their loot in India, and did not send it off to enrich a foreign land as the British did. The Mughals received travellers from the Ferghana Valley politely, enquired about the well-being of the people there and perhaps even gave some money for the upkeep of the graves of their Chingizid ancestors, but they stopped seeing their original homeland as home. By the second generation, let alone the fifth or sixth, they were as "Indian" as any Hindu.

This challenge of authenticity, however, cuts across a wide intellectual terrain. It emerges from those Hindus who share VS Naipaul's view of theirs as a "wounded civilisation", a pristine Hindu land that was subjected to repeated defeats and conquests over the centuries at the hands of rapacious Muslim invaders and was enfeebled and subjugated in the process. To such people, Independence is not merely freedom from British rule but an opportunity to restore the glory of their culture and religion, wounded by Muslim conquerors. Historians like Audrey Truschke, author of *A Sympathetic Biography of Aurangzeb*, have argued that this account of Muslims despoiling the Hindu homeland is neither a continuous historical memory nor based on accurate records of the past. But there is no gainsaying the emotional content of the Hindutva view of the past: it is for them a matter of faith that India is a Hindu nation, which Muslim rulers attacked, looted and sought to destroy, and documented historical facts that refute this view are at best an inconvenience, at worst an irrelevance.

In the Hindutva-centred view, history is made of religion-based binaries, in which all Muslim rulers are evil and all Hindus are valiant resisters, embodiments of incipient Hindu nationalism. The Hindutvavadis believe, in Truschke's words, "that India was subjected to repeated defeats over the centuries, including by generations of Muslim conquerors that enfeebled the people and their land. The belief... that Muslim invaders destroyed their culture, religion, and homeland is neither a continuous historical memory nor is it based on accurate records of the past. But... many in India feel injured by the Indo-Muslim past, and their sentiments [are] often undergirded by modern anti-Muslim sentiments." As K. N. Panikkar has stated, liberal and tolerant rulers such as Ashoka, Akbar, Jai Singh, Shahu Maharaj, and Wajid Ali Shah do not figure in Hindutva's list of national heroes. (Indeed, where many nationalist historians extolled Akbar as the liberal, tolerant counterpart to the Islamist Aurangzeb, Hindutvavadis have begun to attack him too, principally because he was Muslim, and like most mediaeval monarchs of both faiths, killed princes who stood in his way, many of whom happened to be Hindu.)

Communal history continues past the era of Islamic rule. Among those Indians who revolted against the British, Bahadur Shah, Zinat Mahal, Maulavi Ahmadullah, and General Bakht Khan, all Muslims, are conspicuous by their absence from Hindutva histories. And, syncretic traditions such as the Bhakti movement, and universalist religious reformers like Rammohan Roy and Keshab Chandra Sen, do not receive much attention either. What does is the uncritical veneration of "Hindu heroes" like Maharana Pratap (portrayed now in Rajasthani textbooks as the victor of the Battle of Haldi Ghati against Akbar, which begs the question why Akbar and not he ruled the country for the following three decades) and Chhatrapati Shivaji, the intrepid and courageous Maratha warrior, whose battles against the Mughals have now replaced accounts of Mughal kings in Maharashtra's textbooks. (The educational system is the chosen battlefield for the Hindutva warriors, and curriculum revision their preferred weapon.)

A further challenge for the inclusiveness of Indian nationhood is that (with the limited exception of a handful of 'Central Schools' administered through the Union Government's Department of Education'), school systems are run by the respective state governments, which set their own local syllabus and publish state-level textbooks. These tend to extol local or regional heroes—Maharana Pratap in Rajasthan, Shivaji in Maharashtra, Velu Thampi Dalawa or Pazhassi Raja in Kerala—but do little to encourage a pan-national consciousness of Indian history. Very few school students in north India learn about, or have any awareness of, the glories of the Vijaynagara Empire in the south, or the Pallavas and the Cholas before them.

The debates over history are not confined to the distant past alone. Whereas conservatives, in the famous phrase, are "standing athwart history, yelling Stop", the Hindutva nationalists are in fact yelling "turn back! Reverse!" Their reinvention of history is not anchored in a reverence for the past, but in their desire to shape the present by reinventing the past. In 2017, Prime Minister Narendra Modi chose the anniversary of the Quit India movement in 1942 to launch a campaign called *"70 Saal Azadi: Zara Yaad Karo Qurbani"*. ("Seventy years of freedom: remember the sacrifices".) The BJP which, led by PM Modi, has sought to drape itself in the mantle of nationalism, is now seeking to appropriate the freedom struggle for its cause. Ironically, the Quit India movement was an occasion the BJP could well have chosen to criticize rather than celebrate, since it resulted in the jailing by the British of all the leaders and thousands of workers of the nationalist movement, a resultant free hand to the Muslim League to build up a support base it had lacked in the elections of 1937, and thus, strengthened the hands of those who wanted Partition.

But the Modi government has no intention of repudiating Quit India as a Congress folly. It wants to make heroes of freedom fighters, by implication placing them on its own side in a contemporary retelling of history. The complication is that the political cause to which the BJP is heir—embodied in the Jana Sangh, the RSS, and the Hindutva movement—had no prominent freedom fighter of its own during the nationalist struggle for azadi. The BJP traces its origin to leaders who were not particularly active during the nationalist movement. The lack of inspiration for the people in the parent body of the BJP means people like Modi have to look for role models elsewhere.

The process had already begun, lest we forget, in the state of Gujarat, when then Chief Minister Modi moved aggressively to lay claim to the legacy of one of India's most respected Founding Fathers, his fellow-Gujarati Sardar Vallabhbhai Patel, before the 2014 election. In his quest to garb himself in a more distinguished lineage than his party can ordinarily lay claim to, Modi announced plans to construct a giant 550-foot statue of the Iron Man in his state, the largest statue in the world, dwarfing the Statue of Liberty. It is less a monument to the modest Gandhian it ostensibly honours than an embodiment of the overweening ambitions of its builder.

Modi's motives are easy to divine. His own image had been tarnished by the communal massacre in Gujarat when he was chief minister in 2002. Identifying himself with Patel (who is portrayed as the leader who stood up for the nation's Hindus during the horrors of Partition and was firm on issues like Kashmir) is an attempt at character-building by association—portraying Modi himself as an embodiment of the tough, decisive man of action that Patel was, rather than the destructive bigot his enemies decry.

But Patel's conduct during the violence that accompanied Partition stands in stark contrast to Modi's in 2002. Both Patel and Modi were faced with the serious breakdown of law and order in their respective domains, involving violence and rioting against the Muslims. In Delhi, in 1947, Patel immediately and effectively moved to ensure the protection of Muslims, herding 10,000 in the most vulnerable areas to the security of Delhi's Red Fort. Because Patel was afraid that the local security forces might have been affected by the virus of communal passions, he moved Army troops from Madras and Pune to Delhi to ensure law and order. Patel also made it a point to send a reassuring signal to the Muslim community by attending prayers at the famous Nizamuddin Dargah to convey a clear message that Muslims and their faith belonged unquestionably on the soil of India. Patel also went to the border town of Amritsar, where there were attacks on Muslims fleeing to the new Islamic state of Pakistan, and pleaded with Hindu and Sikh mobs to stop victimizing Muslim refugees. In each of these cases, Patel succeeded—and there are literally tens of thousands of people who are alive today because of his interventions.

The contrast with what happened in Gujarat in 2002 is painful. Nor can one imagine Patel saying to an interviewer, as Modi did, that he felt sorry about the killings of Muslims as he would about a puppy run over by a car in which he was a passenger.[9] There is a particular irony to a self-proclaimed "Hindu nationalist" like Modi, whose speeches have often dripped with contempt for Muslims, laying claim to the legacy of a Gandhian leader who would never have qualified his Indian nationalism with a religious label.

Sardar Patel believed in equal rights for all irrespective of their religion or caste. It is true that at the time of partition Patel was inclined to believe, unlike Nehru, that an entire community had seceded. In my biography *Nehru: The Invention of India* (2003) I have given some examples of Nehru and Patel clashing on this issue. But there are an equal number of examples where Patel, if he had to choose between what was the right thing for the Hindus and what was the right thing morally, invariably plumped for the moral Gandhian approach.

An example, so often distorted by the Sangh Parivar apologists, was his opposition to Nehru's pact with Liaquat Ali Khan, the Prime Minister of Pakistan, on the question of violence in East Pakistan against the Hindu minority. The Nehru-Liaquat pact was indeed criticized by Patel and he disagreed quite ferociously with Nehru on the matter. But when Nehru insisted on his position, it was Patel who gave in, and his reasoning was entirely Gandhian: that violence in West Bengal against Muslims essentially took away Indians' moral right to condemn violence against Hindus in East Pakistan.[10] That was not a Hindu nationalist position but a classically Gandhian approach as an *Indian* nationalist.

History has often been contested terrain in India, but its revival in the context of 21st century politics is a sobering sign that the past continues to have a hold over the Hindutva movement in the present. While the Mughals will be demonized as a way of delegitimizing Indian Muslims (who are stigmatized as "Babur ke aulad", the sons of the foreign invader Babur rather than of the Indian soil), the arguments over Patel confirm that he and other heroes of the freedom struggle will be hijacked to the present ruling party's attempts to appropriate a halo of nationalism that none of its forebears has done anything to earn.

The other favourite bugbear of the Hindu nationalists is the Indian liberal, a member of the tribe that used to think of itself as authentically nationalist in terms of its association with, or descent from, the freedom struggle led by the Indian National Congress. We are now accustomed, alas, in our irremediably tedious political controversies, to seeing history used as cannon fodder by the

BJP; given that they are determined to drag us back into the 16th century, I suppose we should be grateful that currently they are restricting themselves to the 20th. Even as they have driven the economy into the doldrums, long before Covid-19 made its appearance (and provided them with an excuse and a smokescreen to cover up their failures on the economic front), the present ruling dispensation has become, in their own phrase, a tukde-tukde gang (a force that seeks to cut India into pieces). They are dividing this country into tukdes: Hindus versus Muslims; Deshdrohis versus Deshbhakts; Raamzaade versus something unprintable; Hindi speakers versus non-Hindi speakers; Us versus Them.

It is bad enough that our Home Minister forgets our history. It would be far worse if he leads the country down a path that repeats it.

20

BHARAT MATA KI JAI

Soon after the BJP came to power in 2014, "Bharat Mata ki Jai"—"Victory to Mother India", an overtly Hindu slogan that postulates the deification of the nation as a mother-goddess—became the latest acid test of Indian nationalism.

Bharat Mata, Mother India, is literally portrayed in iconography in ways identical to that associated with Hindu goddesses: she is usually depicted as a woman clad in a saffron sari holding the Indian national flag, against a back-drop of the map of India, sometimes astride (or accompanied by) a lion, the vahana (divine vehicle) of the goddess Durga. (However, the first known visual portrayal of Bharat Mata, in an Abanindrinath Tagore painting in 1905, has no flag and no map of India. She was depicted in the soft "wash" style of the Bengal School, her benevolent image radiant and glowing, promising bliss and prosperity.)

While the ruling British had long personified their nation through the fig-ure of a mythical "Britannia", there had been no Indian equivalent before the Raj. The term itself seems to have been first used in a Bengali play entitled *Bharat Mata*, written by Kiran Chandra Banerjee and first performed in 1873. There was no earlier scriptural sanction for the idea of Bharat Mata, and the name does not feature in any ancient Hindu text. The concept of Bharat Mata as the personification of India came into existence in the late 19th century along with the rise in nationalist consciousness, and is often credited to the Bengali author Bankim Chandra Chatterjee, whose inspiring book *Ananda Math* gave rise to a passionate patriotism upon its publication in 1882 and was then banned by the British. The scholar B. R. Purohit explains the significance of the Bharat Mata idea in Bankim's novel: "Durga, the goddess and the mother, became one with the country, the greater goddess and the mother. In his well-known novel, *Anandamath*, he presented the country as Goddess

Kali, black because of intense misery, naked because denuded of wealth, with human skulls round her neck because the country was no less than a vast burial ground. But the future India would be like radiant Durga who will annihilate the "demons" and usher in an era of plenty and prosperity.'[1] Bankim's novel included the song "*Vande Mataram*" ("Hail to the Mother!") whose first stanzas are still sung as the "national song" of India, though later verses, with strong Hindu imagery, and anti-Muslim allusions, have been largely ignored.

The Bengali origins of the idea of Bharat Mata are hardly surprising: the very notion of equating a nation with a mother goddess sits comfortably with a region where the worship of Shakti, the divine feminine principle, is common, and various forms of the mother goddess—Chandi, Durga, Kali, and Manasa—are widely revered and popularly worshipped. A little over two decades after the publication of Bankim's book, the Swadeshi movement in Bengal and the agitation to annul the 1905 partition of Bengal occurred, providing the perfect opportunity for both Bharat Mata to be invoked and "*Vande Mataram*" to be sung by nationalists. There was no looking back after that.

Advocates of Hindutva like Savarkar, and sages like Sri Aurobindo, enthusiastically embraced the concept of Bharat Mata, much to the dismay of the broad-minded Tagore, and the scholarly Ambedkar. Savarkar propounded the need for Indian nationalists to offer "whole-hearted love to our common Mother"[2] and recognize her not only as "*Pitarbhu*" but even as a *Punyabhu*," i.e. as motherland and holy land. In a famous episode in 1905, Sri Aurobindo, responding to a question by the nationalist and Hindu revivalist K.M. Munshi about patriotism, pointed to a map of British India and said: "Do you see this map? It is not a map but the portrait of Bharat Mata: its cities and mountains, rivers and jungles form her physical body. All her children are her nerves, large and small...Concentrate on Bharat as a living mother, worship her with nine-fold bhakti."[3]

As the members of the Hindutva movement propagated their concept, "Bharat Mata" became, to their cause, nothing less than the patriotic representation of the land in a divine female form. The depiction of India as a Hindu mother-goddess made it, in their eyes, the religious duty of all Hindus to worship—and protect—the nation. (As Sri Aurobindo had declared in a fiery speech in Bombay in 1907: "What is Nationalism? Nationalism is not a mere political programme; Nationalism is a religion that has come from God; Nationalism is a creed in which you shall have to live. Let no man dare to call himself a Nationalist if he does so merely with a sort of intellectual pride, thinking that he is more patriotic, thinking that he is something higher than those who do not call themselves by that name. If you are going to be a Nationalist, if you are going to assent to this religion of Nationalists, you must do it in the religious spirit. You must remember that you are the instrument of God for the salvation of your own country.")[4] The Rashtriya Swayamsevak Sangh followed suit. In RSS Supremo M. S. Golwalkar's dedication to his polemical *We or Our Nationhood Defined (1939)*, he wrote: 'I offer this work to the public as an [sic] humble offering at the holy feet of the Divine Mother—the Hindu Nation—in the hope that She will graciously accept this worship from an undeserving child of Her Own.'[5] The 'Hindu Nation' is approximated to the 'common Mother' and both are objects of worship. To this day, the RSS conducts its events amid banners emblazoned with images of Bharat Mata holding a saffron flag, and not the Indian tricolour.

Bharat Mata was even installed as a goddess in a Hindu temple in Banaras in 1936, portrayed against a large relief map of British India; another Bharat Mata temple was inaugurated by Prime Minister Indira Gandhi in 1983. But Mahatma Gandhi never used the idea of Bharat Mata in his nationalist messaging, and Rabindranath Tagore openly sought to restrain the Bharat Mata cult. In 1937, he wrote to Congress president Subhash Chandra Bose, a fellow Bengali, protesting against a proposal to declare *Vande Mataram* India's national anthem: "The core of *[V]ande Mataram* is a hymn to goddess Durga: this is so plain that there can be no debate about it...no Mussulman can be expected patriotically to worship the ten-handed deity as "Swadesh"....The novel *Ananda Math* is a work of literature, and so the song is appropriate in it. But, Parliament is a place of union for all religious groups, and there the song cannot be appropriate."[6] This was why Congress took the inoffensive first two stanzas as the "national song" and consciously expunged the rest from its official repertoire.

Pandit Nehru, who abhorred Hindu nationalism, interpreted the idea of Bharat Mata very differently. As he wrote in his monumental *The Discovery of India*:

> Sometimes as I reached a gathering, a great roar of welcome would greet me: *Bharat Mata ki Jai*—Victory to Mother India. I would ask them unexpectedly what they meant by that cry, who was this *Bharat Mata*, Mother India, whose victory they wanted? My question would amuse them and surprise them, and then, not knowing exactly what to answer, they would look at each other and at me. I persisted in my questioning. At last a vigorous Jat, wedded to the soil from immemorial generations, would say that it was the *dharti*, the good earth of India, that they meant. What earth? Their particular village patch, or all the patches in the district or province, or in the whole of India? And so question

and answer went on, till they would ask me impatiently to tell them all about it. I would endeavour to do so and explain that India was all this that they had thought, but it was much more. The mountains and the rivers of India, and the forests and the broad fields, which gave us food, were all dear to us, but what counted ultimately were the people of India, people like them and me, who were spread out all over this vast land. Bharat Mata, Mother India, was essentially these millions of people, and victory to her meant victory to these people. You are parts of this Bharat Mata, I told them, you are in a manner yourselves Bharat Mata, and as this idea slowly soaked into their brains, their eyes would light up as if they had made a great discovery.[7]

For 21st century liberal and patriotic Indians, therefore, the slogan "Bharat Mata ki Jai" has respectable antecedents: it was a rallying cry during the freedom struggle, and even after Independence it is one of the official battle-cries of the Indian army. Given the absence of a scriptural or religious origin for the phrase, liberal Hindus preferred to think of Bharat Mata as a purely nationalist invocation of reverence for the land, rather than a deity. But the Hindu nationalists had other ideas.

Things took a turn in 2016, when the RSS and the BJP, in parallel campaigns, launched a co-ordinated broadside over Bharat Mata ki Jai. On 17 March 2016, the (RSS) joint general secretary Dattatreya Hosabale declared that 'anyone who refused to say "Bharat Mata ki Jai" is anti-national for us'. Then BJP President Amit Shah added two days later: 'Anti-national activity cannot be justified on the plea of freedom of expression.' In March 2016, the BJP's national executive passed a political resolution that declared that refusing to say "Bharat Mata ki Jai" amounted to disrespecting the Constitution. Elected representatives were required to proclaim it, the BJP President challenged audiences he was addressing to chant it with him, and even schoolchildren were instructed to write it on their admission forms. RSS chief Mohan Bhagwat declared that all young Indians must be taught to say "Bharat mata ki jai". A Muslim legislator, Waris Pathan, was suspended from the Maharashtra Assembly soon after for refusing to utter the slogan. A hitherto innocuous phrase suddenly became a litmus test to challenge the nationalist credentials of the unwilling.

Since Bharat Mata involved personifying the nation as a goddess, as Tagore affirmed, the concept was troubling to many orthodox Muslims, Sikhs, and Christians who found the idea offensive to, or at least incompatible with, their own monotheisms. In promoting this idea of Indian nationhood, which privileged one religion, the BJP had yet again launched an assault on the basic ethos of Indian democracy, which recognizes the nation's diversity. As the eminent commentator A. G. Noorani put it: "When the upstarts of the BJP tell us that it is 'anti-national' not to proclaim it, it is because they do not bear loyalty to Indian nationalism, but to Hindu nationalism or Hindutva."[8]

There is a certain irony to the BJP promoting the imagery of the nation as a woman and implicitly glorifying the requirement to protect her, given the overtly patriarchal tilt of Hindu society in the areas in which the RSS holds sway. The proponents of Bharat Mata are overwhelmingly men, who are only too happy to side-line women both in their movement and in society at large. The Hindutva idea of nation and its ideal of nationalism are infused with an overt and dominant element of masculinity. The RSS' founder-President, Hegdewar, resisted frontline participation for women in his movement, and indeed required his pracharaks to undertake vows of celibacy as a prerequisite to work for the organization. He gave in, however, to the idea of a parallel RSS for women, proposed by Lakshmi Bai Kelkar, the mother of one of his volunteers, who persuaded him to authorize the establishment of the Rashtriya Sevika Samiti in 1936. Hegdewar, however, preferred to see this "women's RSS" as a wholly separate organization, working independently along the lines of the Sangh doctrine. A separate women's group, the Durga Vahini, was established in 1991 at the peak of the Ramjanmabhoomi movement (that belligerently sought to destroy the Babri Masjid, a mosque in Ayodhya, and build on the spot where it stood a temple to Lord Ram, whose birthplace the proponents of the movement claimed it was) as a women's affiliate of the Sangh Parivar. It is more closely identified with the aggressive activism of the VHP than the parent RSS, aggressively recruits young women from low-income families, and does not shrink from militant activism, especially against Muslims. The Hindutva movement has never shown much regard for the portrayal in some ancient sources of the autonomous woman as a *swadheena vallabha*, free and subservient to none. Instead its leaders, up to and including its current head, Mohan Bhagwat, have repeatedly articulated the idea that a woman's place is in the home, looking after her husband and nurturing her children. The front bench of the RSS is conspicuously devoid of women leaders, though the Modi BJP government has given prominence to three women ministers (one of whom was dropped before she passed away). Despite these exceptions, the Hindutva movement prefers to worship women as goddesses than to work under them.

To sum up what I have been describing in this chapter, the worship of Bharat Mata as a Hindu goddess undermines the appeal of the slogan to liberal Indian nationalists, and especially those of non-Hindu faiths. The notion of a motherland normally embraces all the people who belong to it, irrespective of faith or creed, but Bharat Mata appears to privilege only a fraternity of Hindus—the ones who worship her—transforming a symbol of the struggle for freedom into the icon of one religious belief. What should have been a rallying cry for national unity instead becomes reduced to a communally divisive instrument of religious polarization.

Hindus like me—or for that matter "cultural Hindus" like Nehru—have no intrinsic objection to Bharat Mata; nor do some Indians of other faiths, seeing the phrase in Nehruvian terms as embodying the land rather than a specific religious deity. But some, particularly devout Muslims, find it uncomfortable to use the phrase because of its religious associations, which marginalize them. They say, "tell us to say *Jai Hind, Hindustan Zindabad, Jai Bharat*, we'll do it—but do not ask us to say *Bharat Mata ki Jai*." That was precisely the point made by the suspended Maharashtra MLA Waris Pathan: "I am willing to say *Jai Hind*. I love my country," he said. "My objection was to their forcing me to say *Bharat Mata Ki Jai*."

To me, this is an unexceptionable stand: the same Constitution that, in our civic nationalism, gives us the right to freedom of speech, also gives us the freedom of silence. We cannot put words in people's mouths. Our democracy and our Constitution respects every Indian's freedom of religion and give every Indian citizen the right to say or not to say something. A Supreme Court ruling in the 1986 Jehovah's Witnesses case (*Bijoe Emmanuel vs State of Kerala*) has even held that a refusal to sing the national anthem is permissible, provided due respect is shown—people may stand while it is sung but refuse to participate if they have objections on religious grounds. If that is true of the sacrosanct national anthem, surely it should apply to a lesser utterance? Indian nationalist history is replete with memorable chants: Jai Hind, of course, but also Sare Jahan se Achha, or even the leftists' favourite Inquilab Zindabad—all these have had tremendous potency during the national movement and continue to resonate with millions even today. People have to accept that history has thrown up a lot of such expressions and "Bharat Mata ki Jai" enjoys no particular precedence—except in the eyes of the Hindutva movement. No Indian should be compelled to mouth a phrase that is nationalistic in the eyes of some, but not in his own. Badri Raina recounts this story:

A political pracharak [Hindutva propagandist] working with people in a slum area was encouraging little slum children to say "*Bharat Mata ki Jai*" (Obeisance to Mother India). At which a little girl with dishevelled and matted hair asked "where is she? Where can we meet her"? The pracharak, rather askance, said "she is everywhere." The little rag picker then wondered why she never comes to meet them, and why, if she is such a caring mother, are they always hungry and destitute.[9]

The Hindutva insistence on thrusting its version of nationalism on all Indians through the imposition of such outward signs of conformity came to the forefront once again over the national anthem. On 30 November 2016, the Supreme Court, egged on by the BJP government, ordered all cinemas to play the anthem before films were screened "for the love of the motherland". The result was a plethora of incidents in which vigilante cine-goers assaulted those in the audience who did not rise for the anthem, including in several cases physically handicapped patrons in wheelchairs. As resentment mounted, it was clear that the order had become counter-productive. On 7 January 2018, a bench led by Chief Justice Dipak Misra quietly modified its own order, making it optional for cinema halls to play the national anthem before every show, and leaving the decision of whether to play the anthem or not to the discretion of individual cinema hall owners, most of whom promptly shelved the scheme.

Between the "civic" nationalist notion of Indian diversity (which Salman Rushdie celebrated as "mongrelization")[10] and the Hindutva supporters' insistence on 'authentic' Indian culture—narrowly interpreted, and uncontaminated by colonial influence or Ganga-Jamuni hybridity—there lies a chasm. Our nationalist heroes created a nation built on an ideal of pluralism and freedom: we have given passports to their dreams. The BJP, with its insistence on the chanting of "Bharat Mata ki Jai", would sadly reduce the soaring generosity of their founding vision to the petty bigotry of majoritarian chauvinism.

PART FOUR

THE ONGOING STRUGGLE FOR INDIA'S SOUL

I have sought to demonstrate, thus far, that India evolved from a classic form of anti-colonial nationalism to a conscious civic nationalism enshrined in its Constitution, and that an alternative approach has been advocated by the proponents of Hindutva, who wish to convert India into an ethno-religious nation-state. In this part, I will examine some of the significant developments in contemporary Indian politics, particularly since the election of the Narendra Modi-led BJP government at the Centre in 2014, that have tended to undermine civic nationalism and promote, if not entrench, its alternative.

21

A PARTITION IN THE INDIAN SOUL

If the ethno-nationalism of the Hindutva movement has posed a fundamental challenge to the "received wisdom" on Indian nationalism for many decades after Independence, it has now reached deeply worrying levels. In the past few years there has been a rash of threats to law and order and the civic nationalism that our founding fathers bequeathed to us—mob rule, vigilantism and lynchings. All these examples of lawlessness undermine both the sanctity of the law as the ultimate arbiter of justice and also faith in the law as the cement that binds the nation together. It is vital that all of us who believe in civic nationalism demand in all the fora available to us that that the primacy of law is reasserted by bringing these self-appointed upholders of justice to justice, to teach them the importance of subordinating their self-righteousness to the majesty of the law.

But, as we have seen, not all agree with the civic nationalist vision of Indian nationhood. Secularism is established in India's Constitution, but these people ask why India should not, like many other countries in the developing world, find refuge in the assertion of what they call its own religious identity. We have already seen the outcome of this view in the horrors that cost perhaps 2000 lives in Gujarat in 2002, and in many of the sectarian riots and lynchings that have occurred since then.

Those riots, like the killing of the Sikhs in reaction to Indira Gandhi's assassination in 1984, were fundamentally violative of the basic ethos of India. India has survived the Aryans, the Mughals, the British; it has taken from each—language, art, food, learning—and grown with all of them. To be Indian is to be a part of an elusive dream we all share, a dream that fills our minds with sounds, words, flavours from many sources that we cannot easily identify.

Chauvinism and anti-minority violence have emerged from the competition for resources in a contentious democracy. Politicians of all faiths across

India seek to mobilize voters by appealing to narrow identities; by seeking votes in the name of religion, caste and region, they have urged voters to define themselves on these lines. As religion, caste, and region have come to dominate public discourse, to some it has become more important to be a Muslim, a Bodo or a Yadav than to be an Indian.

Many of us complacently assumed that the core principles of Indian nationhood were immutable and universally held. But we were wrong; even before Mohammed Ali Jinnah's Muslim League passed its notorious Pakistan Resolution in 1940, demanding the vivisection of the country, the Hindu Mahasabha had in 1937 advanced the theory that Hindus and Muslims were two nations. Savarkar, in his presidential address to the Hindu Mahasabha during its 1937 Ahmedabad session, stated his view clearly: "India cannot be assumed today to be a unitarian and homogeneous nation, but on the contrary, there are two nations in the main; the Hindus and the Moslems, in India."[1] Today's ruling BJP is, after all, the political arm of the RSS, which remains committed to the doctrine of Hindutva and advocates the establishment in India of a Hindu state.

Ambedkar had addressed the subject of majoritarianism in a famous speech on 4 November 1948:

> To diehards who have developed a kind of fanaticism against minority protection, I would like to say two things. One is that minorities are an explosive force which, if it erupts, can blow up the whole fabric of the State. The history of Europe bears ample and appalling testimony to this fact. The other is that the minorities in India have agreed to place their existence in the hands of the majority... They have loyally accepted the rule of the majority, which is basically a communal majority and not a political majority. It is for the majority to realise its duty not to discriminate against minorities.[2]

Today, India is in the grip of the very majoritarianism that Ambedkar had so presciently warned against. Prime Minister Modi's great hero, Sardar Patel, had urged in the Constituent Assembly on 25 May 1949: "It is for us who happen to be in a majority to think about what the minorities feel, and how we in their position would feel if we are treated in the manner they are treated."[3] Given the Government's oft-expressed admiration for the likes of Dr Ambedkar and Sardar Patel, one can only hope that they will abandon their current approach, which reduces individuals to their religious affiliations and denies them their agency as free citizens of our democratic republic. The suggestion that only a Hindu, and only a certain kind of Hindu, can be an authentic Indian is an affront to the very premise of Indian nationalism.

As the past is used by some to haunt the present, the cycle of violence goes on, spawning new hostages to history, ensuring that future generations will be taught new wrongs to set right. We live, Octavio Paz once wrote, between oblivion and memory. Memory and oblivion: how one leads to the other, and back again, has been the concern of much of my fiction. The Kashmiri Indian poet Agha Shahid Ali wrote perceptively: "My memory keeps getting in the way of your history." As I asserted in the last words of my novel *Riot*, history is not a web woven with innocent hands.

The reduction of any group of Indians to second-class status in their homeland is unthinkable. It would be a second partition: and a partition in the Indian soul would be as bad as a partition in the Indian soil. The battle over that second partition that threatens has grown in strength during the years the Modi regime has been in power, and seems likely to gather greater momentum in the remaining years of its term. The remaining chapters in this part parse some of the key recent engagements in the ongoing battle over Indian nationalism.

22

WHERE WE ARE, AND HOW WE GOT HERE

The intense debates that have erupted over the last half-dozen years over Indian nationhood demonstrate that it is again time to reflect on what kind of nationalism we in India are seeking to uphold. The India I have described in Part Two, and the challenge to it from proponents of a Hindu rashtra, are not merely abstract intellectual concepts for academic debates about nationalism. They have underpinned major developments in India's current politics, with critical implications for the everyday lives of millions of Indians.

India, I have long argued, is more than the sum of its contradictions. It is a country held together, in the words of Nehru, "by strong but invisible threads...a myth and an idea, a dream and a vision, and yet very real and present and pervasive". That nebulous quality is what the analyst of Indian nationalism is ultimately left with; it is, as I have said throughout this book, an idea—*the Idea of India*—that Jawaharlal Nehru articulated as pluralism vindicated by history, seeing the country as an "ancient palimpsest"[1] on which successive rulers and subjects had inscribed their visions, without erasing what had been asserted previously. A generation of secular nationalists echoed him, making "unity in diversity" the most hallowed of independent India's self-defining slogans. This conviction is being questioned today, as we have seen, by a new ruling party that has sought to redefine nationalism in more sectarian terms.

The slow but irresistible rise of Hindutva from the 1980s culminated in the victory of a hard-line "Hindu nationalist"—a phrase proudly emblazoned on campaign billboards by Narendra Modi—with a very different view of Indian nationhood from his prime ministerial predecessors. Schooled in the Hindutva doctrines of the RSS—of which he has been a member for most of his life, starting as a *bal swayamsewak* at the age of eight—Mr Modi rejected much of the cosmopolitan secularist assumptions embodied in the core conception of

India adopted by the freedom movement and reflected in the constitutional underpinnings of the Indian republic. He approached India's past and its present differently from those who had adorned the Prime Ministerial office before him. He made no secret of his devotion to the views of Hindutva icons like V. D. Savarkar, M.S. Golwalkar, and Deen Dayal Upadhyaya. His view of Indian history as encompassing twelve hundred years of foreign rule (adding Muslim rulers to the imperial British in his reckoning) differed radically from the historical accounts of India's first Prime Minister, Jawaharlal Nehru. His barely-concealed Islamophobia and condemnation of "minority appeasement" was at odds with the liberal pluralism enshrined in the Constitution, and many decades of Indian political practice. His determination to remake India's institutions in his own image appears to prefigure a desire to fulfil that long-standing desire of the RSS to see India converted into a Hindu ethnonationalist state.

The redefinition of the concepts of Indian nationalism by Narendra Modi and the BJP were given a fresh impetus by his stunning re-election victory (with an enhanced majority) in 2019, made possible by the building up of the most extraordinary personality cult in modern Indian political history, buttressed by larger-than-life imagery, hundreds of thousands of social media warriors, an intimidated "mainstream" media, ubiquitous cameramen, and a slick campaign publicity machinery that was switched on 24/7, all lubricated by 5600 crore rupees [three quarters of a billion dollars][2] of taxpayer funds relentlessly promoting his every move. This was indeed a "Prime Minister with a difference," but not in quite the way the slogan implied—for this was the first Prime Minister who cast a shadow far greater his substance.

This was, as has been affirmed earlier, reflective of a global trend in favour of strongmen leaders, cresting a wave of strident, ethno-religious nationalist politics in many countries in the second decade of the 21st century. But, despite the evident global phenomenon, each country's specific circumstances were dictated by its own distinctive domestic factors. In India's epochal election, Modi was projected by the BJP as a muscular nationalist—the only man who could keep the country safe from terrorists, infiltrators, "anti-nationals," and "termites" seeking to hollow out the sturdy structure of the majoritarian Hindu nation that he was building. It worked.

It was extraordinary, though, that the BJP was able to persuade people to vote their prejudices rather than their economic self-interest. After all, why would a young man who voted for Mr Modi in 2014 expecting to get the job that he needed, vote for him again in 2019 when he still did not have that job? Apparently because he was consumed by fear of and hatred for an Other—

often defined as a Muslim, and additionally as a malign Pakistani general, or a fanatic terrorist despatched by Pakistan—assiduously stoked by the "nationalists" in the ruling establishment. As a result, he saw in Mr Modi his protector, the enabler of his hatred and his shield against its consequences. The cult of the strongman is alive and well and ruling in New Delhi.

The worry for many Indian liberals is that the long-cherished idea of our country as a benign, inclusive state is collapsing. In its place is emerging an India that is less pluralistic, less accepting of difference, less inclusive, and less tolerant than the one we had long celebrated. National ideals have been redefined and repurposed: unity has given way to uniformity; patriotism has been reborn as chauvinism; independent institutions are yielding to a dominant government; democracy is being reshaped into one-man rule.

How did this come to pass? It is a question I began to hear with growing and insistent alarm in recent years from many concerned individuals, a fair number of them concerned friends of India from around the world. The question deserves a serious answer. Today's situation in India is the culmination of three decades of evolving trends in Indian politics, which I would break down into nine factors:

1. *Deepening democracy and its social consequences*: India's democracy, seen wrongly by many observers as a fragile transplant at the onset of independence in 1947, has become deeply entrenched, empowering previously marginalized castes and communities. The implementation of the Mandal Commission proposal in 1989 to provide "reservations", or quotas, in government jobs, universities, and the like to the "Other Backward Classes", or OBCs (such set-asides already existed for the Dalits, once outcastes, and tribals or aboriginal people of India) has led to the rise of the former underclass, who have become a significantly potent political force across the country. Three generations of political empowerment of those once relegated to "backwardness", including people of modest educational attainments, and small-town backgrounds, has ended the dominance of the privileged urban, Anglophone elite around the centre of power in New Delhi that established liberal secularism as India's ruling ethos. A different mentality now prevails in power.

As the journalist and political commentator (and long-time Congress critic) Tavleen Singh observes: "Unlike the old elite, that was generally upper class and upper caste, the new elite is entirely of lower origins and caste. It is defined by its reverence for Modi, a new set of values and a deep hatred of people they believe have done well only because of privilege. They rage

169

against people who speak English. Against those who believe secularism is worth fighting for, those who believe nobody should be told what to eat and drink, those who don't believe the Sanatan Dharma is worth fighting for, and those who believe killing people for their faith is wrong. They reserve real rage for those who believe that avenging the wrongs of history is a flawed idea. This new elite with its new values now dominates political discourse. This new elite believes that its time has finally come."[3]

This may not be the whole story: the journalist Snigdha Poonam reveals a different side of aspirational small-town Indian youth in her conversations with a range of young Indians in tier-II towns, many of whom are desperate to learn English and thrive by doing so.[4] Nor does the BJP represent the "new elite" in its entirety: the newly-risen sections of Indian society are present in every party, and have risen to dominance across the political landscape. But there is no doubting that the changing power equations in Indian society are real enough.

Nowhere is this more apparent than in Milan Vaishnav's study of the nexus among politics, money and muscle in India, showing how, in many parts of (mainly) northern India, criminals flourish by contesting elections themselves, instead of having to seek and win favours of politicians. Vaishnav explains, "By directly contesting elections, criminals could reduce the uncertainty associated with negotiating (and renegotiating) contracts."[5] Criminals join politics for their own self-preservation, to ensure protection from the law, and to gain financial benefits from the offices they might hold. In turn, political parties strapped for the resources needed to contest increasingly unaffordable election campaigns welcome candidates who can finance themselves, pay for the party's campaigns, plus (in many cases) contribute to the party coffers, and help subsidize the party elites. Voters, too, faced with weak rule of law and beset by social pressures, support well-muscled candidates for their ability to "get things done". The fact that the candidate is a criminal is no disqualification in these circumstances, since criminal politicians are more likely to protect their interests and to help them "navigate a system that gives them so little access in the first place".[6]

The anthropologists Anastasia Piliavsky and Tommaso Sbriccoli[7] take this farther, arguing that these figures are often not necessarily seen as 'criminals' but as 'toughs'—'doers' who protect society and provide public goods, stepping in when the state machinery creaks to a halt. In the quest to ensure the proper delivery of services, North Indian politics has moved away from the (Mahatma) Gandhian view of "politics as a site of moral refinement", in one analyst's view, to one that seeks "efficacy, purpose, and performance" to deliver practical results, though the same voters who do this may conduct their own private lives in terms of "what is duty, what is good, what is moral."[8] The success of such criminal "doers" involves a dramatic deepening of democracy, but it is a far cry from the learned constitutionalists who won us our freedom and made up most of our first parliament.

2. *Backlash against cultural globalization*: India, like Turkey and the US, has also witnessed growing resentment of the cosmopolitan secular elites, with their Westernized lifestyles, who jetted off to Davos, and thought of themselves as global citizens but sheltered themselves in gated communities at home. Indian social conservatism shuddered at the breakdown of social mores among the globalized elite, the urban sexual freedoms depicted in films and television. Traditionalists recoiled at women going out to work, dressed in jeans and other non-Indian clothing, returning home late at night after shifts in call-centres attuned to Western work hours, freed from the bonds and the bounds of Indian social custom. An angry "cultural backlash" followed.

3. *Revolt against the political insider class:* Politics was seen as too long the preserve of the denizens of "Lutyens' Delhi", shorthand for the elite governmental enclave in the heart of the capital where the high and the mighty lived. They were seen by their challengers as corrupt, complacent, inefficient, and resistant to change. Modi prided himself in not being captured by the "Khan Market Gang", a reference to the upscale market complex in the heart of Lutyens' Delhi where the elite shops. The first decade of the 21st century saw a growing rejection of all they stood for, including liberalism, secularism, political "insider trading", and sub-optimal ways of governance—a rejection captured, as previously mentioned, in the 2013 uprising of the Gandhian leader Anna Hazare, who held protests throughout the country calling for the country to be cleansed of its corrupted ruling class. This contributed significantly to the initial victory in 2014 of Modi's BJP.

4. *Hunger for liberalization*: The liberalization of the statist Indian economy from 1991 onwards, in response to global market realities, led to the empowerment of an impatient business community, increasingly wealthy, anxious to see more obstacles removed and rent-seekers eliminated, and willing to finance political change in the hope that this would enhance their ability to prosper. Modi and his BJP benefited from this, not least in generous funding from newly wealthy capitalists. He played into their hands by an overtly business-friendly campaign in 2014 that featured

attacks on the public sector—"the government has no business to be in business", he declared—but has not followed through with business-friendly policies. Populists, of course, do not always redistribute wealth; the Moditva approach is to promote identity politics at the expense of social or economic reform. It has become clear that the Modi government has no desire to reduce the power of the state over the economy, since this would diminish its own power. An increasing number of businessmen complain under their breaths about extortion—through campaign contributions and tax terrorism—but those who still cling to faith that Mr Modi will improve the "ease of doing business" as policy and not just as slogan, continue to enable his regime through generous financial contributions.

5. *Global rise of religious consciousness:* The worldwide phenomenon of increasing religiosity over the last quarter-century, especially Islamic, found its counterpart in Hindutva revivalism in India. Partly this was in reaction to the onset of Wahhabi/Salafi ideas, coming into India from the Gulf via shiny new mosques glowing with Saudi-financed prosperity. As Indian Muslims, too, began more consciously to identify with the global Muslim umma, it led them to redefine how to be Muslim in ways that alienated them more visibly from Hindus. In parallel to the visible changes in the way Islam was practised in India rose a greater Hindu consciousness, abetted by the popularity of television serials on the great epics, the Ramayana and the Mahabharata; concerns about "Muslim appeasement" following such steps as the Government passing a law to overturn a Supreme Court ruling that would have awarded alimony to a divorced Muslim woman, Shah Bano; and the popularity of the BJP-led Ram Janmabhoomi agitation. All this prompted an upsurge in Hindu nationalism and helped the spread of the Rashtriya Swayamsevak Sangh or RSS and the rise in popularity of the BJP.

6. *Social transformation in urbanizing India:* Beyond the developments I have explored in points 1 and 2 above, a gradual transformation of Indian society is being reflected politically in a change in the nature of support for the Hindutva movement that requires attention in greater detail. The economic reforms launched in 1991, and their continuation for the next three decades during the era of the information revolution, has promoted not just capitalism but processes of modernization and urbanization that have accelerated social and attitudinal change across India. Traditional values, the caste system, and social conformity were easier to maintain in an India with limited mobility, one governmental television channel, and restricted autonomy for women and the young. Liberalization, the creation of new and hitherto unknown jobs in the cities, the phenomenon of

women staffing all-night call centres, and earning their own salaries, and the profusion of news and entertainment options, providing glimpses of alternative ways of living, all contributed to a breakdown of the old mores and the creation of a "new" rising urban middle-class, including in smaller towns. These "dreamers" chronicled by the journalist Snigdha Poonam, mostly small-town Indian youth, are less constrained by the traditional assumptions and customs that had shackled their parents.[9]

Thanks in part to the enhanced educational and job opportunities made available to the "backward classes," after the adoption of the Mandal report in 1990, this new class was made up of people from different castes, marked only by their training, their sense of initiative, their adventurousness in breaking free of the old shackles, and their willingness to embrace change. Parochial and caste identities mattered less in a world in which people who would formerly never have mingled with each other increasingly shared the same workspaces and enjoyed similar personal and professional experiences.

While elsewhere this would have led to the creation of a free and more liberal society, in India, paradoxically, it facilitated the BJP project of consolidating a Hindu identity that transcended caste, location, and even class. The loosening grip of social orthodoxy on people, the increased frequency of marriage across caste lines, the overwhelming disapproval of untouchability (and the practical impossibility of practising it in urban areas, where you have no idea who you are rubbing shoulders with on the bus, in the street, or in an office elevator) also made it possible to think of oneself as belonging to a larger category of community than in the past—to a national community rather than to a caste, a region, or a place. This form of social modernity could have taken India in a different civic nationalist direction, but instead the rise of the Hindutva movement harnessed it to a consciousness of common Hindu identity, yearning to assert itself.

But it could not be the narrow, intolerant, decidedly pre-modern Golwalkar version of Hindutva, with its reverence for caste, its religious and social orthodoxy, and its marginalization of women. Hindu nationalism was mounted as a social movement of this kind at the very time that the country's economy was globalizing. This meant that, as Thomas Blom Hansen put it, Hindutva promised to recuperate an allegedly suppressed cultural authenticity, even as it sought to be integrated, on an equal basis, into global modernity.[10] Hindutva, too, had to change with the times: it needed to find a 21st century champion, one who could credibly be imagined as leading the nation with a trishul in one hand while clicking a computer mouse with the other.

In Narendra Modi, who (as I argued in *The Paradoxical Prime Minister*) transformed Hindutva into "moditva", the moment found the man.

The RSS/BJP have traditionally portrayed conventional social hierarchies as intrinsic to Indian culture, while condoning communal and caste-based violence against the lower castes and minorities. But in the interests of their own political viability, they have now had to expand their appeal to the OBCs and Dalits, telling them to look beyond their caste to their common Hinduness. Moditva gave many OBCs and Dalits a sense of pride and belonging to a larger cause; some of them, as the political analyst Christophe Jaffrelot has shown, gained a sense of identity by fighting for the cow.[11]

Yet, Jaffrelot has demonstrated that the rise of the BJP has also promoted the interests of upper-caste Hindus, the urban middle class, and business elites, who had been resentful of what they perceived as an unfair advantage for lower castes through reservations. These elites are back in power under the new dispensation: in the Hindi belt, India is again seeing the disproportionate dominance of upper caste MPs and MLAs, whose numbers had been sharply brought down after the Mandal reforms, which had empowered the OBCs and Dalits to elect more legislators. The inequality spawned by the new meritocracy of money has also bred a greater acceptance of hierarchy. Modi's success depended on upper-caste Hindus reacting against years of positive discrimination measures promoted by Congress governments; by promoting "Hindu unity" rather than lower-caste empowerment, and articulating a populist discourse of an "outsider" battling the entrenched forces of privilege and dynasty, he has put more upper-caste members into parliament than there has ever been since the 1980s. This, Jaffrelot adds, "is what populists are so good at across the world: to help elite groups which are losing ground to resist new, emerging social forces by delegitimizing socio-economic factors of politicisation."[12]

7. *India-Pakistan dynamics*: This rise in Hindu consciousness occurred at a time when the militarized Islamic state next door, Pakistan, stepped up its campaign of inciting, financing and leading terrorism in India, at first through militancy in Kashmir and subsequently through overt military hostility such as the attempt to seize the heights of Kargil, from which Pakistani troops were repulsed after a short but bloody war in 1999. Growing hostility to Pakistan, and the repeated failure of several attempts to make peace with it, intensified consciousness that it was Hindus who were being targeted. Modi and the BJP were seen as most likely to "stand up to Pakistan". The Indian air raid on a terrorist training camp in Balakot in Pakistan on 26 February 2019, in response to a bombing in Pulwama

in Indian Kashmir, was seen as a proof of a new determination to take the fight to the enemy, and won Modi additional support. However, it remains to be seen if Modi's underwhelming response (of which more, later on in this section) to Chinese aggression in the Galwan valley in Ladakh in June 2020, in which 20 Indian soldiers tragically lost their lives, will dent his image, and that of the BJP.

It is one of the astounding features of contemporary Indian politics that the forces who fought and made sacrifices for Indian freedom—today loosely called the liberals—have surrendered the "nationalist" tag to the votaries of Hindutva who are descended from elements who either stayed away from the independence struggle or actively collaborated with the British Raj. Today, the Hindutva movement has redefined nationalism on its own terms, marginalized the standard-bearers of civic nationalism and mobilized violence on behalf of its interpretation of Indian interests. Liberalism, diversity, pacifism and pluralism are portrayed as flabby weaknesses, preventing the full development of the nation and undermining India's ability to develop a strong and "modern" society that can present a robust face to the world and hold its own among the rest. As Hansen puts it, "the strong, homogeneous nation [advocated by Hindutva] is a sign of modernity; it bestows protection, sovereignty, self-confidence and political integrity on its citizens."[13] Putting Pakistan in its place is a corollary to this endeavour.

8. *Demography*: India is the world's youngest major country, with 65% of its population under 35. Young India is anxious for change and progress, tired of the old politics (especially of the messy coalitions that reigned from 1989 to 2014, and the political oscillations they embodied), and want India to be self-confident, assertive, and ready to take on the world. Modi's strutting confidence spoke to their urge for a leader who would fulfil their desires, although, as is widely known, his performance on the economic front has been poor; however, Modi's ability to promote himself to the masses is unparalleled, and opinion polls confirm that he has been able to increase his popularity despite his woeful track record on multiple fronts. Indeed, ethno-nationalist populism and identity politics serve as a valuable distraction from the economic slowdown, and from the ineptitude that has caused it.

9. *Technology*: The sweeping transformations brought about by technology led to social media becoming ubiquitous, with sites like Twitter, Facebook, and WhatsApp becoming major influencers and recyclers of prejudice. Social media reinforces people's worst beliefs by recycling

thoughts people might not have dared express in the past; it makes people realise their prejudices are not trifling but are widely held even if reprehensible. Suddenly bigotry became respectable, and shared animosity towards Muslims, previously concealed under a veneer of civility, was not just declaimed from political platforms but became an electoral asset. Prejudice paid off.

All these nine factors, inter-related and mutually reinforcing, came to a head when the moment found the messenger—Narendra Modi, charismatic orator of unchallengeable Hindutva credentials, tough and efficient CEO of Gujarat (again, a triumph of self-promotion), marketed to the previously hesitant as a no-nonsense administrator who would preside over economic growth, and aided and abetted by a skilled campaign manager in his Svengali, Amit Shah. His populism portrayed him both as one of the masses, an outsider, a chaiwallah, a man of the people, *and* as a superman, capable of prodigious feats since childhood, a messianic figure arisen to deliver India from bondage to a corrupt and dynastic elite.[14] India was ready for Modi and voted for him in 2014 and 2019. We are living with the consequences now, but these nine factors explain how we got here.

The social and cultural implications of this moment sustain the Moditva version of nationalism. Hindutva ideology has permeated the state apparatus and formal institutions, and Hindutva activists in the Hindi heartland exert control over civil society through vigilante groups (like the *gau-rakshak samitis*, or cow protection committees), cultural policing (such as through the "anti-Romeo squads" unleashed by Uttar Pradesh), and the tactical use of violence.[15] Tavleen Singh says that this faux version of nationalism and its adherents "translates politically as not criticising Modi or his policies (especially on Kashmir) because to do this is to criticise India and this, in their view, is tantamount to supporting "jihadist" Pakistan. The new elite has utter disdain for such "western" habits as eating meat and drinking wine. It also has utter disdain for reading books that come from foreign lands. The only books, languages, history and religions that they consider worthwhile are those they believe come from "Indic" sources. They believe that India will only prosper when their interpretation of "Indic" values is imposed upon Indians, and these pivot around their version of Hinduism which in fact more resembles Islam than the Sanatan Dharma."[16]

As I have noted, the Modi/BJP vision of Indian nationhood reduces it to a slogan—"Hindi, Hindutva, Hindustan". It would be instructive, in the rest of this section, to go deeper into what this means for the continued contestations over Indian nationalism.

23

THE RENEWED MODI-FICATION OF INDIA

The second-term government of Prime Minister Modi began with the brisk passage of a slew of legislation, including the criminalization of the practice of instant Islamic divorce, or "triple talaaq" (*talaaq-e-biddat*), and the dismantling of the special status given to Jammu and Kashmir under Article 370 of the Indian Constitution (of which more later), as examples of firm and decisive actions, both of which directly or indirectly targeted Muslims. The Government's boosters had, understandably, less to say on the economy, which has been in freefall for much of Modi's second innings, a process that was accelerated by the Covid-19 pandemic, the attendant "lockdown" and its deleterious effects, or on relations between religious communities, which have never been more polarized.

There is no doubt that Modi remains immensely popular personally. This may mystify his critics, since his record of accomplishment is so dismal, but as I have remarked, one of the reasons for this is that he is exceptionally skilled when it comes to portraying himself in a positive light. As a result, he comes across to most people as a decisive, no-nonsense leader with a hard head, willing to break with tradition, and attempt bold solutions to the nation's intractable problems. The reality that most of the out-of-the-box solutions he has attempted have done more harm than good does not seem to bother most voters, who give him full marks for trying. His demonetization of 86% of India's currency in 2016 was, the 2020 pandemic aside, probably the single most disastrous blow to the Indian economy since Independence, costing millions of jobs and causing severe damage to India's growth story, but an election-winning plurality of voters—44% in Uttar Pradesh a few months later, and 37% in the national elections of 2019—seem to have believed his intentions were good. His abrogation of the special status of Jammu and Kashmir was undertaken while locking down the entire state, arresting political leaders, and denying its population telephone and internet connections; while it is still unknown what will happen when the lid is fully off the pressure-cooker, the interim verdict in the rest of India is of unstinting support. As the columnist Keerthik Sasidharan observed: "Modi understands the great truth of democracy better than any politician of his generation: if the idea of personal sincerity and hard work is consistently drummed in, the people are willing to provide considerable latitude as far as outcomes are concerned."[1]

This leaves many in India scratching their heads. Modi's genius at marketing himself notwithstanding, how can many of his own actions, and those of his government be seen as anything other than authoritarian, harmful, vindictive, sectarian, illiberal, and essentially undemocratic? Here is a Prime Minister who has up-ended practically every civilized convention in Indian politics, unleashing law-enforcement authorities to pursue flimsy charges against an array of Opposition leaders (and locking up a former Home and Finance Minister for 101 days without trial), promoting ministers whose divisive discourse against Muslims has left them and other minorities fearful, and so thoroughly intimidated the media and its owners that his press coverage is an embarrassment to India's long tradition of an independent and uncowed media. Ministerial offices have been demeaned by such episodes as a minister ceremonially garlanding suspected killers in his own garden, or another minister exhorting a crowd to "shoot the traitors" (though it sounds even cruder in the original Hindi—"Desh ke gaddaron ko/ Goli maaro saalon ko"). At the same time, democratic and parliamentary conventions have been cast to the winds: not only is the Opposition demonized as illegitimate, the most elementary pretence of co-operation with, and respect for, the other side has been abandoned. On a more personal note, since I was myself the victim of this, for the first time in the entire history of India's parliamentary standing committees, the long-standing bipartisan foreign-policy tradition, under which the Chairmanship of the External Affairs Committee always goes to a member of the leading Opposition party, has been discarded, with the BJP assigning to itself the right to hold its own government accountable in international affairs.

Many of his admirers say it was past time to have a tough leader at the helm after decades of "too much" soft-hearted democracy and ineffectual coalition government. To those of us whose faith in Indian democratic practice is absolute, it is a sobering matter to realize that perhaps its roots were shallower than we had allowed ourselves to think. In its place we have a fervent nationalism that extols every Indian achievement, real or imagined, and brooks no dissent—the mildest disagreement or protest is promptly labelled 'anti-national' or even 'seditious'. Almost every independent institution has been hollowed out and made into an instrument of the government's overweening dominance; while this is less surprising of the tax authorities, the financial investigative agencies, and the enforcement and intelligence-gathering machinery of the government, even famously autonomous bodies like the Election Commission and the judiciary have not been exempt from such concerns. Political freedom has ceased to be a virtue in itself; control (by the authorities) and conformity (by everyone else) is now preferred. The scholar and commentator Pratap Bhanu Mehta writes that "it is difficult to remember a time when…the premium on public and professional discourse marching to the state's tune was as high."[2]

Communal relations have suffered a major setback under BJP rule, with the ongoing alienation of the Muslim community across India a stark reality acknowledged even by some of the Government's staunchest defenders.[3] As I have remarked, India was a famously inclusive land, a haven for the persecuted of all nations and faiths for three thousand years; today, it rejects Rohingya refugees because they are Muslims, and announces an intention (since shelved) to draw up a National Register of Citizens to exclude "foreigners" (defined as anyone living here or even born here after 1971, which would have potentially rendered stateless millions who know no other home). There are murmurs of a new push to eliminate the personal laws that minority communities are allowed to retain to govern their family practices, and the pushing through of a national "anti-conversion" law aimed at restricting missionary activity.

The very character of the country is being changed before our eyes, by a government with no respect for any of the conventions established and practised by its predecessors since Independence. "Boldness", it seems, is all that matters. The increasing worry for liberal democrats like myself is that maybe this is really what the Indian public, modestly-educated and misguided by the ruling party's skilful propaganda, really wants. As Pratap Bhanu Mehta asks: "Is, somehow, this exaltation of power, control and nationalism a completion of our own deepest desires?"[4] If what has taken place this far sets the tone for the remainder of the Modi government's second term in office, the warning is clear—this will cease to be the India Mahatma Gandhi led to freedom.

A striking feature of the stamp the BJP government has attempted to put on the nation is the manner in which the essence of civic nationalism has been distorted to serve the authoritarian agenda of the ruling party. The project of remaking the DNA of India starts, like other classic autocratic projects, with the identification of an enemy, real or imagined, to conjure up the alarming bogey of "the Other". As I have commented earlier, India's citizens are offered a range of forms in which this enemy can be identified: the malign neighbouring nation of Pakistan, with its Islamism, its fomenting of terrorism against India, its peddling of drugs across the border; the usual set of "traitors from within", including Islamic radicals and sympathizers of Pakistan (including those who applaud that country's victories in cricket matches) and more generally, adherents of different religions from that practised by the "majority community"; and third, the weak-kneed liberals who have spent decades appeasing the first two, especially the intellectuals among them, spouting their left-liberal sophistry in English, the hated language of the colonizers. These enemies have, of course, to be put in their place with a combination of methods—inducements for those whose cupidity, ambition or avarice considerably exceed any devotion to principle; intimidation for those whose financial or social position makes them vulnerable to the tax raid, the false case, the threat of arrest, bankruptcy, or public humiliation; and, when necessary, force, whether the policeman's lathi against unruly student protestors or vigilante violence against misbehaving (or uppity) minorities.

In parallel with such endeavours, of course, it is necessary to promote legitimacy for the state's actions. The Modi regime has done this through the aggressive assertion of a belligerent form of nationalism in which the government's ideological agenda is portrayed as synonymous with the national interest. The corollary to this assertion is, inevitably, that any opposition to it is anti-national, if not treasonous; this explains the trigger-happiness with which BJP-ruled states slap sedition cases on their critics, since clearly their criticism itself is proof that they are traitors to the nation. Critics are routinely urged by Government ministers to "go to Pakistan", the mere choice of destination itself pointing to the traitorousness of their opposition. The new nationalism essentially redefines loyalty to the country as loyalty to the ruling party rather than the country, sentimentally defined as patriotism by the liberals. The conflation of the nation with the government, the government with the ruling party, and both with the Prime Minister, has given India, for the first time, a larger-than-life ruler who literally embodies the nation and looms above its democratic institutions.

Mr Modi is very clever about positioning himself as above the mundane fray. Whenever he speaks—which, outside election campaigns, is infrequently (he even delegates responses to parliamentary questions marked for the Prime Minister to a Minister of State in his office, while he sits in silence, listening impassively)—it is almost like a constitutional monarch. He delivers homilies and platitudes in weekly radio broadcasts and staged public interactions with schoolchildren, panchayat heads and the like in a sage tone, while the dirty work of attacking institutions, pushing the boundaries, provoking the Opposition and dog-whistling about the minorities is left to subordinates. This means that he is always capable of claiming a blemish-free official record because technically he himself does not often incite. While he invariably greets an outrage perpetrated by his supporters with silence—condoning by failing to condemn—he reserves the possibility of a belated statement of piety when absolutely unavoidable, as when the raging Islamophobia encouraged by his party in the early weeks of the Covid-19 pandemic created a backlash across the Muslim world that threatened serious international embarrassment for his government: after several days, Modi issued a tweet[5] saying that the virus knew no religion, the mildest possible rebuke calculated to appease his foreign critics. At some level he is aware that he must make pious remarks and pay lip service to ideas he does not believe in because, clearly, they still matter to enough people at home and abroad. But he does so from his official "@PMOIndia" account, not his personal "@NarendraModi" one, as if aware that he is merely performing a ritual, the prime ministership as performance theatre, while the real work of remaking Indian nationalism in his preferred image goes on through his underlings.

As he bestrides the nation like a colossus, the Prime Minister entrenches the consent of the citizenry by militarizing his redefined nationalism and promoting veneration for the coercive apparatus through which he runs the state. The new idiom of respect for power extends to all those in uniform—the police, the military, the paramilitary—and even some out of uniform, the vigilante mobs sponsored or at least encouraged by the ruling establishment to exact the compliance of the unruly. The language of respect for the forces comes into play on every conceivable occasion—in Facebook memes during the disaster of demonetization asking "if our soldiers can stand 24/7 on the borders to defend our nation, why can't we stand 8 hours in a bank queue?", in Parliamentary debates on Kashmir, in election speeches railing against terrorist threats real and imagined, in television programmes featuring comic-opera, be-whiskered retired generals raising fearsome prospects of insurrection and war. All this serves two purposes, to exalt the purveyors of force as pillars of robust nationalism, and to divert the attention of the populace from other problems the government has created and spectacularly failed to resolve.

Needless to say, any questioning of the actions of the men in uniform, selflessly serving the nation, is by definition anti-national. Thus, the government denounces as " unpatriotic" the demand for the withdrawal of the Armed Forces Special Powers Act, allowing the military to shoot civilians in trouble zones with impunity; it condemns reports of human rights abuses and other excesses in Kashmir as disloyal to the unity and integrity of the country; it tars the Congress Party's advocacy of a reading down of the Sedition Act to bring it into conformity with Supreme Court decisions (which for the last six decades have affirmed that only violence or incitement to it can be deemed seditious) as the shameful indulgence of traitors; it portrays those politicians who cast doubt on the Government's account of the air-raid on Balakot, or question the propriety of the Rafale deal, as giving aid and comfort to the nation's enemies; it justifies the brutality of the UP police against protesters, or the inaction and complicity of the Delhi police in the riots in that city in 2020, as justified to uphold the sovereignty of the nation and the authority of its government. Through this militarized nationalism every coercive action of the Indian state becomes legitimate, and the relentless drumbeat of propaganda, on both the "mainstream" media and the tributary streams of social media, ensures the acceptance by the broader public of this version of reality. And to add to it all, the public, in buying into the government's ideological agenda, enjoys the added glow of virtuous nationalism, since it has been led to believe that disagreement or scepticism about the government's intentions only gives succour to the enemies of the nation.

But the Modi government's military credibility took a serious blow in June 2020, when the Chinese People's Liberation Army encroached upon territory India had long claimed along the Line of Actual Control that (in the absence of an agreed, demarcated border) separates the two countries. For all the rhetorical bombast, the Prime Minister proved helpless to prevent the unilateral redrawing of the LAC in the Galwan Valley and Pangong Tso areas of Ladakh. Worse still, his statement claiming the Chinese had not intruded on Indian soil (a typical piece of bluster intended for domestic political compulsion) was seized upon by Chinese propagandists to justify China's claims to what had previously been disputed territory. This inept performance, strategic paralysis, and clumsy messaging, especially in the face of the deaths of twenty Indian soldiers, did nothing for the morale of the very soldiers from whose shoulders Mr Modi and his BJP like to fire the empty bullets of their nationalism.

24

THE ETIOLATION OF DEMOCRATIC INSTITUTIONS

Besides its other alarming acts of commission and omission, the Modi government has also been responsible for the enfeebling of the nation's autonomous institutions. In the BJP conception of Indian nationalism, uniformity and obedience to the nationalist cause trumps the case for autonomous institutions sanctified in the capacious civic nationalism of the established idea of India. Their efforts to bring these institutions to heel in the service of their nationalist project has been extensive and sweeping.

Among the prominent casualties was the Reserve Bank of India, the country's central bank. The announcement that a non-banker, Shaktikanta Das, a former IAS officer, would take over as the 25th Governor of the Reserve Bank (RBI) was a clear signal of the erosion of its independence from government control, following the abrupt departure of Urjit Patel, who, citing 'personal reasons', stepped down from the helm, following a well-publicized standoff with the BJP-led central government.[1]

History certainly seems to have an interesting way of repeating itself: Just a few years back, Patel was the government's blue-eyed boy, widely regarded as the most acceptable choice to succeed his predecessor, Raghuram Rajan, who, despite a stellar record, was not offered an extension by the Modi government.[2] Unfortunately for him, in an era where the currency of a 'Patel' has reached historic heights in the country, this Patel is now remembered for having had the shortest tenure as India's top banker in over three decades.[3]

At a time when the autonomy of the bank has been slowly but surely compromised, as argued by another senior official who was soon to resign— Deputy Governor Viral Acharya—[4] the decision to select someone who was seen to be possibly more 'amenable' towards the whims of the ruling party, naturally drew flak—particularly given how thoroughly the RBI was discredited by the demonetization episode, in which it was widely denounced for failing to perform its fiduciary duties and earned the sobriquet "the Reverse Bank of India" for its frequent reversals of stance.

A spate of similar high-profile departures across the board during the tenure of the Modi government is a telling sign that all is not well. Between the exits of Patel and Rajan in 2018 and 2016 respectively, the country also witnessed the departure of Arvind Subramanian (the former Chief Economic Advisor, who stepped down prematurely in June 2018, and has since been a trenchant critic of the government he used to advise), Arvind Panagariya (Vice-Chairman of the Niti Ayog who, rumour has it, wasn't much liked by the RSS) and the economist Surjit Bhalla (member of the Prime Minister's Economic Advisory Council)—prompting one journalist from CNBC to point out: "It's hard for any government to match the record levels of staff turnover at President Donald Trump's White House, but Indian Prime Minister Narendra Modi's administration appears to be slowly catching up."[5]

This trend is a striking reflection of a much larger atrophy within India's premier public institutions under the Modi regime. A list of such institutions would include financial regulators like the RBI; the investigative agencies (notably the Central Bureau of Investigation); the Election Commission, which organizes, conducts, and rules on the country's general and state elections; the upper echelons of the Armed Forces; institutions of accountability like the Central Information Commission; the national exam-conducting bodies that test tens of millions of schoolchildren every year in highly competitive examinations that could make or break their futures; the elected legislatures; the judiciary, headed by the Supreme Court; and even the free press. Regulatory bodies suffer from similar problems: insufficient authority, weak human resources, overlapping mandates, lack of legitimacy, and political interference. Every one of these priceless institutions, so carefully nurtured over the years, has come under threat in the time that Modi has been in office.

Part of the reason behind this systemic onslaught stems from the Moditva doctrine and the inherently autocratic concentration of power that has developed into a definitive feature of this credo. What does this mean? Moditva articulates a cultural nationalism anchored in the RSS political doctrine of Hindutva, but extending beyond it. On top of the foundation of Hindutva, it builds the idea of a strong leader, powerful and decisive, who embodies the nation, and will lead it to triumph. When a similarly dominant leader, Indira Gandhi, attempted a similar degree of assertion over India's institutions, she declared an Emergency, and suspended many democratic processes, only to restore them fully after 22 months, hold a free election, lose it comprehensively, and relinquish power. Modi's assault on India's democracy is more subtle and more enduring: the changes he is bringing about to India's democratic institutions involve nothing as blunt as emergency decrees, but fundamentally alter the assumptions of their functioning in ways that will inevitably cripple them as effective custodians of the nation's freedom. The danger to liberal constitutionalism is clear.

The Moditva blend of a charismatic ruler, corporatism, an imagined Utopia ("*achhe din*"), an evocation of ancient glories, an "exacerbated nationalism", and Islamophobia, reminds one of Umberto Eco's famous list of the key ingredients of what he dubbed Ur-Fascism,[6] if one allows for the substitution of anti-Semitism by Islamophobia. Still, as I explained at length in *The Paradoxical Prime Minister*, I am not prepared to use the "f" word for the Modi regime. It has become a term of political abuse rather than of understanding. And surely Il Duce went much farther than the BJP would dream of. "The free press was abolished, the labour unions were dismantled, and political dissenters were confined on remote islands", Eco says, whereas of Moditva, the same sentence would have to be rewritten as "the free press was emasculated, the labour unions were ignored, and political dissenters were denied prominent platforms in the mainstream media." Some developments in current Indian politics seem to bode ill for our institutions, as we have seen, but these were much worse under Fascism: "Legislative power became a mere fiction and the executive power (which controlled the judiciary as well as the mass media) directly issued new laws", Eco writes of Mussolini's rule.

Nonetheless, it is instructive to note how many of the fourteen common factors of what Umberto Eco describes as "Eternal Fascism" seem to resonate with relevance when applied to the second-term Modi regime in India. The cult of traditionalism, with BJP grandees tripping over each other to evoke the glories of ancient India; the rejection of modernism, not in the sense of usable technology but of the scientific temper, of the alleged depravity of the modern world and the decadence of modern lifestyles; the cult of action for its own sake and a distrust of intellectualism; the view that disagreement or opposition is treasonous; a fear of difference rather than the ready acceptance of diversity; racism (transmuted, in the Indian context, to Islamophobia); the appeal to a frustrated middle class that is "suffering from an economic crisis or feelings of political humiliation, and frightened by the pressure of lower social groups"; the identification of an external enemy (Pakistan) and a scarcely veiled xenophobia; the tendency to see enemies simultaneously as omnipotent and weak, conniving, and cowardly; the rejection of pacifism (evident in Hindutva's ambivalent relationship with Mahatma Gandhi); the overt contempt for weakness (particularly scorned by the RSS); the cult of heroism, especially built around the image-projection of Narendra Modi; hypermasculinity (celebrated in repeated evocations of Mr Modi's supposed 56-inch chest); the selective populism, relying on chauvinist definitions of "the people" that the movement claims to represent (as Eco puts it, "citizens do not act; they are only called on to play the role of the People"); and finally, the heavy usage of "newspeak" and an impoverished discourse of elementary syntax and resistance to complex and critical reasoning. As Umberto Eco says, these factors are all to be found to a greater or lesser degree in Ur-Fascism, and the world must be vigilant whenever they arise. The green shoots of every one of the elements in his list, alas, have begun to sprout in India.

Autonomous public institutions threaten the dominance of the Moditva doctrine because, by design, they are independent institutions, with specialized mandates, commitments, and accountabilities, and they consequently challenge, through merely their independent functioning, Modi's oversized cult of personality. Naturally, when these institutions refuse to convert themselves into rubber stamps for whatever the ruling party wants them to do (as the standoff between the RBI and the Centre that led to Patel's resignation illustrated) the government's response appears to be to cut these institutions off at the knees or interfere with the institutional independence that is a defining feature of these bodies.

Under the BJP, another well-publicized war of attrition has been taking place within the Central Bureau of Investigation, memorably described as a "caged parrot".[7] Its investigations and indictments, once seen as the gold standard of Indian crime-fighting, are now too often seen as purely politically motivated. Matters came to head when the agency's Director and Special Director sparred openly, leaving Indians with Keystone Cops-style TV visuals of the agency raiding its own offices and court cases being brought against each other by the top two investigators. When the government was finally forced to respond to a rapidly deteriorating situation, that its solicitor described as a 'fight between two Kilkenny cats',[8] its response was far from reassuring, and raised even more concerns. First, it tasked the Central Vigilance Commission, an organization that has supervisory powers over the CBI only in matters of corruption, with conducting a free and fair inquiry. Then, against any existing precedent or law, the CVC recommended that both officers be sent on indefinite leave—which the government promptly acted upon; in doing so, it wilfully ignored the Delhi Special Police Establishment Act, which provides security of tenure to the Director, an essential requirement for the institutional independence of the post.[9] It then exonerated the officer who was known to be close to Mr Modi, even though the charges against him were reportedly well substantiated. There are other issues as well—including the Special Director's alleged proximity to members of the ruling party, his involvement with politically biased investigations and, most worryingly, the controversial background of the new interim Director who ran the CBI in the absence of the top two—that have significantly hurt the reputation of the agency.

Similarly, the judicial system, traditionally above the cut-and-thrust of the political fray, has come under withering scrutiny since January 2018, when the four most senior judges of the Supreme Court (including one, Ranjan Gogoi, who would eventually become Chief Justice) held an unprecedented press conference to question the decisions of then Chief Justice Dipak Misra in allocating cases to his favourite judges as "master of the roster". Their elliptical comments appeared to imply that the Chief Justice was unduly seeking outcomes to favour the government. Another point of contention was the inordinate delay in the elevation of the then Chief Justice of the Uttarakhand High Court, who had been selected by a collegium of judges for a seat at the Supreme Court, but whose transfer had faced obstacles from the government, on account of actions he had taken against them in the state. When he finally made it to the bench he had suffered a loss of several months of seniority, making it impossible for him ever to ascend in the normal course to the position of Chief Justice.

This technique—the use of inertia as a tool to achieve political objectives—is a hallmark of the BJP's abuse of institutions: vacant positions are left unfilled despite the availability of full information well in advance on when individuals are going to retire, weeding out possible contenders who will retire too during the pendency, thus paving the way for the political favourite.

Chief Justices of India are supposed to be free of political interests, but in April 2018 several Opposition parties circulated an equally-unprecedented Impeachment Motion against Chief Justice Misra in the upper house, the Rajya Sabha. Though this was rejected by the Rajya Sabha Chairman, the Vice-President of India, two MPs moved the Supreme Court to challenge his rejection, only to find the Chief Justice naming a bench favourable to him to hear their appeal. They then withdrew their case, but the image of the judiciary took a beating from all this, from which it will not easily recover. The performance of the impugned Chief Justice's successor, Ranjan Gogoi, was even more troubling, though he was never impeached. His role in reducing the fiercely independent apex court to an "Executive

Court", sub-serving the Government's agenda, has been scathingly portrayed by legal luminaries.[10]

Mr Gogoi's tenure as Chief Justice became even more controversial when he was accused of sexual harassment in April/May 2019; he dismissed the allegations after constituting himself as the judge in his own case. He presided over the remarkably opaque functioning of the Supreme Court's Collegium, changing none of the practices to which he had objected, as one of the four dissenting judges, during his predecessor's tenure. He decided that a respected liberal judge, Justice Akil Kureshi, was not "fit" to serve as Chief Justice of the Madhya Pradesh High Court, for reasons never explained, while exiling him to the Tripura High Court, which meant that either the judge's "unfitness" was clearly unsubstantiated or his reassignment was a deliberate insult to the latter court. The ex-Chief Justice also made astonishing statements from the Bench, notably telling a man who had been jailed for satirical speech that "jail is the safest place for you", or advising a woman seeking her constitutional rights to move freely throughout the territory of India under Article 19(1)(d) that "Srinagar is a cold place, why do you want to move around?" His partisan stand on the disposal of petitions seeking the observance of international standards of non-refoulement in respect of the Rohingya refugees did no credit to the ex-Chief Justice's respect for established standards of international humanitarian law. And his refusal to entertain human rights claims, including habeas corpus petitions, connected to the lockdown in Kashmir and the detention of Kashmiri political leaders without trial, on the grounds that the Court had "no time", reflect an unconscionable attitude towards civil and constitutional rights.

At the same time the Gogoi Court was ever ready to oblige the government in a slew of cases, ranging from the National Register of Citizens in Assam to the Babri Masjid/Ram Janmabhoomi dispute (a "land dispute" of interest to the Hindutva movement that was fast-tracked, while Kashmiri cases involving constitutional principles went unheard), and to allow it to submit inconvenient material to the Court's attention in "sealed covers". In the words of the legal analyst Gautam Bhatia, "ex-Chief Justice Gogoi oversaw a drift from a Rights Court to an Executive Court. That is, under his tenure, the Supreme Court has gone from an institution that—for all its patchy history—was at least formally committed to the protection of individual rights as its primary task, to an institution that speaks the language of the executive, and has become indistinguishable from the executive."[11] This is Mr Gogoi's legacy and added to the considerable damage done over the Modi years to the institutional credibility of the Supreme Court. But since it fulfils the "nationalist" agenda of the previously independent judiciary largely marching in lockstep with the government, criticism in mainstream media has been muted or non-existent.

The Gogoi tenure was capped by his unprecedented appointment, within weeks of his retirement, to a nominated seat in the Rajya Sabha, the Upper House of the Indian parliament. The offer of such a position and its immediate acceptance brought to mind the warning issued by the late BJP leader Arun Jaitley when he was in Opposition:

> Pre-retirement judgements are influenced by a desire for a post-retirement job.... But this clamour for post-retirement jobs is adversely affecting [the] impartiality of the judiciary of the country and…it should come to an end....

> The tendency of judges to follow the ballot box, to get carried with the times, has to be avoided. The judiciary is the lifeline of a democracy, and if people lose faith in it, they lose faith in democracy itself.[12]

But even while Jaitley was alive, a former Chief Justice, P. Sathasivam, was appointed by the Modi Government to the post of Governor of Kerala. That Chief Justices, like Caesar's wife, should be above suspicion, now seems to be a principle honoured in the breach in Mr Modi's India.

India's Election Commission has enjoyed a proud record of independence and boasts decades-long experience of conducting free and fair elections, despite its members usually being retired civil servants appointed by the Government of the day for fixed tenures. While in the past, Election Commissioners have largely enjoyed a reputation for integrity, this took a severe blow in 2018, when a BJP-appointed Chief violated the convention of announcing election dates for all impending state elections at the same time. A quarter century ago, the Commission had introduced a Code of Conduct that prohibits government expenditure to impress voters once election dates are announced. With the BJP, which was in power in both the Centre and in Gujarat state in 2018, scrambling to impress voters in Gujarat through last-minute schemes, and pre-election freebies, the EC came under pressure to delay the election announcement there as long as possible. Giving in, it surprisingly declared the dates for elections in Himachal Pradesh, a state that normally goes to the polls at the same time as Gujarat, thirteen days before the latter, citing a specious need to permit flood relief work in Gujarat (which the Code of Conduct would not in fact have disallowed).

Former Election Commissioners condemned the decision,[13] even as the Gujarat government and the Prime Minister himself took advantage of the delay to announce a series of pre-election giveaways. It does no good to

Indian democracy to see a shadow fall over the very institution that guarantees free and fair elections, especially at a time when reports of data manipulation by the likes of Facebook and Cambridge Analytica began to raise doubts over the security of the Electronic Voting Machines (EVMs) on which ballots are cast.[14] But Mr Modi had shown his contempt for the institution during his early days as Chief Minister of Gujarat, when he had taken a dig at then Chief Election Commissioner, J. M. Lyngdoh, at a public rally near Vadodara in August 2002. "Some journalists asked me recently, 'Has James Michael Lyngdoh come from Italy?'," Modi declared, spelling out the CEC's full name to highlight its Christian antecedents. "I said, I don't have his *janam patri*, I will have to ask Rajiv Gandhi. Then the journalists said, 'Do they (Lyngdoh and Sonia) meet in church?' I replied, 'Maybe they do'."[15] Lyngdoh, to his credit, was undeterred, but Mr Modi had made his expectations of the Election Commission clear.

The concern that under BJP rule, the Election Commission was behaving like a government department, became more acute when the Delhi High Court threw out an EC decision to disqualify twenty Aam Aadmi Party (AAP) members of the Delhi Legislature (MLAs) on technical grounds, an action that could have benefited the BJP had by-elections to their seats followed. The Court termed the decision "bad in law" and "violating principles of natural justice".[16] How had an institution widely hailed as the impartial custodian of India's democratic process allowed itself to be brought to such a sorry pass? The answer lay clearly with the ruling party at the Centre, which was seen as pressuring the institution to act according to its wishes.

The Modi Government has also not hesitated to politicize the Armed Forces, not just bypassing time-honoured principles of seniority in appointing the Army Chief, but by elevating a former General to the Council of Ministers and repeatedly using the Army in its political propaganda. The exploitation of a military raid in hot pursuit of rebels in Myanmar, and of the 2016 "surgical strikes" along the Line of Control with Pakistan for party election propaganda (and the declaration of a belated 'Surgical Strikes Day' for the same purpose)—something that Congress governments had never done despite having authorized several such strikes earlier—as well as the electoral exploitation of the Balakot raid, whose precise impact remains shrouded in controversy, marked a particularly disgraceful dilution of the principle that national security issues require both discretion and non-partisanship. The strong and well-established tradition of separation between the civilian and the military spheres in India is eroding because of the use of the army by the BJP, reciprocated by the public interventions of army generals in the media on issues that previously were seen as the domain of civilian politicians alone. The politicization of the army could easily result in the militarization of politics, though so far this has remained at the rhetorical level. At the same time, the BJP government appears to be happy to let the Army function with obsolete equipment, shortages in aircraft, ammunition, and spares, and lower than average spending on modernization—all of which suggests that when it comes to walking the talk, the government prefers partisan posturing over visible action.

This was clear in the 2018 Karnataka state elections which saw the Prime Minister, no less, falsely denouncing India's first prime minister for allegedly having insulted two Army Chiefs from the State. The principle that the Army should be kept out of politics, as the then Army Chief himself had publicly requested,[17] and that the military was above regional or religious loyalties, was disregarded in Mr Modi's flagrant exploitation of the Indian military for short-term purposes. This went even further when in 2019 the government created a new position of Chief of the Defence Staff and appointed the outgoing Army Chief, Gen. Bipin Rawat, to it in 2020, despite a number of statements by the general on political parties and foreign policy that had widely been criticized as inappropriate for a military officer.[18] The assumption by many in the media that his appointment was ensured by his departing from convention[19] to please his political masters did no credit either to the general or his government.

As for the "temple of democracy", the Indian Parliament, its work has been reduced to a farce as allies and supporters of the ruling party repeatedly bring sessions to a standstill through disruptions orchestrated by the Government. There could be no more stark indictment of the failure of Parliament to evolve as a public institution than the progressively downward trend in frequency of sittings, accompanied by more frequent disruptions, both of which have undermined the critical deliberative role of a parliament, which the government has been treating as a notice-board for the announcement of its decisions rather than a consultative body. It seemed as if the Government was willing to destroy the "temple" rather than permit prayers against its misrule to be heard there. (The government's lack of interest in parliamentary accountability was brought home when, three months after Parliament was suspended because of the coronavirus in March 2020, neither it nor its Committees were allowed to be convened either physically or virtually.) And when there is a rare opportunity for sensible debate on matters of serious importance to the country, the preference of the Modi regime is the following: The government will propose; the Opposition will oppose;

if matters come to a head, and a vote is called, the government's brute majority will dispose.

All this is, of course, sought to be justified on nationalist grounds, particularly the argument that opposition and dissent are by definition anti-national. The BJP's loudly proclaimed fear of "anti-nationalism" is, in itself, anti-national, since Indian nationalism and Indian democracy are inextricably linked. An attack on one is an attack on the other. The fear is that ethno-nationalism is taking India towards a peculiar hybrid, a "dictatocracy" which preserves the forms of democracy while brooking no dissent against its dictates.

Nowhere is this more apparent than in the ongoing persecution of India's more liberal universities. The government seems entirely unconscious of the classic prescription that the supreme purpose of the university in our republic is to create well-formed minds which can participate in a democracy, whose future depends on citizens' capacity to scrutinize their elected officials. One purpose of the university is to help us expand our minds in service of that democracy. In a deliberative democracy, universities are meant to be hotbeds of argument, debate, and dissent rather than centres of conformity. Universities are where young people find themselves—in many cases through engagement, political passion, ideological fervour, and personal involvement—in causes larger than their own academic careers. Many—perhaps most—students grow up in the process, and outgrow the more extreme views they adopted out of youthful zeal. Two of my most obdurately leftist classmates at St Stephen's, for instance, are now conservative pundits associated (in one case, till recently) with the BJP. They would undoubtedly be embarrassed to be reminded of the fervour with which they espoused positions that they would dismiss with scorn today.

Perhaps more important, the Indian state is not so feeble that a few irresponsible slogans shouted by misguided students can destroy it. But undermining the democratic ethos of the Indian Republic can destroy the essence of the state, and of the grand national experiment our nationalist leaders embarked when the country became free in 1947. By branding dissent as "anti-national" and so illegitimizing it, our BJP rulers are betraying the founding idea of an India "where the mind", in Tagore's immortal phrase, "is without fear".[20]

One can criticize the government of the day and be loyal to the nation. To define dissent as anti-national is to betray the nationalism of a freedom struggle that was itself built on dissent. We must celebrate a robust and pluralistic Indian democracy, not the fearful brand of governance espoused by the current government, which sees treason in every tweet and a traitor under every desk.

A favoured instrument of the "Hindu nationalists" in their drive to curb the freedom of universities is the sedition law. Jawaharlal Nehru, whose name adorns the university most vociferously targeted by the stormtroopers of Moditva—JNU—considered the sedition law "objectionable and obnoxious".[21] Nehru—along with a host of British-era nationalist leaders (including Bal Gangadhar Tilak, Annie Besant, Bhagat Singh, and Mahatma Gandhi himself)—was a target of the sedition law, Section 124A, and told Parliament in 1951 that "it should have no place both for practical and historical reasons… in any body of laws that we might pass. The sooner we get rid of it the better.". Yet seven decades later, this now-antiquated law continues to be an instrument to silence critical voices, especially student voices. The arrest in February 2016 of student leader Kanhaiya Kumar and his union colleagues under 124A, and the decision four years later to prosecute him; and the filing of an FIR in October 2019 under the same provision against 49 intellectuals who wrote a letter to the Prime Minister deploring mob-lynching, are merely two egregious examples of the misuse of the sedition law that no other democracy would permit to occur. It is essential to clarify and restrict its application to instances in which there is a direct and immediate incitement to violence, as has been interpreted by the Indian Supreme Court as well as judiciaries across the democratic world.

The BJP attack on universities is planned, deliberate, and dangerous to India's democracy. The events at JNU (and the suicide in January 2016, as a result of harassment, by a Dalit student in Hyderabad, Rohit Vemula) are evidence that we have failed to protect our students and scholars from political interference by individuals and organizations that used arbitrary processes to uproot academic freedom. From Dinanath Batra's RSS-supported curriculum in Haryana and Gujarat on "moral science" (which, of course, is neither particularly 'moral' nor 'scientific') to the politically-driven harassment of Vemula and the sacking (also in January 2016) of social activist and Magsaysay awardee Prof. Sandeep Pandey for his dissenting views at Banaras Hindu University, a deeply disturbing pattern emerges which points to an ominous political project, to exact conformity by striking at the intellectual fount of challenges to it, the universities.

The BJP's fear of college students is evidence of their low opinion of the nature of Indian democracy that has flourished since Independence. They seem to believe India's freedom to be so frail as to collapse in the face of dissent that characterizes the spirit of the nation in the first place. The flag that our soldiers have died for, even as the JNU disturbances were going on, stands for a larger idea of freedom than the intolerance of our present authorities accommodates. It is time for the government to live up to the ideals embodied in that flag.

India's free press, which ought to be calling the government's actions to account, has seemingly been cowed by the overweening power of the government. A process combining intimidation and co-optation has ensured the minimum of critical voices in the so-called "mainstream" media are raised against such behaviour. If the de-institutionalization of Indian governance proceeds like this, the greatest danger facing India will be that of the public losing faith in the system altogether—with incalculable consequences for the country's biggest asset, its democracy.

This is already taking place in many other parts of the world. In a widely discussed paper, Harvard scholars Yascha Mounk and Roberto Stefan Foa argue that the health of liberal democracies across the world is falling (the scientific term being 'democratic deconsolidation'), and that former 'consolidated democracies' around the globe confront imminent degeneration.[22] Drawing on data from the World Value Survey (1995–2015), they show that there has been a considerable dilution of support for democracy and a growing impatience in the democratic process, especially among the so-called 'millennial' generations (those born after the 1980s), and that we can no longer assume that once a country upholds democratic institutions for a steady period of time, fosters strong civil society traditions, and attains a degree of wealth, the future of democracy is secure in its hands. It is, we are told, a fallacy, and we must always guard against complacency. Conversely, the same data suggests that support for non-democratic or authoritarian models of governance is rising in many democracies. India is among the worst: the percentage of Indian respondents answering that "a strong leader who does not have to bother with parliament and elections" is a "good" way to "run this country" crossed 70%, behind only Russia and Romania; even Pakistan came 7th, with 62% expressing the same sentiment.[23] While for many people the mere conduct of reasonably free and fair elections is taken to be proof of democracy, civic nationalism can only flourish if the system maintains checks and balances, promotes consensus, and ensures institutional autonomy. Otherwise countries tumble slowly but irresistibly into becoming illiberal democracies. The Mounk-Foa data show India, under Mr Modi, in the vanguard of this trend, a development corroborated by a recent CSDS-Azim Premji University survey, where over 50% of respondents in 4 large states of the country expressed a preference for an authoritarian alternative to our existing democracy.[24]

THE ETIOLATION OF DEMOCRATIC INSTITUTIONS

This certainly does not bode well for the future of our Indian democracy. If the assault on our institutions persists, the confidence that the people of India have in these bodies will erode steadily and this will weaken the very pillars of the democracy that we take for granted today. Political parties and the ruling powers of the day will come and go, but these institutions are the enduring pillars of any democracy. Their independence, integrity and professionalism are meant to inure them from the political pressures of the day. As stewards of our constitutional system, Governments have an extra responsibility to behave with great maturity and restraint, because something done now for short-term gain sets a precedent that can later be exploited by even more unscrupulous elements in power for more drastic and dangerous changes. Increasingly in Modi's India, that ability to think long-term about the health of national institutions is missing.

25

THE ASSERTION OF HINDI

The Hindutva alternative to Indian civic nationalism has historically also been impatient with the notion of Indian multi-lingualism, which it sees as a babel undermining national unity rather than the proud showcase of diversity that civic nationalism celebrates. It has been a long-standing policy plank of the Hindutva movement that Hindi, the language of the northern and central Indian states, where the party has sunk its deepest roots, should be the "national language" of India.

India has no "national language"; it has two official languages, English and Hindi, with co-equal status in the Central Government, the courts, and other national institutions. Attempts to promote Hindi nationwide led to stiff resistance from non-Hindi-speaking states in the early 1960s, with language riots claiming lives in the southern state of Tamil Nadu. The compromise achieved at the time—a "three-language formula", which required each Indian to learn English, Hindi and the language of his or her own state, with a South Indian language to be taught in Hindi-speaking states—has been largely honoured in the breach over the last five decades.

At that time, the man who had been the last Governor-General of India before it became a republic, and the only Indian to have held that title—Chakravarti Rajagopalachari, universally known as Rajaji—had cautioned that the opposition to English was counter-productive: "Xenophobia is an outmoded form of patriotism. It is a sign of immaturity to feel shame in using a world language in our high affairs. Over and over again the inescapable injustice of imposing Hindi is sought to be covered by a cry against the foreign character of English. English is no more foreign than our legal or parliamentary or administrative procedure, all which have been firmly adopted and confirmed for future use also."[1] Ambedkar, too, had expressed the view that the utility of a single language nationwide in the administration and the justice system required the continuation of English as a matter of practical convenience.

On the conflation of Hindi with nationalism, Rajaji was trenchant: "The Hindi programme is a disruptionist programme. He who warns ought not to be looked upon as unfriendly. It is a bad day for us all if criticism such as mine is put down to want of patriotism…Is not just and fair dealing by all the geographically distributed people of this great country as important at least as national pride? Justice is at the root of successful democracy and it is perilous to ignore it. The installation of Hindi as the Union and inter-State all-India language—the honour that now belongs to English by reason of the history of the last one hundred and fifty years—will result in inequality and injustice…."[2]

He also gave short shrift to the argument that Hindi was a language of the Indian masses while English was used only by the deracinated elites: "When the Hindi protagonists are speaking of the masses they are obviously thinking of the masses of the Hindi area only; they ignore the masses in non-Hindi India who are no less in number."[3] Nationalism, he feared, was being used to conceal the naked self-interest of the Hindi-speakers of the north: "Love of oneself may easily masquerade as love of language, and love of language as love of country. Let us not deceive ourselves or others with chauvinistic slogans".[4]

But deluding ourselves is a favoured pastime in New Delhi. A brief flash-point over the language issue erupted again in 2019 when a draft National Education Policy was circulated which sought to make Hindi compulsory in non-Hindi speaking states. After a predictable outcry from non-Hindi-speaking states, the proposal was swiftly withdrawn by the new Minister for Human Resource Development (a published author in Hindi). But the larger issues raised by this ill-advised move still cause worry in the South.

The proposal of the MHRD-appointed Kasturirangan Committee, which provoked an uproar in the southern states, stemmed from the contentious clause that declared that "the study of three languages by students in the Hindi-speaking states would continue to include Hindi and English and one of the modern Indian languages from other parts of India, while the study of languages by students in the non-Hindi-speaking states would include the regional language, Hindi and English."[5]

This was understandably perceived by the aggrieved states as part of a recurring tendency by the BJP-led Central government to try and impose the mandatory learning of Hindi among the predominantly non-Hindi speaking peninsular population of the country. In response, the BJP, whose outreach in states like Tamil Nadu and Kerala was emphatically rejected in recent general elections, was forced to backtrack, including by getting two of its newly inducted Tamil-speaking Cabinet Ministers, neither elected from Tamil Nadu but appointed to the Rajya Sabha from other states, to publicly offer clarifications (in Tamil).

But the issue here is actually much larger than the New (or Newer) Education Policy. On the surface, the issue at hand appears to be the government's attempt to implement the 'three-language formula', a guideline that was formulated in 1968 to ensure the equitable pan-Indian distribution of at least one common language—and, therefore, help promote ideals like national unity and integration, but also for practical purposes—such as creating a widely understood common language (either Hindi or English) that citizens would use to deal with their government.

But in the five decades since, successful implementation has largely failed across the country, for two divergent reasons. At an ideological level, in states like Tamil Nadu, with its proud history of Dravidian sub-nationalism, the question of being required to learn a northern language like Hindi has always been contentious, with anti-Hindi agitations a recurring episode in the state since 1937. In the northern states, there is simply no demand for learning a southern language, and so no northern state has seriously implemented the three-language formula.

The current reality is that most students in the southern states (with the exception of Tamil Nadu) continue to learn Hindi as either their second or third language. But look elsewhere in the country, and one finds very few instances of a student learning either Malayalam or Tamil, or even having the option to do so, as part of their school curriculum. This, in turn, is complemented by other problems, such as the lack of local language options for exam-goers of many of our national competitive exams.

One solution is to focus on the improved implementation of the 'three-language formula' by ensuring that it is both flexible (and therefore allows alternate options for students who do not wish to learn Hindi) and equitable (in that it ensures the availability of southern languages in the North and vice versa).

And then there are practical issues. While a Malayali or Tamilian can see the practical advantages of learning English as a vehicle of empowerment and personal advancement, she does not always see the same advantage in learning Hindi. For the native Hindi speaker, his language is an element of his identity; his advocacy of Hindi is cultural and emotional. A southerner who does not see Hindi as part of his identity needs a good reason to acquire mastery of an unfamiliar tongue. But if the BJP is trying to provide him one, it's the wrong one.

Compulsion is rarely a good argument in a democracy. But the real fear is far more fundamental: that the advocacy of Hindi is merely the thin end of a more dangerous wedge. It has more to do with the ideological agenda of those in power who believe in a nationalism of 'one language, one religion, one nation,' or 'Hindi-Hindu[tva]-Hindustan'. This is anathema to those Indians who grew up and believe in a diverse, inclusive India whose languages are all equally authentic. The Hindutva brigade's attempts to impose cultural uniformity in India will be resisted staunchly by the rest of us; the opposition to Hindi is based on our fear that such cultural uniformity is really what the advocacy of this language is all about.

The quest for uniformity is always a sign of insecurity, and the BJP is no exception: if you do not conform, they seem to be saying, I will feel threatened by you. Their display of majoritarianism has gone to the point where it threatens to undermine the very social fabric that has held the country together since Independence.

The only India that will work and thrive is one which provides a space for all of us to grow equally and without discrimination from the state. If Hindi becomes more than first among equals—if it is the de facto language of administration and courts, as it has become that of national politics—then Singh, Shukla, and Sharma will have the joy of flourishing in a language they have spoken from their mothers' laps, while Subramaniam, Reddy, and Menon would be floundering in a system they cannot comprehend. That is a formula that will destroy the country.

The southern states have had good reason to worry about the growth of northern cultural chauvinism, already manifested socially in issues like the attempted ban on the consumption of beef, a common source of protein in the south, and in the BJP government's decision in May 2018 to change the terms of reference of the 15th Finance Commission and use the 2011 census figures as the benchmark for revenue sharing, which would reduce the share of revenue for the South (where the population growth rate has declined due to concerted emphasis on family planning).

In the longer term, there is a looming political concern regarding whether the carefully balanced arrangement of the distribution of Lok Sabha seats under the 91st Amendment, which expires in 2026, and which the BJP may not be inclined to renew, will end up disenfranchising the southern states by punishing them for their success in curbing population.

We will return to these last two issues later in the book, as we contemplate the future of Indian nationalism. But this latest episode of Hindi assertion is, perhaps, most worryingly, seen by many in the south as an ominous indication of the direction the country is likely to head towards under the BJP.

26

THE CITIZENSHIP AMENDMENT ACT
AND THE NATIONAL REGISTRY OF CITIZENS

The "elephant in the room" when discussing Indian nationhood, of course, is a recent challenge to, arguably, the most fundamental aspect of Indianness, through a law, the Citizenship (Amendment) Act (CAA). It is, without question, the first law to question a basic building block of our nation—that religion is not the determinant of our nationhood and, therefore, of our citizenship. As is well known, the implications of this law immediately created an increase in tensions and a wave of protests around the country, leading to an eruption of violence in the nation's capital that claimed fifty-six lives and left hundreds injured. It has also hurt the perception of India as inclusive state which honours the equality of all and guarantees that the state will not practice religious discrimination.

At a time when India's major national priority ought to have been its flailing economy, whose plummeting growth rate had already aroused widespread alarm, even before the coronavirus struck, the Modi government plunged the country into an unwanted political crisis of its own making with the CAA. With its penchant for shock-and-awe, the Government pushed through parliament legislation that fast-tracks citizenship for people fleeing persecution in Pakistan, Afghanistan, and Bangladesh—provided they are not Muslim.

By excluding members of just one community, the new law is antithetical to India's secular and pluralist traditions. As I argued in parliament, it is not just an affront to the basic tenets of equality and religious non-discrimination that have been enshrined in our Constitution, but an all-out assault on the very notion that our forefathers gave their lives for during the nationalist movement.

As I have said earlier in this book, in the twilight of our freedom struggle, Indian nationalists split on the issue of whether religion should be the determinant of nationhood. Those who believed that it should, led by Mohammed Ali Jinnah and his followers, held out for Pakistan, a separate country for Muslims. The rest, led by Mahatma Gandhi and Jawaharlal Nehru, argued passionately that religion had nothing to do with nationhood. Their vision led to a free country for all people of all religions, regions, castes and languages—the foundational vision of India which the Modi government has now betrayed.

The implications—constitutional, political, social and moral—are profound. The Act paves the way not just for declaring immigrants to be illegal if they happen to be Muslim, but coupled with an even more problematic National Register of Citizens the government announced that it intends to create, (though it has since been deferred), would allow it to disenfranchise any Indian Muslim who is unable to prove his antecedents. Many Indians, especially the poor, do not have documentary evidence of when and where they were born; even birth certificates have only become widespread in recent decades. While non-Muslims would, thanks to this Act, get a free pass, similarly undocumented Muslims would suddenly face the onus of proving they are Indian.

It is, in many ways, a breath-taking departure from over seven decades of democratic practice in a country that was proud of its impressive record of managing stunning levels of diversity. As the legal scholar Gautam Bhatia has shown, the Constitution articulates "a vision of Indian citizenship that is interwoven with Indian constitutional identity as a whole: secular, egalitarian, and non-discriminatory. Drawing upon universal humanist principles—and in specific and conscious contrast to the State of Pakistan—the Constituent Assembly crafted an idea of citizenship that rejected markers of identity, whether ethnic or religious."[1] As Partition refugees streamed across the border in the largest exodus then known to humanity, fleeing religious violence, Alladi Krishnaswamy Ayyar, a veteran lawyer, advised the Assembly that "It is for you to consider whether our conception of citizenship should be universal, or should be racial or should be sectarian."[2] The Constituent Assembly specifically debated whether it should recognize nationality (in an ethnic sense) or citizenship (in a non-racial, "universal" sense) before opting for the latter. As K. M. Munshi observed:

After all we are not making a law of nationality. We are only enacting two indispensable conditions, namely, persons born in India and naturalised according to the law of the Union shall be citizens. The world is divided between the ideas of racial citizenship and democratic citizenship, and therefore, the words 'born in India' become necessary to indicate that we align ourselves with the democratic principle.[3]

Conversely, P. S. Deshmukh spoke for those who wanted an explicitly religious basis for citizenship: he proposed that "every person who is a Hindu or a Sikh by religion and is not a citizen of any other State, wherever he resides" should be eligible to be Indian. This was rejected after a debate in which Ayyar reminded the Assembly that "we are plighted to the principles of a secular State."[4] The Constitution, in other words, linked citizenship very specifically to the idea of a non-communal, non-denominational polity, without distinction of religion, race, caste or class: the idea of India again. The "rigorously universal and non-discriminatory language" of the constitutional provisions for citizenship, in Bhatia's words, "were never intended to be read in isolation. Rather, they formed one strand in a web of harmonious and mutually reinforcing principles, which, woven together, made up the Constitution." Citizenship was linked to "a coherent and morally consistent political vision" of Indian nationhood.[5]

This was the constitutional background to the practice of Indian secularism, which took pride in the fact that its citizenship was held by people of all conceivable religions and ethnicities. Foreigners—including former US President George W. Bush—had admired the fact that despite being home to 180 million Muslims, India had produced hardly any members of ISIS or Al-Qaeda. Indians would point with pride to the fact that this was because Indian democracy gave Muslims an equal stake in the country's well-being. We can no longer say that now.

The religious bigotry that partitioned the country with the founding of Pakistan has now been mirrored in pluralist India. As I told my fellow Parliamentarians, that was a partition in the Indian soil; this is now a partition of the Indian soul.

Inevitably, mass protests erupted, as the CAA made its way through Parliament, particularly in the North-Eastern states bordering Bangladesh who fear their local identities will be eroded by the legitimization of new citizens, and among Muslims and secularists nationwide. Though for the most part the protests have been peaceful, the authorities responded with force, three teenage protestors were shot dead in Assam, curfews imposed and internet and telephone services suspended in some areas. Riots in the nation's capital took dozens of lives. This self-inflicted wound will take a long time to heal.

The nationwide crisis was preceded by a localized crisis in the state of Assam. Seventy-one years after the Partition of India, and forty-seven years after the subsequent rebirth of the former East Pakistan as Bangladesh, one of the legacies of the messy division of the subcontinent came back to haunt the country in 2018. The decision to publish a National Register of Citizens (NRC) in Assam threw into doubt the citizenship, and the future, of some four million human beings, with incalculable consequences for the peace of the region.

As we know, the departing British partitioned India in 1947 on the basis of religion, in order to create a Muslim state, Pakistan, out of Muslim-majority provinces in the West and East of India. East Pakistan seceded in 1971 to form Bangladesh after a brutal and genocidal campaign by the Pakistani army had driven some ten million refugees to India. Once India had vanquished Pakistan in war, and the Pakistani army in the East surrendered, the refugees streamed back home to newly-independent Bangladesh. But some, perhaps, stayed on in India, merging seamlessly into the population.

Over the course of the next few years, they were joined by millions of other migrants from Bangladesh, fleeing economic hardship and land scarcity in an overcrowded country. While those who slipped into the Indian state of West Bengal easily assimilated with their fellow Bengalis, those who made new homes in the north-eastern state of Assam were culturally, linguistically, ethnically, and religiously different from the majority of their Assamese neighbours. Fearing they were being squeezed out of land and job opportunities in their own country, Assamese students began mass protests in the 1980s, which occasionally erupted into violence and made Assam all but ungovernable. A pair of savage massacres of Bengali Muslim migrant groups, including of some 3000 in the Assamese village of Nellie in 1983, revealed the extent of the crisis. The agitation was only defused when then Indian Prime Minister Rajiv Gandhi concluded an "Assam Accord" in 1985, pledging to identify all those who had migrated illegally from Bangladesh into Assam since 1971.

This was easier said than done, and despite semi-official estimates of twenty million illegal immigrants from Bangladesh, an assortment of tribunals set up to identify foreigners failed to spot more than a few thousand over the years. No concrete action was taken, and the problem was left to simmer for decades by successive governments. But the election of the hard-line Hindu-nationalist BJP government of Narendra Modi in 2014 revived the process, under Supreme Court supervision. When it concluded the main phase of its work at the end of July 2018, it published the NRC, a list of persons who could provide proof of antecedents in Assam preceding the Accord's cut-off date of 1971. Just over 4 million people who could not, found themselves rendered, in effect, stateless. After appeals and revisions, this was reduced to a "final" list of 1.9 million non-citizens.

The register was full of anomalies: one half of a pair of twins was found eligible, the other not; a soldier who had fought with distinction in India's last war, and been decorated for it, was deemed to be a non-citizen; and strikingly, some 1.6 million of those declared to be unable to prove they were Indian, turned out to be Hindus. The ruling BJP had hoped simultaneously to take credit for having identified "foreigners", mostly Bangladeshi Muslims, and to shelter behind the protection of the Supreme Court's supervision of the process. Soon enough, with its Hindu supporters outraged at the results, the BJP itself had to denounce the exercise, calling for its abandonment. The CAA was clearly intended to save the party's face by providing a route to citizenship for the non-Muslims omitted, leaving only the intended victims of the exercise, Bengali Muslims, out.

Throughout the preparation of the NRC in Assam, the BJP had pretended that this was a neutral exercise that had nothing to do with politics. But, at bottom, the exercise is indeed intensely political—since it is about who can own land, claim jobs and vote in BJP-ruled Assam. Once the result turned out to be not what they had hoped for, a different solution had to be found through the CAA. But this created a new headache for the Modi government—the hostility of BJP-ruled Assam, which wanted to reduce the pressure of migrants of any faith, and the resentment of Muslims and liberals everywhere else, who don't want Muslims singled out for exclusion.

Whatever the size of the final list of foreigners deemed ineligible for Indian citizenship, it is assumed that the excluded will be overwhelmingly, if not entirely, Bengali Muslims. The question that bedevils Assam today is: what will happen to them? Some speak glibly of deporting them to Bangladesh. But there is no deportation agreement in place between New Delhi and Dhaka, and Bangladesh has made it clear that it assumes no responsibility for people who are not on its soil. Will they be turfed out of their homes in Assam and find themselves with no place to go?

Some suggest the setting up of camps to house these people temporarily till Bangladesh can take them back, a prospect that has human rights groups horrified—not least since that day of repatriation may never come. Indeed, Bangladesh is one of the few neighbouring countries with which the Modi government has been able to maintain good relations. Creating a migration crisis, or worse still, attempting forced deportations, will destabilize a relationship that is vital to India.

The human implications of the NRC list are also troubling. Many who may indeed have come to India after 1971 (and are therefore deemed ineligible under the terms of the Accord) have lived in Assam for over four decades and know no other home. Can they now be stripped of the rights they have exercised in democratic India most of their lives?

It has been cynically suggested that a principal purpose of the exercise in Assam has been to strip Bengali Muslims of the right to vote. In a state of 26 million inhabitants, disenfranchising 4 million could have a significant impact on the electoral fortunes of the ruling party, which is not known to enjoy much support among India's Muslim electorate. But the legal implications of such an action have yet to be parsed, and will be open to challenge in the courts.

The Congress had first proposed an NRC in Assam to fulfil the terms of the Assam Accord, but now both the Congress and the BJP have found it a deeply flawed exercise. One shudders to imagine the same flaws replicated on a national scale, as Home Minister Amit Shah repeatedly declared he wanted to conduct a nationwide NRC.[6] If the Government carries out an all-India citizenship documentation exercise, millions of people born and raised here, who know no other home, will get excluded as many will not be able to "prove" their citizenship. Then this Act can be used by the Government to protect favoured communities to the exclusion of Muslims, whom they want to disenfranchise. What would you do to those excluded? They have lives and homes here, and you can't deport them elsewhere because no one will accept them. Would you build concentration camps for them as "stateless" people, as the Government is aiming to do in Assam? For how many generations? We would rightly earn the condemnation of the world. Employed in tandem, both the CAA and the NRC would have disastrous and ominous implications for our nation and the values that have been central to our polity.

So far, the crisis created by the NRC in Assam has been contained, but as tensions mount on both sides of the issue, the risk of an eruption is ever-present. Is an Accord arrived at in 1985, setting a cut-off date in 1971, necessarily the best framework to resolve the issue in 2020 and beyond? Can democratic India afford to ignore the human rights of a few million people who have been living on its soil for decades? While protecting India's sovereignty and the integrity of its citizenship are laudable principles, can they be applied in practice to create stateless people whose lives would suddenly be plunged into limbo? There are no clear answers to any of these questions, though passionate voices on both sides of the argument have no doubt what those answers should be.

* * *

Moving beyond the specific issues raised by the CAA in Assam is the larger issue with the Act that has propelled nationwide protests against it—the far more profound betrayal it embodies of the very basis of Indian nationhood.

It is worth reiterating some of the points I have already made to show just how destructive the CAA can be to the essence of India. The CAA modifies a 1955 Act, and grants the right of Indian citizenship to Hindus, Sikhs, Buddhists, Jains, Parsis, and Christians fleeing the neighbouring countries of Afghanistan, Bangladesh and Pakistan. It is the first time any law of this nature has specified religious groups by name, and the omission of one community is striking. Ironically, it also goes against our historic legacy that Hindus were proud to lay claim to. Swami Vivekananda had famously told the World Parliament of Religions in Chicago in 1893 that he was proud to speak for a land that has always offered refuge to the persecuted of all nations and faiths. India lived up to Vivekananda's values in giving shelter to Tibetan refugees, the Bahai community, Sri Lankan Tamils, and ten million Bangladeshis—the largest refugee exodus in human history—without ever asking about their religion. India has for 3,000 years offered refuge to the persecuted of various lands, and has never excluded a specific religious group. But Muslims have been very deliberately left out of the purview of the law and therefore denied asylum from persecution on the same conditions as other communities.

This is a shameless performance by a government which, as recently as 2017, refused to entertain any discussion on developing a National Asylum policy, which I had proposed in Parliament in a Private Member's Bill and shared personally with the then Home Minister, his Ministers of State, and his Home Secretary. If the government genuinely cared about refugees, why has it consistently refused to accept the need for an objective asylum policy, based on international standards and objective criteria, or come up with one of their own? We remain the only major democracy without a national asylum law; but when I raised the issue again in the Lok Sabha in 2019, Home Minister Amit Shah declared he would never permit any such thing.

This Act would not just alienate an entire community based on faith. It would completely disregard all other forms of persecution recognized in international law—persecution on the basis of ethnicity, gender, sexual orientation, political opinion. It would create a climate of hatred and discrimination against one community. A democratic India should offer shelter and even citizenship to persecuted minorities from our neighbouring countries, but without specifying their religious affiliations. The government now seeks credit for going the extra mile in granting citizenship to refugees, whereas, in reality, it doesn't even want to take the basic steps required under international law to reify the determination of refugee status or ensure formal legal treatment of refugees.

The Act's supporters in the BJP are belligerent about their bigotry. "If Hindus cannot find a home in India, where can they?" is their refrain. The implicit argument is that India is a natural Hindu homeland; Muslims have other countries they can lay claim to. The shocking thing about this argument is that, in one piece of bigoted legislation, it sweeps aside the fundamental premise of Indian nationalism. The CAA is not just an affront to the basic tenets of equality and religious non-discrimination that have been enshrined in Articles 14 and 15 of our Constitution, but an all-out assault on the basic assumptions of the Republic. Western dictionaries might define "secularism" as the absence of religion, but such a notion is foreign to India: religion is far too deeply rooted in all our communities to be wholly absent from Indians' perceptions of themselves.

I have already explained, in a previous chapter, that irreligiousness can never be popular in our country; every religion flourishes in India. But secularism as an Indian political idea had little to do with Western ideas privileging the temporal over the spiritual. Rather, it arose from the 1920s onwards in explicit reaction to the communalist alternative. Secular politics within the nationalist movement rejected the belief that religion was the most important element in shaping political identity. Lala Lajpat Rai, who unusually served both the Hindu Mahasabha and the Congress, explained it well: "I am a Hindu and not altogether free from bias," he wrote. "But I am always prepared to place myself in the position of the Muslims and look at things from their point of view. In my suggested solutions of these differences I have always kept the pure nationalist point of view, having studiously tried to free my mind from that bias which favours the Hindu community".[7] Indian secularism throughout the freedom struggle and after Independence meant recognizing that India had a profusion of religions, none of which should be privileged by the state.

All the cant about "genuine" and "pseudo" secularism boils down in the end to simply this. Prof Amartya Sen has put it rather well in declaring that political secularism involves merely "a basic symmetry of treatment of different religious communities".[8] This kind of secularism is actually the opposite of classic Western notions of secularism, as I have said in *Why I Am A Hindu*, because in effect it actively helps religions to thrive, by recognizing all religions as equal, in pursuance of Swami Vivekananda's dictum, "Ekam Sat, vipraah bahuda vadanti". ["There is One Truth; the sages call it by different names."]

Our secularism recognizes the diversity of our people and ensures their continued commitment to the nation by guaranteeing that religious affiliation will be neither a handicap nor an advantage. No Indian need feel that his birth into a particular faith automatically disqualifies him from any profession or office. That is how the political culture of our country reflected "secular" assumptions and attitudes. As we have already noted, though the Indian population was 80% Hindu and the country had been partitioned as a result of a demand for a separate Muslim homeland, three of India's Presidents were Muslims, and Muslims have occupied, on merit, the highest offices in the land, from that of Chief Justice to cricket captain.

The critics of secularism in the ruling BJP want an end to India in which this kind of "secularism" is practised. Hindu chauvinism has tended to portray itself as qualitatively different from Muslim sectarianism. Yet, as far back as 1958, Prime Minister Jawaharlal Nehru had warned against the dangers of Hindu communalism, arguing that the communalism of the majority was especially dangerous because it could present itself as nationalist: since most Indians are Hindus, the distinction between Hindu nationalism and Indian nationalism could be all too easily blurred. Obviously, majorities are never seen as "separatist", since separatism is by definition pursued by a minority. But majority communalism is, in fact, an extreme form of separatism, because it seeks to separate other Indians, integral parts of our country, from India itself. This is what we are seeing with the contemptible campaign to rename places bearing Muslim names. The Hindutva movement is the mirror image of the Muslim communalism of 1947; its rhetoric echoes the bigotry that India was constructed to reject. Its triumph would mark the end of the Indian idea.

With the zeal of the recent convert, the former Congressman who is now the BJP's leading strategist in the Northeast, Himanta Biswa Sarma, declared that the Act was necessary to prevent the region from "going to Jinnah". Ironically, what the Act actually does is to surrender to Jinnah. By reducing India to a non-Muslim state, it buys into the underlying scheme of Pakistan, which asserted that adherence to the religion of Islam was what made Muslims a separate nation.

The BJP seems unconcerned that its Hindu-nationalist agenda will unleash an atmosphere of suspicion, fear and bigotry that will sweep across the country, claiming Indian citizens as victims, generating chaos in the name of nationalism. As Pradeep Chhibber puts it: "In current-day India, the word Hindu, especially as it is being deployed by Narendra Modi and Amit Shah's BJP, has virtually no moral connotation.... It seems that in the current BJP conception there are no principles of justice, no philosophy, no compassion associated with the word Hindu. Just 'us' versus 'them'."[9]

The link between the Act and the proposed nationwide National Register of Citizens (NRC), requiring people to show documentary evidence that they are citizens of India, is the essence of the problem. In Assam, the NRC has been implemented in a very strict manner, whereby even spelling differences in documents have caused rejections. This will disproportionately hurt poor, rural, marginalized, and tribal people, as most do not have the required documents. Even ministers in Mr Modi's cabinet—most famously former Army Chief V. K. Singh[10]—do not have reliable documentation of their date and place of birth. If the poor have no documents, they could be declared as illegal migrants and face imprisonment.

Mr Shah's statements in various interviews made it clear that any person excluded by the NRC can seek protection under the rules of the Act without documentary evidence—but no Muslim can do so. Only Muslims without documents will face punitive action. When the NRC comes, the onus will be on the Muslim resident of India to prove that he is indeed Indian; those without documents will then be stripped of citizenship, while an undocumented non-Muslim from a foreign country will not need documents to claim citizenship.

Mr Shah argues that the three countries named in the Act have been selected because their official State religion is Islam and non-Muslims face persecution in these countries. The idea that Muslims cannot be persecuted in Muslim countries is absurd: just ask the Ahmediyas and many Shias in Pakistan, or atheist bloggers in Bangladesh, or just individuals who disagree with Islamist communalism, like Taslima Nasreen or Daud Haider, both of whom were given refuge by India in more enlightened times. But there are non-Muslims in those countries who risk persecution and yet have been excluded from the ambit of the law. Atheists, who are often condemned for apostasy in Islamic states, have also been omitted from the law, as have Jews and Baha'is.

A state's official religion or lack thereof does not necessarily correlate with the degree of persecution. For instance, Rohingyas in Myanmar faced genocide, even though Myanmar (which has a Buddhist majority) is not officially a Buddhist country. There are other anomalies and problems with the CAA. Sri Lanka has been excluded, even though Sri Lanka's official religion is Buddhism, and Sri Lankan Tamils, who are mainly Hindus, have faced

THE CITIZENSHIP AMENDMENT ACT

religious and ethnic persecution. Nearly 100,000 have sought refuge in Tamil Nadu, but it seems the BJP is only interested in Hindus who can speak Hindi! Since there is no consistent principle involved, and since the government has no asylum law to establish by an individual assessment whether or not a person faces religious persecution, the government has indeed made an arbitrary classification. That fails the test of fairness that Mr Shah claims his Act passes.

International law recognizes five types of persecution: race, religion, nationality, membership of a particular social group, or political opinion. In 2011, India decided to give long-term visas to persons facing persecution on these grounds as well as two additional grounds—sex and ethnic identity. The Government has not explained why one form of persecution (religious) has more importance than the other six under this new law.

The distinction between a Muslim facing religious persecution and a non-Muslim facing religious persecution is arbitrary. If the Government feels that Muslims in these countries don't face religious persecution, then logically the standard should be that only persons facing religious persecution can apply. If it is a general standard, then everyone's claim of religious persecution can be assessed individually—but the CAA instead presumes persecution based on religious affiliation alone.

The plain fact is that the government has not thought through the implications of its Act. It seems another hasty and arbitrary decision, the sort that Modi has become notorious for—like demonetization in 2016, which the Prime Minister declared would only hurt black-moneyed fat cats, and ended up hurting everyone else; the abrupt midnight imposition of a new nation-wide Goods and Services Tax, which disrupted millions of unprepared and untrained businesses; and the unplanned coronavirus lockdown in 2020, which gave a billion people less than four hours' notice to suspend their lives before shutting down planes, trains, and inter-state transport, causing a crisis of millions of migrant workers trudging home on foot and the loss of over 200 lives. The CAA's declared purpose is one thing; its consequences will create victims among innocent but undocumented Indians. No wonder our thoughtful young people came out into the streets to declare, "not in our name". The spontaneous and long-lasting protests (they went on until finally ended by the national "lockdown" necessitated by the coronavirus contagion) have inspired every democrat in the nation. Students, office-goers, artists, ordinary Indians of every description stood up to be counted.

A University-gold medallist refusing to receive her medal from the Governor of her state in protest; individuals forming a human chain at their gathering so that Muslim protestors could break for their afternoon namaaz;

students speaking passionately in defence of their protests to police and the media; the ordinary women of Shaheen Bagh in Delhi protesting night after night in the bitter cold; and above all ordinary Indians' determination to stand up and continue their resistance, day after day, in the face of all the forces of intimidation arrayed against them by the state—all this elicited admiration, applause, and of course, the inevitable attempts to discredit and intimidate. Amongst these attempts was the predictably crude one by the BJP to delegitimize the protests as being those of Muslims alone. "You can tell who is protesting by their clothes," Prime Minister Modi notoriously declared,[11] clearly implying traditional Muslim attire. "Look at all the beards, skull caps and hijabs at these protests," a ruling-party sympathizer said to me with grim bigotry. "It will just drive more Hindu votes to our side."

Indeed, Muslims were often at the forefront of these protests. It is their place in India, after all, and their rights as Indian citizens, that are being targeted by our divisive government. But they are by no means alone. Many, perhaps more, non-Muslim Indians have joined them, because they see the CAA/NRC as an assault on the India they hold dear.

These Indians realize the importance of Dr B R Ambedkar's sage warning to the nation in the constituent Assembly on 4 November 1948, which we have already quoted, reminding his listeners that the minorities" have loyally accepted the rule of the majority, which is basically a communal majority and not a political majority. It is for the majority to realize its duty not to discriminate against minorities."[12] The "communal majority" Ambedkar referred to is of the community as a whole, which includes all Hindus, and not only political majority of those Hindus voting for the BJP. This communal majority must resist the persistent efforts of the BJP and its supporters to portray the CAA/NRC protests as being of, by, and for Muslims alone. It is no accident that many protestors, of all faiths, have chosen to recite secular nationalist poetry at their protests, and to repeatedly, and with feeling, sing the national anthem. When I inaugurated a rally of the Muslim Coordination Council outside the Raj Bhavan in Thiruvananthapuram, I made it a point to go there from a temple with the sandalwood paste from the priest's prasadam visible on my forehead. The message was: *You are not alone; believing Hindus are with you too.*

It is vital for all Indians to understand what's at stake for the Muslim community, and also for the India of which they are an integral part. The best answer to this assault is to strengthen the support base for the resistance by appealing to all Indians of every faith to support it. That is indeed what most of the protestors did. They understood that you can't fight Hindutva communalism by promoting Muslim communalism. They knew that identity politics will destroy the very India that made them safe in their identities.

The BJP, which prefers to polarize the electorate before every election, is looking for an opportunity to paint this agitation in communal colours, as Hindu vs Muslim. I said to Muslim protestors: Don't give it to them. Don't facilitate the other side's efforts to divide opinion on communal lines. Say you are fighting for your rights as an Indian, and every right-thinking Indian will empathize with you. India's resistance to injustice embraces all communities. I don't have to be Muslim to object to Muslims being discriminated against. By creating a republic where all faiths are safe, India's Constitution protects Muslims as well as others. We're all in this together.

But the incredible assertion by Home Minister Amit Shah, in a response to me in the Lok Sabha in December 2019, that the Citizenship Amendment Act (CAA), which we shall discuss in the next Part, was "necessary" only because in 1947 Congress divided India on religious grounds, was such a breathtaking piece of effrontery that it deserved a response.

My initial reaction was that Mr Shah must not have been paying attention in history class: Had he never heard of Mohammed Ali Jinnah, the "two-nation theory", the Muslim League's Pakistan Resolution of 1940? Could he seriously believe that Partition wasn't the demand of the League, voted for by a significant plurality of India's Muslims in 1946? Did he actually consider that Mahatma Gandhi's Indian National Congress, the flag-bearer for six decades of a united nationalist movement, a party that had been led multiple times by Muslims and actually served under a Muslim President (Maulana Azad) in the crucial period from 1940 to 1945, wished to divide India on religious lines?

Any elementary reading of the history of our nationalist movement will take you to Mohammed Ali Jinnah, the "two-nation theory", and the Muslim League's Pakistan Resolution of 1940—and confirm everything I have just put forward. As we have seen, our nationalist movement did not divide on ideological lines (Marxists versus capitalists, for instance), nor on geographical lines (North versus South); it divided on one principle alone, which was whether religion should be the determinant of nationhood. Partition was the demand of the League, which argued that their religion determined their political identity, a proposition voted for by a significant plurality of India's Muslims in 1946.

But Mahatma Gandhi's Indian National Congress rejected the logic of the League. They argued that religion did not determine Indianness, that their freedom struggle was for the rights of every Indian, and the Constitution they wrote enshrined the principle of equality for Indians of all faiths. How on earth can anybody with even a basic knowledge of the past argue with a straight face that the Congress divided India on religious lines?

But are we really? The BJP's reinvention of Indian nationalism involves, as we have seen, the fabrication of history to serve their ends: this is not really about history, it's about politics. The BJP Home Minister said that his party had no choice but to introduce the CAA since Congress had partitioned the country on grounds of religion—a preposterous argument to historians. But it was propounded only because his BJP, hero-worshippers of V. D. Savarkar, who first propounded the two-nation theory as President of the Hindu Mahasabha before Jinnah seized upon the same idea, had continued its tiresome political tactic of ascribing to the Congress Party responsibility for any error, tragedy, or event that had cast a blight upon the country. Partition was bad, ergo blame it on the Congress.

In an appearance in New Delhi on 13 February 2020, Mr Shah made a second assertion: that a series of statements from 1947, two by Mahatma Gandhi, and one in a resolution of the Congress Working Committee in November that year, demonstrated India's commitment to giving refuge to persecuted Hindu and Sikh refugees from Pakistan—therefore, today's Congress Party was going back on its revered leaders' commitments.

Amit Shah is not alone in distorting history to blame the Congress Party for the sins of others. The BJP employs another variant of this tactic—to say that Congress had already done what it is now attacking the BJP for doing. Thus, the BJP functionary Ram Madhav said in November 2019 that legislation similar to the Citizenship Amendment Bill (CAB) (the precursor to the CAA) "was enacted by the Jawaharlal Nehru government" and that the Congress' 1950 Immigrants (Expulsion from Assam) Act 'establishes' that Jawaharlal Nehru had specifically exempted minorities from being expelled from Assam. According to PTI, Mr Madhav said: "The Nehru government had passed a similar Act in 1950 for expulsion of illegal immigrants from the erstwhile Pakistan and categorically said minorities of East Pakistan wouldn't be [expelled] under the Act".[13]

It hardly needs to be said that this, too, is false and misleading, and that the attempt to compare the 1950 Act with the CAB reveals the opposite. Clause two of the 1950 Act, entitled 'Power to order expulsion of certain immigrants', has the following provision: "Provided that nothing in this section shall apply to *any person* [emphasis added] who on account of civil disturbances or the fear of such disturbances in any area now forming part of Pakistan has been displaced from or has left his place of residence in such area and who has been subsequently residing in Assam".

This provision makes it explicit that the people exempted are *any persons who fear being sent back to Pakistan*—a category that includes people of all religions and not just non-Muslims. Therefore, Mr Madhav's claim that the Nehru Act, like the BJP's, protected only the minorities of East Pakistan, is false. When I moved an amendment in the Lok Sabha suggesting precisely what the 1950 Act did—that instead of mentioning specific religions and excluding others, the CAA merely speak of "persecuted persons"—it was shouted down with vociferous enthusiasm by BJP MPs. The BJP's attempt to mischaracterize the Congress stand of 1947 or 1950 is a cynical and dishonest manoeuvre to score petty political points today.

To return to Mr Shah's statement about the Mahatma's commitments to refugees, it should be said that on this occasion Mr Shah is accurately quoting the Mahatma but the quotes are divorced from context: the Congress did indeed accord refugees fleeing Pakistan during the Partition of the country the rights of Indian citizens, which they had lost not because they had crossed a border but because a border had crossed over them.

No one disagrees with that stand; the Congress Party supported the Mahatma then, and still does. It was nonetheless appalling and distressing to see the Modi government's Home Minister selectively quote the father of our nation, whose ideals have been wilfully disregarded by the BJP, in an attempt to legitimize their desecration of the very national unity Gandhiji gave his life for. By reproducing his utterances without their context, the Home Minister was perpetrating another affront to a man who had spent his lifetime advocating Hindu-Muslim unity, a man who fought till the very end the idea that religion should determine nationhood, which is sadly the idea that the BJP has embraced. If he had continued to quote the Mahatma, Mr Shah would have also found the following words from the same period: "*To drive every Muslim from India...would mean war and eternal ruin for the country. If such a suicidal policy is followed, it would spell the ruin of ...Hinduism in the Union. Good alone can beget good. Love breeds love. As for revenge, it behooves man to leave the evil-doer in God's hands....The idea that India should only belong to Hindus is wrong. That way lies destruction.*"[14]

It is destruction, indeed, to which Mr Shah and the government he is part of is leading us. Ironically enough he found unlikely allies in the most improbable place—across the border—where my denunciation of his ruling party for ushering in a Hindutva version of Pakistan in our country was fiercely condemned by Pakistani liberals. Asad Rehman in *Dawn* and Yasser Latif Hamdani in *The Print* both criticized me by name for venturing to suggest that

Partition was Mr Jinnah's fault. In their telling, the man who had once been hailed by Sarojini Naidu as the ambassador of Hindu-Muslim unity was blameless: it was Hindu illiberalism, and Gandhiji's use of Hindu religious concepts to stir the masses, that had led Jinnah to demand a separate country.

For these Pakistani liberals, their Quaid-e-Azam was an apostle of decency, secularism and liberality, who wished to run Pakistan as a state where minorities could feel totally at home. They do not explain why, then, he wanted a confessional basis for his state, as homeland for India's Muslims. The phrase "two-nation theory", and the attendant bigotry of Mr Jinnah's speeches averring that Muslims are a separate nation, is never mentioned. They cannot explain why, even today, a citizen of Pakistan hailing from a minority community has the words "non-Muslim" stamped on his passport, rather like the yellow Star of David that Jews were obliged to sport in Nazi-occupied Denmark.

No attempt to reinvent Pakistan as an example of enlightened liberalism will wash in the face of its ruling ideology, its odious practices of religious and sectarian discrimination, its procrustean blasphemy laws, and resultant persecution of minorities, especially those from the poorest sections of Pakistani society, its forced conversions of Hindus and Christians, and its incubation of an alphabet soup of Islamist terrorist organizations. Well might Pakistani liberals want to wish these realities away, but this intolerant incubus is precisely what Indian liberals were proud that we were not—and passionately believed we could never be.

So Pakistani liberals, in their anxiety to defend Jinnah, unwittingly give aid and comfort to the political cynicism of Amit Shah, president of a party that expelled the redoubtable Jaswant Singh for hailing Jinnah as a broad-minded hero. Jinnah had many good qualities, but freedom from communal bigotry was not one of them. The fact that Jinnah drank whisky, enjoyed bacon and sausages, and married a Parsi does not make him a liberal—it just makes him a hypocrite.

Hypocrisy, of course, is hardly absent on India's side of the border. But India's liberal Hindus have stood by their Muslim fellow-citizens in resisting the CAA and, at least for now, in thwarting the launching of a nationwide NRC. We believe in an India of pluralism and diversity, not of religious bigotry and identity politics. We believe in an India that is secure in itself and confident of its place in the world, an India that is a proud example of tolerance, freedom and hope for the downtrodden and the marginalized. This is not the "New India" the BJP seeks to create. It is, instead, a betrayal of the country's liberal constitution, and a log on the funeral pyre of India's civic nationalism.

27

KASHMIR AND THE END OF AUTONOMY

As I have noted, Mr Modi likes to practice what American generals call "shock and awe". The most egregious examples of this have been mentioned in the previous chapter—the utterly misguided abrupt demonetization of 86% (in value) of India's currency, and the sudden lockdown of the country against Covid-19 in March 2020—and resulted in consequences that the nation is still dealing with. In August 2019, he added one more to the growing list of dramatic snap decisions whose repercussions he did not appear to have fully calculated.

On 5 August 2019, Mr Modi shocked the nation with an announcement on Kashmir that could well turn out to be the political equivalent of demonetization. After seven decades of assuring the people of Jammu and Kashmir, and the international community, that the state would continue to enjoy special autonomous status under the Indian Constitution, the Modi government announced that day that it had unilaterally divided the state, carving out a Union Territory in the high plateaux and hills of Ladakh in the eastern half of the state, and reducing the remainder—still named Jammu and Kashmir—from the status of a state to that of a Union Territory. The resultant outcry brought the vexed question of Kashmir back onto the top of the international agenda.

When the British quit India in 1947, the 544 "princely states" (nominally ruled by assorted potentates but owing allegiance to the British Raj) were required to accede to either of the two new states, India or Pakistan. The Maharajah of Jammu and Kashmir—a Muslim-majority state with a Hindu ruler—dithered over which of the two to join, and flirted with the idea of remaining independent. Pakistan, determined to wrest the territory, sent in a band of irregulars, who made considerable inroads before being distracted by the attractions of rapine and pillage. The panicked Maharajah, fearing his state would fall to the marauders, acceded to India, which promptly para-dropped troops who stopped the invaders (by now augmented by the Pakistan Army) in their tracks. India took Pakistan's invasion to the UN as an issue of international aggression. When a cease-fire was declared, India was left in possession of roughly two-thirds of the state of Jammu and Kashmir.

To ascertain the wishes of the Kashmiri people, the UN mandated a plebiscite, to be conducted after the Pakistani fighters had withdrawn from the territory they had captured. India had insisted on a popular vote, since the Kashmiri democratic movement, led by the fiery and hugely popular Sheikh Abdullah, was a pluralist movement associated with India's Congress Party rather than with the Muslim League that had demanded the creation of Pakistan, and New Delhi had no doubt that India would win a plebiscite. For the same reason, Pakistan refused to withdraw from the territory it had occupied, and the plebiscite was never conducted. The dispute has festered ever since.

Four wars (in 1948, 1965, 1971 and 1999) have been fought across the cease-fire line, now dubbed the Line of Control (LoC), without materially altering the situation. In the late 1980s, a Pakistan-backed insurrection by some Kashmiri Muslims, augmented by foreign militants infiltrated across the LoC, and supplied with arms and money by Pakistan, began. Both the mili-tancy, and the response to it by Indian security forces, have caused great loss of life, damaged property, and all but wrecked a Kashmiri economy depen-dent largely on tourism and the sale of handicrafts and carpets. In the process, both countries have suffered grievously: India, whose citizens have been killed in large numbers, and which has had to deploy over half a million men under arms to keep the peace, and Pakistan, whose strategy of "bleeding India to death," through insurgency and terrorism, has accomplished little of value, while making its military enormously powerful within Pakistan and dispro-portionately well-resourced (largely thanks to Kashmir, the Pakistani Army controls a larger share of its national budget than any army in the world).

Amid this stalemate, the revocation of Article 370 of the Constitution of India (and of Article 35A, which permitted Kashmir to define its "state sub-jects" and to restrict the rights of others to acquire or inherit property in the state) is meant to be a game-changer. The government's defenders argue that autonomy had only enhanced a sense of separateness in the Kashmir valley, that it had not prevented the region experiencing large-scale separatist vio-lence, that it had permitted a growing Islamicization marked by the ethnic cleansing of the Hindu Pandits from their traditional homes in the Valley, and that the special status prevented progressive Indian laws and court rulings (such as those assuring affirmative action to "Scheduled Castes", the Dalit community) applying to the state. All this is true, but it had happened despite Article 370, not because of it.

The stripping of special status, apologists also argue, would ensure more economic development in the state, since non-Kashmiris would be free to buy land and would invest more freely. Indeed, in the first two weeks since the revocation was announced, the Governor publicly invited out-of-state investors for a conference; big corporations, including India's biggest, Reliance, have conveyed their intention to start projects in the state; and Bollywood producers have been tripping over themselves to book all possible titles for future blockbusters to be made in and about the state. Most distastefully, politicians in other states have suggested their gender-balance problems could be more easily overcome through the import of fair Kashmiri girls.[1] All of these initiatives fizzled out in the sullen lockdown that followed in the area for several months afterwards.

Many, however, worry that, as with demonetization and Modi's Covid-19 strategy, the short- and medium-term damage caused by this decision will greatly outweigh the theoretical long-term benefits. First and foremost, is the violence to India's democratic culture: the government has changed the basic constitutional relationship of the people of Jammu and Kashmir to the Republic of India without consulting them or their elected representatives. Indeed, it locked them up, depriving Kashmiri democrats of the very voices that had spoken for them within the Indian constitutional space. One former Chief Minister, Omar Abdullah, was incarcerated for 232 days; another, Mehbooba Mufti, and veteran Congress leader and former Union Minister, Saifuddin Soz, clocked nearly a year each under house arrest.

It could also be done to other states in the future. The Kashmir episode was a reminder of a timeless lesson—that constitutional promises made by governments should never be broken, especially through manoeuvres that are so questionable, because that sets a precedent that, if emulated elsewhere in the country, could in due course destabilize the whole republic.

The legal sleight of hand that enabled the changing of the status of Jammu and Kashmir was blatant. By claiming that (as the Indian Constitution requires) the concurrence of the State of Jammu and Kashmir was obtained, when it was under the President's Rule, and translating 'State' to mean the Governor New Delhi itself had appointed, the government had, in effect, taken its own consent to amend the Constitution! Worse, the decision was brought to Parliament (where the ruling party's majority guaranteed its prompt passage) without consultation with the local political parties; with the

Jammu and Kashmir state legislature suspended for more than six months; and, with democratically elected political leaders under "preventive" arrest.

There is no question that the legal issues merit more detailed consideration, and the public, which has largely applauded the outcome, needs to be fully apprised about any legal trickery that might have taken place. Equally, the Indian people need to know whether Constitutional provisions were breached or worked around.

A few basic facts: Article 370 was conceived as a temporary measure until the Constituent Assembly of Jammu and Kashmir was formed, and it was left to the Constituent Assembly of J&K to determine the constitutional relationship between the rest of India and the state. It is because the primacy in such matters lies with the people of J&K, that Article 370 (3) states that Article 370 could only cease to exist through a Presidential order *after* obtaining the recommendation of the Constituent Assembly of J&K to end the operation of the article.

The Constituent Assembly of J&K enacted the Constitution of J&K, whose Article 147(c) prevents the state's legislative assembly from doing anything that would affect the constitutional relationship with India, as provided in the Constitution of India. Thus, they accepted Article 370 as the permanent constitutional relationship between the Union and the state, an interpretation upheld in successive Supreme Court judgements.

The permission of the people of J&K, through an elected body, is a condition precedent to interfere with its special status under Article 370. Clause 3 of Article 370 makes it clear that one cannot amend the article without the recommendation of the constituent assembly.

However, the Government tried to be clever, by amending Article 367 to indirectly amend Article 370, saying that the constituent assembly shall mean the legislative assembly. What was the purpose of this amendment? Because it could then argue that due to the operation of the President's rule in the state, the role of the legislative assembly had devolved upon the Parliament in New Delhi—which could give the recommendation instead of the legislative assembly, because the assembly had been dissolved.

However, the Government had completely ignored the well-established position in law that whatever you cannot do directly, you cannot achieve indirectly. It did not have the right to amend Article 370 without obtaining the consent of the people; it, therefore, could not indirectly amend it in the absence of their consent. The Supreme Court has recognized that while something can be formally legal, the substance of it can be unconstitutional, a judgement that on this matter the Supreme Court has, in its wisdom, chosen not to make.

KASHMIR AND THE END OF AUTONOMY

To summarize: By claiming that the concurrence of the state of Jammu and Kashmir had been obtained, when it was under the President's rule; by translating "state" to mean the Governor the Modi government had appointed; and by interpreting "legislature" to mean the Parliament in New Delhi rather than the body elected to represent the views of the people of Jammu and Kashmir, the Central government showed utter contempt for the people of the State, and for the values of democratic decency that are meant to animate our political culture. In many ways, it is a betrayal of the nationalism that made Kashmiris part of the Indian Union. And the general public in the rest of India, in careless disregard of all this, has applauded the "bold" and "decisive" actions taken by Prime Minister Modi in this regard.

Worse, by locking up democratic parties and their leaders, the government has opened up the space for undemocratic forces. The special status accorded to the State served as a fig-leaf to permit a host of Kashmiri leaders to participate in mainstream politics as defenders of autonomy within India. Now this cover has been stripped away; the state's leading politicians have been rendered irrelevant and powerless to stop extremism. New Delhi had claimed that the government was winning the battle against terrorism—but now it may have given a fresh lease of life to the terrorists, a new injustice for them to cite. The signs are that it may drive more misguided young Kashmiris to join them than ever before and place more of India's brave and beleaguered soldiers in harm's way. Indeed, official figures suggest they already have, judging by the news filtering in of "encounters" in which Indian soldiers and police have lost their lives fighting the very terrorists this move claimed to be eliminating.

Even if the government's lawyers can convince the Supreme Court (where their actions have predictably been challenged) that it is upholding the letter of the law, this action goes against the spirit of Indian democracy and has rightly been described as an act of "garrison governance". Even during the Covid-19 pandemic, the communications blockade in the valley was persisted with, hampering efforts to contain the transmission of the virus. The "lockdown within a lockdown" and the continuing militant violence belittles the government's claims of their constitutional changes being intended to bring about prosperity and economic growth, while also highlighting the growing feeling among Kashmiris that they are second-class citizens. Those of us who have long seen India's democratic diversity as its greatest strength are now confronted by a government that is determined to erase all signs of it and shows scant respect for the Constitution. It is an ominous time for India's pluralists and democrats, its minorities and dissenters.

The precedent this entire affair sets for our democracy is ominous and worrying. Let no one say we have not been cautioned.

* * *

As happens all too often in our country these days, the past was evoked to fight the political battles of the present. The parliamentary debates on the abolition of Article 370 in Kashmir proved no exception. The ruling dispensation's favourite whipping boy, our first Prime Minister Jawaharlal Nehru, again came in for attack, with several BJP legislators criticizing and demonizing Nehru by name and alleging the Kashmir problem was his personal creation. Had Sardar Patel handled Kashmir, they averred, all of Kashmir would have been ours and there would have been no Article 370 to worry about today.

That was an odd claim, because it is a matter of historical record that when dealing with the three contested princely states within India which hesitated to accede to our Union—either because they wanted independence (Hyderabad and Kashmir), or because, defying geography and demography, they wished to join Pakistan (Junagadh)—Nehru and Patel worked together as a team in all three cases. Patel, in fact, was inclined to consider trading Kashmir for the other two, but Nehru would have none of it.[2] Once Pakistan sought to take Kashmir over by force, first by sending armed "irregulars" and then by dispatching its army, Patel was resolute in negotiating the state's accession, sending his aide, V. P. Menon, to win the agreement of the besieged Maharajah.[3]

As to Article 370, the BJP has repeatedly alleged that Nehru came up with it on his own and that Sardar Patel had nothing to do with it. But, in fact, Nehru did not do anything on his own. Maharajah Hari Singh's Instrument of Accession only covered defence, foreign affairs and communications; in Article 7 of the Instrument, he explicitly reserved the right to negotiate other constitutional terms. Though his monarchical despotism was stoutly resisted by the popular leader, Sheikh Abdullah, on this point the Sheikh did not disagree with the Maharajah.

On 15 and 16 October 1949, meetings took place among Sardar Vallabhbhai Patel, Jawaharlal Nehru, and Sheikh Abdullah in the house of Sardar Patel in New Delhi. The Cabinet Minister without Portfolio who was looking after Kashmir, its former Dewan, N. Gopalaswami Ayyangar, took detailed notes. He sent a summary of the notes of these conclusions to Sardar Patel on the 16th itself with the following covering note: *"Will you kindly let*

Jawaharlal Ji know your approval of it? He will issue the letter to Sheikh Abdullah only after receiving your approval."[4]

That approval came the next day from Sardar Patel. Only then was article 370 brought into the Constitution of India on 17 October 1949. In other words, Sardar Patel was party to Article 370 in every detail.

The irony is that only in the parallel universe of the BJP's reinvention of modern Indian history is this even a debateable subject. These records have now been declassified and made available; many scholars have referred to it. Files, notes, minutes of meetings, diaries, and official documents from the period are all open for the scrutiny of historians in the National Archives. Only in Indian politics could controversies be made out of such issues in the face of available documentary evidence.

With Article 370 now having been done away with, all this is now relegated to history. But it is only fitting that we should let the man whom the BJP has depicted as the villain of this saga—the towering nationalist who did so much to win us our Independence and consolidate it, Jawaharlal Nehru, have the last word. What did he say on this subject? *"I say with all respect to our Constitution that it just does not matter what your Constitution says,"* he pointed out in Parliament. *"If the people of Kashmir do not want it, it will not go there. Because what is the alternative? The alternative is compulsion and coercion...*"[5]

And he added in the Lok Sabha in August 1952, exactly 67 years before the BJP government undid the carefully-crafted arrangements that brought Jammu and Kashmir into the Indian Union: *"We have fought the good fight about Kashmir on the field of battle... (and) ...in many a chancellery of the world and in the United Nations, but, above all, we have fought this fight in the hearts and minds of men and women of that State of Jammu and Kashmir. Because, ultimately—I say this with all deference to this Parliament—the decision will be made in the hearts and minds of the men and women of Kashmir; neither in this Parliament, nor in the United Nations nor by anybody else."*[6]

This is sage advice we should all remember today.

Another Indian politician, the socialist leader Jayaprakash Narayan ("JP"), a staunch critic of Nehru's, came to the same conclusion through a different route. JP talked about Kashmiri self-determination within the broader context of global decolonization. In an October 1968 speech in Srinagar, he argued that "the right to self-determination, viewed against" the changes in the world since 1947, "needs to be interpreted afresh in keeping with [the] needs of the people of Kashmir". JP defined self-determination as "the inherent right of every people to determine their ways of life and the form and character of their institutions".[7] But within post-colonial states, which themselves had come into being on a basis of national self-determination and anti-colonial nationalism, the question of self-determination became "an extremely complicated matter". Around the world, "existing nation-states, no matter how haphazardly created, doggedly fight against any of their 'peoples' wanting to break away or to exercise their right to self-determination."

How could one reconcile these two concerns? For JP, the special opportunity arose from the fact that a minority religion in India was the majority in Kashmir. This made him suggest that Kashmir's "majority minority status" might offer a model to the rest of India. Others disagreed: as early as 1963, an Assamese political party warned that East Bengali migration into Assam would create "another 'Kashmir'…by making Assam a Muslim majority state". But inspired by the spirit of Sarvodaya, JP sought to make majority/minority status a strength, rather than a flaw. As Lydia Walker explains it, JP felt that "negotiating the shape of a Kashmir within India defines not only Kashmir, but also India itself".[8] Of course, for JP as for Nehru, the presence of a Muslim-majority Kashmir within India made impossible the Hindutva version of narrow-minded nationalism, even as it made the possibility of future Muslim-majority districts or states reconcilable to the national project.

28

SOFT-SIGNALLING BIGOTRY

At a pre-election rally in 2019 in Wardha in central India, Narendra Modi took to the stage to publicly decry then-Congress President Rahul Gandhi's decision to contest from Wayanad in Kerala, by suggesting that he was "running away from majority-dominated areas" to "take refuge in areas where the majority is in minority".[1] Inspired, his colleagues were quick to parrot their leader's line. Union Minister Ravi Shankar Prasad said Rahul Gandhi may have found Wayanad a "safe seat" since "only 49 per cent of the population… is Hindu"; then-party President Amit Shah called Wayanad a place 'where when a procession is taken out, you cannot make out whether it is India or Pakistan';[2] and UP's Chief Minister Adityanath remarked that the Congress believes that 'Ali (Prophet Mohammed's son-in-law) will help them in the polls…but we think that Bajarang Bali (Lord Hanuman) will help us'.[3]

This was not the first instance where Modi had targeted the Congress leader or the party in such a manner. At an earlier stage, when he publicly derided Rahul Gandhi, then vice president of the party, as a princeling, he did not use the Hindi term 'Rajkumar', preferring the Persian and Urdu 'Shehzada', as if to further damn Gandhi by association with Islamic terminology. When Rahul was appointed party President in December 2017, Modi insinuated that his appointment would mark the beginning of an 'Aurangzeb Raj' in the party.[4] More frequently, Modi has not shied away from labelling the Congress as a party of 'Muslim men' (and also an 'anti-Hindu' party) and has on multiple occasions reiterated his hollow accusation of the Congress's 'minority appeasement.' To be sure, Modi's deplorable obsession with peddling this divisive cocktail of communal messaging is not a new trend and has been documented several times in the last decade. But it is still remarkable how pronounced his bigotry gets when an election is around the corner.

In the immediate aftermath of the 2002 Godhra riots, when Gujarat was going to the polls, as the BJP's CM candidate, Modi openly suggested that there was an active collaboration between Muslims in the state and Pakistani chief 'Mian' Musharraf. Then, in September 2002, while campaigning during his Gujarat Gaurav Yatra, on the note of family planning, Modi mocked Muslims in his state with his 'Hum paanch, hamaare pachees' ("we are five, but we have 25") comment—suggesting that Muslims were out to multiply their numbers to reverse their minority status in the state. In the 2009 and the 2017 campaigns, the 'Mian' barb was resurrected, this time as 'Ahmed Mian', a reference to the faith of Congress leader Ahmed Patel.

Even constitutional authorities have not been spared: Modi has not previously demurred from targeting the Election Commission itself. As I have remarked earlier, he attacked former CEC J. M Lyngdoh on multiple occasions for standing in his way. In the 2002 campaign, when the EC, wary of communal tensions in Gujarat, refused Modi's call for early elections, the latter who was then CM, launched a barely veiled tirade against Lyngdoh, highlighting his Christian faith and suggesting that he was favouring minorities in the state by not calling for early elections, prompting a sharp dressing down from his own party colleague and then Prime Minister Atal Behari Vajpayee.[5]

This is not just a diatribe about how Modi and his BJP have lowered the level of political discourse in India; it is to point out how exactly he does it. In cricket nowadays, the umpires use a "soft signal" when they are unsure of a verdict on an appeal but want to convey to the TV umpire what they really think. This is exactly what Modi is up to: he actively signals his bigotry to his base without necessarily being overt about his distaste for minorities.

During the 2015 Bihar state elections, there was his exhortation not to vote for the 'beef-eating' RJD.[6] Two years later, in Uttar Pradesh, there was his 'kabristan-shamshaan' comment and his 'If there is electricity during Ramzaan there should be electricity during Diwali' (innocuous enough till one recognises the implicit communal message packaged within).[7] In the same year, during the 2017 Gujarat state elections, Modi repeatedly accused his predecessor, Manmohan Singh, and former VP, Hamid Ansari, of colluding with Pakistan with the aim of defeating the BJP in the state elections.[8] Both statements were designed with the specific intent of polarizing the electorate prior to the elections. In 2018, in the midst of the Karnataka state elections, Modi hit out at the Congress' 'celebration of the jayantis of Sultans',[9] a reference to the celebration of Tipu Jayanti in the state.[10] Tipu was, of course, a Muslim ruler.

This brings us to the foundational paradox of Narendra Modi that I have documented extensively in my book *The Paradoxical Prime Minister*. It is striking that the Modi who assured a gathering of Muslim leaders in 2015 that even if they were to knock on his doors at midnight, he would respond, is the same Modi who refuses to wear a Muslim skullcap when one is presented to him (while cheerfully donning all manner of exotic headgear wherever he goes). Silence is also a weapon of soft-signalling: when he refuses to condemn instances of communal violence, he implicitly condones it.[11] This is not behaviour worthy of a true nationalist, who ought to be resolute against anything that would divide his nation and so weaken it.

The Modi who has effusively embraced Muslim heads of state in the Arab world, is the same Modi who keeps Indian Muslims at an arm's length. As has been stated, the BJP is the first governing party in the history of independent India to come to power without a single elected Muslim member of the Lok Sabha, including from Uttar Pradesh, which contributes eighty of these seats, and where nearly a fifth of the population are Muslims. The very fact that the BJP finds itself unable to put up electable Muslim candidates in any constituency speaks volumes about the party's attitude to Muslims and of the attitudes of Indian Muslims to it—as well as of the views of its core voters, whose bigotry would not predispose them to vote for a Muslim, not even one contesting on their own party's symbol.

Ideally, Modi should stop this divisive and infantile practice. The incumbent of the country's top post must be above such bigotry: his language should demonstrate an appreciation that a prime minister of India must be a leader of all Indians and not one with an ostentatiously-displayed blind spot for certain minorities. Our country deserves better than the BJP's torch bearer for bigotry that Modi has become, as a result of which he has lost the moral integrity to lead this nation. Yet if Hindu nationalism is what the PM aspires to, his signals may not really be that soft after all. With the government on a warpath against the fundamental assumptions of the Indian republic, the unspoken fear among the country's democrats is that the worst is yet to come.

29

AYODHYA

ENSHRINING HINDU RASHTRA

The renegotiation of the past in the Modi era towards the construction of a Hindu state reached its zenith, from the point of view of BJP supporters, when the Supreme Court, after eight years of deliberations, finally settled one of the most protracted inter-religious conflicts in India's turbulent history, with its verdict in 2019 on a disputed site in Ayodhya.

Ayodhya, a dusty town in India's largest state, Uttar Pradesh, acquired international prominence when, in 1992, as I have mentioned earlier, a howling mob of Hindu extremists tore down a Muslim mosque, the Babri Masjid, which occupied a prominent spot in a town otherwise overflowing with temples. The mosque had been built in the 1520s by a Muslim noble, Mir Baqi, in the name of India's first Mughal emperor, Babur, on a site traditionally believed to have been the birthplace of the Hindu god-king Ram, the hero of the 3000-year-old epic, the Ramayana. The Hindu zealots who destroyed the temple vowed to replace it with a temple to Ram. In other words, they wanted to avenge history by undoing the alleged shame of half a millennium ago.

India is a land where history, myth, and legend often overlap; sometimes we, as a people, cannot tell the difference. Many Hindus claim the Babri Masjid stood on the exact spot of Ram's birth and had been placed there by Babur to remind a conquered people of their subjugation. However, many historians argue that there is no proof that Babur demolished a Ram temple to build his mosque. Popular sentiment amongst Hindus rose, clamouring for the status quo to be changed, and was seized upon by the BJP in the mid-1980s to resurrect the party's fortunes. A nationwide "rath yatra" led by party President L.K. Advani, calling for the mosque to be replaced by a temple, whipped up passions across north India. A"Ram shilan puja" was inaugurated, requiring Hindus in every village and town across the Hindi heartland to bake consecrated bricks to be transported to Ayodhya to construct a temple. A number of riots broke out, one of which I have anatomized in some detail in my 2001 novel, *Riot*. In vain did rationalists and secular democrats plead with the agitators to let old wounds heal: to destroy the mosque and replace it with a temple, they averred, was not righting an old wrong but perpetrating a new one.

The Archaeological Survey of India, however, confirmed the existence of the ruins of an ancient temple beneath the demolished mosque—though no one could be sure it was a temple to Ram. (One of the archaeologists on the team was a Muslim, Dr K. K. Muhammad, who has published and spoken extensively about the findings.) This provided further fuel to the Hindutva campaign. In December 1992, the government of Prime Minister Narasimha Rao requested the President of India to seek the opinion of the Supreme Court on the question of "whether a Hindu temple or any other religious structure existed prior to the construction of the Ramjanmabhoomi-Babri Masjid". It took the Court two years of reflection to respond that this question was "superfluous and unnecessary and does not require to be answered". In the meantime, a howling, chanting mob assaulted the mosque and reduced it to rubble, setting off a fresh wave of rioting that claimed hundreds of lives, including in a series of bomb blasts a thousand kilometres away, in Bombay.

The question that now arose was what was to be done with the ruins: restore the largely unused mosque, construct a temple on the site, or find a different solution for the premises altogether. Politicians unanimously ducked, deciding to leave this inflammatory issue to the courts. The dispute remained intractable, and dragged on interminably through various levels of the judiciary. A 2010 verdict of the High Court of Uttar Pradesh, the state in which Ayodhya is located, proposed rather Solomonically to divide the disputed property three ways, a solution acceptable to none of the disputants. All the litigants appealed to the Supreme Court, where the matter was finally resolved in late 2019, nearly twenty-seven years after the mosque's destruction.

The court judgement gives the disputed site to a Trust to be established by the central government to build and operate a Ram temple, thus satisfying Hindus, while righting the wrong done to Muslims by requiring the State to provide five acres of land at an unspecified "prominent site" in Ayodhya for a new mosque. The outcome means that a land dispute that featured the criminal destruction of property has been settled in favour of the destroyers, but it is a measure of the issues at stake that those who lost out in the judge-ment—the Muslims of the area—held their peace.

The Supreme Court's judgement was greeted with widespread appeals across political lines to respect the verdict, in the hope that it would finally bring closure to this contentious issue. Though many were troubled that a mere "land dispute" should have been given such high priority by the Court, and others questioned the contradiction implicit in the Court's describing the mosque's destruction as criminal vandalism but awarding the disputed land to the Hindu side anyway, the broad consensus in the country was that, at a time when so much of India's social fabric was under stress, all con-cerned should accept the Supreme Court's judgement as the last word on this matter.

The Supreme Court verdict both affirmed and undermined India's civic nationalism. The Court ruled that a Ram Mandir should be built on the spot, and that the religious sentiments of the Hindus had to be respected—imply-ing both that such sentiments were of greater weight than legal provisions, and that the religious sentiments of the minorities were of less consequence than that of the majority, even though the demolition of the Babri Masjid was illegal. This has led some commentators to speak of "judicial majoritarian-ism—or even judicial populism".[1] On the other hand, by settling the matter in a detailed judgement, the Court's decision can be seen as an affirmation of constitutional processes, restoring the balance after the vandalism and vio-lence that had marked the dispute for a generation.

To most Indian Muslims, the dispute is not about a specific mosque; the Babri Masjid had lain largely unused for half a century before its destruction, most of Ayodhya's Muslims having emigrated to Pakistan in 1947. Rather, it was about their place in Indian society. The destruction of the mosque felt like an utter betrayal of the compact that had sustained the Muslim commu-nity as a vital part of India's pluralist democracy. Its replacement by a temple will seem to many a humiliating insult. Others, however, feel it will buy peace for the community, taking an issue off the table that had poisoned Hindu-Muslim relations across north India. With Ayodhya settled, many hope the Hindus will have no major reason to pursue claims of "revenge" against Muslims. For several decades the road to Paradise for both sets of believers had stumbled into the pothole of Purgatory. What the highest court did was to craft a solution that no political process could have arrived at indepen-dently, but took the dispute off the streets. Otherwise the violence might have gone on, spawning new hostages to history, ensuring that future genera-tions would be taught new wrongs to set right.

The Court's verdict should ideally be seen as the start of a process of healing for a nation that must come together as one. The fact that this longstanding dispute has been resolved with a judicial decision and not another communal riot, reminds the country that democratic India can overcome its most fundamental difficulties within the rule of law and in the spirit of oneness that animated the nation's struggle for freedom. At the same time its projection as a triumph for a reinterpretation of the Indian national idea, and as a building block in the construction of a new Hindutva version of India, remains deeply troubling.

What is important, therefore, is for India to rededicate itself today to the remnants of its civic nationalism, strained but not shattered by the dispute. It is still possible to affirm the best ideals for which our nation has stood—democracy, unity and faith in the indestructible pluralist ethos of India. And in so doing, Ayodhya could still permit India to leave behind a problem of the 16th century as it makes its way through the 21st.

PART FIVE

THE ANXIETY OF NATIONHOOD

As is evident from the preceding sections, Indian nationalism, in precept and practice, had acquired a significantly identifiable character in the decades after the country won freedom but is being pressed to undergo fundamental change today. During the anti-colonial struggle against the British, the nationalist movement had many of the characteristics of classic ethno-cultural national-ism—the Indian people, harking back to their ancient civilization, fought for self-determination against the foreign oppressor. Upon Independence, and with the writing of a secular and liberal democratic Constitution, India's nationalism became a form of civic nationalism, though no political leader specifically used the term. Today, with the ascent of a "Hindi-Hindu[tva]-Hindustan" sentiment in the ruling circles of the country, India's nationalism is being forced to change into a combination of religious, linguistic, and cul-tural nationalism, its liberal-democratic trappings increasingly discarded in the pursuit of a loyal conformity that alone, in the eyes of the dominant establishment, is acceptable as truly nationalist.

To what degree can the version of nationalism propagated by the Modi government be reconciled with what had been built up, promoted and cele-brated in the preceding nearly seven decades of independence? The decision of Prime Minister Modi to embrace Mahatma Gandhi points to one possible approach: to subsume icons of the previous conception of Indian nationalism into the revised Hindutva version. Gandhiji was an unabashed Hindu, who unhesitatingly adopted the symbols and imagery of his faith in advocating an inclusive Indianness. Might this permit the "Hindu nationalists" an entry point into arrogating his legacy for themselves?

235

30

GANDHI'S HINDUISM VS HINDUTVA

At the present time, Mahatma Gandhi's idea of India—the very idea of Gandhi, one might say—is in danger of being swept aside by prevailing ideological currents. Today, when the standing of his historic detractors is at an all-time high, Gandhiji has been criticized for weakness, for having bent over too far to accommodate Muslim interests, and for his pacifism, which is seen by the jingoistic Hindutva movement as unmanly.

The Mahatma was killed, with the name of Rama on his lips, for being too pro-Muslim; indeed, he had just come out of a fast he had conducted to coerce his own followers, the ministers of the new Indian government, to transfer a larger share than they had intended of the assets of undivided India to the new state of Pakistan. Gandhiji had also announced his intention to spurn the country he had failed to keep united, and to spend the rest of his years in Pakistan, a prospect that had thrown the spluttering government of Pakistan collectively into a green funk.

But that was the enigma of Gandhiji in a nutshell: idealistic, quirky, quixotic, and determined, a man who answered to the beat of no other drummer, but got everyone else to march to his tune. Someone once called him a cross between a saint and a Tammany Hall politician; like the best crossbreeds, he managed to distil all the qualities of both and yet transcend their contradictions.

In his immortal 'Tryst with Destiny' speech to the nation on the midnight of 15 August 1947, Jawaharlal Nehru spoke of the Mahatma as "embodying the old spirit of India" whose message would be remembered by "succeeding generations."

What was that message? The Mahatma was the extraordinary leader of the world's first successful non-violent movement for independence from colonial rule. At the same time, he was a philosopher who was constantly seeking to live out his own ideas, whether they applied to individual self-improvement or social change: his autobiography was typically subtitled 'The Story of My Experiments with Truth'.

No dictionary imbues "truth" with the depth of meaning Gandhi gave it. His truth emerged from his convictions: it meant not only what was accurate, but what was just and, therefore, right. Truth could not be obtained by "untruthful" or unjust means, which included inflicting violence upon one's opponent. To describe his method, Gandhi coined the expression satya-graha—literally, "holding on to truth" or, as he variously described it, truth-force, love-force or soul-force. He disliked the English term "passive resis-tance" because satyagraha required activism, not passivity. If you believed in the truth and cared enough to obtain it, Gandhi felt, you could not afford to be passive: you had to be prepared actively to suffer for the truth.

So non-violence, like many later concepts labelled with a negation, from non-cooperation to non-alignment, meant much more than the denial of an opposite; it did not merely imply the absence of violence. Non-violence was the way to vindicate the truth not by the infliction of suffering on the oppo-nent, but on one's self. It was essential to willingly accept punishment in order to demonstrate the strength of one's convictions.

This was the approach Gandhi brought to the movement for India's inde-pendence—and it worked. Where sporadic terrorism and moderate consti-tutionalism had both proved ineffective, Gandhi took the issue of freedom to the masses as one of simple right and wrong and gave them a technique to which the British had no response. By abstaining from violence, Gandhi wrested the moral advantage. By breaking the law non-violently, he showed up the injustice of the law. By accepting the punishments imposed on him, he confronted his captors with their own brutalization. By voluntarily imposing suffering upon himself in his hunger-strikes, he demonstrated the lengths to which he was prepared to go in defence of what he considered to be right. In the end, he made the perpetuation of British rule an impossibility.

What lessons does Gandhi offer to us in today, beyond their historical reso-nance? One thing must be faced: Gandhiji's approach could only work against opponents vulnerable to a loss of moral authority—a government responsive to domestic and international public opinion, capable of being shamed into conceding defeat. Equally, that approach required freedom-fighters to possess moral authority, too. The power of Gandhian non-violent civil disobedience rested in being able to say, "to show you that you are wrong, I punish myself." Gandhism, without moral authority on both sides, is like Marxism without a proletariat. Yet that is what we are confronted with in the Modi era—a ruler incapable of shame seeking to drape himself in the moral authority of he who once evoked it.

None of this dilutes Gandhi's greatness, or the extraordinary resonance of his life and his message. While the world was disintegrating into fascism, violence and war, the Mahatma taught the virtues of truth, non-violence and peace. He destroyed the credibility of colonialism by opposing principle to force. And, he set and attained personal standards of conviction and courage which few will ever match. He was that rare kind of leader who was not confined by the inadequacies of his followers.

Yet Gandhi's truth was essentially his own. He formulated its unique content, and determined its application in a specific historical context. Inevitably, few in today's world can measure up to his greatness or aspire to his credo. The originality of his thought, and the example of his life, inspires people around the world today, but we still have a lot to learn from Gandhiji. One wonders if, beyond lip service, we really have.

The lip-service is evident in the attitude of the Hindutva-inspired government of Mr Modi. He was schooled, like other RSS pracharaks, in an intense dislike of Mahatma Gandhi, whose message of tolerance and pluralism was emphatically rejected as minority appeasement by the Sangh Parivar, and whose credo of non-violence, or ahimsa, was seen as an admission of weakness unworthy of manly Hindus. Hindutva ideologue V.D. Savarkar, whom Modi has described as one of his heroes, had expressed contempt for Gandhiji's 'perverse doctrine of non-violence and truth' and claimed it 'was bound to destroy the power of the country'.[1] But Prime Minister Modi, for all his Hindutva mindset, his admiration of Savarkar, and his lifetime affiliation to the Sangh Parivar, has hailed the Mahatma, even using his glasses as a symbol of the Swachh Bharat campaign, linking it to a call to revive Gandhiji's idea of *seva* (service) through the government's 'Swachchta Hi Seva' Campaign.

These may, or may not, represent a sincere conversion to Gandhism. PM Modi is hardly unaware of the tremendous worldwide reputation that Mahatma Gandhi enjoys, and is too savvy a marketing genius not to recognize the soft-power opportunity invoking Gandhiji provides, not to mention the global public relations disaster that would ensue if he were to denounce an Indian so universally admired. Rather like Indian maharajas of earlier eras who concocted genealogies to link themselves to older dynasties, cities, and traditions, in order to create a narrative that would allow them legitimacy, Mr Modi has shown a decided taste for borrowed plumage. He started using for himself, with minor emendation, but without acknowledgement, Nehru's

1947 coinage of the term "Pratham Sevak" (First Servant)[2] as a substitute for "Pradhan Mantri" (Prime Minister; Modi preferred "Pradhan Sevak" which means the same thing); he had already, as we have seen, sought to drape himself in the raiment of Sardar Patel; and, as a Gujarati, he clearly saw merit in tracing some sort of descent, however elliptical, from Mahatma Gandhi. There may, therefore, be an element of insincerity to his newfound love for the Mahatma, as well as a shrewd domestic political calculation.

But the ambivalence speaks volumes: when many members of Modi's BJP call for replacing Gandhiji's statues across the country with those of his assassin, Nathuram Godse, the PM seeks to lay claim to the mantle of his fellow Gujarati for his own political benefit. At the same time, there is also a tangible dissonance between the official governmental embrace of Gandhiji and the unofficial ideological distaste for this icon, that is privately promoted by members and supporters of the present ruling party, some of whose members have not hidden their view that his assassination was, in their eyes, a patriotic act. Even the Mahatma's declared intention, shortly before his assassination, to spend his remaining days in Pakistan, sits uncomfortably with a party whose leaders' favourite imprecation for its critics is "Go to Pakistan!"

It is well understood that the vision of Gandhiji, an openly practising Hindu, differed greatly from that of his fellow Hindus V. D. Savarkar and M. S. Golwalkar, the principal ideologues of the Hindu Mahasabha and its more militarized alter ego in the post-independence era, the RSS and eventually, the BJP. His Hinduism, open, eclectic and accepting of difference, could have lent itself to a different form of "Hindu nationalism", or a civic nationalism imbued with his Hindu values, and so well suited to managing the diversity of India. But Gandhiji was far too inclusive to have qualified his nationalism with a communal adjective. Savarkar, who had little use for Hindu religious beliefs and practices except as a label for identity formation, never thought much of Gandhi's faith or the principle of non-violence that merged from it. To the Hindutvavadi, nationalism cannot be non-violent because in order to succeed it needs to be coercive and destructive of enemies, and when it succeeds it is expressed through the apparatus of the state, which has a monopoly over violence. Despite being a far more deeply rooted Hindu than Savarkar, Mahatma Gandhi has little place in the Hindutva imagination. Gandhiji embodied the central approach of Advaita Vedanta, which preached an inclusive universal religion. Despite the recent controversy about his earlier views on black Africans (expressed as a young man when he was specifically fighting only for the rights of the Indian community in South Africa), Gandhiji was neither racist nor sectarian—he saw Hinduism as a faith that respected and embraced all other races and faiths. He was profoundly influ-enced by the principles of *ahimsa* (non-violence) and *satya* (truth) and gave both a profound meaning when he applied them to the nationalist cause. He was a synthesizer of cultural belief systems: his signature bhajan of *Raghupati Raghava Raja Ram* had the second line *Ishwara Allah Tero Naam*. This practice emerged from his Vedantic belief in the oneness of all human beings, who share the same atman and therefore should be treated equally.

Such behaviour did not endear him to every Hindu. In his treatise on 'Gandhi's Hinduism and Savarkar's Hindutva' the social scientist Rudolf Heredia places his two protagonists within an ongoing debate between het-erogeneity versus homogeneity in the Hindu faith, pointing out that while Gandhi's response is inclusive and ethical, Savarkar politicizes Hinduism as a majoritarian creed.[3]

But Gandhiji's own understanding of religion, in Heredia's words, "tran-scended religiosity, Hindu as well as that of any other tradition. It is essen-tially a spiritual quest for *moksha* but one rooted in the reality of service to the last and least in the world". Unlike Savarkar, who believed in conformity, Gandhiji was a synthesizer like no other who took care to include Indians of other faiths in his capacious and agglomerative understanding of religion. He took inspiration from not just Advaita Vedanta but also the Jain concept of 'Anekantavada'—the notion that truth and reality are perceived differently by different people from their own different points of view, and that there-fore, no single perception can constitute the complete truth. This led him to once declare that 'I am a Hindu, a Muslim, a Christian, a Parsi, a Jew'. The Mahatma was profoundly moved by an image of Christ on the crucifix in the Sistine Chapel, which he visited during his stopover in Rome while returning home from the failed Second Round Table Conference in London in 1931. He stood there a long time in contemplation and later told an aide: "So deep an impression did that crucifix make on me that it stands out all alone in my mind, and I remember nothing else of my visit to the Vatican."[4]

Hinduism and Hindutva, as I have argued in my recent book *Why I Am a Hindu*, represent two very distinct and contrasting ideas, with vitally different implications for nationalism and the role of the Hindu faith. The principles Gandhiji stood for and the way in which he asserted them are easier to admire than to follow. But they represented an ideal that is betrayed every day by those who distort Hinduism to promote a narrow, exclusionary bigotry.

31

BHARAT VS INDIA

Having explored Gandhiji's Hinduism and vision for India, let us briefly revisit the unpalatable alternative Savarkar, the founding ideologue of Hindutva, offered as an all-embracing credo. Hindutva, as set out in his books and other utterances, was about Hindus rendering "whole-hearted love to our common Mother [India]". As he wrote in his 1922 book, *Hindutva: Who is a Hindu?* 'To be a Hindu means a person who sees this land, from the Indus River to the sea, as his country but also as his Holy Land.' As I have mentioned earlier, Savarkar included within the 'Hindu' fold, in his *Essentials of Hindutva* (1923), any Muslim or Christian who so embraces his idea; it is possible, he writes, for Muslims and Christians to make a choice, "a choice of love". *Essentials of Hindutva* was written as a sentimental love letter to the country, reimagining it through religious ritual and mythology that had been eclipsed by the British, and endowing it with the sacredness of *punya* (merit), a term from the Hindu scriptures. Yet, Savarkar conflated this romantic vision of his homeland with European ideas of the modern state and the modern idea of nationality, together constituting the ideology of Hindutva.

In an attempt to realize the vision of Savarkar and other Hindutva ideologues, the edifice of religious nationalism is being relentlessly constructed in the Modi government's second term. The criminalization of triple talaaq, the abrogation of Article 370, the shutting down of the internet in Jammu & Kashmir, amid the detention of Kashmiri political leaders, the triumphal movement to build a Ram temple in Ayodhya, the Citizenship Amendment Act, and the proposed nationwide National Register of Citizens, are each building blocks in an overt project to show Muslims (and by extension, other minorities) their place in a Hindu nation. These are all precursors to the creation of a second-class citizenship that the statements of some BJP leaders suggest may be on its way. They have been accompanied by a daily toll of petty and not-so-petty incidents and humiliations, lynchings in the name of cow protection, repeated statements of anti-Muslim bias, and strategic silences whenever Muslim rights are violated, that underscore the same message. Anti-Muslim riots are accompanied by the chanting of vicious mob slogans during the rampage, like "Mussalman ka ek hi sthan—Kabristan ya Pakistan" (There's only one place for a Muslim—the graveyard, or Pakistan). As the commentator Samar Halarnkar remarked dispiritedly: "It is difficult, these days, to keep up with and feel outrage against the verbal and physical attacks, boycotts and other forms of prejudice to which Indian Muslims are subject. The overwhelming feeling is despair and disquiet."[1]

While the older Indian nationalist leadership prided itself on its domestic management of diversity and sought global recognition and admiration for the success of the country's large Muslim minority, the newer Hindutva elite, speaking principally (and often, only) in Hindi, and declaiming the glories of Bharat in time-honoured religious allegories and allusions, couldn't care less: it goes about its majoritarian ways indifferent to their impact on India's standing in the world.

The oldest and tiredest cliché of contemporary political discourse is the duality between "Bharat" and "India"—Bharat, rustic, poor, and unlettered, yet timeless and authentic, versus the cosmopolitan, urban, modern, but deracinated and superficial, liberal India to which readers of a book like this largely belong. Many Hindutva leaders have stressed this distinction, indeed made a virtue out of it. When a medical student was raped and murdered in Delhi in 2012, RSS chief Mohan Bhagwat said: "Such crimes hardly take place in Bharat, but they occur frequently in India… Where 'Bharat' becomes 'India,' with the influence of Western culture, these types of incidents happen."[2] Depressingly, in this incident, it was products of Bharat who raped and killed a young girl trying to rise above the limitations of her life opportunities to enter the world of India.

And yet how real is that division? After all, don't the two Indias meet all the time—for instance in politics, in the media, in cinema halls, and on the cricket field? The Indian-origin writer Aatish Taseer does not think so, or at least thinks the decline of one is terminal. The Indian elite, he writes, "thought they lived in a world where the 'idea of India' reigned supreme—but all the while, the constituency for this idea was being steadily eroded. It was Bharat that was ascendant. India's leaders today speak with contempt of the principles on which this young nation was founded. They look back instead to the timeless glories of the Hindu past. They scorn the 'Khan Market gang' …that has become a metonym for the Indian elite. Hindu nationalists trace a direct line between the foreign occupiers who destroyed the Hindu past—first Muslims, then the British—and India's Westernized elite (and India's Muslims), whom they see as heirs to foreign occupation, still enjoying the privileges of plunder."[3] These words seem to place "Bharat" in the Hindutva camp, and "India" in the civic-nationalist one, a distinction underscored in the infructuous attempt by a pro-government lawyer in June 2020 to get the Supreme Court to replace the constitutional name "India" with "Bharat". Still, if the victory of Bharat over India that Taseer sees reflects the success of Hindutva in overturning India's liberal assumptions, then this cultural trope is a useful marker for the ascendancy of Hindu nationalism today.

One example, not as trivial as it sounds, of the irreconcilability of cosmopolitan "India" and Hindutva-inspired "Bharat" lies in their respective attitudes to the cow. In Bharat, the cow is revered because of its multiple roles as a source of nourishment, income, and indeed of life itself; it is admired for producing sattvic or pure foods, including milk, ghee, curd, and the traditional panchgavya (a mixture of five cow products—milk, curd, butter, urine, and cow-dung) used widely for an assortment of purposes, including ritualistic purification. The modern, English-educated Indian often has no time for the traditional Bharatvasi's reverence for the sacred cow, but knows better than to say so in public. Still, he has been watching in growing alarm the accelerated attention and importance given over the past few years to cow protection, with laws being passed, ratified and implemented, restrictions being imposed on the transportation, sale, and slaughter of cows, and severe penalties exacted for the possession or consumption of beef, all enforced by ruthless vigilante mobs disguised as cow protection societies. He is outraged that instant justice is delivered in cases of violence (often merely alleged or allegedly intended) against a cow, in a country where violence against a woman requires years for justice to descend. He declares that the government should have no place in the citizen's kitchen. But in the face of overwhelming popular sentiment, particularly in the vote-rich "cow belt" of Hindi-speaking northern India, he bites his tongue.

Overt contempt for the holy cow of Bharat, is unacceptable across a broad swathe of the political spectrum. Yet Savarkar, as a rationalist reformer, had urged Hindus to care for the cow because of its utility (upayuktavadi), rather than worship it. "Why are cow's urine and dung purifying while even the shadow of a man like Ambedkar is defiling?"[4] he asked pointedly in terms that none of his admirers in the BJP would care to recall today. It is clear that his attitude to the cow would not be welcomed by his own acolytes in today's India. If sentiments denigrating the cow are unwelcome in India, actions are totally unforgivable: When an overzealous Youth Congress worker in Kerala protested a beef ban by publicly slaughtering a calf, he was promptly expelled from the liberal party by its outraged national leadership. Politics aside, the young man's action was unnecessarily cruel—to take a life to make a point—and horrified many who would have otherwise protested the beef ban alongside him.

Whereas the classic liberal position would be that a secular state has no business deciding what people may eat, and that banning beef is an assault on individual freedom, the Congress party, the initiator and principal propagator of Indian secularism, has increasingly made its peace with popular Hindu sentiment. The party has notably acquiesced in recent developments on cow protection, and on the Ram Janmabhoomi temple issue. So much so, that as I address audiences around the country, one of the questions I find myself increasingly being asked is:" Isn't the Congress now practising a form of 'soft Hindutva'? Haven't you become 'BJP Lite'?"

The short answer is, no. I have long argued that any attempt to emulate the BJP will give the voters a choice between the "real thing" and a pale imitation, and most will understandably prefer the original. The Congress is not the BJP in any shape or form, and we should not appear to be attempting to be a lighter version of something we are not. But the question is asked repeatedly, and it requires a fuller answer. The questioners tend to point to Rahul Gandhi's temple visits, Digvijay Singh taking credit for banning beef in his state, Kamal Nath promising gaushalas in every district of Madhya Pradesh, the Congress party's support for Sabarimala devotees in Kerala against the Supreme Court verdict allowing women of reproductive age to worship at that shrine, and for that matter even the fact that I published a book entitled *Why I am a Hindu*, about my faith, to suggest that the Congress party is emulating the BJP in appealing to Hindu sentiment rather than to its own secular traditions.

The respected columnist G. Sampath, writing (ironically enough) in *The Hindu* newspaper in late 2018, even questioned "whether the Congress can emerge as a meaningful alternative to the Bharatiya Janata Party (BJP) and its Hindu majoritarian politics." Repeating the "soft Hindutva" charge, Mr Sampath averred "that even an outright victory for a Congress-led alliance in 2019, however improbable it may seem at present, may not really signify a defeat of communal forces." (Of course, such a victory did not happen; instead, another rout did.) He concluded that "liberals and other good-hearted people hoping that Mr. Gandhi and the Congress would rescue them from Hindutva may be in for a rude awakening."

Such criticisms do not take the Congress' own assurances seriously—that it remains a party for all, the safest refuge of the minorities, the weak and the marginalized, and fundamentally committed to secularism. But that doesn't mean such criticism is justified—the truth is that Congress is the only major party to say all of the foregoing and mean it. The BJP does not even bother to pretend that it has the interests of any of these sections at heart.

Our critics see the Congress party's distinction between Hinduism and Hindutva as specious. They reject its leaders' arguments that the Hinduism respected by Congress leaders is inclusive and non-judgemental, whereas Hindutva is a political doctrine based on exclusion. They are quick to conclude that what the Congress offers is merely a watered-down version of the BJP's political messaging.

Nothing could be farther from the truth. Rahul Gandhi has made it clear that, for all his willingness to proclaim his personal Hinduism, he does not support any form of Hindutva, neither soft nor hard. The Congress understands that whereas Hinduism is a religion, Hindutva is a political doctrine that departs fundamentally from the principal tenets of the Hindu faith. While Hinduism is inclusive of all ways of worship, Hindutva is indifferent to devotion and cares only about identity. Hinduism is open to reform and progress, which is why it has flourished for 4,000 years; Hindutva is reactionary and regressive, with its roots in the "racial pride" ethos that spawned Fascism in the 1920s, which is why it is unlikely to outlast its current peak.

There are more fundamental differences. Congress leaders profess a Hinduism that accommodates a vast amount of diversity and respects the individual and his relationship with the divine; the BJP's Hindutva prefers communal identity politics and seeks to Semitize the faith into something it is not, a uniform monolithic religion. Though Hinduism is a faith of multiple sacred books, it is not a "religion of the book" in the sense that the Semitic faiths are; yet, the late BJP leader, Sushma Swaraj, called for the adoption of the Bhagavad Gita as India's "national book", conflating Indian nationalism with the Hindu religion, despite the existence of so many other religions in the national mosaic. Even the Congress' understanding of Hinduism differs from the BJP's. The Hinduism of Congress leaders rests on Swami Vivekananda's ideas of the acceptance of difference, embracing with respect people of other religions; the BJP's Hindutva seeks to erase differences by assaulting, intimidating and subjugating those of other views.

Why then should the liberal Indian feel any despair in Hindu Congressmen asserting their personal faith? Over my adult life I have built up an extensive collection of Ganeshas—over a hundred little (and not so little) statuettes of

Lord Ganapati, some worthy of worship, some irreverent (such as the god in lawyer's robes or playing a musical instrument) made in various materials from bronze to porcelain—without ever feeling that their ubiquitous presence in my house betokened any overt religiosity on my part. And, even though I make no secret of the fact that I am a believing Hindu, I have no difficulty accommodating within my faith the emancipatory nature of my casteless cosmopolitanism, my secular political convictions, a belief in modern meritocracy, and a strong desire to work for a more egalitarian India. In my understanding, Hinduism is not a totalizing belief system; it offers a way of coping with the complexity of the world. It acknowledges that the truth is plural, that there is no one correct answer to the big questions of creation, or of the meaning of life. The greatest truth, to the Hindu, is that which accepts the existence of other truths.

For me, as a Congressman and a liberal, I find it easy to claim allegiance to Hinduism—a religion that is personal and individualistic, privileges the individual, and does not subordinate one to a collectivity; a religion that grants complete freedom to the believer to find his or her own answers to the true meaning of life; a religion that offers a wide range of choice in religious practice, even in regard to the nature and form of the formless God; a religion that places great emphasis on one's mind, and values one's capacity for reflection, intellectual inquiry, and self-study; a religion that distances itself from dogma and holy writ, that is minimally prescriptive, and yet offers an abundance of options, spiritual and philosophical texts, and social and cultural practices to choose from. These are not the qualities admired by the advocates of Hindutva. In a world where resistance to authority is growing, Hinduism imposes no authorities; in a world of networked individuals, Hinduism proposes no institutional hierarchies; in a world of open-source information-sharing, Hinduism accepts all paths as equally valid. In every case, Hindutva asserts the opposite.

Given these qualities of the Hindu religion I, and others like me, profess, I would say to the troubled liberal, don't lose faith. Hindu Congressmen have nothing to do with the Hindutva that you rightly abhor. Our faith remains true to the tolerant, liberal heart of the religion that has made India, till recently, the safest place for non-Hindus. But that does not remove a very real fear: are we going to be able to prevent the BJP changing that?

32

BENDING THE CONSTITUTION

The rise of identity-based nationalism in India, and its overt avowal of majoritarian sentiment, is, as I have stated at length in this book, clearly occurring at the expense of India's over seven-decade-old attempt to construct a meaningful and effective civic nationalism. Since freedom of speech and association and representative democracy are not totally inconsistent with the majoritarian impulse, civic nationalism must rest on liberal constitutionalism (and functioning, autonomous, democratic institutions) if the country is not to descend into an ethno-nationalist "illiberal democracy".

The great question before us today is, therefore: Will constitutionalism tame Hindutva, or will Hindutva transform the workings of the constitution? Can Hindutva change with the times, particularly since its acolytes are now in power, and for the first time in the history of India, its top three constitutional offices—President, Vice-President and Prime Minister—are all occupied by RSS men?

Three one-hour lectures by RSS Chief Mohan Bhagwat at Delhi's Vigyan Bhavan in 2018, where his organization held a conclave on the "Future of Bharat: An RSS Perspective", have led many to wonder whether the RSS has modified its views on some of the key positions with which it has long been identified. During his lectures, the RSS sarsangchalak explained the Sangh position on some issues in a manner that distanced it from the stands associated with his predecessors, notably the RSS' longest-serving head, M. S. Golwalkar, who had remained, even in death, its principal ideologue.

For instance, the RSS has long held the belief that the Constitution of India is fundamentally flawed: first, because it is full of imported Western ideas, written by Anglophone lawyers in the wrong language; and second, because it rests on a dangerously flawed premise, that of territorial nationalism. As we have seen, Sangh thinkers from Golwalkar to Deen Dayal Upadhyaya have consistently argued that the Constitution wrongly defines the nation as a territory called India and all the people on it, whereas a nation is not a territory but a people—in this case, the Hindu people. The RSS has therefore strongly taken the position that the Constitution must be rewritten to create their warped notion of a Hindu rashtra, an intention of which the novelist and activist Arundhati Roy has written: "That idea turns everything that is beautiful about India into acid."[1] But Mr Bhagwat seemed to abandon this long-held view. The Constitution, he declared in Delhi, is no longer such a flawed document. "The RSS accepts the Constitution. There is not even one example in which the RSS has done anything against the Constitution," Bhagwat declared. "The Constitution is the consensus of our country. Following the Constitution is everyone's duty,"[2] he added.

From anyone else, that would be a mere statement of the obvious; coming from Mohan Bhagwat, it seems an earth-shaking affirmation. What about Hindu rashtra? Bhagwat did not disavow the term; he merely redefined it. "Hindu rashtra," he explained, "does not mean it has no place for Muslims. The day it is said that Muslims are unwanted here, the concept of Hindutva will cease to exist". There was no echo in Bhagwat's speeches of either Mr Golwakar's "*ek hazaar saal ki ghulami*" (thousand years of servitude) or even Mr Modi's "*barah sau saal ki ghulami*" (twelve hundred years of slavery) which had demonized Muslims as foreign invaders who had "enslaved" Indians. I remain sceptical, as I will explain, but I am not indifferent to the changed nuances of what the RSS chief was articulating.

Many in the RSS had held the view that the basis of Indian nationhood was Hinduism. This, some averred, did not exclude people of other religious affiliations; they merely had to acknowledge they were, at bottom, Hindus too. "Some people know they are Hindus but they are not willing to accept it because of political correctness," Mohan Bhagwat declared. "According to us, this entire society is a Hindu society."[3] From this sweeping erasure of difference, Bhagwat went on to argue that no exclusion of any minority group was intended. "*Hum log to sarwalog-yukt Bharat waale log hain, mukt wale nahin*",[4] he stated in an uncharacteristic paean to inclusiveness. ("We want an India that includes everyone, not excludes them.") Bhagwat explained that India's diversity—linguistic, social, cultural and religious—was inescapable. The idea was to celebrate this diversity, and for the RSS to be the thread that tied together the different pearls in the Indian necklace.

In addition, Bhagwat took the RSS away from its traditional strident advocacy of Hindi as the only language for India. He blithely suggested that Indian children should be educated in their mother tongues, including regional languages, and even English should be retained, though "in its place" ("*angrezi hatao nahin, angrezi rakho, per yathaasthaan rakho*"). This may well be because the aspiring middle class, whose support the RSS needs, and actively pursues, wants to learn English, not least because it offers them cultural capital in the globalized world. Such a desire is not incompatible with the RSS' ambition to see India assert its national strength in the international system.

If these statements were a repudiation of much that the RSS had stood for over the previous nine decades, Bhagwat rubbed it in by scarcely bothering to mention Golwalkar, while scattering various other names through his three hours of lectures. Indeed, Golwalkar only came up in the context of a startling admission that the RSS had censored the inflammatory ideas of its erstwhile leader: "As far as *Bunch of Thoughts* goes," said Bhagwat, referring to Golwalkar's classic, hitherto seen as a sort of RSS *Mein Kampf*, "every statement carries a context of time and circumstance…his enduring thoughts are in a popular edition in which we have removed all remarks that have a temporary context and retained those that will endure for ages."[5] This editing out of ideas the RSS no longer wishes to defend is the clearest change of position imaginable. Asked about Golwalkar's view that Muslims were "the enemy", Bhagwat disarmingly explained that in the newly reissued and censored *Bunch of Thoughts*, "You won't find the (Muslim-is-an-enemy) remark there."[6]

The omission of Golwalkar's thoughts from the RSS chief's lectures, and the announcement of a censored version of Golwalkar's book, is arguably a major public signal that the RSS has been rethinking its stand on some of the key issues that have placed it beyond the pale for so many secularists and liberals. As I have stated in this book, and in numerous speeches and writings, the RSS' view of Hindutva had always been based on an idea of the Indian nation in which the Hindu religious identity coincides with the national. With Bhagwat now proclaiming that the RSS believes in pluralism, accepts heterogeneity, and seeks to tie the pearls of diversity in a thread of unity, one might be forgiven for wondering whether he would next pronounce secularism as his organization's credo.

Indeed, some observers welcomed his remarks, seeing them as ending the bigotry with which the RSS has long been associated, and heralding a new more acceptable avatar of the organization. Well-meaning friends asked me, "Shouldn't you applaud Mohan Bhagwat's remarks? What more could he have said to make you happy?" I do not deny that these statements seem to suggest a significant move away from hard-core RSS positions that had troubled secular Indians like myself. And yet, I find myself unconvinced that they represent any real change.

First, Mohan Bhagwat's redefinition of the central concepts of the RSS still stakes out his position on his own terms. He is still thinking of India as a Hindu state, albeit one characterized by tolerance of religious diversity, rather than one seeking to exterminate or drive out its minorities. This is a considerable improvement on Golwalkar, but not an advance on Upadhyaya, and it is still a long way short of the original conception of India as a secular state that grants equal rights to all, sees all faiths as equally valuable to the Indian idea, and treats all faiths with equal respect. The RSS' India is still a Hindu nation, but a benevolent one in which minorities live on the sufferance of the majority, thanks to the kindness and generosity of Hindus. That is not the free India Mahatma Gandhi, Jawaharlal Nehru, and Dr Ambedkar established, in which Hindus were meant to see themselves as equal to, and no better than, their fellow citizens of other faiths.

Bhagwat's remarks made it clear he still sees other faiths as inferior to his own within the Indian ethos. Hinduism certainly has many benevolent features that are unique to it, notably an acceptance of different forms of worship, but it also has its own challenges and inequities to contend with. For Bhagwat to suggest that India can simply be an all-embracing Hindu society in which the identity of the majority, because of their natural inclusiveness, will ensure the well-being of all, is at the very least disingenuous.

This became apparent in his remarks on the contentious issue of the Ram Janmabhoomi temple. The RSS chief did not amend his stand in any way but expressed it in soothing terms: the construction of a grand Ram temple will help, Bhagwat said, to end a major reason for tension between Hindus and Muslims. "If the temple is built in a harmonious way," said the RSS chief, "there will be no more pointing of fingers at Muslims,"[7] a message he left for the final day of the RSS's three-day lecture series. In other words, Bhagwat seemed to be saying to the Muslims, settle problematic issues on our terms and you will face no trouble: a Corleone-style "offer you can't refuse". That is a long way short of the reassurance the RSS believes its chief conveyed to India's minorities.

As Ashutosh Varshney put it: "His is not a discourse about the full and equal citizenship of Muslims. It is hard to escape the inference that for Bhagwat, Muslims may be Indians, but they are secondary Indians. They have produced no Indian heroes; their religion "attacked" India; they must give up beef eating because Hindus are offended by it; accepting Ram as "Imam-e-Hind", they should agree to a Ram Temple in Ayodhya, or the fingers of suspicion will continue to be pointed at them. The welfare of the Muslim community, in other words, depends on Hindu pleasure, not constitutional principles. There is no conception of rights."[8]

In addition, Mr Bhagwat's speeches signal no dilution of the core RSS philosophy, under which individuals should not think of their own interests, but subsume these in the service of society—a repudiation of the concepts of civil liberties and fundamental rights, which the Constitution grants to individual citizens. Essentially, the RSS continues to see society's interests as the supreme priority, to the exclusion of individual interests, in much the same way as Hitler demanded complete immersion in German nationhood, or Mao insisted that the "new Chinese man" emerging from the Cultural Revolution would be completely unselfish and think only of his country. The idea of collective interest is usually used to justify the oppression of the individual citizen, the elimination of the spirit of dissent, and the downgrading of human rights. To some degree, the RSS' apparent change of heart could also be seen as stemming from finally accessing real power and seeing how complicated it is to exercise it in a diverse country like India. People cannot be dragooned or beaten into ideological shape: they have to be persuaded mainly with carrots, the stick only existing for the weak or the recalcitrant, or to send out occasional signals to the core constituency. This newfound moderation, many would suggest, is a tactical shift as much as it is a reflection of changing concerns.

Needless to say, my critics from the BJP's ideological camp could allege that I have been unfair in refusing to take Mr Bhagwat at his word. After all, he accepted India's diversity, embraced minorities, and spoke of inclusiveness. How then could I still object to the RSS's idea of Hindutva? I could sum up my difference with Mr Bhagwat in that hallowed phrase I have mentioned before and that, for all its over-use, has not yet lost its potency: unity in diversity. That's what I believe in, and that's what the Constitution of India, written by the nationalists who fought for our freedom, propounds. Mr Bhagwat doesn't believe in "unity in diversity"; he believes in "diversity in unity". Let me explain.

The first idea assumes that there are various kinds of Indians, with very different views of their own identity, including religious assumptions that differ markedly from each other. Yet, we all belong together, and share a common allegiance to India. I have described this for many years now as my "thali" theory of Indian nationalism. To refresh the reader's memory, I believe that, like a thali, we are a collection of different items in different bowls; since we are in different bowls, the dishes don't necessarily flow into each other, but we belong together on the same platter and combine on your palate to give you a satisfying repast.

Mr Bhagwat's construct is not that of my thali. It is, instead, a jumbled theory of nationalism: we are one dish, with many ingredients all mixed up and cooked together. Yes, individual pieces might stand out in the mash, a carrot here, a potato there, but they are nothing other than parts of the meal. Thus, for him, all true Indians are Hindus; there might be a "Muslim Hindu" here and a "Christian Hindu" there, but they must acknowledge that they are part of the mixed, saffron-hued khichdi and have no identity separate from it. Their diversity, in other words, is subordinate to their common role as part of the larger unity.

These are fundamentally different ideas of what Indian nationalism is all about. Mine sees each identity as valid in itself, and as an equal stakeholder in the larger identity of Indianness. Mr Bhagwat's sees Indianness as the primordial identity to which any other identity is subordinate, and indeed is only tolerated as part of the larger mix. For the Hindutva lobby, India's national culture is Hindu religious culture, and cultural nationalism cloaks plural India in a mantle of Hindu identity. In Mr Bhagwat's Hindutva, the idea of the Indian nation is one in which the Hindu religious identity coincides with the cultural and both equate to the national. He leaves no room for a Muslim to be a Muslim or a Christian to be a Christian and still call herself Indian.

Sure, India is an overwhelmingly Hindu country, but, as we have seen, the founders of our republic consciously did not choose to be a Hindu state. Neither politics nor governance was based on religious principles, and success in no field required a litmus test of faith. The Hindutva project involves an attempt to create an overarching political ideology that would iron out the differences among all the adherents of a highly differentiated and eclectic religious faith, and also suppress the far greater differences with people of other faiths. Accordingly, the RSS idea of Hindu nationalism conflates ideas of religion and culture with those of nation and state. But the really important debate in India is not about Hinduism, not even about "Bharat" and "India", but between the unifiers and the dividers—between those who think all Indians are "us", whichever God they choose to worship, and those who think that Indians can be divided into "us" and "them". Like demagogues elsewhere, India's current rulers find it easier and more politically profitable to appeal to the public's prejudices than to uphold what unites them with others. For Mr Bhagwat and the RSS, only Hindus are "us"; everyone else is "them". That cannot be the basis for the kind of unity that he and his organization claim to promote.

Indeed, the 2019 elections marked the triumph of a narrow-minded Hindu nationalism, evidenced by a string of divisive markers: the BJP's deliberate failure, yet again, to nominate a Muslim candidate to the Lok Sabha in any of the Hindi heartland states; in contrast, the candidacy of Pragya Thakur, accused of terrorist attacks against Muslim targets, who had hailed Mahatma Gandhi's assassin as a hero and a "patriot"[9] who, in her words, would always be one; the electioneering Amit Shah's claim that Muslim migrants from Bangladesh or Myanmar were "termites"[10] whom he would throw out, along with all immigrants who were not Hindu, Buddhist, Sikh or Jain [the list was later expanded to include Christians and Parsis]; Modi's own acerbic comment that Rahul Gandhi's choice of Wayanad as a second constituency was because the minorities were a majority there, implying that Muslims and Christians are a lower order of citizens; and finally, Modi's victory speech on 23 May 2019 gloating that the elections had "exposed" secularists who could no longer "deceive" the country.[11]

It is, of course, pertinent to ask whether we should take the Hindutvavadis' claims to be admirers of the present secular, liberal, Western-influenced Constitution of India to be as sincere as their professions of devotion to Upadhyaya. Will Modi and his tribe, after consolidating their hold on both the Lok Sabha and the Rajya Sabha feel emboldened to tear up the very Constitution to which they have so far so enthusiastically pledged allegiance? A close reading of the works of its principal ideologues, notably Deen Dayal Upadhyaya, suggests that amending the Constitution is likely to be high on the ruling party's priority list.[12] Or will they decide, as Mohan Bhagwat's words seem to suggest, they do not need to, for after all as Ambedkar had warned, the Constitution itself could be perverted in its application to ensure that it protected a majoritarianism it did not envisage?

Whether or not the BJP goes full tilt at rewriting the entire Constitution to establish the Hindu state of its dreams, an obvious first step in that direction is probable. The easy target our ruling party may aim at is to reverse the 42nd Amendment of the constitution, which in 1976 added two words the BJP doesn't like—"secular" and "socialist"—to the Preamble.

During the Constituent Assembly debates, Prof K.T. Shah had tried and failed on November 15, 1948 to achieve inclusion of the words 'Secular, Federalist, Socialist" in the preamble.[13] In the eventual compromise, the majority of the Assembly took the view that the Indian state would indeed be secular but that it was not necessary to use the word in the preamble. The word "secularism", after all, was explicitly Western in origin, emerging from the political changes in Europe that accompanied the Protestant Reformation and the era called the Enlightenment. But many 20th century leaders outside Western Europe were attracted to the concept, notably Kemal Ataturk in

Muslim-majority Turkey, and Jawaharlal Nehru in Hindu-majority India, both of whom saw a secular state as a crucial hallmark of modernity. In India's case, secularism also seemed to Nehru the only way to avoid the religious and communal antagonisms that had partitioned the country when the British left.

The Constituent Assembly debates show the extent to which this logic was accepted by our Founding Fathers. "I accepted this secularism in the sense that our State shall remain unconcerned with religion, and I thought that the secular State of partitioned India was the maximum of generosity of a Hindu dominated territory for its non-Hindu population,"[14] said Lokanath Misra in the debate on 6 December 1948.

But was it necessary to include the word itself in the Constitution? The Chairman of the Drafting Committee, Dr B. R. Ambedkar, thought not. Ambedkar said: "What should be the policy of the State, how the Society should be organised in its social and economic side are matters which must be decided by the people themselves according to time and circumstances. It cannot be laid down in the Constitution itself because that is destroying democracy altogether."[15]

Still, the adoption of Articles 25, 26, 27 and 28 of the Constitution, guaranteeing freedom of conscience and the right to profess, practice, and propagate one's religion, to manage one's own religious affairs and to enjoy the freedom of religious worship, confirmed that the concept of secularism was unarguably implicit in India's constitutional philosophy. But it wasn't Western-style secularism, which meant irreligiousness, which as I have explained, even avowedly atheist parties like the Communists or the southern DMK party found unpopular amongst their voters. Rather, secularism meant, in the Indian tradition, a profusion of religions, none of which was privileged by the state, which (in Amartya Sen's words) preserved an "equidistance" from, and an "equal symmetry" of treatment of, all religions.[16] One can credibly argue that the 42nd amendment merely put a word into the Constitution whose spirit was always deeply embedded in it, and reified in governmental practice. The loss of the word "secularism" will not necessarily make the country less secular, since successive Indian governments had practised the peculiar Indian variant of secularism anyway before the 42nd amendment. Nor can we convincingly protest a further amendment to a constitution we have already amended a hundred times before.

The theory of secularism, as Prof R. S. Misra of Banaras Hindu University has argued, and which I have discussed at length in *Why I Am A Hindu*, is based on *dharma-nirpekshata* ('keeping apart from dharma'), which is impossible for any good Hindu to adhere to. BJP politicians like Rajnath Singh and

Adityanath have argued that Indian governments cannot observe *dharma-nirpekshata* but should follow the precept of *panth-nirpekshata* (not favouring any particular sect or faith). In this, they are not far removed from my argument—which I have made for several years before my entry into Indian politics—that 'secularism' is a misnomer in the Indian context of profuse religiosity, and what we should be talking about is 'pluralism'. I believe the roots of India's pluralism can be found in the Hindu philosophy of acceptance of difference: *ekam sat vipraa bahudha vadanti*, the Truth is one but the learned call it by many names.

Pluralism has meant the active encouragement of religion in this country, in defiance of classical secular theory. Indian secularism cheerfully embraces financial support to religious schools and the persistence of 'personal law' for different religious communities. The Hindutva brigade does not like this, and it is determined to do away with it as a significant step towards the Hindutva project. They claim that there is uncritical acceptance by the Indian establishment of regressive practices among the Muslim community while demanding progressive behaviour from Hindus, support for minority education while denying such aid to Hindus, promotion of "family planning" among Hindus but not among Muslims, cultivation of "vote banks" led by conservative Muslim leaders but the disparagement of their Hindu equivalents, and so on.

This widespread denunciation of the "appeasement" of Muslims seems bizarre when one looks at the statistical evidence of Muslim socio-economic backwardness and the prevalence of discrimination in such areas as housing and employment. Muslims are under-represented in the nation's police forces and over-represented in its prisons. Yet, Hindutva leaders have successfully stoked a perception that government benefits are skewed towards minorities, and thus justified their campaign for Hindu self-assertiveness. Majoritarian opinion is irritated by the prevalence of a practice like Muslim Personal Law, which—dealing as it does with matters of marriage, divorce and inheritance—in no way impinges on the Hindu community. Despite this, the drafting of a Common Civil Code is also on the BJP agenda—once again as a way of putting Indian Muslims firmly in their place.

It is for such reasons that Deen Dayal Upadhyaya had argued that secularism would have to go: in his words, it 'implies opposition of Hindus and appeasement of Muslims or other minorities. We should get rid of this word as soon as possible. It is completely irrelevant in the Indian context.'[17] But to remove the word "secular" would be no ordinary amendment—even if that alone cannot change the secular nature of the Constitution, which was a liberal document before the word was inserted and will remain liberal if it is removed. For the signal it would send would be chilling. It would attack something fundamental and intrinsic to the way our Constitution-makers intended India to be.

The Opposition must and will resist the BJP's attempts—not because the word itself is essential, but because its removal will symbolize an assault on the spirit of Indian pluralism and religious freedom. This spirit, it must be remembered, was not created by the Constitution but reflected in it. Of course, such a change would first have to pass the test of judicial review against the yardstick of the Supreme Court's historic 1973 judgment in *Kesavananda Bharati v. Union of India*, outlining the "Basic Structure" of the Constitution, which is presumed to include secularism. If it survives that test, and if Indian liberals fail in preventing the removal of the word "secularism", we must never stop fighting to preserve its spirit in the political practice of our country.

In his 1917 essay on 'Nationalism in India', Tagore highlighted the challenges of India in "developing a national self-consciousness as well as the need for that consciousness to be grounded in Indian cultural sensibilities." Tagore's view of India as a land whose entire history (for "about fifty centuries at least") was a story of striving to accommodate diversity and difference, did not shy away from acknowledging the constructive role of religion, and specifically Hinduism, in this process. "Towards this realization have worked, from the early time of the Upanishads up to the present moment, a series of great spiritual teachers, whose one object has been to set at naught all differences of man by the overflow of our consciousness of God. In fact, our history has not been of the rise and fall of kingdoms, of fights for political supremacy. In our country records of these days have been despised and forgotten. For they in no way represent the true history of our people. Our history is that of our social life and attainment of spiritual ideals."[18] This sublimated any talk of Indian nationalism into a wider humanism. Tagore said, "My countrymen will gain truly their India by fighting against that education which teaches them that a country is greater than the ideals of humanity."

Before wrapping up this chapter, we should acknowledge that some Hindutvavadis speak of the great spiritual principle of "*Vasudhaiva Kutumbakam*", the world is a family, that I have referred to earlier. This probably has its foundation in the attempts of the leadership of the Sangh Parivar to develop a "Hindu nationalism" that may be chauvinist at home but respectful abroad, and can comfortably embrace other religions, traditions and cultures, so long as they are outside India's borders.

The backlash evident in many Muslim countries in 2020 to the growing intolerance and Islamophobia being expressed in domestic Indian politics suggest that such a simple way out is not possible. It has become evident that the domestic demonization of Muslims that seems so indispensable to the ruling party's continuance in power is incompatible with the international relationships the government wishes to preserve. When a member of one of the UAE's ruling families, Princess Hend Al Qassimi, a self-declared friend of India, speaks out against growing intolerance in the country she loves, it is clear that a wall of diplomatic restraint has been breached. The compartmentalization the BJP seeks is, in effect—"what we do to Muslims in India has nothing to do with our respect for Muslims in other countries"; "we love Muslims abroad, as long as they don't encroach on our Hindu space in India". Needless to say, in a globalized media world, where headlines report continuing discrimination, harassment, and worse against India's Muslim minority, condoned by the government and the ruling establishment, this doesn't work.

The key question remains whether a Hindutva-modified Constitution, assuming that it ever comes to pass, will retain the core principle of independent India, that all adult Indians are deemed equal, irrespective of religion. Or would it consciously embrace the central theme of Hindutva, which would discriminate against non-Hindus? If it did so, it would be true to Hindutva as expounded by Savarkar, Golwalkar and Upadhyaya, but not to the Hinduism of Swami Vivekananda or Mahatma Gandhi, who did not define Indianness in terms of the gods one worshipped, what one ate, the way one dressed or where one went for pilgrimage. But if it did not do so, it would betray a century's worth of political philosophizing in the name of Hindutva, surrendering its tenets to the dominant nationalist stream it had long derided as 'pseudo-secular'. This will be a crucial dilemma for the Hindutva ideologues. Do they take the opportunity given to them by their crushing political majority—which might not endure if they wait too long—to remake the Constitution as their principal thinkers had advocated? It is difficult to imagine that people who have openly disdained and disavowed the Constitution for so long will suddenly abandon their vision of a Hindutva-infused Constitution that sanctions a Hindu majoritarian Bharat to embrace the ideal of a multi-ethnic, multi-lingual and multi-religious polity they despise.

33

BEATITUDES OF BELONGING

I have attempted to summarize in the previous pages some clearly visible trends in Indian society and politics. In this chapter, I will probe a little deeper into the distasteful and dangerous ethno-nationalism that Mr Modi and his cohorts are fomenting.

The BJP's breakthrough in 2014 had already prompted a debate about whether India had graduated from an era of federalized multipolarity, political fragmentation, competitive electoral contests among a multiplicity of parties, and coalition governments often involving strong state (or regional) parties, to a new, dominant-party system centred on a hegemonic BJP.[1] After its storming victory in 2019, the BJP was described by scholars as a "system-defining" party, with its emphasis on Hindu nationalism and what political scientist Suhas Palshikar calls a "new developmentalism"[2] that have allowed the party to saturate the current political space in India. Hindu nationalism has managed to eclipse the Congress Party's legacy of secular nationalism, but today's "developmentalism" is merely the Congress Party's welfarism (that the BJP decried and derided as "povertarianism" in 2014) dressed up as Hindutva-inspired *antodaya*. Still, there is no debating the ascendancy of the Hindu-nationalist narrative. The French political scientists Christophe Jaffrelot and Gilles Vernier have not only acknowledged that the BJP has made the Indian political system "more centralized and less liberal", but have gone so far as to argue that the BJP has changed India "from a de facto Hindu majoritarian state towards a de jure Hindu majoritarian state".[3]

Along with it, inevitably, has come an assault on the underpinnings of the civic nationalism that the Constitution establishes. The veteran editor Harish Khare sees a "mindset" which "seeks legitimacy for itself from the paraphernalia of an elective democracy but uses the democratic mandate to chisel away at the core of democratic arrangement".[4]

261

As I have shown throughout this book, the principal features of the governmental ethos now emerging suggest a deep-seated ethno-nationalism at work. The propping up of an idealized leader who is said to embody the timeless essence of the nation; the increasing autocracy, including the systematic rendering dysfunctional of the institutions designed to curb abuse of power; the overt demonization and repression of a single target community, the Muslims, delegitimized as a treacherous permanent foreign element amidst true Indians; the cultivation and exploitation of bigotry among the masses against that community; the use of symbols and vocabulary anchored in Hindu beliefs and practices, to the exclusion of members of other faith communities from his rhetorical embrace; the division into "us" and "them" with "them" of course being dubbed "anti-national"—all this is out of the standard ethno-nationalist playbook. The quest for absolute power, emerging from a ruthless electoral machine, outrageously well-funded, and supremely efficiently organized, with a take-no-prisoners style of campaigning, and the use of every available technique from inducement to intimidation to ensure control of the vital arena of law-making, the Parliament; the efforts to direct those who enforce the law—the police—and to influence those who interpret it, the judiciary; the curbing of free speech and dissent in all its natural habitats, from educational institutions, especially universities, to the mass media; and the imposition of a single national narrative, a single language, a single religion, a single set of approved slogans, songs and symbols, and a uniform ideology—all of this represents as fundamental a departure as can be imagined from the idea of India celebrated by Tagore, achieved by Gandhi and implemented by Nehru and his comrades.

An essential component of the appeal of Hindu nationalism was its embodiment in one man. People told pollsters they were voting for the leadership of Narendra Modi, whom they saw (or had been persuaded to regard) as a decisive leader, strong, incorruptible, and selfless, who was motivated only by the national interest. Prior to 2014, voter turnout patterns had been higher at state elections than in national ones, since local leaders meant more to voters; with Mr Modi, that factor reversed, with people even voting in state elections to support his party because of his campaigning for it. Mr Modi is credited with almost single-handedly developing and articulating a new nationalist narrative that has broad currency with the voting public.

This new nationalism, as anatomized by the scholars Milan Vaishnav and Jamie Hintson, had four distinct features as revealed in the 2019 elections:[5]

(1) the selective deployment of Hindutva nationalist messaging in those parts of the country where the party felt it would win votes, with passionate

invocations of the Ram Mandir, cow protection, and illegal Muslim immigration to polarize Hindu majority opinion and transcend caste divisions;

(2) an expanded nationalist discourse centred on territorial sovereignty, loyalty to the nation, and resentment toward traditional liberal elites who it painted as out-of-touch, feckless, and compromised by divided loyalties;[6]

(3) muscularity abroad and a reclaiming of what was portrayed as "India's rightful place in the world"; and

(4) developmentalism: the provision of welfare schemes such as the construction of toilets and the supply of cooking-gas cylinders to demonstrate to millions of voters that the government could be a force for positive change in their lives.

These factors helped entrench Mr Modi and the BJP in power, and in the process facilitated their larger ambition of redefining the idea of the nation. Somewhat dismaying to the Hindutvavadis, however, was the narrow basis of the Hindu nationalist appeal, even amid such an electoral triumph: 75 percent of the BJP's parliamentary tally in 2014 came from just eight states in the predominantly Hindi-speaking north, west, and central regions of the country, where its Hindutva message resonated most effectively.

To understand some of the trends that have resulted after the BJP's victory it is important to note that Mr Modi's standing as the principal vote-getter for his party has encouraged some of the worst traits he embodies to become widespread in the political space. The historian and political commentator Ramachandra Guha identified three personal traits in Narendra Modi that, in his view, explained the Prime Minister's failures in office: a deep suspicion of experts and expertise, the building up of a cult of personality around him to mask his own insecurities, and his "Sanghi" communal bigotry. Guha cited several examples of Modi's errors (ones already mentioned in this book) and concluded that "his own megalomania, his own suspicion of experts, his own reluctance to share credit, and his own inability to transcend the sectarian ideology that he embraced as a young man" were squarely to blame for them.[7]

He has been largely responsible for the systematic downgrading of the place of deliberation, discussion, and dissent in the system through the example he has set in the years that he has been in power. A Prime Minister who is a firm believer in top-down, one-way communication, addressing the nation in hortatory speeches, image-building tweets, and platitudinous monthly radio addresses, Modi is yet to hold a single press conference in this country in which he would be required to take any spontaneous questions. Even his television interviews are fawning, scripted affairs, conducted by favoured journalists or celebrities (a movie star, a Bollywood lyricist) who can be relied upon not to pose him anything remotely resembling a challenging question. The ruling party's narrative is tightly controlled, assiduously crafted, and widely disseminated. Opposing viewpoints are dismissed as "anti-national". The delegitimization of dissent is overwhelming, and meets with wide public approval by a public primed to be irritated by "negative politics". As Suhas Palshikar put it, "'Politicising' is a pejorative term reserved for any dissenting view."[8]

Decisions are made by the PM without consultation, not even with his own Cabinet; this was the case, it is widely believed, on demonetization, on Kashmir, and most recently, on the coronavirus lockdown. Modi's total domination of his cabinet and party is apparent not just in his disregard for them but in their subservience. When Modi declares he is a chowkidar (watchman), all party members modify their social media handles to call themselves chowkidars. When Modi appoints senior bureaucrats to key posts, he looks for evidence of personal connections and loyalty to himself;[9] it is no accident, after all, that so many important positions in the Government of India have been assigned to officials of the Gujarat cadre. Since decision-making in private or with a tightly-restricted cabal makes planning impossible, each of these decisions has been followed by disasters that could have been anticipated had a wider group of knowledgeable people been consulted, but the PM's faulty decisions are spun as impressively quick decision-making, his "decisiveness" portrayed as a supreme virtue unrelated to the content or effectiveness of his decisions. "As for the prime minister," one commentator declared, "he is here to keep our morale high and comfort us, while gently massaging our egos."[10] Actual results are irrelevant.

Unfortunately, he has not always managed to keep morale high. His deer-caught-in-the-headlights performance over the conflict with China in the Galwan Valley in Ladakh in June 2020 also betrayed his lack of resolution. The violent incidents on the undemarcated border between India and China, the Line of Actual Control, exposed for many the hollowness of Moditva nationalism. Days of contradictory statements and media links, accompanied by the Prime Minister's usual stoic silence, marked the unfolding of the crisis, leaving the Indian public alarmed, confused and unenlightened. And, as I have remarked earlier, when the Prime Minister spoke, it was to claim there had been no Chinese intrusions into Indian territory, a statement gleefully seized upon by Chinese propagandists to vindicate their position that the incidents had occurred on Chinese land. Modi's dissimulation and lack of resolve were on full display in his efforts to deflect the attempts by the Opposition Congress party and some commentators to raise the key questions: BJP spokesmen were quick to assert that questioning the Prime Minister at a time of national crisis was—of course—anti-national.

As the Ramachandra Guha commented: "Our capacity to tackle these problems, indeed even our ability to adequately understand these problems, is inhibited by the political culture of the day, where the government and the ruling party seek to present the Prime Minister as infallible, and his policies as beyond criticism."[11] And Brahma Chellaney did not mince words even when writing for an international audience: "Modi has himself to blame [for the border setbacks].... With his excessive personalization of policy and stubborn strategic naivete, he has shown himself not as the diplomatically deft strongman he purports to be, but as a kind of Indian Neville Chamberlain."[12]

Since such incompetence cannot be defended on merits, dissent is all the more illegitimized. As Khare puts it, "the Modi crowd believes, sincerely and righteously, in the correctness of its chosen path; it mesmerises itself with the notions of integrity and commitment of its personnel and leaders and their infinite wisdom. It resents democratic opposition.... Millions have paid a heavy price for the regime's arrogance and incompetence. Yet, the government would not countenance any discussion of its mistakes and missteps. Over the years the regime has used a heavy-handed approach to put its critics in their place. It has brought to bear overwhelming resources, power, prestige and skills to fix its critics, however small or scattered."[13]

In Modi's India, the laws, court judgements and public opinion are all arrayed against dissenters; they are seen as enemies of orderly society, whose disruptive political views merely obstruct the all-knowing, always-correct state. As these words are written, a pregnant protestor had spent three months in jail for organizing a peaceful protest against the Citizenship Amendment Act, some prominent Kashmiri politicians were still under house arrest nine months after their incarceration began, and the courts have shown no urgency even in hearing habeas corpus cases or petitions challenging the altered status of the state of Jammu and Kashmir.

In the process, the checks and balances foreseen in the Constitution are also, inevitably, disregarded. I have described in the previous chapter how institutions have been etiolated. The process has gathered pace since the Modi re-election of 2019. Though Modi won a sweeping victory in Parliament, he treats the institution with contempt, barely attending or speaking in the Lok Sabha of which he is a member, treating parliamentary debate as an exercise in occasional declamatory rhetoric, and when he bothers to speak, mocking the Opposition, especially the Congress Party. The umbilical tie between an ascendant ethnic nationalism and charismatic, centralized leadership has consequences. The great flaw is that as institutions crumble, the dependence on one man increases to intolerable levels. One of the flaws of ethno-nationalism is its dependence on the projection of a strong leader: the success of the cause thus depends on the indispensability of one man. As we have seen in Italy, Germany, Portugal, Spain, and Argentina in the course of the 20th century, in an ethno-nationalist populist project led by a charismatic authoritarian figure, a change in leadership, for whatever reason, can lead to an implosion of the movement—which has so identified itself with him that it may find itself unable to stay united or purposeful with his departure. For Hindu nationalism to succeed in contemporary India, it needs Narendra Modi to stay in charge till a Hindu state is well entrenched. Otherwise conflicts over leadership and a divided movement would generate multiple local conflicts, which will be challenging to control politically in a diverse democracy like India. And yet the quality of the larger-than-life leadership offered is itself questionable. As the political commentator Pratap Bhanu Mehta put it:

> What has the prime minister reduced leadership to? Instead of confronting reality, deny it; instead of encouraging criticism, suppress it; instead of socially mediating differences, exacerbate them; instead of taking responsibility, take the credit and pawn the blame; instead of appropriate empathy, revel in a kind of cruelty; and instead of preparing the nation for challenges, constantly trap it in diversions.... His leadership has been totally missing. What has been put in its place is a politics of illusion we have all too easily internalised. India is heading into uncharted waters with no leadership at the helm, just the simulacra of one.[14]

Despite this abject performance, an extraordinary centralization of power has been taking place around Modi. Power emanates from the central government in New Delhi, and within it from the Prime Minister's Office, itself an institution built around an individual. Alongside the Prime Minister, his principal political aide is his former party President, now the Home Minister, in charge of the nation's internal security. If law-making is derided and devalued, law-enforcement has become a mockery. The machinery built specifically to protect the rule of law is in a shambles. The riots in Delhi in early 2020 witnessed policemen in uniform helping a mob throw stones—acts captured on camera by media and broadcast around the world by the BBC. In the words of Pratap Bhanu Mehta: "The idea is to carpet-bomb the Indian republic as we know it, and replace it with a regime that thrives on cruelty, fear, division and violence."[15] The Delhi violence featured a reversion to horrors last witnessed in the nation's capital during Partition, when young men were stripped of their trousers and undergarments to determine if they were circumcised and so Muslim. Mehta adds: "We are back to a barbarism where crowds threaten to strip you to ascertain if you have a right to any civic standing. The purpose is to strip us of all the decencies of ordinary humanity; the only thing that matters will be the identity that can be inscribed on your body."[16]

If law-making and law-enforcement have lost their autonomy and authority, surely the interpretation of the law and the constitution by a fearless judiciary can offer it the ultimate protection? Those who seek comfort in such a thought are drawn up short when a Supreme Court judge openly praises the Prime Minister as a 'versatile genius' and his Chief Justice fails to defend the right to non-discriminatory citizenship, non-refoulement of refugees, the evidence act, federalism, free speech or even that most basic of rights, habeas corpus. Justice Ranjan Gogoi, the Chief Justice in question, widely described as having converted the Court into a branch of the executive, then went on to accept the government's nomination to a seat in the Rajya Sabha. His conduct, Pratap Bhanu Mehta wrote, "has disabused us of any illusions we might harbour about the legitimacy of the Indian Supreme Court.... The authority of the Supreme Court of India rests squarely on two things: the cogency of its reasoning, and the integrity of its judges. Justice Gogoi's track record as justice was to take a wrecking ball to the Indian Constitution and smash it to smithereens". Larger issues of institutional propriety, not to mention the dangers of a precedent that can be followed by other judges under future governments, remain troubling; so too are the broader warning signals emerging from this episode. "In an era where ordinary citizens are struggling to safeguard their citizenship rights and basic constitutional standing,", Mehta concludes, "Justice Gogoi's actions say to us: The Law will not protect you because it is compromised, the Court will not be a countervailing power to the executive because it is supine, and Judges will not empower you because they are diminished men."[17]

The ultimate restraint on authoritarianism taking over India lies in its federalism, especially with many states ruled by other political parties, but the federal aspects of our quasi-federal state are blithely ignored in the central government's headlong rush to dominance. Though the Constitution envisages a federal structure with many powers reserved to the states, the national government tells the states what they can do, and grants or withholds funds the states needs to perform their functions. Nowhere was this more apparent than when the coronavirus pandemic began sweeping the world, and the Modi regime involved a little-known provision of the National Disaster Management Act, 2005, to impose a nationwide lockdown (at just over three hours' notice) without even a pretence of consulting the elected chief ministers of governments in the states. Where President Trump, in the US, had the national "bully pulpit" all to himself, he was obliged constitutionally to leave it to each state governor to decide for himself or herself whether to lockdown their state. Mr Modi, without consultation or even the preparation of a national plan as mandated by law, was simply the "bully" without need for a "pulpit", imposing his wishes on the states, who were meekly obliged to implement the instructions of the central Home Ministry in physical movement and economic activity in their state (though both are, constitutionally, within the purview of the state List rather than the central.) Making matters worse, after the initial months after the pandemic hit, when a phased and gradual lifting of the lockdown had to be managed, the Prime Minister stayed away from taking ownership of the strategy, having instructions issued by a bureaucrat in the Home Ministry and essentially asking state governments to assume the political responsibility for either prolonging the lockdown or ending it prematurely.

Prime Minister Modi is not alone in wanting to have it both ways. Many regional parties are acutely conscious of their dependence on the largesse of the central Government and their vulnerability to the authority of New Delhi. Some have made a Faustian bargain with the BJP: do what you like at the national level as long as you leave us alone in our states. Even in those states where the BJP is not in power but regional parties are, they have proven all too willing to negotiate with the central government in order to navigate their way through its authoritarianism, rather than resist it. The result is a reconfiguration of India's federal diversity in the service of the nationalist project; the BJP's hyper-nationalism remains unchallenged even in the name of federalism.

The intention in India, articulated by successive governments over several decades, and particularly since the adoption of panchayati raj (village self-government) legislation in the early 1990s, was supposed to be greater decentralization of decision-making, in keeping with the tenets of civic nationalism. India had a tradition of local self-government that was destroyed by the British colonial masters in their efforts to exert centralized control in order to extract revenue, through the imposition of a "Collector" in every district, answerable not to the locals but to the imperial government. Self-governance through institutions of local governance was supplanted by top-down British rule.

Independent India sought, fitfully, to revert greater power and authority to institutions of local self-government (while still retaining the Collector and the administrative system around him). This process of increasing decentralization has come to a halt with Mr Modi; worse, the authority of the intermediate layer, the state governments, is now under assault. Mr Modi with his penchant for declaratory rhetoric that proves unconnected to actual intention (like "government has no business to be in business", a statement he has not lifted a little finger to implement) has spoken piously of his faith in "cooperative federalism". This has again turned out to be a mantra without a method. As a sometime admirer commented, Modi "revealed that he was an all too familiar, and tiresome, figure in (the) Indian political economy: a socialist who believed he could turn white elephants into gazelles."[18] The excuse is always the extraordinary circumstances assailing the nation. Decentralization, deliberation, dissent, and debate—indeed the substance of democracy itself—are all treated as dispensable in times of crisis. They are seen as desirable rhetorical ideals best reserved for "normal" times.

As Suhas Palshikar, writing about the coronavirus lockdown, observed: "What we have probably not realised is that at the stroke of midnight on March 24 [2020, when the first lockdown was announced], India suspended 'politics'. The effects of that suspension may not be confined to the mismanagement of the current crisis; they will stay with us. A qualitative shift in the agenda of politics might appear as daydreaming in the present context because, with our love for conformity, we have left no room for criticism, much less for politics."[19] For the several months of lockdown, Parliament remained non-functional, with Committees refused authorization to meet virtually, and governmental accountability to the legislature, for all practical purposes, suspended.

Complicit in this transformation is Indian business. Indian capitalism, except for its brief infatuation with the liberal Swatantra Party in the 1960s, has demonstrated no great track record in defending liberty. But now it appears to have been cudgelled or cajoled into buying into the ruling party's nationalist ideology wholesale. As Mehta observed of Indian business, "It is having to devote all its capital, political funding, philanthropic commitment, media ownership, and even its symbolic capital, to the BJP and RSS.... No opposition, political or in civil society, can now count on that kind of material support."[20] The BJP's income from corporate sources in 2019 was twice the *combined* income of the other six "national" parties; more than 90% of the "electoral bonds" permitting anonymous donors to fund political parties were cornered by the ruling party that had devised this mechanism.

In return, the government seems to have earmarked one aspect of its nationalist project—what has been dubbed "techno-nationalism"—for its favoured private companies, or at least those big companies capable of harnessing the nation's technological prowess for the greater glory of the state. The Modi government appears determined to facilitate the creation of national capabilities in the private sector by smoothing the path for a handful of iconic companies that could, at least domestically, stand up against the global giants seeking to "colonize" the Indian technology space and thus serve as carriers of national power. The blatant retrospective changes of e-commerce rules to the disadvantage of multinational companies like Walmart and Amazon are a clear indication the government sees the promotion of Indian alternatives as a proxy for national power." The nexus of big companies, state power and consumerist populism might be the new carriers of techno-nationalism, instead of the old public sector," writes Mehta. "So one of the oddest manifestations of techno-nationalism ... will be arguments for the subtle promotion of a few big companies, now positioned in their nationalist avatar."[21] This corporatist alliance of big government with big business in the nationalist cause had striking precedents elsewhere, from Germany in the 1930s to China in more recent times, but it leaves little room for others.

Ramchandra Guha has written that all this was prefigured in the "Gujarat Model" pointed to by Mr Modi's backers when he first ran for office on the strength of his dozen years as chief minister of the state of Gujarat. His performance there, Guha points out, "included the relegation of minorities (and particularly Muslims) to second-class status; the centralization of power in the Chief Minister and the creation of a cult of personality around him; attacks on the independence and autonomy of universities; curbs on the freedom of the press; and, not least, a vengeful attitude towards critics and political rivals."[22] These are precisely the same patterns of conduct we have seen in the years of Mr Modi's rule at the Centre: "The communalization of politics and of popular discourse, the capturing of public institutions, the intimidation of the press, the use of the police and investigating agencies to harass opponents, and, perhaps above all, the deification of the Great Leader by the party, the Cabinet, the Government, and the Godi [lapdog] Media—these have characterized the Prime Ministerial tenure of Narendra Modi."[23]

Of course, in India, as elsewhere, populism requires a charismatic leader enjoying a direct rapport with the people. Mr Modi's disregard for the media is because he does not need it; he seeks, and demands, unmediated access to the Indian masses. Social media, providing direct access to the people, is the favourite mode of communication for a populist today. Narendra Modi is no exception. What is new since his early years in Gujarat is the advent, and the ruling party's skilled manipulation, of social media. Benign trends in Indian society—the expanding reach of the mobile phone network, the affordability of inexpensive communications, the development and expansion of broadband connectivity—have proven, in BJP hands, to be politically manipulable to promote majoritarian nationalism. As if the more than four hundred all-news television channels broadcasting pro-government stories 24/7 in every one of India's languages (or manufacturing distractions whenever the government wants the nation's attention deflected) weren't enough, a new mass medium has been born that uses the phone in our hands for its insidious messaging. This digital extremism began at a time when the BJP was in the Opposition and felt its point of view was marginalized in the mainstream national media, but it has developed into a well-organized machine with a formidable presence on Twitter, Facebook, and WhatsApp that reinforce the narrative assiduously propagated by the powers-that-be.

A year prior to the 2014 elections, a study conducted by the IRIS Knowledge Foundation and the Internet and Mobile Association of India (AIMAI)[24] suggested that there were only 160 constituencies (out of 543 in the Lok Sabha) where social media might have made a difference. Those constituencies included those where the election was won by a smaller margin of victory than the number of residents active on social media, and those where over 10 per cent of the population was on social media. It estimated that, by the 2014 election, as many as 80 million Indians would be using social media, and asserted that this was now a vote-bank that no politician can afford to ignore.

If that was true then, it's a lot truer now. The tentative assertions made in that study just two elections ago seem laughable now. I haven't seen a comparable study recently, but the numbers have, of course, grown dramatically since 2014; with some 560 million internet connections in India, of which upwards of 80% are on mobile phones, it would be a foolish politician indeed who ignored its importance as a tool in our democracy.

At the same time, my own view—though I was a pioneering Indian politician in the social media space—is that while social media is vital, no Indian election can be won or lost on social media *alone*. While perhaps a bit more than two-thirds of India's population, and perhaps above 50% of our voters, use social media, there are no reliable studies of how frequently they use it for political news and views. They could be zinging WhatsApp jokes to each other or sharing Facebook snaps of their holiday, rather than discussing the merits of the political parties contending in their constituency. There's still no substitute for mass rallies, street-corner addresses, door-to-door visits, handshakes at marketplaces and busy junctions, and jeep tours.

Consider the numbers. Twitter, the most "political" of social media, has only 27.3 million users in India; it is dwarfed by Facebook and WhatsApp with over 300 million users each. Still, with 543 parliamentary constituencies of some 2 million people each, Twitter is of limited help in political mobilization. Unlike the US, for example, Twitter would be useless for organizing a mass rally in India or even convening a large public meeting. Social media cannot be a substitute for conventional campaigning by individual candidates. But its role in building and sustaining attitudes, and in directing those attitudes towards a particular vision of the nation, is unparalleled. Social media memes, digital posters, and WhatsApp forwards are extensively used for political messaging; in addition, the indirect impact of social media (as a source for "mainstream" media stories) makes it an indispensable communications tool for politicians.

WhatsApp is the favoured medium, first, because 82% of India's mobile phone users have downloaded the app,[25] and second, because it's targeted to specific people; a party can create groups defined by their interests, their caste or religious identity, or a specific issue or cause, and bombard them with messages to reinforce their biases, and convince them the party is with them. The BJP is the master at this technique, running an estimated half a million WhatsApp groups across the country. Its IT cell head, Amit Malviya, famously declared before the 2019 polls that 'The upcoming elections will be fought on the mobile phone.... In a way, you could say they would be WhatsApp elections.'[26]

That could well have been true for the BJP: the party's organization in just one state, West Bengal—a state where it was widely considered to stand no chance against the well-entrenched incumbent ruling regional party, the Trinamool Congress—created and monitored 55,000 WhatsApp groups to influence voters. The party boasted that its Bengal BJP Facebook and Twitter accounts received 220 million engagements and 4 million impressions, respectively, in the two months leading up to the election. Partly as a result, it performed far better than had been expected in the state, winning 18 seats in West Bengal, up from just two in the previous election. In all, the BJP is reported to have spent over 20 crore rupees on its social media electioneering.[27]

The use of social media is far from benign. Disinformation is rife on these BJP groups, including concocted accounts of what leading Congress politicians have said[28] (including, often enough, myself)[29] and photoshopped images seeking to portray traitorous behaviour by Opposition leaders.[30] Truth is optional: the "larger truth" of the nationalist message is all that matters; no wonder the age of social media is dubbed the "post-truth" era. Salacious allegations are lightly, almost insouciantly, issued, widely circulated, and rarely retracted, and the public is enthusiastically whipped up to hound the vulnerable. To adapt an old saw, in today's India, if you don't see social media, you are uninformed, and if you see it, you are misinformed. "Fake news" has been derided enough in the contemporary world, but it exists because it has been manufactured to serve the political interests of its disseminators. The danger, therefore, is that a lot of votes will be cast on the basis of false information. The ruling party's attitude is that all is fair in love, war, and politics, but the collateral damage that is sustained in the process is of Indian democracy itself.

Having been made aware of the political misuse of its messaging services, WhatsApp took steps to limit the damage, limiting forwards, for instance, to just five recipients[31] in order to make it more difficult for lies to go viral. It also decided to block numbers identified by the Election Commission of India as guilty of spreading "fake news".[32] But this has done little to stop the dissemination of disinformation; at best it might slow it down. The BJP benefits from vast armies of people, some paid, and some volunteer, whose job it is to feed the voracious appetites of these WhatsApp groups.[33] Today, the ruling party literally runs lakhs of WhatsApp groups, their memberships arranged by region, issue, and preferred prejudice, manufactures hundreds of TikTok videos every month, and sends out artfully tailored messages that, in Arundhati Roy's memorable phrase, "keep the population on a drip feed of frenzied bigotry".[34]

The fears of democrats are not unfounded: people have been killed on the basis of fake WhatsApp rumours.[35] It is striking that when the Easter church bombings took place in Sri Lanka in April 2019, one of the first reactions of the government was to shut down social media in that country. But the stakes are different when it comes to political messaging: in India, when the government itself has a vested interest in seeing itself re-elected, it tends to turn a blind eye to the excesses of its own partisans. So far, despite regular denunciations by the powers that be, India has seen very little progress in stopping "fake news", arresting its perpetrators, or limiting its spread—other than using the term to justify the selective targeting of journalists critical of the government.

Social media offers a marvellously useful set of communication tools that democratizes the expression of public opinion. But, in the hands of unscrupulous politicians, who see it as a means of manipulation, social media can undermine democracy itself. Once you have voted for the wrong people on the basis of false information, there is nothing you can do about it till the next election. In that chilling fact lies the WhatsApp danger to Indian democracy.

The febrile messaging is so totalitarian in its omnipresence and intolerance of disagreement that it admits no exceptions, not even on its own side. The vilification to which the late BJP Foreign Minister Sushma Swaraj was subjected by members and supporters of her own party in 2018 was a stark indication of the toxicity that has consumed India's social media space.

Ms Swaraj, who had developed something of a reputation for responding to citizens' appeals for her Ministry's services on Twitter, was viciously attacked for the punitive transfer of a passport official, who had made bigoted remarks to an inter-faith couple when they applied for a passport. Her party members, who largely share the anti-Muslim bigotry the official expressed, blamed her for his administrative punishment (a decision taken by the ministry when she was out of the country). They expressed their rage in a flood of excoriating tweets, including referring to her disparagingly as "begum" and urging her husband to beat her for getting out of line.

In the last decade, the BJP has developed a powerful band of cyber-warriors to propagate its message of Hindu chauvinism, contempt for minorities, and hyper-nationalism, coupled with a capacity for Rottweiler-like attacks on political opponents. The social media "troll" has become a vital foot-soldier in the BJP's political campaigns. Cyber-cells of well-paid "trolls" were set up in India and abroad to flood the social media space at all hours, taking on "sickulars" [secularists], "libtards" [liberal "bastards"], "Khangressis" (an allusion to the allegedly pro-Muslim leanings of the Congress Party), and responding ferociously to any statement or action deemed inimical to the BJP's interests. A 2016 exposé, *I Am A Troll: Inside the Secret World of the BJP's Digital Army*, by Swati Chaturvedi, bared the details of the well-oiled and scurrilous machinery that has been set up by the party. A virtual army of paid political pawns operates multiple accounts geared to attacking anyone deemed inimical to the party's political interests or hostile to its Hindu-chauvinist, anti-Muslim ideology. The BJP's cyber hit-squads are indeed so pervasive that it is difficult to express a liberal opinion on Indian social media without being assailed by a flood of insults and abuse.

As a regular victim of these trolls, I have experienced the daily mortification of opening my timeline to be assaulted by a flood of vile negativity. But, for Ms Swaraj, a leading member of the BJP herself, and the very same person who had been spared the indignity of shaving her head by Sonia Gandhi's renunciation of the prime ministership, it was a new experience to be trolled by her own side. She rashly conducted a Twitter poll to seek her followers' support against the textual harassment; a startling 47% supported the trolls instead. Ms Swaraj had merely discovered what the rest of us had long known: that her party has poisoned the social media space with posts of such toxicity that entering social media in India has become like stepping into a mud-wrestling pit. As Dr Frankenstein discovered, you can create a monster, but you can't always control what it does.

If Sushma Swaraj suffered in 2018, even Prime Minister Modi was not spared by the Islamophobes in his camp in 2020. Attempting to soothe Arab anger over anti-Muslim social media posts by Indians, he tweeted, "COVID-19 does not see race, religion, colour, caste, creed, language or borders before striking... We are in this together." This unexceptionable sentiment prompted howls of outrage from his followers, including several whom Mr Modi himself followed on Twitter, with one declaring: "We are NOT in it together @narendramodi sir. We are NOT the ones spitting at cops, we are not the ones hiding foreign nationals in mosques. We are NOT the ones pelting stones at doctors. We are NOT the ones hiding travel history. THEY are. And THEY have a name." Recounting this episode, the journalist Varghese K. George reported: 'Another Twitter user, celebrated and followed by the who's who of the nationalist band, declared that those who continued to "chant Modi, Modi" after reading his tweet were worthy of a universally abusive epithet that literally refers to a woman's genitals.' Almost worse, a Ramzan greeting by Modi on 24 April 2020, blandly issuing bromides wishing everyone "safety, well-being and prosperity", met with a similar rebuff as an anti-Muslim riposte to him was retweeted more often than his own politically-correct post.[36]

Abuse of women journalists and political activists is particularly widespread; not only are their morals called into question and aspersions cast on their looks and sexual conduct, but rape threats are routine. A threat on Twitter by a BJP activist to rape the 10-year old daughter of a Congress party spokeswoman led to his arrest, but this was an isolated incident that does not appear to have discouraged subsequent threats from similar social media misogynistic thugs. The internet is particularly fertile ground for abusive behaviour because of the anonymity it affords and the safe distance the perpetrators keep from their targets. This, coupled with the sense of righteousness that pervades all true believers in a political cause, seems to empower social media users to say anything they like.

It's not just sensibilities they disregard; it's also facts. It is common knowledge that the "fake news" phenomenon has taken over the social media world;

falsehoods are routinely asserted without the most elementary fact-checking. Dishearteningly, this has cost lives, as rumours forwarded on social media, especially on WhatsApp, have led to mob-lynchings of innocent people wrongly suspected to be child-kidnappers, cow-slaughterers or worse. Tens of thousands of Indians from the North-East fled their homes and jobs in major Indian cities in 2012 after fake social media posts used pictures of victims of a Myanmar cyclone to claim they were Muslims butchered in the North-east and Muslim activists, in revenge, started threatening North-easterners elsewhere in India.

It is in the nature of social media, which thrives on sensationalism and unverified information, that falsehoods go viral faster than sanity can be restored by disseminating the truth. But attempts to regulate it should be resisted, because regulating content on the internet opens the door to censor-ship of free expression on other media. There is no easy solution to the conun-drum. But it took a BJP leader to be trolled for the ruling party to realize the horrors it has unleashed on the rest of us. It did not, however, deter the party's cyber-warriors in the least. Social media remains an indispensable tool in the armoury of the foot-soldiers of Indian ethno-nationalism.

The picture this chapter has painted of the rise of what Prime Minister Modi unabashedly calls "Hindu nationalism" also shows how it is entrench-ing itself at the expense of the institutions, practices, and habits that had undergirded India's civic nationalism for seven decades. The much-vaunted "new India" of Mr Modi's imaginings is imposing itself upon a diverse, plu-ralist, and fractious society, which for now appears largely to have acqui-esced in his rule.

But the widespread protests against the Citizenship Amendment Act, which show Indian democracy fighting for its life, and the nationwide dis-gruntlement over the appalling treatment of the migrant workers trudging homeward after Mr Modi's no-notice Lockdown of 2020, suggest that cracks may be developing in the edifice. How the government responds could yet determine whether it goes the way of Hungary, where Viktor Orban used the excuse of the coronavirus pandemic to suspend parliament, and rule by decree, or of Turkey, where Recep Taiyib Erdogan has consolidated power, alternating as President and Prime Minister, and rewritten the Constitution to his taste—or whether, as happened in 1977, the Indian people will reassert themselves and return to their usual ways of being.

One of the strengths of civic nationalism is that it allows people to be themselves, to express their views, and to live as they wish within the larger national framework. Hindu nationalism, on the other hand, seeks to remake

Indians in the image of a new model of Indianness—conscious of themselves as belonging to a single faith community, speaking a single dominant language, following a single set of precepts, and owing allegiance to a single leader. This is the process that has begun; whether it will culminate in the successful conversion of the republic into an entity that is disquietingly majoritarian, ultimately only the Indian people can decide.

34

THE NORTH-SOUTH DIVIDE

The hyper-nationalist desire for uniformity all too often involves riding roughshod over the federalism that keeps a diverse country united. It is not often that a seemingly technical issue points towards a potentially grave challenge for the survival of our nation itself, but that is exactly what happened in 2017. (I mentioned this issue in passing earlier, when discussing the language controversy, but will go into it more fully here.)

A letter sent to ten Chief Ministers and the Prime Minister by Dravida Munnetra Kazhagam leader M.K. Stalin, questioning the "ill-conceived" terms of reference of the Fifteenth Finance Commission, revealed how an apparently thoughtless, but conceivably deliberate, decision by the Modi government opened a Pandora's Box with incalculable consequences for the country.

The Finance Commission is one of the less well-known institutions of our governing system. It is appointed every five years to review and decide how the country's revenue from taxation will be apportioned between the states. The Finance Commission uses various criteria to determine this, including each state's percentage of the national population. But for more than four decades, it has based itself on population figures from the 1971 census.

That may seem odd, since we have had four censuses since 1971, and new numbers have been available to successive Finance Commissions. But the reason for this is very simple, and it was made explicit in relation to an even more vital issue—that of political representation in our Parliament. In 1976, the omnibus 42nd Amendment to the Constitution decided to freeze the allocation of Lok Sabha seats to our states for twenty-five years to encourage population control, by assuring states that success in limiting population would not lose them Lok Sabha seats. In 2001, the NDA Government of Prime Minister Vajpayee extended this arrangement for another twenty-five years; its proposal, which became the 91st Amendment, was unanimously adopted by all parties in both Houses of Parliament.

The thinking behind this policy was clear: it was based on the sound principle that the reward for responsible stewardship of demography and human development by a state could not be its political disenfranchisement. While there is some logic to the argument that a democracy must value all its citizens equally—whether they live in a progressive state or one that, by failing to empower its women and reducing total fertility, has allowed its population to shoot through the roof—no federal democracy can survive the perception that states would lose political clout if they develop well, while others would gain more seats in Parliament as a reward for failure.

This is the carefully balanced arrangement that the Modi government carelessly caused to be undone by instructing the Finance Commission to use the 2011 census figures instead of the 1971 figures, leading Mr Stalin to erupt. Already, when the (earlier) Fourteenth Finance Commission had been asked to take the 2011 figures into account (while still relying principally on 1971), a south Indian analyst wrote, "India rewards the brute demographic advantage of north India over a state's performance." The analyst, R. S. Nilakantan, asked bluntly: "is it fair that the parameters of such progressive transfers ultimately reward poor female literacy?"[1]

Such concerns have resurfaced, and Mr Stalin was not alone in expressing his unease. Then-Karnataka Chief Minister Siddaramaiah in tweets and a Facebook post articulated a strong case; and Pawan Kalyan, the former film star who founded a political party in Andhra Pradesh, did so as well. "Is the success of south Indian states going to be used against them by Union of India?" he tweeted,[2] expressing "genuine concern that population-based formula for sharing tax revenues between states & Centre would hurt south Indian states." The analyst Nilakantan wrote that the Fifteenth Finance Commmission was worse than the Fourteenth, and "the future of the Indian union may well unravel based on its decisions":

> Using 2011 data to allocate resources among states, above all else, is a stunning rebuke of success. Why would a country punish a state so severely for successfully lowering its fertility rate by sending girls to school? What is the message that India is trying to send to Tamil Nadu? Or, to Kerala?

> The bind that Tamil Nadu and Kerala, in particular, find themselves is this: they are at a stage where their success is being used against them by [the central government of] India, which is seeking to aggressively redistribute resources based on brute demographic might. These states made improve-

ments in health to find that the reward for that is to have less money to spend on health; their improvements in education meant they'd have less money to spend on education.[3]

Siddaramaiah's post went much farther, raising a whole host of issues relating to Indian federalism, from Karnataka's ancient history and its right to its own flag, to the importance of honouring the Kannada language and the unfairness of the current tax distribution system: "Historically, the South has been subsidizing the north. … For example, for every one rupee of tax contributed by Uttar Pradesh, that state receives 1.79. For every one rupee of tax contributed by Karnataka, the state receives 0.47. While I recognize the need for correcting regional imbalances, where is the reward for development?"[4] He added that population was an important criterion for the apportionment of central taxes. "For how long", he asked, "can we keep incentivizing population growth?"

The fact is that whereas Tamil Nadu's Gross State Domestic Product is higher than Uttar Pradesh's, but the total budget expenditure of Tamil Nadu for 2018–19 was significantly lower than that of Uttar Pradesh—which benefited from a 36% higher budget outlay than Tamil Nadu despite being a 7% smaller economy. Other iniquities are measurable too: Karnataka meets 72% of its expenses from the state's own taxes; Bihar gets 77% of its expenses from Central taxes. In other words, unlike most federal systems, India's revenues are going disproportionately to its worst-performing states, those with poor levels of education, high rates of fertility and population growth, while the high-performance states in the south get short shrift. These are important questions that the rest of India can ill afford to ignore. The states of the "cow belt"—the Hindi-speaking heartland, once called the BIMARU states—have comprehensively failed to improve their development indicators, notably relating to female literacy and women's empowerment. As a result, their population growth has outstripped that of the southern states. And thanks to the Finance Commission's new formula, that makes them eligible for a larger share of tax revenues.

The fifteenth Finance Commission has no choice but to use the 2011 census, so it cannot dodge this issue indefinitely. True, population figures are just one of several criteria used in the Commission's calculations, and the Commission can reduce the weight it gives to this particular factor in finalizing each state's revenue share, though to what extent it can do so remains to be seen.

But India should pay attention to the greater dangers. While northern states like Bihar, Jharkhand, Madhya Pradesh, Rajasthan, and Uttar Pradesh had a decadal population growth rate of over 20% between 2001 and 2011, southern states like undivided Andhra Pradesh & Telangana, Kerala, Karnataka, and Tamil Nadu grew at less than 16% in the 2001–11 period. My own state of Kerala has the country's lowest growth rate (4.9% in 2001–11, and dropping, it is estimated, to negative growth by 2021). That is one-fifth of Bihar's growth rate. Why should Kerala be punished for its impressive performance by receiving less revenue from the Finance Commission and also losing seats in Parliament, thereby being forced to dilute its voice in national affairs?

The government's answer would be that those are the rules of democracy: one-person-one-vote means the more people you have, the more political clout, and tax rupees, you get. But in a country like India, whose diversity is held together by a sense of common belonging but whose civic nationalism must accommodate a range of states with divergent levels of development, it is essential that all feel that their common nationhood is a winning proposition for them. In a country where regional, religious, and linguistic tensions are never far from the surface, such an answer—"we have more people, so we will have more money and more power"—risks rupturing the fragile bonds that hold us all together. The worry is that the success of southern states in lowering fertility would be rewarded with a loss of political representation when the delimitation of Lok Sabha seats is undertaken on the same basis as the 15th Finance Commission. As Nilakantan, puts it starkly: "the levers of political power are irreversibly skewing towards the demographic might of north India. That makes the south fear economic and cultural hegemony; and it's not an irrational fear....[It's] a slap on the face of democratic progress that the southern states made in the past 70 years."[5]

As it is, the Hindi-Hindu-Hindustan politics of today's BJP is very different from the conciliatory coalition-building of the Vajpayee era when the BJP was last in power. Their blatant majoritarian triumphalism, the brazenness of the Hindi supremacism that infuses their discourse, and the culture of Aryavrat domination that infects their attitudes, have already raised disquiet among many Southern politicians. In addition to the high levels of corruption and venality in public life, highlighted by the brazen inducements offered to Opposition legislators to switch sides and defect to the BJP (in Madhya Pradesh, Gujarat, Karnataka, and elsewhere), the BJP government has been marked by lack of competence at the policy design and formulation levels and further incompetence at implementing government policies equitably. Allied to this is an insensitive and inept management of crucial federal issues, of which the botched allocation to states of funds from the State Disaster Risk Management Fund (SDRMF) for relief measures during the coronavirus lockdown—of amounts which bore no relation to the size of the Covid caseload, the number of migrants in the state or any similar challenges—was alarmingly illustrative.[6] As Harish Khare notes, "three professional associations of epide-miologists, public health practitioners and social medicine experts have called out the clumsy and confused decision-making practised by the Leader-driven power structure."[7] The combination of ineptitude and bigotry has laid the country low; if the Modi government compounds its economic fecklessness with political recklessness, it could plunge India into turmoil.

We have already seen how much the south is aggrieved by the ruling par-ty's aggressive promotion of linguistic nationalism. The three-language for-mula is honoured in the breach by Hindi-speaking states that are complacently soaking up the benefits of their mother tongue's increasing dominance while disregarding their obligation to teach and learn a southern language; mean-while, southern civil servants are suffering the burden of the government's increasing linguistic homogenization, while English is daily disparaged with scant regard for the utility to India of its officialdom mastering a world lan-guage. The financial and political consequences of this attitude threaten the very unity of India, since the South would face political disenfranchisement to go along with its sense of financial victimization—a combination that is bound to generate resentments that can spill over beyond the confines of quotidian politics.

Already some hotheads are calling for serious consideration of secession, and some in the environs of Chennai have begun reviving the case for a "Dravida Nadu". Such an idea may have little appeal beyond a few limited circles in Tamil Nadu, but that does not mean the underlying concerns behind such an idea should be ignored. Ethno-nationalism is not easy to get away with in the midst of linguistic, cultural, and regional diversity, quite apart from the religious divisions that are already bedevilling the Hindu nationalist project. One sober commentator has observed that "The Indian union has made it almost untenable for Tamil and Malayalee societies to thrive in the union as rational self-interested sub-units".[8]

Such concerns should ignite deep disquiet among all well-wishers of Indian democracy, and all true Indian nationalists. The only remedy is to acknowledge that we need a more decentralized democracy, one in which the central share of tax resources is not so crucial, and the political author-ity of New Delhi not so overwhelming. That could make the concerns raised by the new census figures less relevant. But as long as our system is what it is, we need to run it sensitively. That is something that the Modi government failed to do.

How can we flesh out what a decentralized democracy would mean? Former Karnataka Chief Minister Siddaramaiah has argued that India is evolving from a "union of states" into a "federation of states". This may, to some degree, be wishful thinking for now, in an era in which a glib phrase like "co-operative federalism" masks a reality of over-centralization; but there is no reason for us not to consider how to take India in that direction, even though we are not there yet. In our "quasi-federal" system, there is no doubt that the Union currently enjoys the upper hand: after all, in India, the Union created the states, rather than the states coming together to create the Union, and new states have been created in recent years by Acts of Parliament. But that does not mean that the dominance of the Union should extend to the point where the states have little or no autonomy and feel themselves the playthings of New Delhi. It is that perception that made the seemingly technical correction of the Finance Commission's TORs such a major political issue, with serious implications for national unity.

But what would a more federal India look like? The first fear to set at rest is that a more substantive federalism would loosen the bonds that tie all Indians together in a shared nationality. When Karnataka approved its own official state flag in March 2018, alarms went off, and the cry arose that such a flag would constitute a de facto challenge to the Indian flag. But many other federal nations have state flags and state symbols without their national governments feeling in the least threatened. Indeed, recognizing strong regional identities is a mark of a strong and confident state. It only the weak who are reluctant to empower their subordinates.

Indian civic nationalism has also been distinguished by its capacity to promote and celebrate multiple identities. The singularity of Indianness is that it works in the plural. The great Malayali poet Vallathol wrote: "Bharataam ennu kettaal, abhimaana pooritham aavanum antharangam; Keralam ennu kettalo, thilakan choara namukke njerambaglil." ("If one hears the name of India, one's heart must swell with pride; if one hears the name of Kerala, the blood must throb in one's veins.") Similarly the Kannada poet Kuvempu composed a lyric, "Jaya Bharatha Jananiya Tanujathe", hailing Karnataka as the daughter of Bharata, the Indian nation.

In short, the southern states are not really interested in secession; they want a more genuine federalism. Siddaramaiah argued the case for a system where states receive a larger portion of the taxes collected from them; this would permit the relatively well-developed southern states to retain a larger portion of what they currently contribute to the centre. The difficulty with that suggestion, of course, is that it reduces the quantum of funds available to the central government to subsidize India's poorer states. Siddaramaiah argued that "the share of centrally sponsored schemes must go down".[9] That could be the answer: take some revenues from the more affluent states to finance central schemes in the poorer states, but apply those schemes more flexibly so that each state can judge whether it needs them, and also be empowered to tailor these schemes to their needs. This, in turn, would free more funds to be allocated to the states' own priorities rather than to the Centre's.

Siddaramaiah also lamented that "the states do not have a say in making of the country's economic policy". He cited the example of the import of cheap pepper from Vietnam through Sri Lanka as the result of a Free Trade Agreement that states like Kerala and Karnataka had no say in negotiating, though it was their pepper farmers whose livelihoods would be most seriously affected. He proposed a body "on the lines of the GST Council" to discuss "trade policy and agrarian issues so that we have a better say in making policies that affect our farmers... We urgently need a mechanism where the states get a greater say in [the] making of the nation's policies."[10]

This proposal is worth considering. It is time for a second liberalization: just as the original liberalization of 1991 set Indians free from the restrictions of the license-permit-quota Raj, so do we need to liberate the states to grow according to their capacity and through good governance. "The states need greater autonomy to run their economic policies," wrote Mr Siddaramaiah, "borrow internationally as long as they convince the lenders of their credit-worthiness, build the infrastructure of their choice without depending too much for licenses from the centre, and design programs of their choice."[11]

This may sound like a radical idea to those who have been working in recent years to pursue Hindu nationalism as India's Volksgeist. But for the rest of us, in Manmohan Singh's famous phrase about liberalization, (when as Finance Minister he paraphrased Victor Hugo, while presenting the 1991–92 budget), it is an idea whose time has come. The solution suggested by civic nationalism would not, of course, be the same as those preferred by the votaries of ethno-nationalism. That is where the central tension lies.

35

REAFFIRMING CIVIC NATIONALISM AND PATRIOTISM

Where does all this leave us? It is clear that ever since the Narendra Modi government came to power at the Centre, India has been taken away significantly from its established practice of civic nationalism; the direction in which the country has been pushed has become much clearer since the 2019 election. Is India on the verge of ceding the cherished assumptions of its independence to a set of rulers who, in effect, will establish a Second Republic on its soil, seven decades after the first? We have pointed to the dangers of the BJP's brand of Hindu nationalism, in particular the marginalization of minorities, especially Muslims, with the attendant risks of the radicalization of sections of that community; and the side-lining of the non-Hindi heartland, with the risk of growing disaffection in the southern states. Both these developments fundamentally threaten the nationhood nurtured by the nationalist movement against the British and sustained over more than seven decades of Indian democracy.

Pratap Bhanu Mehta has argued that debates over Hinduism versus Hindutva, secularism and pluralism, are, in fact, beside the point. What the ruling BJP had successfully done, he suggested, was to hijack a particular conception of nationalism, which no amount of delving into our tradition—as I sought to do in *Why I Am a Hindu*—could cure. "Let us name the problem for what it is: a deep-seated prejudice against Muslims", he wrote to me in a private email.[1] "This cannot be cured by throwing Vedic thinking at them." The key issue India must confront, he declared, was that of individual and collective membership in a democratic society: who got to be a member? To him, as Renan recognized nearly a century and a half ago, almost every single modern state has a history of exclusion and homogenization, if not genocide, at the heart of its creation and sustenance. The BJP was trying to, if not exclude, at least dilute the rights of Muslims in India, but this challenge

287

could not be resolved, Mehta asserted, by seeking answers in our ancient traditions and values, or in accusing the Hindutva brigade of betraying the inclusive essence of Hinduism, as I had done in my writings. The troubling question was that the BJP's tendencies arose from within democracy, which "(made) the categories of majority and minority politically salient", sought to redefine India's conception of nationalism, and which required (or at least enabled) the state "to intervene in religious practices to emancipate individuals from communities".

I was right, Mehta would concede, in suggesting that ancient Hindu thought did not have a history of theological intolerance, but to him, that was not the issue, anyway. He rightly pointed out that Indian life, despite preaching the acceptance of difference, was full of histories of social intolerance: the iniquities of the caste system would be Exhibit A for such a proposition. Its pluralism often does not descend from the lofty heights of the metaphysical into ordinary people's daily lives. Though the Constitution reflects a conception of modern citizenship for every Indian as a rights-bearing individual, this is not sanctified by history: the history of individual freedom and social equality in India is chequered. Our current Hindu-Muslim problems arise from our historical conditions—going back to invasions more than a millennium ago, oppressions, exactions and conversions, and culminating in Partition: this is what the BJP is harking back to, not the precepts of the Hindu sages. "No amount of tradition can solve this angst," Mehta said to me. "We need political, not metaphysical solutions".

I do not disagree. The real issue, we would both agree, has to do with democracy and liberal constitutionalism. The Constitution grants rights to individual citizens but also to religious groups (by permitting their personal laws, for instance, or recognizing minority institutions). If you have many groups, how will power be shared amongst the different groups? Should we make group identities entirely irrelevant to what rights individual people have and how they are represented? If not, how will power be distributed? This question of power sharing (symbolic, political, and cultural) cannot be solved by throwing the slogans of pluralism or diversity at it, since it is precisely because we are plural that questions of power sharing arise. Groups (castes, religions, regions) compete for shares of the national pie. In Mehta's words, India's pluralism is a fact, not a solution. True enough; but in the acknowledgement of that fact lies the only viable possibility of a solution.

To a thinker like Mehta, the essential conflict in modern India—which I have described as a battle for India's soul—is essentially over individual freedom and equality, and the definition of national values that sustain or enfeeble these. The flaw in conventional exegeses of the idea of India is that it places value on the diversity of cultures, not on the freedoms of individuals within them. "If the range of freedom expands, all kinds of diversity will flourish anyway", Mehta argues. "But this will not necessarily be the diversity of well-defined cultures. It will be something that both draws upon culture and subverts it at the same time.... We need to privilege freedom over identity to protect genuine diversity."[2]

According to Mehta, India's "was a form of toleration compatible with walls between communities.... Our moral discourse is so centred on diversity and pluralism that it forgets the more basic ideas of freedom and dignity.... The problem is not the proliferation of identities; that may be a good thing. The problem is the assumption that these identities are inescapable."

Mehta is right that India's many identities are ineluctable legal categories, which outline what marriage law you are governed by, what property rules you fall under, what institutions you can run—minority status comes with the right to establish and administer one's own schools, hospitals and trusts with specified exemptions from laws applicable to the majority community. In some cases, such provisions are necessary to address historical injustice and continued deprivation, as with the Dalits. But it is troubling that these identities have grown stronger and more inescapable, that they are not a matter of self-definition but assigned and immutable. Politics has increasingly made India a federation of communities, where the conception of Indian citizenship was based on caste and communal identities. He goes on:

> Every community, majority or minority, often appeals to the thought that something must not be imposed on them if they do not consent to it. The problem is that communities do not often extend the same courtesy to individuals within them....India needs to move away from the idea that it is composed of a social contract between communities, to the idea that it should be a zone of individual freedom... [which] recognises that the challenge is not protecting community identities; it is protecting those who breach them.

Majoritarianism, he concludes, is the natural outgrowth of a culture that fails to think beyond majority and minority: "If we care about freedom all kinds of identities will flourish. If we insist on circumscribing identities, neither identities nor freedom will flourish."

This is where the Constitution comes in, and more pertinently its implementation in practice. Justice Dhananjaya Chandrachud of the Supreme Court has argued that "a commitment to pluralism did not imply non-interference where group practices hinder the constitutional vision of an equal citizenship premised on equal dignity, worth and liberty of every individual."³ In other words, group rights exist, but the Court can and does intervene to uphold individual rights when these are compromised by one's group. The challenge in Indian nationalism has always been that of finding ways of acknowledging and accommodating difference. To my mind, this quest for balance between group and individual rights entails one thing: to reaffirm, and to fight for, India's endangered civic nationalism, in the face of the determined effort to replace it with an ethno-religious nationalism as India's ruling credo. This must involve a reassertion of our democracy, and a defiant deepening of the habits of democratic practice and liberal constitutionalism in our political culture, which is in currently the process of wrenching the Indian people away from democracy in the name of identitarian majoritarianism.

* * *

Democracy, Winston Churchill famously wrote, is the worst system of government in the world, except for all the others. One of its defining characteristics is its unpredictability, since democracy reflects the wishes of large numbers of people expressed in the quiet intimacy of the polling booth. The wonders of democracy have repeatedly startled the world as the voters of India have confounded all manner of pundits and pollsters to place the country in the hands of different governments led by different parties or coalitions. India's first prime minister, Jawaharlal Nehru, would have been proud of this. His greatest satisfaction would have come from the knowledge that the democracy he tried so hard to instil in India had taken such deep roots, despite so many naysayers claiming that democracy would never work in a developing country.

As a result, India has managed the process of political change and economic transformation necessary to develop our country and to forestall political and economic disaster. Much as it is tempting to do so, this cannot, in all good conscience, be accredited to some innate beneficence that one acquires along with the right to an Indian passport. Rather, I credit Indian democracy and civic nationalism, rooted in the constitutional rule of law and free elections.

Every Indian general election is immediately the world's largest exercise in democratic franchise—with some 900 million registered voters in 2019, that is hardly surprising. And look what happens in these elections: governments are routinely voted out of office, and voters hold politicians accountable for their development promises. And they do so within India's extraordinary framework of diversity: for instance, as I have often pointed out with pride, in May 2004, India witnessed a general-election victory by a woman leader of Roman Catholic background, and Italian heritage (Sonia Gandhi) making way for a Sikh (Manmohan Singh) to be sworn in as Prime Minister by a Muslim (President Abdul Kalam)—in a country 80% Hindu.

India's democracy has flourished while pursuing some of the most intractable challenges of development the world has known. Of course, fiercely contentious politics remains a significant impediment to India's development, since reforms are pursued with hesitancy as governments keep looking constantly over their electoral shoulders. But this also ensures the acceptance of reforms when they are eventually made.

India has also been proud of being able to demonstrate, in a world riven by ethnic conflict and notions of clashing civilizations, that democracy is not only compatible with diversity, but preserves and protects it. No other country in the world, after all, embraces the extraordinary mixture of ethnic groups, the profusion of mutually incomprehensible languages, the varieties of topography and climate, the diversity of religions and cultural practices, and the range of levels of economic development that India does. Yet Indian democracy, rooted in the constitutional rule of law and free elections, has managed the processes of political change and economic transformation necessary to develop our country. This is an experience that some who are currently in power appear to forget, or devalue.

As I demonstrated in Part Two, India is united not by a common ethnicity, language, or religion, but by the experience of a common history within a shared geographical space, reified in a liberal constitution, and the repeated exercise of democratic self-governance in a pluralist polity. India's founding fathers wrote a constitution for this dream; we in India have given passports to their ideals. Amartya Sen applauds this: "The increasing tendency towards seeing people in terms of one dominant 'identity' ('this is your duty as an American', 'you must commit these acts as a Muslim', or 'as a Chinese you should give priority to this national engagement') is not only an imposition of an external and arbitrary priority, but also the denial of an important liberty of a person who can decide on their respective loyalties to different groups (to all of which he or she belongs)."[4]

So, as I have tried to show throughout this book, the idea of India is of one land embracing many—and many with multiple identities. It is the idea that a nation may endure differences of caste, creed, colour, culture, conviction, cuisine, costume, and custom, and still rally around a democratic consensus. That consensus is about the simple principle that in a democracy you do not really need to agree all the time—except on the ground rules of how you will disagree. The reason India has survived all the stresses and strains that have beset it for over seven decades, and that led so many to predict its imminent disintegration, is that it maintained consensus on how to manage without consensus. That consensus now seems to be in question, as the Indian that was comfortable with the idea of multiple identities and multiple loyalties, all coming together in allegiance to a larger, more plural sense of the nation, is now being forced to yield to a narrower India privileging Hindi-speaking Hindus.

The Indian voter has long since resolved the "bread vs freedom" debate so beloved of intellectuals: the question of whether democracy can literally "deliver the goods" in a country of poverty and scarcity, or whether its inbuilt inefficiencies only impede rapid growth. Some still ask—as they were prone to when three governments fell between 1996 and 1998—if the instability of political contention (and of makeshift coalitions) is a luxury a developing country cannot afford, and whether, as today's young concentrate on making their bread, they should consider political freedom a dispensable distraction. Some argue back that not only is democracy not incompatible with economic growth and progress, it is the only guarantee that growth and progress will be stable and self-sustaining. But they do so with diminishing conviction, in the face of the relentless assault of Moditva.

This is where lies the great battle for Indian nationhood, and for the survival and success of India's civic nationalism. I used to aver that no one identity can ever triumph in India: both the country's chronic pluralism and the logic of the electoral marketplace had made this impossible. In leading a coalition government of twenty-three parties, and then in losing office, the first iteration of the Hindutva-inclined BJP government learned that any party with aspirations to rule India must reach out to other groups, other interests, other minorities. After all, there are too many diversities in our land for any one version of reality to be imposed on all of us. The second iteration—the Modi government—has twice been elected with an absolute majority, for reasons I have explained earlier in the book, and does not need the support of others. Might it, then, emboldened by its current levels of support, remake India's nationalism altogether? I have looked at this question from different angles and tried to provide a satisfactory response, but the battle is still being fought and it is impossible to predict exactly how the future might unfold.

Democracy is a process and not just an event; it is the product of the exchange of hopes and promises, commitments, and compromises which underpins the sacred compact between governments and the governed. Democracy is also about how to lose, and that is something Indians have repeatedly learned, as multiple changes of governments have confirmed. But democracy flourishes within a specific defined framework of nationhood, and that is where India is beset by the uncertain fear that the framework itself is being rattled.

Civic nationalism is vital for India's future. While there is no easy way to cope with the country's extraordinary diversity, democracy is the only technique that can work to ensure all sections of our variegated society the possibility of their place in the sun. Elections and civic institutions are the instrument for ensuring this. What is encouraging for the future of democracy is that India is unusual in its reach; in India, electoral democracy is not an elite preoccupation, but matters most strongly to ordinary people. Whereas in the United States a majority of the poor do not vote—in Harlem, in ten Presidential elections before 2008 (when a credible black candidate, Barack Obama, ran), the turnout was below 23%—in India the poor exercise their franchise in great numbers. It is not the privileged or even the middle-class who spend four hours queueing in the hot sun to cast their vote, but the poor, because they know their votes make a difference.

As Supreme Court Justice Dhananjaya Chandrachud put it, "The making of our nation is a continuous process of deliberation and belongs to every individual."[5] The experiment begun in the middle of the 20th century by India's founding fathers has worked. Though there have been major threats to the nation from separatist movements, caste conflicts, and regional rivalries, electoral democracy has helped defuse them. When violent movements arise, they are often defused through accommodation in the democratic process, so that in state after state, secessionism is defeated by absorption into civic nationalism. Separatism in places as far afield as Tamil Nadu in the South and Mizoram in the Northeast has been defused in one of the great unsung achievements of Indian democracy: Yesterday's secessionists have, in many cases, become today's Chief Ministers. (And thanks to the vagaries of democratic politics, tomorrow's Opposition leaders.)

It's still true that in many parts of India, when you cast your vote, you vote your caste. But that too has brought about profound alterations in the country, as the lower castes have taken advantage of the ballot to seize electoral power. The explosive potential of caste division has been channelled through the ballot box. Most strikingly, the power of electoral numbers has given high office to the lowest of India's low. Who could have imagined, for 3,000 years, that a Dalit woman would rule as chief minister of India's most populous state? Yet Mayawati has done that three times in UP, on the basis of her electoral appeal. And even the ascent of a self-declared "chaiwallah" to the position of prime minister is a testament to the triumph of Indian democracy.

On the 50th summer of India's independence, K. R. Narayanan, a Malayali Dalit—a man who was born in a thatched hut with no toilet and no running water, whose university refused to award him his degree at the same ceremony as his upper-caste classmates—was elected President of India. He led an India whose injustices and inequalities he had keenly felt as a member of an underprivileged community; yet an India that offered—through its brave if flawed experiment in constitutional democracy, secularism, affirmative governmental action, and change through the ballot-box—the prospect of overcoming these injustices. Five years later, he was succeeded by a Tamil Muslim, a fisherman's son who sold newspapers in the street as a boy, and who happened to be the father of India's missile program. Today, the highest office in the land is again occupied by a member of the Dalit community, Ram Nath Kovind, who rose to the top from humble beginnings in Uttar Pradesh, and whose wife was photographed at a sewing machine, making masks for the poor to ward off the coronavirus. If the Presidency symbolizes the Indian State, it is still a symbol of India's diversity, and its egalitarian democracy.

The question of whether democracy and development can go together has also been answered convincingly by India. Some experts have argued that democracy does not lend itself to rapid development—that the compromises that are an essential element of democratic governance, and the need for decision-makers in a democratic society to take the wants of their constituents into account, were distractions that less developed states could ill afford if they were to make the hard decisions necessary to improve their futures.

In its first few decades after independence from Britain in 1947, India was seen as the global poster child for the virtues of democracy, in contrast to its giant neighbour, China, which turned into a Communist dictatorship in 1949. Till the 1970s, it was widely argued that while both countries suffered the horrors of poverty, under-development, and disease, India's was the superior model because its people were free to choose their own rulers. As China surged ahead economically from 1978 onwards, however, the debate changed: it was now argued that China's was clearly the superior economic performance, while India's chaotic democracy held its people back from the efficient pursuit of prosperity.

This was apparent across the board, notably in infrastructure development. If China wanted to build a new six-lane expressway, it could bulldoze its way past any number of villages in its path; in India, if you wanted to widen a two-lane road, you could be tied up in court for a dozen years over compensation entitlements, abetted by passionate demonstrators at the project site, egged on by political parties. But the flip side of India's weakness is its strength: India has mechanisms to deal with dissent, whereas China's suppression of politics could prove unsustainable in the long run, when a more educated populace began to assert its rights.

The old debate has now taken a new twist with the publication by Daniel A. Bell, an American professor at Beijing's Tsinghua University, of the book *The China Model: Political Meritocracy and the Limits of Democracy*, which argues that the authoritarianism intrinsic to China's success is actually a viable model of governance which might in fact be superior to India's (and the West's) liberal constitutionalism. Bell cites the remarkable economic success of an assortment of non-democracies in recent years. Certainly, countries like Singapore and China have prospered in recent decades through benign authoritarianism, built on what Bell calls "political meritocracy". While Amartya Sen famously demonstrated that famines don't occur in democracies with a free press because their governments would be unable to ignore the suffering,[6] Bell argues that China has also avoided famine and done better than democratic India on malnutrition. In other words, you don't have to be democratic to serve your people effectively. That is an argument that could well appeal to some in the current Indian political leadership.

Bell focuses on the methods for choosing political leaders in both systems of government and suggests that authoritarian selection processes, based strictly on merit, guarantee better leadership than the random enshrining of ignorance and prejudice in democratic voting. China's economic success can be attributed, he says, to the way it selects, evaluates, and promotes officials. Despite some weaknesses (notably complacency and corruption), it ensures orderly governance and development, which democracy doesn't necessarily do. The "politically relevant question," he says," is whether democratic elections lead to good consequences."[7]

It's a question India debated once before, exactly forty years ago, when then-Prime Minister Indira Gandhi declared a state of Emergency in 1975, suspended India's civil liberties, locked up the opposition leadership, and censored the press. She argued explicitly then that democracy in India had detracted from development. The issue became known as the "bread versus freedom" debate: the question of whether democracy can literally deliver the goods in a country of poverty and scarcity, or whether its inbuilt inefficiencies only impede the prospects of rapid growth.

That debate was resolved in India by the elections of 1977, which defenestrated the Emergency regime and restored democracy. But the question has not gone away, and the dysfunctional politics of democratic India in recent years has made it seem even more relevant. When, for a quarter of a century, India was ruled by governments in Delhi made up of over twenty political parties, political decision-making was determined by the lowest common denominator: the weakest link in the governmental chain determined its strength. Is that an efficient way of ensuring the well-being of the Indian people? Arguably not. But is the over-centralized, top-down, unitary autocracy being engineered by the Modi government any better?

I am not persuaded that Bell's affirmative answer (for the Chinese version of totalizing nationalism) is the right one. While rapid industrialization and development has pulled millions of Chinese out of poverty, it has often come at great cost in human suffering. China may have grown at breakneck speed—but it has broken necks in the process.

Whatever one might say about India's sclerotic bureaucracy versus China's efficient one, India's tangles of red tape versus China's unfurled red carpet to foreign investors, India's contentious and fractious political parties versus China's smoothly-functioning top-down Communist hierarchy, there's no doubt that India had become, at least until very recently, a strong example of the management of diversity through pluralist democracy. Every Indian had been allowed to feel that he or she has as much of a stake in the country, and at least in principle, as much of a chance to run it, as anyone else.

The legitimacy of democracy in India comes from the faith of the vast numbers of underprivileged rather than the minuscule elite. As has been discussed, it is the poor who turn out in large numbers to vote, because the poor know that their votes matter. They also believe that exerting their franchise is the most effective means of demonstrating what they really demand from the government. Frustration with Indian governments manifests itself in voting against the rulers rather than in revolts or insurrections. The Chinese system wasn't designed to cope with fundamental challenges to it except through repression. But every autocratic state in history has come to a point where repression was no longer enough. If that point is reached in China, all bets are off. The dragon could stumble where the elephant can always trundle on.

One of the problems of the Chinese system is that it is too bureaucratic. It only permits gradual and graduated ascent up the ladder, making it impossible for a young and relatively inexperienced but exciting leader like Barack Obama to emerge. It would fail to pick gifted leaders who were failures in their youth, like FDR, Lincoln, or for that matter Mahatma Gandhi, or Jawaharlal Nehru. Rebels and non-conformists, who have flourished in Indian politics, would never have got to first base in the Chinese system.

The authoritarian Chinese model denies its citizens a say in the kinds of policies the nation should pursue, and eliminates any possibility of mediating among competing value systems, ideologies and political and economic choices. Politics is about more than efficient management—it is also about representing different segments of society and accommodating their views and interests. This only liberal democracy within a framework of civic nationalism can do.

Bell cites the successes of authoritarian systems but does not acknowledge that these successes do not require authoritarianism. The methods employed by China and the other East Asian "tigers" to promote economic growth and development, which include economic competition, use of international markets, spread of education and land reforms, have in fact been consistent with democratic principles. As a result, many formerly authoritarian states in East Asia have become democracies at no cost to their development success stories. And no people who have gained democratic rights have clamoured for a return to the blessings of dictatorship, a clinching refutation of the Bell view.

Indian democracy is a strength, not a weakness. The Chinese system requires consensus and co-operation from top to bottom. It will flounder, and founder, if that consensus ever breaks down. This is why the Chinese model works in a predictable environment, but the Indian model may be better to cope with the perils of an uncertain world. And, just as we are aware—and proud—of modern India's strong democratic traditions, we are also aware of our responsibility to develop—to seek to bring all our people into the twenty-first century with comfortably full bellies and comfortably fulfilling occupations. Democracy and human rights are fundamental to who we are; but human rights begin with breakfast.

So modern India has struggled to come to terms with what has sometimes been seen as the competing demands of freedom and development, just as it has struggled with the need to fully respect diversity and at the same time strengthen and pay homage to our sense of identity. Democracy, as precept and practice, will never wear the mantle of perfection. I have written in my books of the many problems that India faces, the poor quality of much of its political leadership, the rampant corruption, the criminalization of politics. And yet, we go on. To take just one example of how problems are sorted, corruption continues to be tackled by an activist judiciary, and by energetic investigative agencies that have not hesitated to indict the most powerful Indian politicians. (If only the rate of convictions matched the rate of indictments, it would be even better...) The rule of law remains a vital Indian strength. The liberal institutions of our civic nationalism give every member of our polity an opportunity to pursue their constitutional rights. The Congress-led UPA government (2004–2014) ensured the rearming of India's rights regime (with the Right to Information Act, the Mahatma Gandhi National Rural Employment Guarantee scheme, the Right to Education Act and other liberal entitlements such as to food security and welfare), along with near-double-digit economic growth, a dramatic drop in the number of Indians living below the poverty line, and even a nuclear deal with the US. It is that form of democracy, informed by Nehru's vision, and undergirded by civic nationalism, which built an entire edifice of rights for Indians, that is under threat from today's hyper-nationalist forces. These forces need to be defeated, for, as I have shown throughout this book, the India of tomorrow will only flourish if it resists the undermining of its strengths by a rampant Hindu nationalism, strengthens its civic institutions and shores up its liberal democracy. That is the challenge that awaits India in the 21st century.

PART SIX

RECLAIMING INDIA'S SOUL

As we discussed in Part One, the idea of nationalism evolved from sentiments based on notions of blood, soil, and belonging, to what is known as civic nationalism. The world appeared to have moved significantly away from the nationalism of identity to the nationalism of citizenship. In Part Two, I described how India developed and sustained an idea of itself, anchored in its history but sustained by a pluralist democracy that was anchored in a constitutional civic nationalism. In a globalized world of multiple belongings, in which people tend to be affiliated in different ways, and to different degrees, to more than one collectivity, the notion of identity-based "rootedness" had appeared almost quaint—until developments in many democracies in the last decade demonstrated that it was no anachronism.

India, in recent years, has reflected in its own political experience the global resurgence of nationalism. Around the world, questions are being asked about the future of nationalism, the viability of the idea of the nation, and the survival of the nation-state. As identitarian ethnic nationalism reasserts itself in the third decade of the 21st century, can it afford to revert to the old models of the 20th? As the post-coronavirus world seems to be retreating behind protective and protectionist barriers, are we witnessing a revival of the nationalism of primordial identities? If so, will the characteristics of the idea of nationalism be reaffirmed, or change, and in what way? If not, are there alternatives to the civic nationalism that seemed to represent the direction of the modern nation-state? And where will, and should, India go?

36

WHERE DO WE GO FROM HERE?

The BJP government of Narendra Modi, charged by its fervour for Hindutva, appears determined to promote its version of ethnic nationalism. As I have shown in the book, it has already acted on the following ingredients of its redefined ethno-nationalist project:

- to establish a shared myth of common Hindu identity for Indian nationhood, derived from a common ancestry, justified by rewriting Indian history, promoting new "national" slogans like "Bharat Mata ki jai", introducing a religious test for citizenship through the CAA, building a Ram Mandir at Ayodhya and so on;
- to entrench its conception of majoritarian nationalism through such devices as the signalling of soft bigotry against minorities, the use of mob violence and riots targeting Muslims, "cow vigilantism", the criminalization of triple talaaq, and the assault on the autonomy of Jammu and Kashmir and the disposal of Article 370; and
- to secure a Hindu ethnic nationalism through effective centralization and top-down unitary rule by a strongman leader. As we have seen, this has entailed (a) the promotion of "Moditva" and the personality cult around the Prime Minister (b) the remaking of the national ethos through what I have dubbed the Modi-fication of India (c) the subversion of India's institutions and their subordination to a central agenda, and (d) the weakening of federalism and its practices by ensuring that financial resources and political clout shift irretrievably towards the Hindi heartland of northern India.

The Constitution of India established the shared norms on which self-government rests, in particular the statutory equality of every citizen, irrespective of religion, region, or language. India's civic nationalism is both created by and reflected in its provisions. The Constitution granted representation not to an Indian's pre-determined identity (religion or caste) but to each individual's expression of agency. The governments it commands are supposed to be committed to the welfare of the country's weakest citizens. Though poverty, social discrimination and caste tyranny still persist, the Constitution offers the victims protection and redress. Amid the myriad problems of India, it is constitutional democracy that has given Indians of every imaginable caste, creed, culture, and cause the chance to break free of their lot. This rests on a core assumption of civic nationalism: the development and strengthening of free institutions that ensure pluralism, protect diversity, and guarantee the integrity of the state.

Our liberal, inclusive, and just Constitution, based unambiguously on the principles of civic nationalism, has been the bedrock of our society, a guiding document that historically secured the inalienable rights of all Indians. It has not only consolidated and distilled the best of our democratic values, ideas for which our forefathers gave their lives at the height of our nationalist struggle, but has served to liberate the collective aspirations of our people. In the remarkable work of the Constituent Assembly, the Constitution served as a reminder that our country was always greater than the sum of our differences and that our diversity of thought, expression, and ideology was, and can be, our greatest strength. The Constitution allowed each Indian to create their individual political identity and thus collectively to fashion the nation's destiny. But, as Dr Ambedkar warned, a Constitution is only as good as those who work it. That is where, sadly, India seems today to be falling short.

A respected Indian Muslim jurist and scholar, Faizan Mustafa, surprisingly took his exasperation with Hindutva farther than one might have expected, by suggesting an end to the hypocrisy of promoting a Hindu rashtra in a supposedly secular state. He wanted to grasp the bull by the horns:

> Minorities, too, are now fed up with this facade of secularism, with all state institutions tilting towards one religion. Perhaps some kind of Hindu Rashtra can help us bring peace.... A Hindu Rashtra will certainly sound the death knell of the idea of India that celebrated diversity and will lower our international standing, but minorities should not worry too much about it. Just like several other modern theocracies, a Hindu Rashtra could guarantee substantial rights to religious minorities. ... We, too, may declare Hinduism to be the official religion of the state and, like England, give equal rights to all citizens, ensuring freedom of religion and prohibiting discrimination on the basis of religion.[1]

Mustafa hopes that a Hindu rashtra can incorporate "genuine liberalism, substantive equality, modernity and, above all, state responsibility towards religious minorities with the guarantee of freedom and cultural autonomy". This, he hopes, might "bring to an end the project of hate and polarisation." It is a pious hope: surrender rarely leads to the victor conceding the demands of the vanquished. If Hindutva did all that Mustafa asks for, it would no longer be the guiding spirit of the fantasy land the ideologues want. Surrendering to this dystopia, far from ending the Hindutva project, will merely whet the appetite for more hatred and polarization.

As I have shown in Parts Three and Four, the alternative "Hindu nationalist" vision of the BJP has fundamentally threatened the assumptions of India's constitutional civic nationalism. Its return to power at the helm of government in 2019, and the breath-taking speed with which it has subsequently introduced and cleared far-reaching legislation such as the RTI (Amendment) Bill, the UAPA Bill, the Citizenship Amendment Act, and the abrogation of Article 370 with the Jammu and Kashmir Re-organisation Bill during its first year's Parliamentary sessions, and the careless disregard for the sentiments of the South in such matters as the promotion of Hindi and the terms of reference of the Finance Commission, have presented a fundamental threat to the future of the freedoms that we have taken for granted, every one of them grounded in the tenets of civic nationalism since our Independence from colonial rule in 1947.

Far more worrying, however, is the remarkable shift in pace in the ruling party's ambition from their first innings to their second. They have gone from whispering about changing the Constitution to openly undermining it, from suggesting that some Indians are first and others are last, to openly ensuring that from Kashmir to Kanyakumari the very experience of Indianness, and what it means to be an Indian, is different, and from asserting control over independent national institutions to openly using them as instruments of their political agenda. All of this makes it abundantly clear that the present ruling dispensation is remaking the country into a populist, communalist, chauvinist, authoritarian, slickly-marketed, and power-hungry kakistocracy supported by stoked-up vigilante mobs—all in the name of a democratically-elected government, and at the expense of those public institutions that were intended to safeguard the rights of all Indians. They do this in the name of what Prime Minister Modi has dubbed "New India".

In the Old India, fought for by the blood of our forefathers, and birthed in the crucible of our national struggle, the fundamental premise that was ultimately forged was that of access to a historically inalienable set of freedoms— the freedom of choice being prime. The freedom to choose what government you wanted, the freedom to choose what set of convictions to resonate with, the freedom to choose who to love, and how to love, the freedom to choose what to wear, eat, drink, and speak, the freedom to move freely within the sovereign borders of the republic, and the freedom to choose whether Ram or Rahim (or Jesus or Jehovah) was the force that guided and moved the cosmos. All of these were freedoms enshrined in our Constitution and embedded not just in the letter and spirit of the law, but into the lived experience of India and its peoples.

So, when Prime Minister Modi speaks of a 'New India', and defines it as an India free from the shackles of casteism and communal tension, an India that successfully solves its endemic problems of corruption, nepotism, and terrorism, an India where every woman, man, and child would be given an empowered and dignified standard of living, thanks to a society that harnesses India's entrepreneurial spirit to become an economic powerhouse, he is not wrong. Rather, he is merely reiterating a historic commitment to the freedoms that were preserved and guaranteed in the Old India.

But, as usual, between the rhetoric and the reality there falls a great shadow. For all these statements and ideals (which one can find very little to disagree with), one is struck by the complete lack of any idea of how our country is going to achieve any of this. And, on the contrary, plenty of evidence of the opposite: whether it is the 'Achhe Din' of 2014 or the 'New India' of the present, under the BJP government, these phrases appear to be a mere smokescreen for the real agenda that this government has pursued since coming to power. The road to New India appears littered with the wreckage of all that was good and noble about the old India.

In its place, an ugly distortion of the Indian idea is rising, an India where an especially dangerous and perverted form of ethno-nationalism is being fostered and—in this India that is being sought to be created a narrow-minded majoritarianism prevails, where incidents of communal violence proliferate, driven by mob-lynching zealots, and gau-rakshak vigilantes. In this grotesque New India, driven by Hindu zealots, *Bharat Mata Ki Jai* and *Jai Shri Ram* have become rallying cries of bigotry rather than the beautiful slogans Indians are free to use or not as they wish. Human beings have been assaulted and killed in the name of cow protection. Muslims and Dalits have been particularly victimized: the father of an Air Force serviceman, a 15-year-old boy returning from Eid shopping, a dairy farmer transporting cows with a permit, Dalits doing their job of skinning a dead cow, have all been casualties of this New India. In fact, as Pratap Bhanu Mehta fittingly asked: "How did this fantasy of hope, painted in the colours of a nation marching to one tune and one purpose, completely blanket out the actual republic of fear?

If this 'republic of fear' was only hinted at in the first term of Modi's BJP government, in its second term it has become a clearly illustrated reality, as the previous chapters have described. Partly this may be because the Hindu-nationalist agenda has not proved to be easy to implement. Mistakes made in the first term, and the demonstrated lack of competence on a whole range of issues, from demonetization to the implementation of GST to the handling of the Covid-19 lockdown, to the Chinese attacks along the LAC, have obliged the BJP establishment to dig their heels in on their core principles, partly out of fear of failure and in reaction to backlashes they did not anticipate.

The British also ruled India as an "empire of fear" for this very reason: as historians have shown, the colonial regime was constantly fearful, even paranoid, because they were unsure of whether or not they really understood what they were doing.[2] The BJP government has begun showing similar symptoms. Their populism is built on the exploitation of fear: the nativist fear of foreigners (migrants, minorities, threatening neighbours), the middle class fear of competition from rising socio-economic groups (OBCs, Dalits, Muslims, migrants), the identitarian fear of demographic eclipse (from Muslim over-procreation, "love jihad", and the like), the nationalist fear of territorial fragmentation (caused by a left-liberal-Kashmiri "tukde-tukde gang", abetted by Pakistan, determined to break India into pieces), and the traditionalist fear of the unfamiliar ruptures of globalization. The "Hindu nationalists" have an ideology they want to implement but the resistance they have run into—from the CAA protests to unruly, suffering but defiant migrant workers—causes doubts and prompts them into exaggerated counter-reactions as a way of masking their confusion. It is ironic that in their strutting hyper-nationalism, bereft of any real understanding of the country's history and heritage and devoid of any commitment to the true idea of India they most resemble the imperialist bluster of the British Raj.

The Covid-19 pandemic showed up the Modi government from the time the first cases began to be detected—its multiple failures in dealing with the crisis, whether in terms of dealing with the catastrophic human cost of the disease or the collapse of the economy, were difficult to hide. At the same time the outbreak facilitated nationalist projects in many countries, including India. The signs are evident: the pandemic has confirmed, for many, that in times of crisis, people rely on the nation-state to shield them; that global supply chains are vulnerable to disruption and are therefore unsustainable; that dependence on foreign countries for essential goods (such as pharmaceuticals, or even the ingredients that go into making them) could be fatal; that the demand for more protectionism and "self-reliance" (Mr Modi's call for "*atma-nirbharta*"), for bringing manufacturing back home or at least closer to home, is not regressive but prudent; and that countries cannot always expect useful help from their neighbours and allies. It has also convinced many (who needed little convincing) that foreigners are to be feared, that strict border and immigration controls are essential, that free trade should be restricted, and that national interests should trump international cooperation. To many, including those around Mr Modi, the answer lies in strong government, in putting the nation's needs over individual citizens' freedoms, and in dispensing with democratic niceties, from federalism to parliamentary oversight, in what the government deems to be the national interest.

Support for strongmen (many of whom have used the present crisis to shore up the authority and power invested in them) may therefore increase exponentially and reduce the likelihood of international pressure on Modi's BJP government to honour democratic ways. Already this pandemic period seems to have ushered in an increased fear of the 'Other', as unfounded rumours and accusations against people blamed on the basis of their national, religious, ethnic or regional identity have had a field day in many countries. In India, citizens from the north-eastern states have suffered racial discrimination because of their supposedly "Chinese" features. Social media and nativist populism have amplified prejudices; the fact that a puritan Muslim sect, the Tablighi Jamaat, had held a major gathering just before the lockdown, whose attendees spread the infection to many states when they returned home, was used to justify open bigotry and discrimination against Muslims. The atmosphere created by the virus has empowered those who seek to spread another contagion, that of communal hatred and bigotry, in the cause of Hindu nationalism.

Another risk thrown up by the government's response to the pandemic, that may help further its nationalist project, is the increasing reach of the surveillance state. Already the BJP government had expanded the reach of the Aadhaar scheme—initially conceived by its predecessor UPA government as a means of providing verifiable secure identities to the poor to permit the direct transfer of government benefits to them—as an all-embracing mandatory means of amassing biometric information on every citizen, even linking it to people's mobile phone numbers and bank accounts. Though the Supreme Court partially put the brakes on this digital over-reach, the government was undeterred, continuing to use Aadhaar to create a national database of Indian residents, going well beyond the provision of government benefits. During the coronavirus outbreak, concern about the inadequacies of existing data systems to monitor and track the spread of the virus' transmission was used to justify the development of dedicated apps and tools to track, along with GPS, Bluetooth and cell-phone towers, a person's data, their travel history, contact with other individuals and possible proximity to known carriers of the virus. The government has already made its "Aarogya Setu" app, reliant on these tools, compulsory for every government employee and is trying to extend its reach to every citizen.

Post-Covid India is unlikely to give up these useful instruments of surveillance and control. China has already shown the way to a form of "digital Leninism"; India's is heading towards "digital nationalism". India could well see an enhanced deployment of surveillance and data gathering under the guise of preventing a similar scenario in the future, despite Supreme Court rulings on individuals' right to privacy. Ethno-nationalism, the sort of nationalism the BJP government favours, requires authoritarian means to maintain its consolidation; it would be surprising if the government does not take steps to ensure greater surveillance and data generation to keep tabs on Opposition leaders, dissenters, media and others who might not be enthusiasts of its nationalist project.

37

FIGHTING BACK

The ethno-religious nationalism avidly promoted by the Modi government risks turning the nation's democracy against itself. History is replete with examples of democracy being used as a stepping stone to power by nationalist parties that then proceed to subvert or even dismantle it and substitute it with their own authoritarianism. The formula is well known: weaken the independent institutions, demolish the autonomous checks and balances, stifle dissent, persecute and prosecute the critics, suspend genuine politics and replace it with mass rallies, parades, celebrations and entertainments, while treating the populace to "bread and circuses". The Modi government seems well on its way to goose-stepping down this familiar path.

Yes, India in the 2020s is not Italy in the 1920s or Germany in 1930s. True, the BJP has expressed no public determination to dismantle democracy, which, in any case, has been entrenched in the Indian body politic for decades now. The old excesses of ethno-nationalist regimes came in a different era, and the circumstances are unrecognizably different from those that preceded the Second World War. But is the BJP's majoritarian triumphalism all that different from the ideologues of an earlier era trumpeting "the will of the majority" over the wishes of the minority?

And, when Opposition politicians point to the fact that the BJP won its sweeping majorities in Parliament with merely 31% and 37% of the national vote in 2014 and 2019 respectively—suggesting that the BJP's majoritarianism is really the tyranny of the *minority*—and the ruling party's votaries respond that Prime Minister Modi embodies the will of the majority, whether or not he can claim a majority vote, does it not suggest some chilling reminders from history? Hitler, after all, had answered the same objection in a speech to industrialists in Dusseldorf in 1932. A majority vote, or "the supremacy of mere numbers", Hitler argued then, "is not rule of the people, but in reality the rule of stupidity, of mediocrity, of half-heartedness, of cowardice, of weakness, and of inadequacy… Thus, democracy will in practice lead to the destruction of a people's true values."[1] The impatience with democracy that is visible at the heart of the ethno-nationalist project, the invoking of majority will on the basis of a mandate from a minority, and the co-opting of the language of national will in the service of their own programmes, are not unique to today's India. When the 69%, and now 63%, who disagree with the BJP's agenda are dismissed as anti-nationals by those who delude themselves into believing they are on a historic mission to carry out the will of the people, there are uncomfortable echoes of past nationalist excesses elsewhere from which Indians seem not to have learned enough.

This is ethno-nationalist populism in full spate, portraying itself as the embodiment of the will of the pure and virtuous masses, anti-elitist (since the old elites are, of course, immoral, corrupt, self-serving, and "out of touch with the people"). Populism reduces democracy to electoral victory, which it then portrays as a referendum on the popular will. Accordingly, it discredits the importance of those non-elected autonomous institutions that are supposed to provide checks and balances on the overweening power of the state—the judiciary, media, civil society, NGOs, the Election Commission, the Reserve Bank, and so on—insisting that they honour the electoral verdict, rather than subvert it through their institutional functioning. Being unelected, they have no right, the populists say, to constrain the popularly elected government, and when they go too far, they will have to be brought to heel.

The de-legitimization of dissent is the inevitable corollary to this identification of state and nation. Thus, even a legitimate protest, constitutionally permitted under the established rules of our democracy, against the Citizenship Amendment Act in Uttar Pradesh in late 2019, was not just forbidden, but the protestors were subjected to swingeing fines and the confiscation of their property. A young woman who had helped organize one of the protests, Sarfoora Zagar, was punitively jailed without bail for months, though she was pregnant. As Tavleen Singh wrote: "The Modi government is so thin-skinned that even mild criticism is seen as an attack. Dissent is seen as sedition, and if you happen to be a dissenting Muslim, you risk being labelled a traitor. If you are a dissenting businessman, you risk being raided by the tax department. If you are a dissenting journalist, you risk being silenced in more ways than one. There is little doubt that there is more repression in the air of our dear Bharat Mata than at any other time except during the Emergency."[2]

In a remarkable lecture delivered at the Gujarat High Court, Supreme Court Justice Dhananjaya Chandrachud remarked: "The silencing of dissent and the generation of fear in the minds of people go beyond the violation of personal liberty and a commitment to constitutional values—it strikes at the heart of a dialogue-based democratic society which accords to every individual equal respect and consideration."[3] Justice Chandrachud added: "Homogeneity is not the defining feature of Indianness. Our differences are not our weakness. Our ability to transcend these differences in recognition of our shared humanity is the source of our strength. Pluralism should thrive not only because it inheres in the vision of the Constitution, but also because of its inherent value in nation building." This was not a dictum that India's ethno-nationalist government is inclined to heed. Under the present government, dissent is portrayed as seditious, protests are 'anti-national', and free speech is censored through economic pressure on media owners and outright political intimidation—all of which are illustrations of the petty intolerance and chauvinism that passes for a ruling ideology in today's times.

When in the Opposition, the BJP had regularly expressed its impatience with the traditions and institutions of Indian civic nationalism that obstructed their desires. The Congress party that was in power was said to be discredited by dynasticism and contaminated by its leader's foreign origins and in any case alleged to be devoted to "minority appeasement". Institutions of government and bureaucracy were portrayed as being self-seeking and riddled with corruption. The autonomous bodies upholding free elections, anti-corruption probes, sound monetary policy, and federalism were all derided as complicit in the emasculation of the nation. Cases against BJP leaders "proved" that the judges were part of the enemy establishment and out of touch with the real justice sought by the people. The press was dismissed as hopelessly biased and sold out to the "sickularists"; the news was either "paid" or fake, and dispensed by "presstitutes". The universities were demonized as bastions of radical Marxism that promoted seditious and anti-national ideologies. The trade unions were sneered at as full of vested interests that stood in the way of progress. The protective institutions of liberal democracy and civic nationalism were thus "exposed" as hollow creations, not fit for the grand and noble purpose of national renewal that the BJP sought.

Inevitably, when the same BJP came to power, it reduced—or sought to reduce—all these institutions to the very caricature of themselves that they had portrayed. Only that this time it was the BJP actually performing the subversion by bringing every one of these institutions to heel in the service of its transcendent agenda. A well-regarded annual "democracy report" for 2020 describes India as an "autocratizing" country, comparable to Hungary and Turkey, and well on the way to forfeiting its standing among the ranks of the world's liberal democracies.[4] As Nehru said of Hindu fundamentalism, and its adherents, after Gandhiji's assassination: "We must face this poison, we must root out this poison, and we must face all the perils that encompass us, and face them not madly or badly, but rather in the way that our beloved teacher taught us to face them."[5]

If India is to reclaim its soul, the urgent national challenge is to restore, empower and renew the very institutions of civic nationalism that the BJP has commandeered and weakened. These are the institutions that can best protect the minorities and the marginalized, that protect free speech and the expression of unfashionable opinions, that elevate principles and values above the interests of politicians in power, that offer shelter and aid to the vulnerable, and so create the habits and conventions that make democracy the safest of political systems for ordinary people to live under. This is what true civic nationalism is about, the only nationalism suited to India, anchored in liberal constitutionalism, and not some fraudulent, dangerous, primitive, regressive form of ethno-religious nationalism that is guaranteed to destroy all that is noble, good and beneficial to every Indian. Indians should be speaking of a common future more than of a divided past; in that common sense of purpose would lie the basic premise of belonging.

Like most democratic civic nationalists, I want a New India, too. It will be a New India where you won't get lynched for the food you eat, marginalized for the faith you hold dear, criminalized for the person you love or imprisoned for making use of fundamental rights guaranteed by your own Constitution. Instead, we must look forward to a 'New India' that celebrates and welcomes pluralism, an idea vindicated by history itself, and one that is uniquely suited to our country. To me, this new India must be fundamentally rooted in the idea of India that our founding fathers believed in—an idea anchored, as Justice Chandrachud put it, "in the guarantee of individual liberty and the protection of a plural polity". After all, as I've asked in a different context, if you don't know where you are coming from, then how can you know where you are going?

38

LIBERAL CONSTITUTIONALISM AND PATRIOTISM

There has been mounting concern in academic circles about the decline of liberal constitutionalism worldwide, including in the west.[1] Liberal constitutionalism is a typical attribute of civic nationalism, based on a written constitution that encodes individual rights, provides for judicial review, grants rights of political participation in conditions of political equality, requires periodic democratic elections, and is committed to the rule of law (which includes fair administrative and judicial functions that operate in the interests of all citizens and retain autonomy from political or governmental authority). Francis Fukuyama famously saw these elements as the default governance option for the post-Cold War world: "at the end of history, there are no serious ideological competitors left to liberal democracy,"[2] he opined. The global rise of populist ethno-nationalism has destroyed that illusion: the dominant players in the biggest and most influential countries of the world have all undermined liberal constitutionalism, where they have not dispensed with altogether, as China's Xi and Russia's Putin have done.[3]

Civic nationalism, on the other hand, derives strength from liberal constitutionalism, and makes common cause with both national tradition and the internationalism of our common humanity. It is true that ideologies, especially if they seek mass appeal, do not offer technocratic programmes. They offer a way of seeing the world, not just a blueprint for governance. It is the spirit of civic nationalism that will capture the public imagination, more than the formal institutions of liberal constitutionalism—but it is the latter that sustains the spirit. In India, the staunch nationalist poet Subramania Bharati (1882–1921) was in many ways an early exponent of patriotic civic nationalism. In the words of his great-grand-daughter, Mira T. Sundara Rajan,

His own nationalism, unshakably rooted in internationalism and individualism, and inspired by his deep reading of ancient Indian literature, was as clear-sighted as it was passionate. A firm believer in reason and science, he was always the first to acknowledge the shortcomings of the past and the moral failings of tradition, whether in India or elsewhere. His appeal was to our common humanity, and neither tradition nor history could ever be a valid reason for denying it. His rallying cry was, "Nalla kalam varuguthu!"—"the best of times lies ahead!" Krutha yugam, the epoch of goodness, always lay ahead; there was never any excuse to cease moving forward.[4]

Internationalism was a key aspect of his approach, as it was of Nehru's. For Bharati, "nationalism could never mean a turning inward, a focus on national interest in the narrow sense, to the exclusion of the world at large. On the contrary, the world's problems were India's, and India's were the world's; so, too, were the shared ideals of culture, nature, and humanism".[5]

Those shared ideals are attainable if one pursues them from a platform of patriotism, the sibling of civic nationalism—the benign, tolerant, unthreatening love for one's country with all its myriad strengths and weaknesses. As we have seen, India does not need the dangerously intolerant and vicious nationalism promoted by Modi's BJP; it needs the freedom and justice and equality promised to every citizen of the country by the Constitution—classic civic nationalism, in short. Civic nationalism twinned with patriotism would be a means of giving every Indian their rightful, honoured place in the India of the twenty-first century and beyond.

Patriotism, linked to a civic tradition, can be traced back at least to Cicero, who wrote of patriotism two millennia ago as incorporating both love and duty:

> Yet, being the sort of man I was, I did not hesitate to brave the wildest storms and almost the very thunderbolts themselves to protect my countrymen, and, by risking my own life, to win peace and security for the rest. For our country did not give us life and nurture unconditionally, without expecting to receive in return, as it were, some convenience, providing a safe haven for our leisure and a quiet place for our relaxation. No, it reserved the right to appropriate for its own purpose the largest and most numerous portions of our loyalty, ability, and sagacity, leaving to us for our private use only what might be surplus to its needs.[6]

For Cicero, love of homeland was an extension of filial love for one's home: Rome is mother to all Romans, she has nurtured them, she needs to be protected by her sons in her hour of need. But the Romans were not merely sustaining liberty through their ideas of patriotism: they did follow policies of exclusion and slavery, and used patriotism to justify war and imperial expansion. In France, the self-proclaimed patriots of the Revolution stressed their love of country, but met resistance to their ideas with the slogan, "let impure blood water our fields." So patriotism can be harnessed to unworthy ends. We see this when the noble sentiment of patriotism is misappropriated by those who advocate what we have described as "bad nationalism".

But patriotism that is compatible with civic nationalism offers hope. This love of homeland is what Martin Heidegger calls the rootedness of one's being (*Dasein*).[7] One is rooted in the land in which one was raised and educated, or perhaps chose to work and live in; that rootedness is patriotism. The Indian poet and scholar Badri Raina put it well: "Home was something entirely different from a fine house equipped with all the comforts that material advancement makes available. Home evoked the memory of sights, sounds, smells, cadences of social interaction, attitudes to time, space, money, the deep oneness with the languages we are born into and in which our imaginations embellish our realities".[8] A renewed call to patriotism—not an empty jingoistic patriotism, certainly not ethnic nationalism masquerading as love of country, but a true, good, kind patriotism, rooted in the streets and neighbourhoods, the soil and songs, the ballot-boxes and courts, and above all the people of our country, a patriotism that celebrates pluralism, that inheres in free democratic institutions and is coupled with the soaring ideals of civic nationalism enshrined in our Constitution—offers hope for India's redemption.[9]

A rampant ethnic nationalism can only propose top-down national solutions to the anxieties of nationhood. Local patriotism, which is the grassroots constituent of the larger national patriotism I have referred to in the previous para—the attachment of the peasant to his land, of the poet to his language—is either sentimentalized or looked down upon. But we live in a world where it is increasingly essential to be both local and national. The response to the COVID pandemic has highlighted the need for a country like India to be simultaneously local and national, as bureaucratic instructions issued from Delhi have proven to be out of touch with the realities in distant states and districts.

This was already apparent from the experience of dealing with environmental degradation: the *Swachh Bharat* (Clean India) campaign could not succeed through press releases from the capital and photo-ops of leaders draped in national flags, but only with effective local efforts. The COVID crisis has also made it clear that we cannot fight a pandemic nationally without taking the "local" along; central diktats could not prevent the virus from spreading. The migrant crisis showed that Indians are tied emotionally to the places they are from, much more than to the places they live in for the temporary exigencies of work: in Raina's poetic words, "even our patriotism may shrink to pieces of land that speak to our souls."[10] And the economic crisis brought about by the COVID lockdown needs national solutions but simultaneously highlights the importance for all Indians to support the local farmer, the corner shopkeeper, the returned migrant, the small businessperson, the unemployed factory worker, and so on.

One of Ernest Renan's pithy observations was that a nation's citizens must have a shared joy, a shared sorrow, and a shared dream, of which a 'shared sorrow', he felt, was most important: if you cannot cry together, he said memorably, you are not a nation. The COVID pandemic has revealed many fault lines in Indian society—the plight of the migrant workers to which so many in the establishment were indifferent, the demonization of Muslims, the privations of the poor and unemployed, the lockdown-within-a-lockdown in Kashmir, the challenges faced by Indian workers and students stranded abroad—which suggest that, perhaps, a substantial percentage of Indians do not have a shared sense of sorrow, that vital ability to cry together. In his powerful 2015 book, *Looking Away: Inequality, Prejudice and Indifference in New India*, the activist Harsh Mander wrote with passion of the indifference and lack of sympathy of India's aspiring middle-classes for the less-fortunate. He described the Indian rich and middle-class to be "among the most uncaring in the world".[11] Five years later, viewing the attitude of state and society to the working poor whose lives were disrupted by the coronavirus-inspired lockdown, Mander asked for "civilisational introspection": "Will we recognize the abject collapse of our moral centre? Will we at last learn lessons of solidarity, equality and justice?"[12]

The political scientist Suhas Palshikar does not seem to think we will, because Moditva has nullified the possibility: "The lack of popular protest is more because of the success of the regime in constructing and popularising a narrative that not just delegitimises but simply denies the existence of suffering, injustice and victimhood.... This narrative posits two contrasting social camps. One is the nation. It represents unity, progress and a possible millennium. All else is fragmentary and divisive. So any voice speaking of a particular group's suffering becomes a hurdle in the march of the nation; any coalition of the marginalised by definition assumes an anti-national tenor."[13] This brings us back to the point that ethno-nationalism destroys decency and compassion, but patriotism, undergirded by civic nationalism, provides the antidote. We can only do what Harsh Mander seeks, of course, out of a shared patriotism that embraces every Indian in a common narrative of hope.

All of this can be translated into a celebration of local patriotism, of love for one's roots within a civic nationalism that respects others' love of their roots; as the war against the pandemic has to be fought locally and nationally, so too its success could lie in the reassertion of Indian patriotism as the sum of hundreds of local patriotisms. Patriotism, as we have discussed, is linked to one's sense of home. "Home," as Badri Raina puts it, is "simply a cadence of unselfconscious living that informs everything from our palate to the structure of our interactions."[14] A cadence of unselfconscious living: this is a feeling that resonates with each of us. My idea of patriotism is that it expresses something you can't take away from me without changing me into someone else. For some Indians that patriotism is most deeply felt in their own little patch of it—their village, their district, their state. For someone like me, a Keralite brought up in Bombay, Calcutta and Delhi, my patriotism is pan-Indian. My love for India is part of who I am; I belong to India as India belongs to me. With my national feeling simultaneously rooted in different corners of the country, my patriotism admits and embraces the differences that make up my India. I admire its wonders, rail against its failings, express exasperation at its peculiarities, but always, in each case, out of my deep-seated love for my country, my desh, my watan, my nation. Both kinds of patriotism, local and national, taken together, safeguarded in the Constitution and co-existing in fraternity with others, preserve the pluralist essence of the idea of India.

One of the political clichés of my childhood in India was the phrase "national integration". Politicians were forever advocating it, and even tax policies actively encouraged it: "entertainment tax" was often waived on films that promoted "national integration", such as the Bollywood blockbuster *Amar, Akbar, Antony*, about three brothers separated at birth who grow up to be Hindu, Muslim, and Christian but who unite in the course of the film to defeat the bad guys. But such fantasies apart, what attitude, what frame of mind, in practice, does national integration require? The progressive writer, columnist, and filmmaker Khwaja Ahmed Abbas put it best: "The integrated Indian", he wrote, "is the one who regards India and everything in India as belonging to every Indian."[15] That is true patriotism—when a Malayali can get a lump in his throat hearing a Bengali sing D. L. Ray's *"Ami ei desheter janma jano, ei desheter mori"* ["I was born in this land and will die in it"], pine for the coffee house on his Delhi University campus, celebrate the festivals of his Bombay classmates, and be moved to an inexpressible longing by the aroma of freshly-steamed idlis in a Kerala village. Yes, that is my experience of patriotism, and it is as authentically Indian, I believe, as the "Go to Pakistan!" aggression directed at me by slogan-shouting, black-paint-wielding BJP protestors outside my MP office. Perhaps even more so.

Where ethno-religious nationalism divides and alienates, the patriotism enabled by civic nationalism unites and empowers our people. This is emphatically not the "bad nationalism" propagated by those who arrogate to themselves the privilege of deciding which patriot is anti-national. As Raina describes it:

> Thus, were I to echo the sentiment "India first" I would not mean by that India above all, but to express the sentiment of the least inhabitant of my country who might wish her little hutment to be clean and attractive because, simply, it was a space closest to her existence.

> I came to realize that such attachment to the concrete conditions of our grooming and lived being constitutes patriotism, whereas projecting that concrete into an unfelt abstraction that has never any basis in fact or reality comprises nationalism.[16]

It is time to reaffirm the patriotic 'Idea of India' enshrined in our constitution in order to build a New India that will cherish and uplift each and every one of us. This requires a conscious effort to defend the besieged institutions of civic nationalism, restore their autonomy, and ensure their effectiveness. To truly build a new India, we will need to separate the powers and roles of the legislature, the judiciary, and the executive to ensure that the first two do not become mere rubber-stamps for the third. This may require, as I argued in detail in my book *India Shastra*, the adoption of a Presidential form of government, with a clear separation of powers, in order to ensure both efficiency and democracy. Elected chief executives at all levels of government, from village heads and town mayors to state governors and the national president, would have the mandate, the authority, and the resources to deliver solutions in their respective areas, to be accountable to independent elected legislatures, and an autonomous judiciary, and to face the voters at the end of fixed terms. The existence of multiple power-centres would ensure decentralization and prevent the emergence of a hyper-nationalist strongman, while celebrating patriotism and the best features of civic nationalism at all levels.

Of course, Indianness is constantly being remade, in a continuous process of deliberation and democratic discourse, a process that must continue (and that civic nationalism permits and encourages) in perpetuity. To defend and strengthen our civic nationalism, with its unique overlay of everything that is good and valuable about India, we will also need to undertake a careful retelling of a modern Indian history that is comprehensive, embraces all experiences, and refuses to see the past through the prism of any one faith. Swami Vivekananda spoke of the religion professed by the majority in this country, Hinduism, as one that does not merely tolerate other faiths but accepts them as they are. This acceptance of difference has been key to our country's survival, making, as I have remarked in this book and elsewhere, 'unity in diversity' the most hallowed of independent India's self-defining slogans. It is that unity we seek, not uniformity; it is consensus we must pursue, not conformity.

All this requires a rearmed liberalism, with a mass movement for the restoration of our civic nationalism. To restate the basic premise of the book, and that which gives it its title, the struggle for India's soul is a battle between two ideas—the idea of a civic nationhood of pluralism and institutions that protect our diversity and individual freedoms pitted against the ethno-religious nationalism of a Hindu state. To wage that battle effectively, Indian liberalism needs new ideas, precepts, narratives and heroes. It must be rooted in genuine patriotism and refuse to cede ground to the Hindutva devotees on nationalism. It also needs as wide a social coalition as Gandhiji was able to build for his nationalism. And it probably also needs to move out of the liberal enclaves to the urban neighbourhoods, the slums, the rural hamlets, and the streets of India. We will have to ensure that the South is not provoked into political disgruntlement by Hindi chauvinism, financial inquity or centralized government. Muslims and other minorities must enjoy the assurance that they are integral parts of the Indian nationalist narrative. Only by maintaining civic nationalism, and its commitment, through liberal constitutionalism, to a democratic and pluralistic ethos, can New India be able to fulfil the aspirations of all Indians.

To those who will protest that my critique assumes malign intentions on the part of the government where there are none, and that the Moditva "New India" upholds a vision of freedom and prosperity for all, I would respond in the words of a great American jurist, Justice Brandeis, nearly a century ago: "Experience should teach us to be most on our guard to protect liberty when the government's purposes are beneficial. Men born to freedom are naturally alert to repel invasion of their liberty by evil-minded rulers. The greater dangers to liberty lurk in insidious encroachment of men of zeal, well-meaning but without understanding."[17]

This is not just a political battle against the party in power or the government of the day, but an existential issue that transcends the moment. Post the current era of Moditva, the genie will still be out of the bottle. Hyper-nationalism will still be around, mistrust between Hindus and Muslims will persist, the gulf between Bharat and India will have widened, the hollowness of weakened institutions will exist, the chasm between versions of history will remain, the abandonment of unifying civic principles in favour of divisive and exclusionary slogans will continue, the gaps between north and south may have increased, and the abusiveness on social media will continue. The need for a solution that can heal the wounds of this era and bind the nation together would remain. This must involve a sense of commitment to the common good, the willingness to incorporate one's particularistic identity and interests into a larger accommodation of the identity and interests of others, and the realization that all Indians are part of an all-embracing civic nationalist community undergirded by a liberal constitution, suffused by common values, and striving for a shared future.

There is manifestly a need for reclaiming patriotism from the ethnonationalists, who have sought to arrogate a monopoly over it, and to do so through a social movement that seeks to rebuild an India that works for every Indian. This would rest on a sound structure of civic nationalism, recognizing our shared history, a shared vision, and at heart a set of shared values, that respect our diversity and pluralism, and value our multiple "local patriotisms" as building-blocks for our Indian patriotism. Democracy is essential in this construct, since one of the reasons democratic choices are accepted by those who voted otherwise is the presumption that the other side is, after all, part of the same national community and is as entitled to its choice as you are. Majoritarianism is circumscribed by the acceptance of clear restraints upon it: your rights cannot be compromised by the will of my majority. In Indian civic nationalism, patriots are willing to make some sacrifices for other patriots and for maintaining the integrity of the nation they share.

My response to those who fear that group identities are swamping our liberal constitution's guarantee of individual rights and freedoms is that this understanding of patriotism means acknowledging the loyalty many Indians have to their communities, while accepting the commonalities that make us a national community. Everyone feels a greater sense of responsibility for those closest to them, people with whom they have long-lasting social relations and shared moral beliefs. There is nothing wrong in such group loyalties provided communities are not permitted to violate the individual rights of their members. The sum of our local patriotisms infuses our national patriotism on the basis of shared values, faith in inclusiveness, an ethos of fellow-feeling and a willingness to serve the common good. The American scholar Amitai Etzioni has argued that "a good society cannot be centred only on liberty and individual rights but also must attend to the common good, expressed in terms of social responsibilities to others and to one's communities".[18] If we accept that we have many local communities that together make up our national community, and that our common good can be balanced with respect for both community and individual rights and interests, we can over-come the divisive polarization that currently bedevils our politics.

My advocacy of the common good is not intended to supersede the indi-vidual rights of any Indian but, rather, to balance these rights by taking into account the rights of the groups and local communities to which she may choose to belong. At the same time, affirming the common good requires patriots to resist the capture of our shared assets by special individual inter-ests—whether crony capitalists favoured by the government of the day or by clamorous community groups demanding special privileges for their mem-bers. All this calls for capable governance, skilled, humane and inclusive leadership, and the ability to make difficult decisions—essential attributes of a successful democracy, operating within the liberal constitutionalist frame-work of civic nationalism.

Etzioni explains that the hoary terms unity and diversity apply very well to the construction of an effective patriotism, provided one balances them well: "All members of a given society will fully respect and adhere to select core values and institutions that are considered part of the basic shared frame-work of the society (the unity component). At the same time, every group in society is free to maintain its distinct subculture—those policies, habits, and institutions that do not conflict with the shared core (the diversity compo-nent). Respect for the whole and for all is the essence of this position, with respect for the community (which itself may be recast over time) taking pre-cedence over diversity if and when these two come into conflict (unless the claims of community infringe on basic liberties and minority rights)".[19]

At the same time, we must also be conscious that preserving our ideo-logical commitment to pluralism, acceptance and the freedom provided by our democratic systems is only one half of the battle. Providing a decent standard of living to the people of India, particularly those from economi-cally vulnerable groups, is the second commitment that we must undertake in our blueprint for a 'New India'. Indians endure poverty and malnutri-tion, made worse by the economic ravages of the pandemic. Meanwhile the planet faces a new existential crisis: climate change. The impact of decades of unchecked growth and "development" is clearly visible in India as else-where, with rising temperatures causing repeated natural disasters and climate catastrophes—tsunamis, cyclones, hurricanes and the like—which have already scarred the first two decades of the twenty-first century. To ensure people are pulled out of poverty in a sustainable way, while being shielded from the hatreds and divisions of communal politics, are the twin challenges India must rise to.

Our new India must be an India that respects all religions, all faiths, all beliefs, all cultures, all languages, all regions, all castes, all classes—and all individual citizens. That Idea of India is under threat today from those who seek not just to rule India, but to change India's very heart and soul into something it has never been and was never meant to be. Our patriotism must be anchored in unity, not division; promote inclusion, not exclusion; encourage all identities, and privilege none; encourage growth and uplift the downtrodden. It must celebrate a sense of belonging, not hostility to an Other. Above all, our patriotism must give us a nationalism of hope, not fear.

Only then will we be able to look a questioner in the eye and say with upright stance and uplifted gaze: *"This is my nation. I am proud to say that I am an Indian."*

EPILOGUE

WINNING THE STRUGGLE FOR INDIA'S SOUL

This book has been a paean to an India where it does not matter what religion you practice, what language you speak, what caste you were born into, what colour your skin is, and a celebration of a civic nationalism that affirms that in India it should only matter that you are Indian. A paean, I said—not an elegy, and certainly not a dirge. It is possible to wrest back for India's civic nationalists the India that the proponents of Hindutva have been seeking to transform. Our choice is clear. We can have a new India that belongs to all of us, led by a government that works for all of us. Or we can have a new India that belongs to some, and serves the interests of a few. That is the difference between the civic nationalism enshrined in the constitutional republic and the ethno-religious-linguistic nationalism of the Hindutva movement.

I believe we must build this New India on solutions to our major challenges. But it must remain an open society, a rich and diverse and plural civilization, one that is open to the contention of ideas and interests within it, unafraid of the prowess or the products of the outside world, wedded to the democratic pluralism that is India's greatest strength, and determined to liberate and fulfil the creative energies of its people.

At the same time this will require our educated youth, untainted by the bigotries and communal prejudices of the religious nationalists, to come to the forefront to sustain liberal democracy. This book is a call to action by those who see the merits of civic nationalism, to rise to defend it against the regressive depredations of those who wish to set the clock back to an ancient era that in fact never existed outside their fevered imaginations.

The idea of India, articulated by our founders, and carried forward by those who believed in their soaring vision, matters because it is the only idea that can keep India together. It has worked for many decades in addressing the severe problems the British left us with. This idea and the practice of civic nationalism is not just woolly-headed liberal talk, but a practical and hard-headed vision of what India needs to both survive and thrive. A Hindu state will end up dividing India; a liberal, democratic India, rooted in civic nationalism, undergirded by liberal constitutionalism, welded together by a common purpose, and striving for a shared destiny, will unify the nation in an inclusive sense of belonging.

The scholar David Baker was born in 1932 in Perth, Western Australia, on the shores of the Indian Ocean, and developed an early fascination with India. His academic career as a historian saw him specializing in modern Indian history, particularly the rise of the nationalist movement in the Central Provinces and Berar, on which he has published the definitive book. Dr Baker is highly regarded internationally in his field, particularly as an authority on central-regional dynamics in the emergence of the modern Indian state and society, and has published numerous papers in major peer-reviewed journals: a typical essay, in *Modern Asian Studies*, is called "Colonial Beginnings and the Indian Response: The Revolt of 1857–58 in Madhya Pradesh".[1] But rather than pursue a career as an expert on modern Indian history in a Western institution like Oxford or Cambridge, or his own country's Australian National University, David Baker decided he wished to stay in India, and took up a teaching position, in 1969, at St Stephen's College in Delhi University. Half a century later, he is still there.

I met him in 1972. He was both my teacher as well as the "block tutor" (the faculty member in residence) at Mukharji East, my student accommodation block in college. We immediately took to each other. A slim, spare, rather ascetic figure, Baker lived frugally, devoting himself to books and ideas. With the casual racism that Indians profess to be incapable of, the college had decided they could not have a white man teaching Indians their own nationalism, and he was asked, therefore, to teach British history, a subject that was far removed from his academic concerns. But, if that was the price of staying in his beloved India, David Baker decided he would pay it. Even while pursuing his own field research and scholarly work on modern India, he read up his British history, and taught it to freshmen diligently and rigorously. His "tutorials" to small groups of students were outstanding and highly valued.

When I met him, David Baker had applied, much to everyone's surprise, for Indian citizenship, and the authorities were giving him the run-around. "They treated me as if I was trying to smuggle myself into Heaven, and that it was their duty to throw up as many obstacles as possible," he chuckled. "It was only my persistence that made them give up!" In the first couple of decades after Independence, there had been a handful of cases of "white men going native" in this way—the scientist J.B.S. Haldane and the anthropologist

Verrier Elwin were the best-known examples—but so great were the inconveniences of an Indian passport in those days of foreign exchange restrictions, limited international travel, and hard-to-obtain visas, that many who were entitled to one would have been only too happy to exchange places with Dr Baker. He persisted, refusing, to his credit, to call upon the distinguished network of Stephanian alumni in key positions in the Indian government to cut corners for him. It took years, many forms to be filled in, and many frustrating trips (by bus, in his case) to government offices, but in the end the government officials mystified by his quest could find no irregularity in his application, and David Baker became a citizen of India. Well into his 80s now, he lives in Delhi, researching and writing a history of St Stephen's College.

I asked him once why he wanted to be Indian, and his response was simple: "I feel Indian," he said. "It's the country I love, the place whose history matters most to me, the nation whose aspirations I share. It's India's people I love. It's where I am most comfortable. I wouldn't dream of living anywhere else, so I felt I should confirm that this is where I belong by taking on the passport as well."

India must always remain a country that appeals to other David Bakers, other M. A. R. Shaikhs, and other Ansar Husain Khans. The revival of our beleaguered civic nationalism must be both civic and nationalist, in the "good" sense of a benign patriotism that embraces and includes, rather than excludes and divides. When J. B. S. Haldane acquired Indian citizenship late in life, he wrote, in response to being hailed as a "citizen of the world": "No doubt I am in some sense a citizen of the world. But I believe with Thomas Jefferson that one of the chief duties of a citizen is to be a nuisance to the government of his state. As there is no world state, I cannot do this [as a "citizen of the world"]. On the other hand, I can be, and am, a nuisance to the government of India, which has the merit of permitting a good deal of criticism, though it reacts to it rather slowly. I also happen to be proud of being a citizen of India, which is a lot more diverse than Europe, let alone the U.S.A, the U.S.S.R or China, and thus a better model for a possible world organization".[2]

A world organization seems an increasingly remote prospect in these hyper-nationalist times. But a democratic, pluralist India, reflecting the diversity Haldane spoke of, exists and deserves the protection of every patriot, especially one who, like this author, takes the patriotic duty of being a nuisance very seriously. Such an India can not only survive but thrive, if we reassert and rebuild the civic nationalism in which our Constitution embeds it. We must remain faithful to our founding values of the twentieth century if we are to conquer the looming challenges of the twenty-first.

NOTES

1. THE EMERGENCE OF NATIONALISM

1. Liah Greenfeld, *Nationalism: A Short History*, Brookings 2019, p. 5, p. 16.
2. Guido Zernatto and Alfonso G. Mistretta, 'Nation: The History of a Word', *The Review of Politics*, Vol. 6, No. 3 (Jul., 1944), pp. 351–366.
3. Stephen Metcalf, "Neoliberalism: the idea that swallowed the world," *The Guardian*, 18 August 2017.
4. Ibid.
5. Ibid.
6. Tyler Stiem, "Statue Wars: What Should We Do with Troublesome Monuments?", *The Guardian*, 26 September 2018, https://www.theguardian.com/cities/2018/sep/26/statue-wars-what-should-we-do-with-troublesome-monuments?CMP=share_btn_link.
7. Jonathan D. Ostry, Prakash Loungani, and Davide Furceri, "Neoliberalism: Oversold?", International Monetary Fund/ FINANCE & DEVELOPMENT, June 2016, Vol. 53, No. 2.
8. Quinn Slobodian, *Globalists: The End of Empire and the Birth of Neoliberalism*, Harvard University Press, 2018).
9. Kenichi Ohmae, *The Borderless World* (NY: Harper Business, 1990).
10. Keerthik Sasidharan, "An equal and opposite reaction," *The Hindu*, March 12, 2017, https://www.thehindu.com/society/an-equal-and-opposite-reaction/article17449394.ece
11. Ece Temelkuran, *How to Lose a Country: The 7 Steps from Democracy to Dictatorship* (London: Fourth Estate, 2019).
12. Yascha Mounk and Jordan Kyle, "What Populists Do to Democracies", https://www.theatlantic.com/ideas/archive/2018/12/hard-data-populism-bolsonaro-trump/578878/
13. David Goodhart, *The Road to Somewhere: The Populist Revolt and the Future of Politics* (London: Hurst, 2017).
14. Quoted by Margaret Canovan, "Trust the People! Populism and the Two Faces of Democracy", *Political Studies* 47, no. 1 (March 1999): p. 12.
15. https://www.theguardian.com/politics/2018/oct/12/theresa-mays-brexit-speech-had-shades-of-hitler

16. Ibid.

17. Aihwa Ong, Flexible Citizenship: The Cultural Logics of Transnationality (Duke University Press, 1999).

18. Theresa May, 2016 Conservative Party Conference speech, (Birmingham, UK, October 5, 2016), https://www.mirror.co.uk/news/uk-news/theresa-mays-speech-conservative-party-8983265

2. A VERY RECENT IDEA

1. Quoted in Keerthik Sasidharan, "A Clash of Nations", The Hindu, July 15, 2018.

2. Thomas Hobbes, Leviathan (1651), full downloadable text available at https://www.holybooks.com/leviathan-by-thomas-hobbes-download-free-pdf-here/

3. https://www.brown.edu/Departments/Joukowsky_Institute/courses/islamiccivilizations/7966.html

4. Kautilya, Arthashastra, Translated by R. Shamasastry. (Bangalore: Government Press, 1915). Full downloadable text available at: https://en.wikisource.org/wiki/Arthashastra

5. Abhishek Kaicker, The King and the People (Oxford University Press, 2020).

6. Argenson, René Louis de Voyer d',Considérations sur le gouvernement ancient et present de la France, Amsterdam: Marc Michel Rey, 1764. [accessed on Google Scholar, books.google.com]

7. Dusan Kecmanovic, The Mass Psychology of Ethno-Nationalism (Springer, 1996)

8. Ernest Gellner, Nations and Nationalism (London, 1983).

9. Partha Chatterjee Nationalism: A Derivative Discourse (University of Minnesota Press, 1993), p. 34

10. Homi Bhabha, "Introduction: narrating the nation," Nation and Narration, ed. Homi Bhabha (Routledge, 1990): 2–3.

11. Homi Bhabha,"DissemiNation: time, narrative, and the margins of the modern nation," Nation and Narration, ed. Homi Bhabha (Routledge, 1990): 292, 300.

12. Speech before the Chamber of Deputies, May 26, 1927, in Benito Mussolini, Discorsi del 1927, (Milan: Alpes, 1928), p. 157.

13. Benedict Anderson, Imagined Communities: Reflections on the Origin and Spread of Nationalism, 2d ed. (London: Verso, 1991), p. 5

14. Salman Rushdie, Midnight's Children (Viking, 1981; Vintage paperback, 2010).

3. THE SIGNIFICANCE OF CULTURE

1. A. Azfar Moin, The Millennial Sovereign: Sacred Kingship and Sainthood in Islam (Columbia University Press, 2012).

2. http://pastdaily.com/wp-content/uploads/2015/11/JFK-In-Paris-JUne-2–1961.mp3. From NBC Radio—JFK In Paris—June 2, 1961—Gordon Skene Sound Collection.

3. Ahmed, Nazneen. (2012). The poetics of nationalism: Cultural resistance and poetry in East Pakistan/Bangladesh, 1952–71. Journal of Postcolonial Writing. 50. 1–13.

4. Llobera, J.R., *The god of modernity: The development of nationalism in western Europe.* (Oxford: Berg, 1994), p. 144.
5. Gellner, "Culture and Organisation", in Nationalism, London: Weidenfeld & Nicolson,1997. pp. 8–9
6. Weber (1948:179)
7. Smith (1995:68)
8. Bipin Chandra Pal, "Hinduism and Indian Nationalism," Published in *The Spirit of Indian Nationalism*, 1910, pp. 22–48.

4. THE PRISM OF IDENTITY

1. Benedict Anderson, *Imagined Communities: Reflections on the Origin and Spread of Nationalism, 2d ed.* (London: Verso, 1991), p. 3.
2. Karl Popper, *The Open Society and Its Enemies*, vol2, 4th rev. ed (London: Routledge and Kegan Paul, 1962), p. 49.
3. Yuval Noah Harari, *Sapiens: A Brief History of Humankind.*
4. Smith (1995:68).
5. Hobsbawm, 1993b.
6. Smith, 1986:148.
7. 1. Hans Kohn, *Prelude to Nation-States: The French and German Experience, 1789–1815* (Princeton, N.J.: Van Nostrand, 1967), p. 32
8. Umut Özkirimli, "The nation as an artichoke? A critique of ethnosymbolist interpretations of nationalism," *Nations and Nationalism* 9 (3), 2003, 339–355.
9. Ibid.
10. Ernest Gellner, *Nations and Nationalism* (London, 1983),
11. For details, see Kapil Komireddi, "Show No Mercy: The Tragedy in Xinjiang," *The Critic*, 8 June 2020, https://thecritic.co.uk/show-no-mercy-the-tragedy-in-xinjiang/
12. Aleksander Hemon, "Fascism is Not an idea to Be Debated," *Literary Hub*, Nov 1, 2018, https://lithub.com/fascism-is-not-an-idea-to-be-debated-its-a-set-of-actions-to-fight/
13. Michael Ignatieff, *Blood and Belonging*, 1997, pp 34–71.
14. Jürgen Habermas, *Inclusion of the Other: Studies in Political Theory* (John Wiley & Sons, 2015).
15. Ernest Renan, "*Qu'est-ce qu'une nation?*", 1882 lecture
16. Ibid.
17. All quotes from Tagore, unless otherwise specified, are from his book *Nationalism*, (New York: Macmillan: 1917).
18. https://www.goodreads.com/author/show/1181319.Sarat_Chandra_Chattopadhyay
19. Quoted by his disciple Arrian in *Discourses*. Bishop of St. David's, *The Christianity of Stoicism: or Selections from Arrian's Discourses of Epictetus*, trans. Carter, Carmarthen: 1822.

20. Otto Bauer, *the Question of Nationalities and Social Democracy (1907)* in Gopal Balakrishnan and Benedict Anderson, eds., *Mapping the Nation* (London: Verso, 2012) p. 52.

21. Quoted in R. Taras, *Liberal and Illiberal Nationalisms*(Springer, 2002). P. 13

22. Ernest Gellner, Culture and Organisation, in *Nationalism*, London: Weidenfeld & Nicolson,1997 p. 9.

5. WHAT MAKES PATRIOTISM DIFFERENT

1. William A. Galston, "In Defense of a Reasonable Patriotism," Brookings Institution, July 23, 2018, https://www.brookings.edu/research/in-defense-of-a-reasonable-patriotism/.

2. Badri Raina, "Why the Wren is a Patriot and not a Nationalist," *Mainstream*, VOL LVIII No 25, New Delhi, June 6, 2020, http://www.mainstreamweekly.net/article9454.html

3. Christopher Alan Bayly, *Origins of Nationality in South Asia: Patriotism and Ethical Government in the Making of Modern India* (Oxford University Press, 1998) p. 27.

4. Alasdair MacIntyre, *A Short History of Ethics: A History of Moral Philosophy from the Homeric Age to the Twentieth Century*, (University of Notre Dame Press, 1998)

5. Badri Raina, "Why the Wren is a Patriot and not a Nationalist," *Mainstream*, VOL LVIII No 25, New Delhi, June 6, 2020, http://www.mainstreamweekly.net/article9454.html

6. John H. Schaar, *Legitimacy in the Modern State* (collected essays) New Brunswick, NJ: Transaction Press, 1981, p. 287.

7. Senator Carl Schurz, Remarks in the Senate, February 29, 1872, *The Congressional Globe*,Vol. 45, p. 1287. https://www.bartleby.com/73/1641.html.

8. "Mark Twain Quotes." BrainyQuote.com. BrainyMedia Inc, 2020. 21 June 2020. https://www.brainyquote.com/quotes/mark_twain_386139.

9. Carlo Ginzburg, "The Bond of Shame," *New Left Review 120*, Nov-Dec 2019.

10. Arthur Schopenhauer, Essays and Aphorisms.

11. Quoted in Amitai Etzioni, *Reclaiming Patriotism*, University of Virginia Press, 2019, p. 60.

12. Raina, op.cit.

13. Acton 1972, 163

14. Ernest Gellner, *Nations and Nationalism*, New York: Cornell University Press, 1983. p. 138

15. George Orwell, "Notes on Nationalism", *Polemic*, October 1945, reprinted by Penguin Books, 1963. Also available in full on https://www.orwellfoundation.com/the-orwell-foundation/orwell/essays-and-other-works/notes-on-nationalism/ [All Orwell quotes are from this essay].

16. Frank DiKotter, How to be a *Dictator: The Cult of Personality in the Twentieth Century*, London: Bloomsbury, 2019.

17. Kedourie, *Nationalism* (1960), p. 72.

18. Quoted as the epigraph of Amitai Etzioni, *Reclaiming Patriotism*, (University of Virginia Press, 2019)
19. https://www.forbes.com/quotes/186/.
20. J. Scheff,., *The Bloody Revenge: Emotions, Nationalism and War*, Boulder, CO: Westview Press, 1994.p. 58.
21. Dilip D'Souza and Joy Ma, *The Deoliwallahs: The True Story of the 1962 Chinese-Indian Internment*, Pan Macmillan, New Delhi, 2020)
22. Fukuyama, Francis, *The End of History and the Last Man*, New York: The Free Press, 1992.p. 201.
23. Orwell, op.cit., note 54.

6. JANUS-FACED NATIONALISM

1. for more details, see Adrian Waters, "Gabriele D'Annunzio's Fiume Enterprise: 100 Years On," *Italics Magazine*, September 12, 2019, https://italicsmag.com/2019/09/12/gabriele-dannunzio-fiume-enterprise-100-years-on/
2. Tom Nairn, *The Break-up of Britain: Crisis and neo-nationalism*. London: Verso, 1981.
3. Tom Nairn, *Faces of Nationalism: Janus Revisited* London: Verso, 1998.
4. Etienne Balibar, "Racism and nationalism" In Balibar, E., & Wallerstein, I. (eds.), *Race, nation, class: Ambiguous identities*. (London: Verso, 1991).
5. Lea Brilmayer, "The Moral Significance of Nationalism", 71 *Notre Dame Law Review* 7, (1995), Available at: http://scholarship.law.nd.edu/ndlr/vol71/iss1/2.
6. William Tyler Page, "The American's Creed," 1917, http://www.ushistory.org / documents/creed.htm.
7. Hans Kohn, *The Idea of Nationalism: A Study In Its Origins And Background*, *(1944)*, reprinted Transaction Publishers, 1967.
8. Ernest Gellner, *Nations and Nationalism*, (New York: Cornell University Press, 1983) p. 138
9. Amitai Etzioni, *Reclaiming Patriotism*, (University of Virginia Press, 2019), p. 7.
10. Quoted in S. Irfan Habib, *Indian Nationalism*, (Delhi: Aleph, 2018).
11. Mark Jurgensmeyer, *The New Cold War: Religious nationalism confronts the secular state*, Berkeley: University of California Press, 1993. p. 15
12. J. R. Llobera, *The God of Modernity: The development of nationalism in Western Europe*, Oxford: Berg, 1994.p. 211.
13. Quoted in Dusan Kecmanovic, T*he Mass Psychology of Ethno-Nationalism* (Springer, 2013) p. 201.

7. THE ERA OF GLOBALIZATION

1. Arnold Toynbee, *Surviving the Future*, London/ New York: Oxford University Press, 1971.
2. Stanley Hoffman, 'On the Political Psychology of Peace and War: A critique and an agenda', *Political Psychology*, 7, 1968, 1–21.
3. Liah Greenfeld, *Nationalism: A Short History*, Brookings 2019, p. 34.

4. Speech to the Bombay Assembly, quoted in S. Irfan Habib, *Indian Nationalism* (Delhi: Aleph, 2018).

5. Benjamin Barber, *Jihad vs. McWorld: How Globalism and Tribalism Are Reshaping the World* (Times Books, 1995).

6. J. Braunthal, *The Paradox of Nationalism*, London: St. Botolph, 1946,. p. 5.

7. Jonathan Maunders, "A Potted and Bloody History of NATO," *History*, October 29, 2016, https://www.counterfire.org/articles/history/18584-keep-the-russians-out-the-americans-in-and-the-germans-down-a-potted-and-bloody-history-of-nato

8. https://yougov.co.uk/topics/politics/articles-reports/2015/07/14/decline-british-patriotism

9. https://worldpopulationreview.com/countries/most-patriotic-countries/

8. THE BETTER NATIONALISM

1. Theodor Adorno, *Minima Moralia: Reflections on a Damaged Life*, (1974,Translated from German by E.F.N.,Jephcott) London: Verso, 2005. p. 103.

2. Anthony Smith, *Nationalism and Modernism: A critical survey of recent theories of nations and nationalism*, (London: Routledge, 1998).pp. 40–41.

3. Kanishk Tharoor, "Cosmopolis: *The past through a distilled lens*", BLink, *The Hindu Business Line*, December 2019.

4. "America: the Failed State," Francis Fukuyama, *Prospect*, December 13, 2016, https://www.prospectmagazine.co.uk/author/francis-fukuyama

5. Yoram Hazony, *The Virtue of Nationalism* (New York: Basic Books, 2018).

6. Rich Lowry, *The Case for Nationalism* (New York: Broadside Books, 2019).

7. Jill Lepore, *Foreign Affairs*, citing Jill Lepore, *This America: The Case For The Nation*, New York: Liveright, 2019.

8. Brian Barry, *Democracy, Power, and Justice: Essays in Political Theory*, Oxford, 1989.

9. Tyler Stiem, "Statue Wars: What Should We Do with Troublesome Monuments?", *The Guardian*, 26 September 2018, https://www.theguardian.com/cities/2018/sep/26/statue-wars-what-should-we-do-with-troublesome-monuments?CMP=share_btn_link

10. THE BASICS

1. E. P. Thompson in *The Guardian*, 1980, quoted in https://www.weforum.org/agenda/2017/08/seventy-years-after-india-declared-independence-where-is-it-now/.

2. B. R. Ambedkar, 'A Nation Calling for a Home', in *Pakistan or Partition of India*. (Bombay, 1940).

3. Satish Chandra Mittal, *India Distorted: A Study of British Historians in India*, Vol. 1, (Delhi: M.D. Publications, 1995, p. 162.

4. Quoted by Pranab Mukherjee, President of India, Independence Day Address 2015, full text in *Indian Express*, August 15, 2015, https://indianexpress.com/article/india/

india-others/full-text-president-pranab-mukherjees-address-on-eve-of-independence-day/.

5. Diodorus Siculus, *Bibliotheca historica*, Vol. II., Translated by C.H. Oldfather, *Library of History: Loeb Classical Library*. (Cambridge, MA: Harvard University Press, 1935).

11. THE CHALLENGE OF DEFINITION

1. Quoted in Ramachandra Guha, "The Brexit of 1947," *Scroll*, June 24, 2016, https://scroll.in/article/810548/the-brexit-of-1947-scotland-is-more-like-spain-than-bengal-is-like-the-punjab

2. Diana L. Eck. *India: A Sacred Geography* (Harmony Books, 2013).

3. Jayaprakash Narayan, quoted in S. Irfan Habib, *Indian Nationalism*, (Delhi: Aleph, 2017) [*emphasis added*].

4. Rabindranath Tagore, NATIONALISM (San Francisco: Book Club of California, 1917) pp. 15–16

5. Jayaprakash Narayan, quoted in S. Irfan Habib, *Indian Nationalism*, (Delhi: Aleph, 2017)

6. Romila Thapar, *On Nationalism* (Aleph 2016), p. 3 [*emphasis added*].

7. Quoted in S. Irfan Habib, *Indian Nationalism*, (Delhi: Aleph, 2018)

8. Quoted in Ramachandra Guha, "The Brexit of 1947," op.cit., https://scroll.in/article/810548/the-brexit-of-1947-scotland-is-more-like-spain-than-bengal-is-like-the-punjab

12. WE ARE ALL MINORITIES IN INDIA

1. Dhananjay Mahapatra, "SC stresses on expiry date for quota," *Times of India*, April 14, 2008, at http://timesofindia.indiatimes.com/articleshow/2949805.cms?utm_source=contentofinterest&utm_medium=text&utm_campaign=cppst

2. Tagore, *Nationalism, op.cit.*

13. THE CONSTITUTION AND INDIAN NATIONHOOD

1. Jawaharlal Nehru, *Words of Freedom*, Delhi: Penguin Books India, 2010.

2. B. R. Ambedkar, "The Grammar of Anarchy," Speech to the Constituent Assembly, 25 November 1949.

3. Ambedkar's 1942 Bombay radio address, quoted in Luis Cabrera, *The Humble Cosmopolitan* (Oxford University Press, 2019), p. 277.

4. Madhav Khosla. *India's Founding Moment: The Constitution of a Most Surprising Democracy* (Harvard University Press, 2019)

5. Ronad Dworkin, *Freedom's Law: The Moral Reading of the American Constitution* (Harvard University Press, 1997), Introduction.

6. Quoted in Bhanu Dhamija, "Why Ambedkar Didn't Like India's Constitution," *The Quint*, 14 April 2018, https://www.thequint.com/voices/opinion/why-ambedkar-did-not-like-indian-constitution. Despite this self-disparagement, Ambedkar's stature has grown enormously since his passing; in his lifetime he lost almost every

election he contested, including two runs for the Lok Sabha, but today he is arguably amongst the most revered of Indians, his birthday the occasion of a five-night
vigil by his devoted followers, his statues across the country second only in number to those of Mahatma Gandhi.

7. Ibid.

8. Ibid.

9. Rabindranath Tagore, *Gitanjali: Song Offerings* (1912, reprinted by Pomona Press, 2007.

10. Tagore, *Nationalism*, op.cit

11. Ramachandra Guha, "An Unlikely Nation", *New Statesman*, 2 August 2007, https://www.newstatesman.com/asia/2007/08/democratic-india-british.

12. Vallabhbhai Patel, *The Collected Works of Sardar Vallabhbhai Patel*, vol. I (Delhi: Konark Publishers, 1990).

13. Quoted in S. Irfan Habib, *Indian Nationalism* (Delhi: Aleph, 2018). Emphasis added.

14. A LIVING DOCUMENT

1. Justice Dhananjaya Chandrachud, JUSTICE PD DESAI MEMORIAL LECTURE 2020, 15 February, 2020, Gujarat High Court, text at: https://images.assettype.com/barandbench/2020–02/f3dad31d-ed51–4ddb-af39–5d9138bf6162/Justice_DY_Chandrachud___Justice_PD_Desai_Memorial_Speech.pdf.

2. Amartya Sen, *THE ARGUMENTATIVE INDIAN: Writings on Indian History, Culture and Identity* (Farrar, Straus and Giroux, 2006) p. 273.

3. Jean-Jacques Rousseau, *The Social Contract, translated by Maurice Cranston (*Penguin Books, 2001).

4. Lala Lajpat Rai, "A Study of Hindu Nationalism," *Hindustan Review* and *Kayastha Samachar*, September–October, 1902. (Vol. VI, nos. 3–4) pp. 249–54.

15. "INDIC CIVILIZATION" AND INDIANNESS

1. Gerard Fussman, Étude des civilisations de l'Himālaya et de l'Asie centrale", La Lettre du College de France, https://doi.org/10.4000/lettre-cdf.756, pp 24–25

2. For the full text of the letter, see https://www.rediff.com/news/1999/may/17pawar2.htm, May 17, 1999.

3. Bal Gangadhar Tilak, Speech delivered at Ahmednagar, 31 May 1916, from S. Irfan Habib, *Indian nationalism* (Delhi: Aleph, 2018) p. 29.

4. *Indian Express*, May 18, 1999.

5. Ashutosh Varshney, "Is Sonia Indian?", https://www.rediff.com/news/1999/apr/21sonia.htm, 21 April 1999

6. *The Times of India*, May 20, 1999

7. Quoted in Paul R. Deltman, *India Changes Course: Golden Jubilee to Millennium* I(London: Praeger, 2001), p. 135

8. Amartya Sen, *The Argumentative Indian*, op.cit., p. 136.

9. Ibid., p. 18.

10. B.R. Ambedkar, 'A Nation Calling for a Home', in *Pakistan or Partition of India*. (Bombay, 1940)

11. Ibid.

12. Maroof Raza, "1965 War: A Tale of War and Three Brothers", *Open magazine*, 27 Aug, 2015 https://openthemagazine.com/voices/1965-war-a-tale-of-war-and-three-brothers/

16. THE DOCTRINE OF HINDUTVA

1. Bombay: Veer Savarkar Prakashan, (1st edition 1923)

2. Cited during the Constituent Assembly debates by Minoo R Masani, quoted in https://thewire.in/labour/labour-laws-constituent-assembly-protection-working-class

3. V. D. Savarkar, *Essentials of Hindutva* (Bombay: Veer Savarkar Prakashan, (1st edition 1923)

4. Ibid.

5. *Sri Guruji, the Man and his Mission* (author unspecified), Rashtriva Swayamsevak Sangh, Nagpur, 1973

6. V. D. Savarkar, *Hindutva*, p. 3.

7. M. S. Golwalkar, *We, or Our Nationhood Defined* (3rd edition, Nagpur: Bharat Prakashan, 1945)

8. M. S. Golwalkar, *Bunch of Thoughts* (4th impression, Bangalore: Vikrama Prakashan, 1968)

9. M. S. Golwalkar, *We, or Our Nationhood Defined* 3rd edition, Nagpur: Bharat Prakashan, 1945).

10. Vaibhav Purandare, *Savarkar: The True Story of the Father of Hindutva*, (Delhi: Juggernaut, 2019).

11. Vikram Sampath, *Savarkar: Echoes from a Forgotten Past, 1883–1924*, (Delhi: Viking Penguin, 2019).

12. Golwalkar, *We, or Our Nationhood Defined*, pp. 52–53. Some scholars have recently begun to suggest that this book, though it bore Golwalkar's name, was not authored by him. The fact that he claimed authorship and promoted the book extensively, while not repudiating any of its tenets in his lifetime, vitiates the force of this disclaimer. Whether he wrote it or not, he was happy to claim its contents as his own work.

13. M. S. Golwalkar, *We, or Our Nationhood Defined* 3rd edition, Nagpur: Bharat Prakashan, 1945.

14. Golwalkar, *We, or Our Nationhood Defined*, pp. 15, 16. Subsequent Golwalkar quotes are from this book and his *Bunch of Thoughts, op.cit.*

15. V. S. Naipaul, *Among the Believers: An Islamic Journey*, London: Penguin Books, 1982.

16. M. S. Golwalkar, *Bunch of Thoughts* (4th impression, Bangalore: Vikrama Prakashan, 1968).

17. Golwalkar, *We, or Our Nationhood Defined*.

17. HINDU RASHTRA UPDATED

1. Bipin Chandra Pal, "Hinduism and Indian Nationalism," Published in *The Spirit of Indian Nationalism*, 1910, pp. 22–48.
2. Ibid.
3. The quotes from and relating to Upadhyaya's views may be found in K. S. Bharathi, *The Political Thought of Pandit Deendayal Upadhyaya*, New Delhi: Concept Publishing Company, 1998, p. 86; C. P. Bhishkar, *Pt. Deendayal Upadhyay: Ideology & Perception—Part 5: Concept of The Rashtra*, New Delhi: Suruchi Prakashan, 2014, p. 4; & V. V. Nene, *Pandit Deendayal Upadhyaya: Ideology and Perception*, trans. by M. K. Paranjape and D. R. Kulkarni, New Delhi: Suruchi Prakashan, 1988.
4. Deen Dayal Upadhyay, *Rashtra Jeevan Ki Disha* (Lucknow: Lohit Prakashan, 1971).
5. Ibid.

18. A "HINDU PAKISTAN"

1. Hegde, quoted in "We are Here to Change the Constitution," *Indian Express*, 26 December 2017, https://indianexpress.com/article/india/anantkumar-hegde-we-are-here-to-change-the-constitutionsecular-mos-4998737/
2. Govindacharya quoted in *National Herald*, 1 October 2017, https://www.national-heraldindia.com/eye-on-rss/we-should-remove-secularism-socialism-from-the-constitution-govindacharya

19. THE FABRICATION OF HISTORY

1. Orwell, *Nationalism*, *op.cit.*
2. Romila Thapar, *On Nationalism* (Delhi: Aleph, 2016), pp. 31–35.
3. Tony Joseph, *Early Indians* (Delhi: Juggernaut, 2018).
4. Romila Thapar, *On Nationalism* (Delhi: Aleph, 2016), pp. 35.
5. Ibid. pp., 14–15
6. Ambedkar's 1942 Bombay radio address, quoted in Luis Cabrera, *The Humble Cosmopolitan* (Oxford University Press, 2019), p. 277.
7. Amartya Sen, *THE ARGUMENTATIVE INDIAN: Writings on Indian History, Culture and Identity* (Farrar, Straus and Giroux, 2006) p. 2 73.
8. See, for instance, Modi's remarks in the Lok Sabha on 9 Jun 2014, *"Barah sau saal ki gulami"*: https://www.firstpost.com/politics/1200-years-of-servitude-pm-modi-offers-food-for-thought-1567805.html
9. Reuters, "Interview with BJP Leader Narendra Modi," July 12, 2013, http://blogs.reuters.com/india/2013/07/12/interview-with-bjp-leader-narendra-modi/
10. For a detailed account of this episode, Shashi Tharoor, *Nehru: The Invention of India* (Penguin Books, 2003).

20. BHARAT MATA KI JAI

1. B. R. Purohit, *Hindu Revivalism and Indian Nationalism* 1990, p. 79.

2. Quoted in Chetan Bhatt, *Hindu Nationalism: Origins, Ideologies and Modern Myths* (Routledge, 2020) p. 98.

3. Sumathi Ramaswamy, "Maps and mother goddesses in modern India." *Imago Mundi* 53 (January 2001): 97–114. https://doi.org/10.1080/03085690108592940.

4. Sri Aurobindo's speech in Bombay on 19 January 1907 at the invitation of Bombay National Union, quoted in S. Irfan Habib, *Indian Nationalism* (Delhi: Aleph, 2018) p. 7.

5. M. S. Golwalkar, *We or Our Nationhood Defined: A Critique With the Full Text of the Book*, by Dr Shamsul Islam (Delhi: Pharos Media, 2006).

6. Express News Service, "The song and dance over Vande Mataram", *Indian Express*, 12 November 2009, http://archive.indianexpress.com/news/the-song-and-dance-over-vande-mataram/540277/

7. Jawaharlal Nehru, *The Discovery of India* (Delhi: Penguin, 2008).

8. A. G. Noorani, *On Nationalism*, (Delhi: Aleph Book Company, 2016), p. 102.

9. Badri Raina, "Why the Wren is a Patriot and not a Nationalist", *Mainstream*, VOL LVIII No 25, New Delhi, June 6, 2020, http://www.mainstreamweekly.net/article9454.html

10. Richard Jenkins, *Rethinking Ethnicity* (Sage, 2008), p. 32.

21. A PARTITION IN THE INDIAN SOUL

1. Quoted in Sharik Laliwala, *The Wire*, 8 August 2018, https://thewire.in/history/quit-india-movement-hindu-mahasabha-british.

2. Dr B.R. Ambedkar, *Constituent Assembly Debates*, Vol. 7, 4 November 1948, https://www.constitutionofindia.net/constitution_assembly_debates/volume/7/%C2%AD1948–11–04

3. Sardar Valbhbhai Patel, *Constituent Assembly Debates*, Vol. 8, 26 May 1949, https://www.constitutionofindia.net/constitution_assembly_debates/volume/8/1949-05-26

22. WHERE WE ARE, AND HOW WE GOT HERE

1. Jawaharlal Nehru, *The Discovery of India* (Delhi: Penguin, 2018)

2. https://economictimes.indiatimes.com/news/politics-and-nation/govt-has-spent-over-rs-5200-cr-in-ads-since-2014–15-rathore-in-ls/articleshow/67077392.cms

3. https://indianexpress.com/article/opinion/columns/narendra-modi-bjp-lutyens-delhi-amit-shah-6133916/.

4. Snigdha Poonam, *Dreamers* (London: Hurst, 2018).

5. Milan Vaishnav, *When Crime Pays: Money and Muscle in Indian Politics* (Yale University Press, 2017, and HarperCollins India, 2017)

6. Ibid.

7. Anastasia Piliavsky and Tommaso Sbriccoli, "The ethics of efficacy in north India's *goonda raj* (rule of toughs)", *Journal of the Royal Anthropological Institute* 22(2), 2016, pp 1–19.

8. Keerthik Sasidharan, "The clash of conceptual end goals," *The Hindu*, March 26, 2017, https://www.thehindu.com/opinion/columns/the-clash-of-conceptual-end-goals/article17664159.ece

9. Snigdha Poonam, *Dreamers* (London: Hurst, 2018).

10. Thomas Blom Hansen, "Globalisation and Nationalist Imaginations: Hindutva's Promise of Equality through Difference", *Economic and Political Weekly*, Vol. 31, No. 10 (Mar. 9, 1996), pp. 603–616.

11. 'Not Hindu Nationalism, But Society has changed': Christophe Jaffrelot', *The Wire*, 25 January 2020, https://thewire.in/religion/christophe-jaffrelot-rss-narendra-modi

12. 'History Was Accelerated in the Wake of BJP's 2019 Victory': The Wire Interviews Christophe Jaffrelot', *The Wire*, 24 January 2020, https://thewire.in/politics/christophe-jaffrelot-bjp-india-caa-part-one.

13. Ibid, p. 603

14. See Shashi Tharoor, *The Paradoxical Prime Minister* (New Delhi: Aleph, 2019).

15. Angana P. Chatterji, Thomas Blom Hansen & Christophe Jaffrelot (Eds.), *Majoritarian State: How Hindu Nationalism is Changing India*, (London: Hurst, 2019).

16. https://indianexpress.com/article/opinion/columns/narendra-modi-bjp-lutyens-delhi-amit-shah-6133916/.

23. THE RENEWED MODI-FICATION OF INDIA

1. Keerthik Sasidharan, "Modi Amongst a Million Mutinies", *The Hindu*, 20 April 2019, https://www.thehindu.com/opinion/columns/modi-amidst-a-million-mutinies/article26896421.ece

2. https://indianexpress.com/article/opinion/columns/narendra-modi-bjp-hundred-days-kashmir-lockdown-5980799/

3. Swapan Dasgupta, https://www.telegraphindia.com/opinion/hindus-and-muslims-are-no-longer-talking-to-each-other-in-the-bjp-s-new-india/cid/1699328

4. Pratap Bhanu Mehta, "A hundred days on, Modi 2.0", *Indian Express*, September 10, 2019

5. https://twitter.com/PMOIndia/status/1251839308085915649?s=20

24. THE ETIOLATION OF DEMOCRATIC INSTITUTIONS

1. https://www.washingtonpost.com/world/2018/12/12/whats-behind-potentially-catastrophic-fight-indias-central-bank/?utm_term=.520df0a5d897

2. https://www.thehindu.com/business/Economy/rajans-tenure-extension-opposed/article8608109.ece

3. https://economictimes.indiatimes.com/industry/banking/finance/banking/urjit-patel-resigns-as-the-rbi-governor/articleshow/67026103.cms

4. https://economictimes.indiatimes.com/industry/banking/finance/banking/here-is-the-full-text-of-rbis-deputy-governor-viral-v-acharyas-speech-in-mumbai/articleshow/66384553.cms

5. https://www.cnbc.com/2018/12/11/rbi-reserve-bank-of-india-governorurjit--patel-resigns.html

6. Umberto Eco, "UR-FASCISM", *The New York Review of Books*, June 22, 1995, http://www.nybooks.com/articles/1856

7. "A caged parrot", Reuters, May 10, 2013. https://in.reuters.com/article/cbi-supreme-court-parrot-coal/a-caged-parrot-supreme-court-describes-cbi-idINDEE94901W20130510

8. https://theprint.in/governance/a-brief-history-of-the-cats-of-kilkenny-why-they-were-linked-to-cbis-internal-feud/159387/. [Kilkenny cats destroy each other in the course of their fighting.]

9. https://scroll.in/article/899443/in-sending-the-cbi-director-on-leave-the-centre-has-stretched-the-law-to-its-limits

10. For a scathing (and comprehensive) indictment, see Gautam Bhatia, "The Troubling Legacy of Chief Justice Ranjan Gogoi", *The Wire*, March 16, 2020. https://thewire.in/law/chief-justice-ranjan-gogoi-legacy.

11. Ibid.

12. "What Arun Jaitley Said on Post-Retirement Jobs for Judges," *Outlook*, 3 September 2014, https://www.outlookindia.com/blog/story/what-arun-jaitley-said-on-post-retirement-jobs-for-judges/3376

13. See, for instance, https://www.thehindu.com/news/national/gujarat-poll-schedule-delay-raises-suspicion/article19846992.ece, Oct 12, 2017

14. Anupam Saraph, "Is this my vote?", *Frontline*, May 24, 2019: https://frontline.thehindu.com/cover-story/article27058245.ece

15. Monobina Gupta, "The Legacy of a Different CEC," *The Wire*, 6 May 2019, https://thewire.in/politics/election-commission-jm-lyngodh-modi-model-code

16. https://timesofindia.indiatimes.com/india/hc-sets-aside-ec-disqualification-of-20-aap-mlas-asks-for-fresh-hearing/articleshow/63436712.cms

17. https://indianexpress.com/article/india/military-defence-forces-should-be-kept-away-from-politics-army-chief-bipin-rawat-4970733/

18. Shoaib Daniyal, "Why Army Chief Rawat's Comments Should Worry All Indians Who Care About Democracy," *Scroll*, Feb 22, 2018: https://scroll.in/article/869669/why-army-chief-rawats-comments-about-assam-party-should-worry-all-indians-who-care-about-democracy

19. For instance: "Last week, Gen Bipin Rawat drew criticism from the opposition parties after he publicly criticised people leading protests over the new citizenship law, saying leadership is not about guiding masses to carry out arson and violence across the country. There were also sharp reactions from activists and military veterans who accused him of making political remarks, thereby compromising the long-held convention in the Army of not wading into political matters. In his three-year tenure as Army Chief, he has faced allegations of not remaining politically neutral." https://www.indiatoday.in/india/story/gen-bipin-rawat-appointed-as-first-chief-of-defence-staff-1632705-2019-12-30

20. Tagore, *Gitanjali* (1917)

21. Satya Prakash, "To repeal or not", *The Tribune*, September 10, 2018, https://www. tribuneindia.com/news/archive/nation/to-repeal-or-not-nehruvian-dilemma-on-sedition-law-650444

22. Roberto Stefan Foa and Yascha Mounk, "The Signs of Deconsolidation," *Journal of Democracy*, January 2017, Vol 28, Issue 1, pp. 5–16.

23. Ibid., p. 7

24. https://thewire.in/books/people-vs-democracy-yascha-mounk-populism

25. THE ASSERTION OF HINDI

1. From Irfan Habib, *Indian Nationalism* (Delhi: Aleph, 2017)

2. Ibid.

3. Ibid.

4. C. Rajagopalachari, 'Claims of Hindi Examined', *Swarajya*, 1 February 1958.

5. https://www.thehindu.com/news/national/what-is-the-three-language-formula/article27698700.ece

26. THE CITIZENSHIP AMENDMENT ACT AND THE NATIONAL REGISTRY OF CITIZENS

1. Gautam Bhatia, "Citizenship and the Constitution," Yale University Law School paper,17 April 2020, https://papers.ssrn.com/sol3/papers.cfm?abstract_id=3565551

2. Quoted in Bhatia, ibid.

3. Parliament of India, Constituent Assembly Debates, Vol. III (29th April, 1947) (speech of K.M. Munshi).

4. Constituent Assembly Debates, Vol. 9, 11 August 1949, http://loksabhaph.nic.in/writereaddata/cadebatefiles/C11081949.html. For a fascinating summary of the debate, see Aditya Chatterjee, "How the Constituent Assembly Debated (and Rejected) Citizenship by Religion",*The Wire*, 10 February 2020, https://thewire.in/religion/caa-citizenship-religion-constituent-assembly

5. Gautam Bhatia, "Citizenship and the Constitution," Yale University Law School paper,17 April 2020, https://papers.ssrn.com/sol3/papers.cfm?abstract_id=3565551

6. He did so five times: See this Dec 20, 2019 article in *Scroll:* https://scroll.in/article/947436/who-is-linking-citizenship-act-to-nrc-here-are-five-times-amit-shah-did-so.

7. Lala Lajpat Rai, "Communalism and Nationalism", *The People*, 12 September 1926.

8. Amartya Sen, *the Argumentative Indian*, op.cit.

9. Pradeep Chhibber, https://theprint.in/opinion/modi-shah-bjp-reduced-hindu-to-ethnic-identity-without-moral-compass/335760/, 17 December, 2019.

10. https://timesofindia.indiatimes.com/india/Gen-VK-Singh-loses-battle-for-age-tries-to-save-some-honour/articleshow/11843085.cms

11. https://economictimes.indiatimes.com/news/politics-and-nation/those-indulg-ing-in-arson-can-be-identified-by-their-clothes-narendra-modi-on-anti-caa-protest/articleshow/72687256.cms

12. Dr B.R. Ambedkar, *Constituent Assembly Debates*, Vol. 7, 4 November 1948, https://www.constitutionofindia.net/constitution_assembly_debates/volume/7/%C2%AD1948-11-04

13. Press Trust of India, PTI News, 8 December 2019, http://www.ptinews.com/news/11054172_India-duty-bound-to-give-citizenship-to-persecuted-minorities--Madhav

14. Urvish Kothari, "Modi wrongly quoted Mahatma Gandhi on Pakistan's Hindu & Sikh refugees to defend CAA", *The Print*, 25 December, 2019: https://theprint.in/opinion/modi-wrongly-quoted-mahatma-gandhi-on-pakistans-hindu-sikh-refugees-to-defend-caa/340323/

27. KASHMIR AND THE END OF AUTONOMY

1. Stated by the Chief Minister of Haryana, no less! https://www.news18.com/news/india/now-we-can-bring-kashmiri-girls-for-marriage-haryana-cm-khattar-at-beti-bachao-event-2265427.html

2. See Saifuddin Soz, *Kashmir: Glimpses of History and the Story of Struggle* (Delhi: Rupa, 2018); Rajmohan Gandhi, *Patel: A Life*, (Ahmedabad: Navjivan Trust, 1991); and https://scroll.in/article/884176/patel-wanted-hyderabad-for-india-not-kashmir-but-junagadh-was-the-wild-card-that-changed-the-game

3. See the detailed account of the historian Srinath Raghavan in https://www.nationalheraldindia.com/opinion/srinath-raghavan-busts-myths-around-jawahar-lal-nehru-kashmir-policies

4. The text of the letter is reproduced in full in A.G. Noorani, *Article 370: A Constitutional History of Jammu and Kashmir* (Delhi: Oxford University press, 2014).

5. Quoted in B. S. Yediyurappa, "Jawaharlal Nehru was adamant on special status for Jammu and Kashmir", *Economic Times*, September 25, 2019: https://economictimes.indiatimes.com/news/politics-and-nation/view-jawaharlal-nehru-was-adamant-on-special-status-for-jammu-and-kashmir/articleshow/71286035.cms?utm_source=contentofinterest&utm_medium=text&utm_campaign=cppst

6. Ibid.

7. Quoted by Lydia Walker, https://amp.scroll.in/article/935119/fifty-years-on-jayaprakash-narayans-views-on-kashmir-hold-pointers-for-the-present

8. Ibid., https://amp.scroll.in/article/935119/fifty-years-on-jayaprakash-narayans-views-on-kashmir-hold-pointers-for-the-present

28. SOFT-SIGNALLING BIGOTRY

1. https://indianexpress.com/elections/wanted-to-show-i-am-with-them-rahul-gandhi-on-choosing-south-indias-wayanad-ticket-5654547/. The Congress appealed this to the Election Commission as hate speech, but were denied by the EC: https://

indianexpress.com/elections/narendra-modi-election-commission-of-india-mcc-minority-rahul-gandhi-5703702/

2. https://www.indiatoday.in/elections/lok-sabha-2019/story/hindus-minority-in-wayanad-so-rahul-gandhi-picked-it-says-pm-modi-1495806-2019-04-06

3. https://www.deccanherald.com/national/national-politics/if-cong-sp-have-faith-in-ali-we-have-bajrang-bali-727915.html

4. https://www.ndtv.com/india-news/gujarat-assembly-election-2017-pm-narendra-modis-aurangzeb-raj-dig-at-congress-after-rahul-gandhis-n-1783312

5. "PM raps Modi for remarks on Lyngdoh", *Times of India*, 24 August 2002, https://timesofindia.indiatimes.com/india/PM-raps-Modi-for-remarks-on-Lyngdoh/articleshow/20086174.cms

6. https://economictimes.indiatimes.com/news/politics-and-nation/pm-modi-wades-into-beef-controversy-with-attack-on-lalu-prasad/articleshow/49269981.cms

7. https://www.huffingtonpost.in/2017/02/19/if-you-provide-power-supply-for-eid-then-you-should-also-do-it_a_21717084/

8. https://timesofindia.indiatimes.com/india/pak-working-with-cong-to-beat-bjp-in-guj-polls-pm/articleshow/62014443.cms

9. https://www.livemint.com/Politics/00fGvhpmazRQ7jPo86QpdI/Karnataka-elections-2018-Congress-celebrating-jayantis-of-S.html

10. Ibid.

11. https://www.hindustantimes.com/india/if-you-knock-at-midnight-i-will-respond-pm-modi-to-muslim-leaders/story-yicZRZixKbYgkEgRaLkTnM.html

29. AYODHYA: ENSHRINING HINDU RASHTRA

1. 'History Was Accelerated in the Wake of BJP's 2019 Victory': The Wire Interviews Christophe Jaffrelot', *The Wire*, 24 January 2020, https://thewire.in/politics/christophe-jaffrelot-bjp-india-caa-part-one

30. GANDHI'S HINDUISM VS HINDUTVA

1. Quoted in James W. Douglass, *Gandhi and the Unspeakable: His Final Experiment with Truth* (Orbis Books, 2012) p. 96.

2. Embossed plaque at the Nehru Memorial Museum, Teen Murti Bhavan, New Delhi, bearing Nehru's quote *'is desh ki janta hame pradhan mantri na kahe, pratham sevak kahe'*, visited 27 May 2009. Also cited in: https://www.deccanherald.com/lok-sabha-election-2019/word-pradhan-sevak-was-used-first-by-nehru-raj-728372.html

3. Rudolf C. Heredia, 'Gandhi's Hinduism and Savarkar's Hindutva', *Economic and Political Weekly* 44 (29) 2009, pp. 62–67.

4. Sudheendra Kulkarni, 'Why Gandhi Resonates in Rome', *Indian Express*, 2 October 2013, https://indianexpress.com/article/opinion/columns/why-gandhi-resonates-in-rome/

31. BHARAT VS INDIA

1. https://scroll.in/article/958724/why-the-slow-drip-of-anti-muslim-poison-in-india-is-now-a-flood
2. https://www.indiatoday.in/india/story/rapes-happen-in-india-not-bharat-rss-chief-mohan-bhagwat-blames-western-culture-for-gangrapes-150752–2013–01–04
3. Aatish Taseer, "India Is No Longer India", *The Atlantic*, May 2020, https://www.theatlantic.com/magazine/archive/2020/05/exile-in-the-age-of-modi/609073/
4. https://scroll.in/article/763503/read-what-vd-savarkar-wrote-care-for-cows-do-not-worship-them

32. BENDING THE CONSTITUTION

1. Arundhati Roy, "India: Intimations of an Ending", 22 November 2019, https://www.thenation.com/article/archive/arundhati-roy-assam-modi/
2. "Muslims, Constitution, Hindutva…: How Mohan Bhagwat is Allaying Fears at RSS Meet", News18.com, September 19, 2018, https://www.news18.com/news/politics/muslims-constitution-hindutva-how-mohan-bhagwat-is-allaying-fears-at-rss-meet-1882165.html
3. https://news.rediff.com/commentary/2018/sep/19/being-hindu-doesnt-mean-we-dont-want-muslims-rss-chief/3ca6e5f75af2e8bc7a2ea24ed227b71f
4. https://www.firstpost.com/india/rss-advocates-inclusion-mohan-bhagwat-systematically-refutes-rahul-gandhi-sangh-critics-in-day-one-speech-5208171.html
5. https://www.tribuneindia.com/news/archive/column/sangh-is-the-soul-657436
6. Ibid.
7. https://indianexpress.com/article/india/uniform-civil-code-is-not-just-about-hindu-muslim-rss-chief-mohan-bhagwat-5365535/
8. https://indianexpress.com/article/opinion/columns/a-new-rss-mohan-bhagwat-5387095/
9. She said this on the campaign trail: https://www.hindustantimes.com/lok-sabha-elections/lok-sabha-elections-2019-nathuram-godse-a-patriot-says-bjp-s-pragya-thakur/story-uq5EU9OWje7r5tmORd7UsK.html [May 13, 2019]. She then repeated it in Parliament [Nov 27, 2019]: https://scroll.in/latest/945096/pragya-thakur-again-refers-to-nathuram-godse-as-a-patriot-this-time-in-the-lok-sabha
10. https://www.indiatoday.in/elections/lok-sabha-2019/story/bjp-amit-shah-hindu-refugees-mamata-bannerjee-1499691–2019–04–11
11. Ashutosh Varshney, "Transfiguring India", *Indian Express*, 27 May 2019, https://indianexpress.com/article/opinion/columns/narendra-modi-bjp-rahul-gandhi-lok-sabha-elections-2019–5749518/
12. See Shashi Tharoor, https://theprint.in/opinion/anantkumar-hegde-has-only-repeated-what-hindutva-founders-said-about-the-constitution/24848/
13. Adrija Roychowdhury, *Indian Express*, June 4, 2020, https://indianexpress.com/article/research/anant-kumar-hegde-secularism-constitution-india-bjp-jawaharlal-nehru-indira-gandhi-5001085/

14. Constituent Assembly Of India Debates (Proceedings)-Volume Vii, *Monday, the 6th December 1948*, http://164.100.47.194/loksabha/writereaddata/cadebatefiles/C06121948.html

15. https://www.thestatesman.com/opinion/ambedkars-vision-secular-constitution-1502618002.html

16. Amartya Sen, *The Argumentative Indian, op.cit.*

17. Quoted in Shashi Tharoor, *Why I am a Hindu*,Aleph, 2018.

18. Rabindranath Tagore, NATIONALISM (San Francisco: Book Club of California, 1917) pp. 15–16.

33. BEATITUDES OF BELONGING

1. Milan Vaishnav and Jamie Hintson, "The Dawn of India's Fourth Party System," Carnegie Endowment for International Peace, Paper, Sept 05, 2019, *https://bit.ly/2Sf7DV4*

2. Suhas Palshikar, "Towards Hegemony: BJP Beyond Electoral Dominance," Economic and Political Weekly 53, no. 33 (August 18, 2018): 36–42.

3. Christophe Jaffrelot & Gilles Verniers, "A new party system or a new political system?", *Contemporary South Asia*, June 19, 2020, https://www.tandfonline.com/doi/abs/10.1080/09584935.2020.1765990?journalCode=ccsa20

4. Harish Khare, "Beyond the legal counsel's predicament, "*the Hindu*, June 6, 2020, https://www.thehindu.com/opinion/lead/beyond-the-legal-counsels-predicament/article31761429.ece

5. Milan Vaishnav and Jamie Hintson, "The Dawn of India's Fourth Party System," Carnegie Endowment for International Peace, Paper, Sept 05, 2019, *https://bit.ly/2Sf7DV4*

6. Suhas Palshikar, "Towards Hegemony: BJP Beyond Electoral Dominance," Economic and Political Weekly 53, no. 33 (August 18, 2018): 36–42. See also Devesh Kapur, "Modi's India is Aspirational, Assertive—and Anti-elite," Washington Post, May 29, 2019, https://www.washingtonpost.com/opinions/2019/05/29/modis-india-is-aspirational-assertive-anti-elite/?utm_term=.0a81fe8e3814

7. Ramachandra Guha, "3 Traits of Modi That Have Cost India Dearly", NDTV.com, June 9, 2020, https://www.ndtv.com/opinion/3-traits-of-modi-that-have-cost-india-dearly-by-ramachandra-guha-2242669.

8. Suhash Palshikar, "An ecrie quiet," *Indian Express*, April 1, 2020: https://indianexpress.com/article/opinion/columns/india-lockdown-quarantine-coronavirus-cases-deaths-6340978/

9. https://economictimes.indiatimes.com/news/politics-and-nation/key-members-from-narendra-modis-government-in-gujarat-take-crucial-positions-at-centre/articleshow/45040948.cms?from=mdr; https://thewire.in/government/all-the-prime-ministers-men; https://theprint.in/india/governance/in-modi-govt-just-4-of-ias-officers-are-from-gujarat-cadre-but-they-hold-the-key-posts/129239/; https://

thefederal.com/news/elevation-of-gujarat-cadre-ias-officers-to-top-posts-stirs-a-hornets-nest/

10. Sidharth Bhatia, *The Wire*, https://thewire.in/politics/narendra-modi-speech-simplistic-message May 13, 2020

11. Ramachandra Guha, "On China, Modi Acted Very Much Like Nehru", *ndtv.com*, 22 June 2020, https://www.ndtv.com/opinion/curious-parallels-between-nehru-and-modi-on-china-by-ramachandra-guha-2250121

12. Brahma Chellaney, "India's appeasement policy toward China unravels", *Japan Times*, 22 June 2020, https://www.japantimes.co.jp/opinion/2020/06/08/commentary/world-commentary/indias-appeasement-policy-toward-china-unravels/#.Xu-qPmgzYyx

13. Harish Khare, "Beyond the legal counsel's predicament, "*The Hindu*, June 6, 2020, https://www.thehindu.com/opinion/lead/beyond-the-legal-counsels-predicament/article31761429.ece

14. Pratap Bhanu Mehta, "India is heading into uncharted waters with no leadership at the helm, just the simulacra of one", *Indian Express*, 16 June, 2020, https://indianexpress.com/article/opinion/columns/pm-modi-coronavirus-crisis-economy-india-china-border-dispute-6460702/

15. https://indianexpress.com/article/opinion/columns/delhi-violence-riots-police-caa-npr-6288323/

16. Ibid.

17. https://indianexpress.com/article/opinion/columns/ranjan-gogoi-supreme-court-rajya-sabha-6320869/

18. Keerthik Sasidharan, "Modi Amongst a Million Mutinies", *The Hindu*, April 20, 2019, https://www.thehindu.com/opinion/columns/modi-amidst-a-million-mutinies/article26896421.ece

19. Ibid.

20. https://indianexpress.com/article/opinion/columns/sedition-charge-against-celebrities-mob-lynching-narendra-modi-6061361/

21. https://indianexpress.com/article/opinion/columns/the-new-techno-nationalism-technology-elections-5703564/

22. https://www.ndtv.com/opinion/give-us-kerala-model-over-gujarat-model-any-day-by-ramachandra-guha-2216254

23. Ibid.

24. https://www.livemint.com/Consumer/5HG6ozPQITQ9LHM6MhOfzN/The-BJPs-mobile-strategy.html

25. http://www.businessofapps.com/data/whatsapp-statistics/

26. https://www.nationalheraldindia.com/book-extract/india-whatsapp-election

27. Saumya Tewari, "How Smart, Viral Content Helped BJP Trump Congress on Social Media," Mint, June 4, 2019, https://www.livemint.com/politics/news/how-smart-viral-content-helped-bjp-trump-congress-on-social-media-1559663323348.html.

28. https://www.hindustantimes.com/india-news/decoding-fact-free-world-of-whatsapp/story-LQ79X96OOKrGo7MHuW3TMP.html
29. https://factly.in/shashi-tharoor-didnt-say-that-he-will-even-hit-the-shivling-with-a-chappal-if-needed-to-oust-modi/
30. https://www.thequint.com/news/webqoof/congress-rahul-gandhi-photo-morphed-adil-ahmad-dar-pulwama-attack-fake-news
31. http://time.com/5512032/whatsapp-india-election-2019/
32. https://inc42.com/buzz/whatsapp-deactivating-numbers-spreading-fake-news/
33. http://time.com/5512032/whatsapp-india-election-2019/
34. Arundhati Roy, "Intimations of an Ending", *the Nation*, Nov 22, 2019, https://www.thenation.com/article/archive/arundhati-roy-assam-modi/
35. http://time.com/5512032/whatsapp-india-election-2019/
36. https://twitter.com/narendramodi/status/1253695904764309504?s=20. See also Varghese K. George, "Hindutva's extremist Twitterati now target Modi for Muslim appeasement", The Hindu, May 9, 2020, https://www.thehindu.com/opinion/op-ed/comment-hindutvas-extremist-twitterati-now-target-modi-for-muslim-appeasement/article31545353.ece

34. THE NORTH-SOUTH DIVIDE

1. Nilakantan R. S., "How the 14th Finance Commission punishes Tamil Nadu," *The Wire*, 21 April 2017: https://thewire.in/economy/federalism-vs-14th-finance-commission
2. https://twitter.com/pawankalyan/status/965064871426445313?lang=en
3. Nilakantan R. S., "The 15th Finance Commission May Split Open Demographic Fault Lines Between South and North India", *The Wire*, 15 Feb 2018: https://thewire.in/economy/fifteenth-finance-commission-threatens-split-open-demographic-fault-lines-south-north-india
4. https://economictimes.indiatimes.com/news/politics-and-nation/south-subsidises-north-karnataka-cm-siddaramaiah/articleshow/63340369.cms?from=mdr
5. Nilankantan R. S, "The Economics and Politics Behind Dravida Nadu or South Indian Sub-Nationalism", *the Wire*. 20 March 2018; https://thewire.in/economy/economics-politics-behind-dravida-nadu-or-south-indian-subnationalism.
6. Nilankantan R. S, "Fifteenth Finance Commission and the Muddied Financial Response to COVID-19", *the Wire*. 6 April 2020. https://thewire.in/political-economy/15th-finance-commission-states-covid-19
7. Harish Khare, "Beyond the legal counsel's predicament," *The Hindu*, June 6, 2020, https://www.thehindu.com/opinion/lead/beyond-the-legal-counsels-predicament/article31761429.ece
8. Nilakantan R. S., "The 15th Finance Commission May Split Open Demographic Fault Lines Between South and North India", *The Wire*, 15 Feb 2018: https://thewire.in/economy/fifteenth-finance-commission-threatens-split-open-demographic-fault-lines-south-north-india

9. https://www.thequint.com/voices/opinion/ka-is-allowed-to-demand-greater-federal-autonomy-siddaramaiah

10. https://hi-in.facebook.com/Siddaramaiah.Official/posts/regional-identity-feder-alismsome-time-in-july-last-year-tv-studios-in-delhi-were/602181456793987/

11. Ibid.

35. REAFFIRMING CIVIC NATIONALISM AND PATRIOTISM

1. Private email dated 1 January 2020 from P.B. Mehta to the author

2. The quotes from here onward on the next two pages are from Pratap Bhanu Mehta's essay, "India: From Identity to Freedom," in Nidhi Razdan (ed.), *Left, Right and Centre: The Idea of India*, (Delhi: Penguin Random House India, 2017)

3. Justice Dhananjaya Chandrachud, JUSTICE PD DESAI MEMORIAL LECTURE 2020, 15 February, 2020, Gujarat High Court, text at: https://images.assettype.com/barandbench/2020–02/f3dad31d-ed51–4ddb-af39–5d9138bf6162/Justice_DY_Chandrachud___Justice_PD_Desai_Memorial_Speech.pdf

4. Amartya Sen, *The Idea of Justice* (NY: Belknap, 2009)

5. Justice Dhananjaya Chandrachud, JUSTICE PD DESAI MEMORIAL LECTURE 2020, 15 February, 2020, Gujarat High Court, text at: https://images.assettype.com/barandbench/2020–02/f3dad31d-ed51–4ddb-af39–5d9138bf6162/Justice_DY_Chandrachud___Justice_PD_Desai_Memorial_Speech.pdf

6. Michael Massing, "Does Democracy Avert Famine?", *New York Times*, 1 March 2003, https://www.nytimes.com/2003/03/01/arts/does-democracy-avert-famine.html

7. Daniel A. Bell, *The China Model: Political Meritocracy and the Limits of Democracy* (Princeton University Press, 2015).

36. WHERE DO WE GO FROM HERE?

1. Faizan Mustafa, "Minorities, too, are fed up of this façade of secularism", *Indian Express*, March 21, 2020, https://indianexpress.com/article/opinion/columns/narendra-modi-govt-6324468/

2. See, for instance, Kim Wagner, *Amritsar 1919—An Empire of Fear and the Making of a Massacre* (Yale University Press, 2019).

37. FIGHTING BACK

1. https://www.historylearningsite.co.uk/modern-world-history-1918-to-1980/weimar-germany/text-of-the-dusseldorf-speech-of-1932/

2. https://indianexpress.com/article/opinion/columns/delhi-riots-violence-shiv-vihar-maujpur-babarpur-chand-bagh-6304413/

3. Justice Dhananjaya Chandrachud, JUSTICE PD DESAI MEMORIAL LECTURE 2020, 15 February, 2020, Gujarat High Court, text at: https://images.assettype.com/barandbench/2020–02/f3dad31d-ed51–4ddb-af39–5d9138bf6162/Justice_DY_Chandrachud___Justice_PD_Desai_Memorial_Speech.pdf

4. Anna Lührmann, Seraphine F. Maerz, Sandra Grahn, Nazifa Alizada, Lisa Gastaldi, Sebastian Hellmeier, Garry Hindle and Staffan I. Lindberg. 2020. "Autocratization Surges—Resistance Grows", *Democracy Report 2020*, Varieties of Democracy Institute (V-Dem). https://www.v-dem.net/media/filer_public/f0/5d/f05d46d8–626f-4b20–8e4e-53d4b134bfcb/democracy_report_2020_low.pdf

5. Nehru's speech on Gandhi's assassination, January 30, 1948, https://thewire.in/history/light-gone-lives-nehrus-words-gandhis-assassination

38. LIBERAL CONSTITUTIONALISM AND PATRIOTISM

1. See, for instance, Tom Ginsburg, Aziz Z. Huq and Mila Versteeg, "The Coming Demise of Liberal Constitutionalism?", *The University of Chicago Law Review*, Vol. 85, No. 2 (March 2018), pp. 239–256

2. Francis Fukuyama, *The End of History and the Last Man*, (NY: Free Press, 1992), p 211.

3. On Putin, for instance, see Grigory Yavlinsky, "On the Putin System: How A Dictator maintains his power," *Literary Hub*, April 2, 2019, https://lithub.com/on-the-putin-system-how-a-dictator-maintains-his-power/

4. Mira T. Sundara Rajan, "Subramania Bharati: The Eternal Revolutionary," *The Hindu*, September 12, 2017, https://www.thehindu.com/news/national/subramania-bharati-the-eternal-revolutionary/article19670435.ece

5. ibid.

6. Cicero, cited in Plato's *Republic*, translated by R. Jowett (Oxford, 1881), Book 1, 7–9 p. 6

7. Martin Heidegger, "The Ontological Priority of the Question of Being." *Being and Time* (Translated by John Macquarrie & Edward Robinson). London: S.C.M., 1962.

8. Badri Raina, "Why the Wren is a Patriot and not a Nationalist", *Mainstream*, VOL LVIII No 25, New Delhi, June 6, 2020, http://www.mainstreamweekly.net/article9454.html

9. I am indebted to Professor Pradeep Chhibber for conceiving this idea.

10. Badri Raina, "Why the Wren is a Patriot and not a Nationalist", *Mainstream*, VOL LVIII No 25, New Delhi, June 6, 2020, http://www.mainstreamweekly.net/article9454.html

11. Harsh Mander, *Looking Away: Inequality, Prejudice and Indifference in New India* (New Delhi: Speaking Tiger, 2015).

12. Harsh Mander, "A moment for civilisational introspection", *The Hindu*, May 30, 2020, https://www.thehindu.com/opinion/lead/a-moment-for-civilisational-introspection/article31705361.ece

13. Suhas Palshikar, "Where's our George Floyd?", *Indian Express*, June 11 2020, https://indianexpress.com/article/opinion/columns/george-floyd-migrant-workers-suffering-outrage-over-injustice-6452914/

14. Badri Raina, "Why the Wren is a Patriot and not a Nationalist", *Mainstream*, VOL LVIII No 25, New Delhi, June 6, 2020, http://www.mainstreamweekly.net/article9454.html

15. K. A. Abbas, column of 29 June 1968 in *Blitz*, reprinted in *Bread, Beauty and Revolution*, New Delhi: Jaico, 1982.
16. Badri Raina, "Why the Wren is a Patriot and not a Nationalist", *Mainstream*, VOL LVIII No 25, New Delhi, June 6, 2020, http://www.mainstreamweekly.net/article9454.html
17. Justice Louis Brandeis, *Olmstead v. United States*, 277 U.S. 479 (1928)
18. Amitai Etzioni, *Reclaiming Patriotism*, (University of Virginia Press, 2019), p. 10.
19. Ibid., p. 99.

EPILOGUE: WINNING THE STRUGGLE FOR INDIA'S SOUL

1. David Baker, https://doi.org/10.1017/S0026749X00013913, Published online by Cambridge University Press: 28 November 2008.
2. Ramachandra Guha, *India After Gandhi: The History of the World's Largest Democracy*, Pan Macmillan, 2008, pp. 769–770.

ACKNOWLEDGEMENTS

This book has been the work of many years of reflection and argument, sometimes in the columns of India's lively press, and in recent years particularly in the free space afforded by a number of online publications. Some of the issues raised here were first aired, in somewhat different form, in my opinion columns in *The Week, The Print, The Quint, Open* Magazine, and Project Syndicate, to all of which publications I am most grateful.

In the writing of this book, I have benefited from invaluable research assistance, especially in regard to the vast amounts of scholarship on the issue of nationalism, from Prof. Sheeba Thattil, Katherine Abraham, and John Koshy, whose frequent kindness, forbearance, advice, suggestions and diligent support are gratefully acknowledged. My niece Ragini Tharoor Srinivasan, and my sons Kanishk Tharoor and Ishaan Tharoor, no mean scholars themselves, offered perceptive, insightful, and erudite critiques of my initial thoughts on nationalism that greatly sharpened my understanding and discussion of the issues. The historian Manu Pillai, once my closest aide, read an early draft of the manuscript closely and offered multiple useful comments and suggestions that reflected both his wide knowledge of the subject of this book and his familiarity with my own thinking. Dr Shruti Kapila and Professors Pradeep Chhibber and Pratap Bhanu Mehta were kind enough to comment constructively on an earlier version of the book, suggesting further reading and adding the rigour of their scholarship to my amateur theorizing. My thanks, too, to my friends Keerthik Sasidharan, who shared invaluable insights from his extensive reading and writing, Joseph Zacharias, who offered his own highly original and provocative thoughts on Indian politics, and Isheeta Ganguly, who introduced me to Tagore's patriotic songs. I have benefited enormously from each of them, and thank them most warmly for their inputs. But as always, sole responsibility for the final product, its content and conclusions, rests with me alone.

David Davidar, my publisher for over three decades, was, as usual, an irreplaceable source of perceptive editorial judgement, and robust common sense. For his inspiring faith in my ideas and my writing, no words of appreciation can ever suffice. Let me say, once again, that this book would not exist without him.

BIBLIOGRAPHY

BOOKS, ARTICLES, SPEECHES, WEB SOURCES AND LEGAL CITATIONS

Books

Abbas, Khwaja Ahmad, *Bread, Beauty and Revolution*, New Delhi: Marwah Publications, 1982.

Acton, Lord, *Nationality: Essays on Freedom and Power*, Gloucester: Peter Smith, 1972.

Adeney, Katharine and Sáez, Lawrence (eds), *Coalition Politics and Hindu Nationalism*, London: Routledge, 2005.

Adorno, T. W., *Minima Moralia: Reflections on a Damaged Life*, trans., Jephcott, E.F.N., London: Verso Books, 2005.

Alter, Joseph S., *Gandhi's Body: Sex, Diet and the Politics of Nationalism*, Philadelphia: University of Pennsylvania Press, 2000.

Ambedkar, B. R., 'A Nation Calling for a Home', in *Pakistan or The Partition of India*, Bombay: Thackers, 1940.

Anderson, Benedict, *Imagined Communities: Reflections on the Origin and Spread of Nationalism*, London: Verso Books, 1983, 1991 (second edition).

Anderson, Kevin B., *Marx at the Margins: On Nationalism, Ethnicity and Non-Western Societies*, Chicago: University of Chicago Press, 2010.

Andersen, Walter and Damle, Shridhar D., *Messengers of Hindu Nationalism: How the RSS Reshaped India*, London: Hurst Publishers, 2019.

Andrews, C. F. (ed.), *Speeches and Writings of M. K. Gandhi*, third edition, Madras: G. A. Natesan & Company, 1922.

Ansari, M. T., *Islam and Nationalism in India: South Indian Contexts*, London: Routledge, 2016.

Anter, Andreas, *Max Weber's Theory of the Modern State: Origins, Structure and Significance*, London: Palgrave Macmillan 2014.

Armstrong, John Alexander, *Nations Before Nationalism*, Chapel Hill: University of North Carolina Press, 1982.

Balibar, E., 'Racism and Nationalism', Balibar, E., & Wallerstein, I., (eds.), *Race, Nation, Class: Ambiguous Identities*, London: Verso Books, 1991.

BIBLIOGRAPHY

Barry, Brian, *Democracy, Power, and Justice: Essays in Political Theory*, London: Oxford University Press, 1989.

Barker, Ernest, *Social Contract: Essays by Locke, Hume and Rousseau*, London: Oxford University Press, 1946.

Bayly, Christopher, *Origins of Nationality in South Asia: Patriotism and Ethical Government in the Making of Modern India*, New Delhi: Oxford University Press,1998.

Beiner, Ronald (ed.), *Theorizing Nationalism*, New York: State University of New York Press, 1999.

Bell, Daniel A., *The China Model: Political Meritocracy and the Limits of Democracy*, Princeton: Princeton University Press, 2015.

Berberoglu, Berch (ed.), *The National Question: Nationalism, Ethnic Conflict and Self Determination in the 20th Century*, Philadelphia: Temple University Press, 1995.

Bharathi, K. S., *The Political Thought of Pandit Deendayal Upadhyaya*, New Delhi: Concept Publishing Company, 1998.

Bhatt, Chetan, *Hindu Nationalism: Origins, Ideologies and Modern Myth*, Oxford: Berg Publishers, 2001.

Bhishkar, C. P., *Pt. Deendayal Upadhyay: Ideology & Perception—Part 5: Concept of The Rashtra*, New Delhi: Suruchi Prakashan, 2014.

Billig, Michael, *Banal Nationalism*, London: Sage Publications, 1995.

Bishop of St. David's, *The Christianity of Stoicism: or Selections from Arrian's Discourses of Epictetus, trans. Mrs Carter*, Carmarthen: 1822.

Blom Hansen, Thomas, *The Saffron Wave: Democracy and Hindu Nationalism in Modern India*, Princeton: Princeton University Press, 1999.

Braunthal, J., *The Paradox of Nationalism*, London: St. Botolph, 1946.

Breuilly, John, *Nationalism and the State*, Manchester: Manchester University Press, 1993.

———— (ed.), *The Oxford Handbook of The History of Nationalism*, Oxford: Oxford University Press, 2013.

Brosius, Christiane, *Empowering Visions: The Politics of Representation in Hindu Nationalism*, London: Anthem Press, 2004.

Brown, Michael E., *Nationalism and Ethnic Conflict*, Cambridge: MIT Press, 1997.

Busch, M. A., *Rise and Growth of Indian Nationalism: Non Violent Nationalism, Gandhi and his School*, Baroda: Atmaram Press,1939.

Calhoun, Craig, *Nationalism*, Minneapolis: University of Minnesota Press, 1997.

Chatterjee, Partha, *Nationalist Thought and the Colonial World: A Derivative Discourse*, London: Zed Books, 1986.

Chattopadhyay, Swati, *Representing Calcutta: Modernity, Nationalism and the Colonial Uncanny*, London: Routledge, 2005.

Cheah, Pheng, *Spectral Nationality: Passages of Freedom from Kant to Postcolonial Literatures of Liberation*, New York: Columbia University Press, 2003.

Chopra, Rohit, *Technology and Nationalism in India: Cultural Negotiations from Colonialism to Cyberspace*, New York: Cambria Press, 2008.

BIBLIOGRAPHY

Corbridge, Stuart and John Harriss, *Reinventing India: Liberalization, Hindu Nationalism and Popular Democracy*, Cambridge: Polity Press, 2000.

Delanty, Gerard and O'Mahony, Patrick, *Nationalism and Social Theory: Modernity and the Recalcitrance of the Nation*, London: Sage Publications, 2002.

Díaz-Andreu, Margarita, *A World History of Nineteenth-Century Archaeology: Nationalism, Colonialism and the Past*, New York: Oxford University Press, 2007.

Dikötter, Frank, *How to be a Dictator: The Cult of Personality in the Twentieth Century*, London: Bloomsbury, 2019.

Eagleton, Terry, Jameson, Fredric and Said, Edward W., *Nationalism, Colonialism and Literature*, Minneapolis: University of Minnesota Press, 1990.

Earnest, David C., *Old Nations, New Voters: Nationalism, Transnationalism and Democracy in the Era of Global Migration*, New York: State University of New York Press, 2008.

Fanon, Frantz, *The Wretched of the Earth*, trans. Constance Farrington, New York: Grove Press, 1963.

Fukuyama, Francis, *The End of History and the Last Man*, New York: The Free Press, 1992.

Gandhi, Rajmohan, *Patel: A Life*, Ahmedabad: Navjivan Trust, 1991.

Gans, Chaim, *The Limits of Nationalism*, New York: Cambridge University Press, 2003.

Gellner, Ernest, *Nations and Nationalism*, New York: Cornell University Press, 1983.

————, *Nationalism*, London: Weidenfeld & Nicolson, 1997.

Gerth, H. H. and Mills, C., Wright, (eds.), *From Max Weber: Essays in Sociology*, New York: Oxford University Press, 1946.

Ghassem-Fachandi, Parvis, *Pogrom in Gujarat: Hindu Nationalism and Anti-Muslim Violence in India*, New Jersey: Princeton University Press, 2012.

Gould, William, *Hindu Nationalism and the Language of Politics in Late Colonial India*, New York: Cambridge University Press, 2004.

Gowalker, M. S., *We or Our Nationhood Defined*, Nagpur: Bharat Prakashan, 1945 (third edition).

Golwalker, M. S., *Bunch of Thoughts*, Bangalore: Vikrama Prakashan, 1968 (fourth impression).

Graham, Bruce Desmond, *Hindu Nationalism and Indian Politics: The Origins and Development of the Bharatiya Jana Sangh*, Cambridge: Cambridge University Press, 1990.

Greenfeld, L., *Nationalism: Five Roads to Modernity*, Cambridge: Harvard University Press, 1992.

————, *Nationalism: A Short History*, Washington D. C: Brookings Institution Press, 2019.

Grosby, Steven and Leoussi, Athena S., (eds.), *Nationalism and Ethnosymbolism: History, Culture and Ethnicity in the Formation of Nations*, Edinburgh: Edinburgh University Press, 2007.

Guichard, Silvie, *The Construction of History and Nationalism in India: Textbooks, Controversies and Politics*, London: Routledge, 2010.

Habib, Syed Irfan, *Indian Nationalism: The Essential Writings*, New Delhi: Aleph Book Company, 2017.

BIBLIOGRAPHY

Hallet Carr, Edward, *Nationalism and After*, London: Macmillan, 1945.

Harari, Yuval Noah, *Sapiens:A Brief History of Humankind*, London: Harvill Secker, 2014.

Hazony, Yoram, *The Virtue of Nationalism*, New York: Basic Books, 2018.

Hechter, Michael, *Containing Nationalism*, New York: Oxford University Press, 2000.

Herb, Guntram H. and Kaplan, David H., (eds.), *Nations and Nationalism: A Global Historical Overview, Volume 1, 1770 to 1880*, California: ABC-CLIO, 2008.

Hertz, Frederick Otto, *Nationality in History and Politics: A Psychology and Sociology of National Sentiment and Nationalism*, London: Routledge & Kegan Paul, 1957.

Hobsbawm, E. J., *Nations and Nationalism Since 1780: Programme, Myth, Reality*, Cambridge: Cambridge University Press,1990.

Hobsbawm, Eric and Ranger, Terence, (eds.), *The Invention of Tradition*, Cambridge: Cambridge University Press, 1983.

Ignatieff, Michael, *Blood and Belonging: Journeys into the New Nationalism*, Toronto: Penguin Books,1993.

Jaffrelot, Christophe, *Hindu Nationalism: A Reader*, Princeton: Princeton University Press, 2007.

Johnson, Gordon, *Provincial Politics and Indian Nationalism: Bombay and the Indian National Congress 1880 to 1915*, Cambridge: Cambridge University Press, 1973.

Joseph, Tony, *Early Indians*, New Delhi: Juggernaut Books, 2018.

Jurgensmeyer, M., *The New Cold War: Religious Nationalism Confronts the Secular State*, Berkeley: University of California Press, 1993.

Khan, Mohibbul Hasan, *History of Tipu Sultan*, Calcutta: Bibliophile Ltd., 1951.

Kaicker, Abhishek, *The King and the People: Sovereignty and Popular Politics in Mughal Delhi*, New York: Oxford University Press, 2020.

Kecmanovic, Dusan, *The Mass Psychology of Ethnonationalism*, New York: Plenum Press, 1996.

Kedourie, Elie, *Nationalism*, London: Hutchinson, 1960.

Kohn, Hans, *Nationalism: Its Meaning and History*, Florida: Krieger, 1965.

———, *Prelude to Nation-States: The French and German Experience, 1789–1815*, Princeton: Van Nostrand, 1967.

Kinnvall, Catarina, *Globalization and Religious Nationalism in India: The Search for Ontological Security*, New York: Routledge, 2006.

Khurshid, Salman, *Visible Muslim, Invisible Citizen: Understanding Islam in Indian Democracy*, New Delhi: Rupa Publications, 2019.

Low, D. A., *Britain and Indian Nationalism: The Imprint of Ambiguity 1929–1942*, Cambridge: Cambridge University Press, 1997.

Löwith, Karl, *Max Weber and Karl Marx*, London: Routledge,1993.

Mander, Harsh, *Looking Away: Inequality, Prejudice and Indifference in New India*, New Delhi: Speaking Tiger, 2015.

Marx, Anthony W., *Faith in Nation: Exclusionary Origins of Nationalism*, New York: Oxford University Press, 2003.

McCrone, David, *The Sociology of Nationalism: Tomorrow's ancestors*, London: Routledge, 1998.

BIBLIOGRAPHY

Moin, A. Azfar, *The Millennial Sovereign: Sacred Kingship and Sainthood in Islam*, New York: Columbia University Press, 2012.

Moore, Margaret, *The Ethics of Nationalism*, Oxford: Oxford University Press, 2001.

Motyl, Alexander J., *Encyclopedia of Nationalism: Leaders, Movements and Concepts, Volume 2*, California: Academic Press, 2001.

Naipaul, V. S., *Among the Believers: An Islamic Journey*, London: Penguin Books, 1982.

Nairn, T., *The Break-up of Britain: Crisis and Neo–nationalism*, London: Verso Books, 1981.

Nandy, Ashis, *The Illegitimacy of Nationalism: Rabindranath Tagore and the Politics of Self*, New Delhi: Oxford University Press, 1994.

Nene, V. V., *Pandit Deendayal Upadhyaya: Ideology and Perception, trans. by M. K. Paranjape and D. R. Kulkarni*, New Delhi: Suruchi Prakashan, 1988.

Noorani A. G., 'Nationalism and Its Contemporary Discontents in India', *On Nationalism*, New Delhi: Aleph Book Company, 2016.

Noorani, A. G., *Article 370: A Constitutional History of Jammu and Kashmir*, New Delhi: Oxford University Press, 2014.

Norman, Wayne, *Negotiating Nationalism: Nation-building, Federalism and Secession in the Multinational State*, Oxford: Oxford University Press, 2006.

Ohmae, Kenichi, *The Borderless World: Power and Strategy in the Global Marketplace*, New York: Harper Business, 1990.

Ong, Aihwa, *Flexible Citizenship: The Cultural Logics of Transnationality*, Durham: Duke University Press, 1999.

Orsini, Francesca, *The Hindi Public Sphere 1920–1940: Language and Literature in the Age of Nationalism*, New Delhi: Oxford University Press, 2002.

Özkırımlı, Umut, *Theories of Nationalism: A Critical Introduction*, London: Macmillan, 2000.

——— (ed.), *Nationalism and its Futures*, New York: Palgrave Macmillan, 2003.

Pal, Bipin Chandra, 'Hinduism and Indian Nationalism', *The Spirit of Indian Nationalism*, London: Hind Nationalist Agency, 1910.

Poonam, Snigdha, *Dreamers: How Young Indians Are Changing Their World*, London: Hurst Publishers, 2018.

Purandare, Vaibhav, *Savarkar: The True Story of the Father of Hindutva*, New Delhi: Juggernaut Books, 2019.

Purohit, B. R., *Hindu Revivalism and Indian Nationalism*, Sagar: Sathi Prakashan, 1965.

Rajagopal, Arvind, *Politics after Television: Religious Nationalism and the Reshaping of the Public in India*, Cambridge: Cambridge University Press, 2004.

Razdan, Nidhi (ed.), *Left, Right and Centre: The Idea of India*, New Delhi: Penguin Random House, 2017.

Regan–Lefebvre, Jennifer, *Cosmopolitan Nationalism in the Victorian Empire: Ireland, India and the Politics of Alfred Webb*, London: Palgrave Macmillan, 2009.

Rothermund, Dietmar, *The Phases of Indian Nationalism and Other Essays*, India: Nachiketa Publications, 1970.

Rowe, David E. and Schulmann, Robert, *Einstein on Politics: His Private Thoughts and Public*

Stands on Nationalism, Zionism, War, Peace and the Bomb, Princeton: Princeton University Press, 2007.

Sampath, Vikram, *Savarkar: Echoes from a Forgotten Past, 1883–1924*, New Delhi: Viking Penguin Books, 2019.

Savarkar, V. D., *Essentials of Hindutva*, Bombay: Veer Savarkar Prakashan, 1923 (first edition).

Schaar, John H., *Legitimacy in the Modern State*, New Brunswick: Transaction Press, 1981.

Scheff, T. J., *The Bloody Revenge: Emotions, Nationalism and War*, Boulder: Westview Press, 1994.

Schopenhauer, Arthur, *Essays and Aphorisms*, London: Penguin Books, 2014.

Seal, Anil, *The Emergence of Indian Nationalism, Competition and Collaboration in the Later Nineteenth Century*, Cambridge: Cambridge University Press, 1968.

Searle-White, Joshua, *The Psychology of Nationalism*, New York: Palgrave Macmillan, 2001.

Shakir, Moin, *Gandhi, Azad and Nationalism*, New Delhi: New India Press, 1977.

Sharma, Jyotirmaya, *A Restatement of Religion: Swami Vivekananda and the Making of Hindu Nationalism*, New Haven: Yale University Press, 2013.

———, *Hindutva: Exploring the Idea of Hindu Nationalism*, New Delhi: HarperCollins, 2015.

Silvestri, Michael, *Ireland and India: Nationalism, Empire and Memory*, London: Palgrave Macmillan, 2009.

Skey, Michael and Antonsich, Marco (eds.), *Everyday Nationhood: Theorising Culture, Identity and Belonging after Banal Nationalism*, London: Palgrave Macmillan, 2017.

Smith, Anthony D., *Ethno Symbolism and Nationalism: A Cultural Approach*, New York: Routledge, 2009.

———, *Nations and Nationalism in a Global Era*, Cambridge: Polity Press, 1995.

———, *Nationalism and Modernism: A Critical Survey of Recent Theories of Nations and Nationalism*, London: Routledge, 1998.

———, *Nationalism: Theory, Ideology, History*, Cambridge: Polity Press, 2010.

———, *The Ethnic Origins of Nations*, Oxford: Basic Blackwell, 1986.

Soz, Saifuddin, *Kashmir: Glimpses of History and the Story of Struggle*, New Delhi: Rupa Publications, 2018.

Spencer, Philip and Wollman, Howard, *Nationalism: A Critical Introduction*, London: Sage Publications, 2002.

Stalin, J., *Marxism and the National Question 1913*, Moscow: Foreign Languages Publishing House, 1947.

Stuart Mill, John, *On Liberty*, London: John W. Parker & Son, 1859.

Stuart, Robert, *Marxism and National Identity: Socialism, Nationalism and National Socialism During the French Fin de Siècle*, New York: State University of New York Press, 2006.

Tagore, Rabindranath, *Nationalism*, Norwood: Norwood Press, 1917.

———, *Nationalism*, New York: Macmillan, 1917.

———, *Nationalism*, San Francisco: Book Club of California, 1917.

BIBLIOGRAPHY

Tamir, Yael, *Why Nationalism*, New Jersey: Princeton University Press, 2019.

Thapar, Romila, 'Reflections on Nationalism and History', *On Nationalism*, New Delhi, Aleph Book Company, 2016.

Temulkuran, Ece, *How to Lose a Country: The Seven Steps from Democracy to Dictatorship*, London: Fourth Estate, 2019.

Tharoor, Shashi, *Why I Am a Hindu*, New Delhi: Aleph Book Company, 2018.

————, *India: From Midnight to the Millennium*, New York: Arcade, 1997.

Toynbee, Arnold, Wakaizumi, Kei, *Surviving the Future*, London: Oxford University Press, 1971.

Tsang, Rachel and Woods, Eric Taylor, (eds.), *The Cultural Politics of Nationalism and Nation-Building: Ritual and Performance in the Forging of Nations*, London: Routledge, 2014.

Tucker, Robert C., (ed.), *The Marx-Engels Reader*, New York: W.W. Norton & Company, 1978.

Tuteja, K. L., and Chakraborty, Kaustav, (eds.), *Tagore and Nationalism*, New Delhi: Springer, 2017.

Upadhyay, Deen Dayal, 'Rashtra Jeevan Ki Disha', *The Direction of National Life*, Lucknow: Lohit Prakashan,1971.

Vaishnav, Milan, *When Crime Pays: Money and Muscle in Indian Politics*, New Haven: Yale University Press, 2017, & New Delhi: HarperCollins, 2017.

van der Veer, Peter, *Religious Nationalism: Hindus and Muslims in India*, Berkeley: University of California Press, 1994.

Viroli, Maurizio, *For Love of Country: An Essay on Patriotism and Nationalism*, New York: Oxford University Press, 1995.

Volcic, Zala and Andrejevic, Mark, (eds.), *Commercial Nationalism: Selling the Nation and Nationalizing the Sell*, London: Palgrave Macmillan, 2016.

Wagner, Kim, *Amritsar 1919—An Empire of Fear and the Making of a Massacre*, New Haven: Yale University Press, 2019.

Weber, M., *From Max Weber* (H. Gerth & C. Wright Mills, eds. & trans.) London: Routledge and Kegan Paul, 1948.

Wright, Julia M., *Ireland, India and Nationalism in Nineteenth-Century Literature*, New York: Cambridge University Press, 2007.

Articles, Chapters in Books and Speeches

Bhabha, Homi K., 'Introduction: Narrating the Nation', *Nation and Narration*, (ed.), Bhabha, Homi K., London: Routledge, 1990.

————, 'DissemiNation: Time, Narrative, and Margins of the Modern Nation', *Nation and Narration*, (ed.), Bhabha, Homi K., London: Routledge,1990.

Cabral, Amilcar, 'National Liberation and Culture', *Unity and Struggle: Speeches and Writings*, trans. Michael Wolfers, New York: Monthly Review Press, 1979.

Hansen, Thomas Blom, 'Globalisation and Nationalist Imaginations: Hindutva's Promise of Equality through Difference', *Economic and Political Weekly*, Vol. 31, No. 10, 9 March 1996.

BIBLIOGRAPHY

Hobsbawm, E., 'Nationalism thrives with history as handmaiden', *The Australian 1*, December 1993.

Hoffman, S., 'On the Political Psychology of Peace and War: A critique and an agenda', *Political Psychology*, 7, pp. 1–21.

Mehta, Pratap Bhanu, 'India: From Identity to Freedom',in Razdan, Nidhi (ed.), *Left, Right and Centre: The Idea of India*, New Delhi: Penguin Random House, 2017.

Munshi, K. M., Speech delivered in the Parliament of India, Constituent Assembly Debates, Vol. III, 29 April 1947.

Mussolini, Benito, Speech before the Chamber of Deputies, 26 May 1927, *Discorsi del 1927*, Milan: Alpes, 1928.

Nazneen, Ahmed, 'The Poetics of Nationalism: Cultural resistance and poetry in East Pakistan/Bangladesh, 1952–71', *Journal of Postcolonial Writing*, Vol. 50, 2012, pp. 1–13.

Ngũgĩ wa Thiong'o, 'Towards a National Culture', *Homecoming: Essays on African and Caribbean Literature, Culture and Politics*, London: Heinemann,1972.

Ozkirimli, Umut, 'The Nation as an Artichoke: A Critique of Ethnosymbolist Interpretations of Nationalism', *Nations and Nationalism*, 2003, Vol. 9, No. 3 pp. 339–55.

PTI, 'PM Modi wades into beef controversy with attack on Lalu Prasad', *Economic Times*, 8 October 2015.

Rai, Lala Lajpat, 'A Study of Hindu Nationalism', *Hindustan Review* and *Kayastha Samachar*, Vol. VI, No. 3–4, September–October 1902, pp. 249–54.

———, 'Communalism and Nationalism', *The People*, 12 September 1926.

Renan, Ernest, 'Qu'est-ce qu'une nation?' [What is a Nation?], 1882 lecture.

Sri Aurobindo, Speech delivered in Bombay at the invitation of Bombay National Union, 19 January 1907.

Tilak, Bal Gangadhar, Speech delivered in Ahmednagar, 31 May 1916.

Web Sources

Abhinav Garg, 'HC sets aside EC disqualification of 20 AAP MLAs, asks for fresh hearing', *Times of India*, 24 March 2018.

Ankur Bhardwaj, 'WhatsApp To Block Numbers Which Spread Misinformation During Elections: Report', *Inc42*, 13 April 2019.

Anupam Saraph, 'Is this my vote?', *Frontline*, 24 May 2019.

Arundhati Roy, 'India: Intimations of an Ending', *The Nation*, 22 November 2019.

Ashutosh Varshney, 'A new RSS?', *Indian Express*, 5 October 2018.

Asit Ranjan Mishra, 'NSC members resign after row over NSSO employment report', *Live Mint*, 30 January 2019.

Bhanu Dhamija, 'Why Ambedkar Didn't Like India's Constitution', *The Quint*, 14 April 2018.

Billy Perrigo, 'How Volunteers for India's Ruling Party Are Using WhatsApp to Fuel Fake News Ahead of Elections', *Time*, 25 January 2019.

BIBLIOGRAPHY

C. Rajagopalachari, 'Claims of Hindi Examined', *Swarajya*, 1 February 1968.

'Rajaji in 1968: "Hindi Is, At Best, The Language Of A Large Minority"', *Swarajya*, 14 September 2016. <https://swarajyamag.com/from-the-archives/rajaji-in-1968-hindi-is-at-best-the-language-of-a-large-minority>

Deeksha Bhardwaj, 'A brief history of the cats of Kilkenny & why they were linked to CBI's internal feud', *The Print*, 6 December 2018.

Devesh Kapur, 'Modi's India is Aspirational, Assertive—and Anti-elite', *Washington Post*, 29 May 2019.

Dhananjay Mahapatra, 'Gen VK Singh loses battle for age, tries to save some honour', *Times of India*, 11 February 2012.

D. P., Bhattacharya, 'Key members from Narendra Modi's government in Gujarat take crucial positions at Centre', *Economic Times*, 5 November 2014.

ET Online, 'Here is the full text of RBI's deputy governor Viral V Acharya's speech in Mumbai', *Economic Times*, 27 October 2018.

———, 'Urjit Patel resigns as RBI Governor', *Economic Times*, 11 December 2018.

Express Web Desk, 'Defence forces work best in a secular environment, should be kept away from politics, says Army chief', *Indian Express*, 6 December 2017.

'Fake Picture of Rahul Gandhi "Meeting" Pulwama Attacker Goes Viral', *The Quint*, 15 February 2019.

Fukuyama, Francis, 'America: the failed state', *Prospect Magazine*, 13 December 2016.

Fussman, Gérard, 'History of India and Greater India', Himalayan and Central Asian Civilizations. First European Colloquium of the European Society for the Study of Himalayan and Central Asian Civilizations, 27–28 April 2009, pp. 24–25. <https://doi.org/10.4000/lettre-cdf.756>

Gautam Bhatia, 'The Troubling Legacy of Chief Justice Ranjan Gogoi', *The Wire*, 16 March 2020.

———, 'Citizenship and the Constitution', Yale University Law School paper, 17 April, 2020. <https://papers.ssrn.com/sol3/papers.cfm?abstract_id=3565551>

Harsh Mander, 'A moment for civilisational introspection', *The Hindu*, 30 May 2020.

Ian Straughn, 'ARCH0650: Islamic Civilizations: The Formative Periods', Course, Joukowsky Institute for Archaeology and the Ancient World. <https://www.brown.edu/Departments/Joukowsky_Institute/courses/islamiccivilizations/7966.html>

IANS, 'If There Is Electricity In Ramzan, It Should Also Be There On Diwali, Says Modi In UP', *Huffpost*, 19 February 2017.

Joanna Slater, 'What's behind the "potentially catastrophic" fight at India's central bank', *Washington Post*, 12 December 2018.

Jonathan Davis and Andy Hollis, 'Theresa May's Brexit speech had shades of Hitler', Letters, *The Guardian*, 12 October 2018.

Kanishk Tharoor, 'Cosmopolis: The past through a distilled lens', *Hindu Business Line*, 31 December 2019.

Lydia Walker, 'Fifty years on, Jayaprakash Narayan's views on Kashmir hold pointers for the present crisis', *Scroll.in*, 28 September 2019.

BIBLIOGRAPHY

Mansoor Iqbal, 'WhatsApp Revenue and Usage Statistics (2020)', *Business of Apps*, 24 April 2020. <http://www.businessofapps.com/data/whatsapp-statistics/>

Maroof Raza, '1965 War: A Tale of War and Three Brothers', *Open*, 27 August 2015.

Milan Sharma, 'Was sidelined, govt not releasing job figures, says National Statistics Commission chief PC Mohanan on why he quit', *India Today*, 30 January 2019.

Milan Vaishnav and Jamie Hintson, 'The Dawn of India's Fourth Party System', *Carnegie Endowment for International Peace*, Paper, 5 September 2019. <*https://bit.ly/2Sf7DV4*>

Monobina Gupta, "The Legacy of a Different CEC," *The Wire*, 6 May 2019.

Most Patriotic Countries 2020. <https://worldpopulationreview.com/countries/most-patriotic-countries/>

Mukul Dube, 'Read what VD Savarkar wrote: Care for cows, do not worship them', *Scroll.in*, 20 October 2015.

Nilakantan R. S., 'How the 14th Finance Commission punishes Tamil Nadu', *The Wire*, 21 April 2017.

———, 'The 15th Finance Commission May Split Open Demographic Fault Lines Between South and North India', *The Wire*, 15 February 2018.

———, 'The Economics and Politics Behind Dravida Nadu or South Indian Sub-Nationalism', *The Wire*, 20 March 2018.

———, 'Fifteenth Finance Commission and the Muddied Financial Response to COVID-19', *The Wire*, 6 April 2020.

Niraja Gopal Jayal, 'What Happens to Democracy When It Abandons Liberalism', *The Wire*, 7 June 2018.

Nyshka Chandran, 'India is about to get its 3rd central bank governor in 3 years. Markets are concerned', *CNBC*, 11 December 2018.

Pradeep Chhibber, 'For Modi and Amit Shah, the word "Hindu" is devoid of a moral compass. It's just us vs them', *The Print*, 17 December 2019.

Prasanna Mohanty, 'GDP base year row: What's the problem with re-basing India's growth calculations', *Business Today*, 13 November 2019.

Pratap Bhanu Mehta, 'We might enter an 'RSS meets Jio' ideological world', *Indian Express*, 1 May 2019.

———, 'A hundred days on, Modi 2.0: Its purpose is the show of power, nationalist fervour, social control', *Indian Express*, 10 September 2019.

———, 'Serial authoritarianism picks out targets one by one, and tires out challenges', *Indian Express*, 10 October 2019.

———, 'The Delhi darkness: Our rulers want an India that thrives on cruelty, fear, division, violence', *Indian Express*, 29 February 2020.

———, 'The Gogoi betrayal: Judges will not empower you, they are diminished men", *Indian Express*, 20 March 2020.

PTI, 'Karnataka elections 2018: Congress celebrating jayantis of Sultans for vote bank politics, says PM Modi', *Live Mint*, 6 May 2018.

———, 'Govt has spent over Rs 5,200 cr in ads since 2014–15: Rathore in LS', *Economic Times*, 13 December 2018.

BIBLIOGRAPHY

————, 'Those indulging in arson "can be identified by their clothes": Narendra Modi on anti-CAA protest', *Economic Times*, 15 December 2019.

Puja Mehra, 'Rajan's tenure extension opposed', *The Hindu*, 17 May 2016.

R. Rajagopalan, 'Elevation of Gujarat cadre IAS officers to top posts stirs a hornet's nest', *The Federal*, 17 April 2020.

Rajmohan Gandhi, 'Patel wanted Hyderabad for India, not Kashmir–but Junagadh was the wild card that changed the game', Scroll.in, 27 June 2018.

Rakesh Vuppu, 'Shashi Tharoor didn't say that he will even hit the Shivling with a chappal, if needed, to oust Modi', *Factly*, 26 April 2019.

Rezaul H. Laskar, 'If you knock at midnight, I will respond: PM Modi to Muslim leaders', *Hindustan Times*, 3 June 2015.

Rohan Venkataramakrishnan, 'Who is linking Citizenship Act to NRC? Here are five times Amit Shah did so', Scroll.in, 20 December 2019.

Ross Colvin and Satarupa Bhattacharjya, 'A "caged parrot"—Indian judge describes top police agency', Reuters, 10 May 2013.

Samar Halarnkar, 'Why the slow drip of anti-Muslim poison in India is now a flood', Scroll.in, 10 April 2020.

Samarth Bansal and Kiran Garimella, 'Fighting fake news: Decoding "fact-free" world of WhatsApp', *Hindustan Times*, 5 March 2019.

Sanjay Pandey, 'If Cong, SP have faith in Ali, we have Bajrang Bali', *Deccan Herald*, 10 April 2019.

Sanya Dhingra, 'In Modi govt, just 4% of IAS officers are from Gujarat cadre, but they hold the key posts', *The Print*, 4 October 2018.

Saumya Tewari, 'How Smart, Viral Content Helped BJP Trump Congress on Social Media', *Live Mint*, 4 June 2019.

Sharik Laliwala, 'During the Quit India Movement, the Hindu Mahasabha Played the British Game', *The Wire*, 8 August 2018.

Shashi Tharoor, 'The cat is finally out of the bag: Hindutva leaders' utter disdain for the Indian Constitution', *The Print*, 26 December 2017.

Shivam Shankar Singh, 'India's WhatsApp election', *National Herald*, 18 March 2019.

Shoaib Daniyal, 'Why Army Chief Rawat's Comments Should Worry All Indians Who Care About Democracy', Scroll.in, 22 February 2018.

Sidharth Bhatia, 'The Simple, and Simplistic, Messaging of Modi's Lectures Is a Big Hit With His Audience" *The Wire*, 30 May 2020.

Sruthisagar Yamunan, 'By sending the CBI director on leave, the Centre has stretched the law to its limits', Scroll.in, 24 October 2018.

Suhas Palshikar, 'Towards Hegemony: BJP Beyond Electoral Dominance', *Economic and Political Weekly, Vol.* 53, No. 33, 18 August 2018, pp. 36–42.

————, 'An eerie quiet', *The Indian Express*, 1 April 2020.

Sunil Prabhu, 'PM Narendra Modi's 'Aurangzeb Raj' Dig As Rahul Gandhi Set To Become Congress Chief', NDTV, 4 December 2017.

Supriya Shrinate, 'Urjit Patel's resignation is a note of protest: Raghuram Rajan', *Economic Times*, 11 December 2018.

BIBLIOGRAPHY

Swapan Dasgupta, 'Hindus and Muslims are no longer talking to each other in New India', *The Telegraph*, 22 August 2019.

Swati Chaturvedi, 'All the Prime Minister's Men', *The Wire*, 9 May 2018.

Tavleen Singh, 'PM Modi's real "parivartan" has gone almost unobserved because of India's new elite', *Indian Express*, 24 November 2019.

————, 'There is more repression in the air than at any other time except during the Emergency', *Indian Express*, 8 March 2020.

TNN, 'Pakistan working with Congress to beat BJP in Gujarat polls: PM', *Times of India*, 11 December 2017.

Venkatesh Upadhyay, 'The BJP's mobile phone strategy', *Live Mint*, 16 September 2013.

Vijaita Singh, 'ECI decision to not announce Gujarat poll dates surprises former CEC S.Y. Quarishi', *The Hindu*, 12 October 2017.

Web Desk, 'Hindus minority in Wayanad, so Rahul Gandhi picked it, says PM Modi', *India Today*, 6 April 2019.

Will Dahlgreen, 'Patriotism in Britain reduces with each generation', *YouGov*, 14 July 2015. <https://yougov.co.uk/topics/politics/articles-reports/2015/07/14/decline-british-patriotism>

Legal Citations

1. Dr. Rajendra Prasad Agarwal vs Union Of India And Another on 18 May1993. Equivalent citations: AIR 1993 All 258.

2. As far as the National Anthem Case there are two citations, one the case in India and the case on the basis of which the Judgment was factually delivered.
   Court relied on decision of the High Court of Australia in Adelaide Company of Jehovah's Witness v. Commonwealth, (1943) 67 C.L.R 116.
   Bijoe Emmanuel & Ors vs State Of Kerala & Ors on 11 August 1986.
   Equivalent citations: 1987 AIR 748, 1986 SCR (3) 518.

3. Shah Bano Case—Ahmed Khan v. Shah Bano Begum [1985 (1) SCALE 767 = 1985 (3) SCR 844 = 1985 (2) SCC 556 = AIR 1985 SC 945].

4. Babri Masjid—Dr. M. Ismail Faruqui Etc, Mohd. ... vs Union Of India And Others on 24 October 1994.
   Equivalent citations: AIR 1995 SC 605 A.

5. Case on Sedition—Kedar Nath Singh vs State Of Bihar on 20 January 1962.
   Equivalent citations: 1962 AIR 955, 1962 SCR Supl. (2) 769.

6. Iltija vs Union Of India on 26 February 2020.
   Writ Petition(s)(Criminal) No(s). 81/2020.

INDEX

INDEX

INDEX

INDEX

INDEX

INDEX

INDEX

Wilde, Oscar, 41

World Bank, 6

World Trade Organization, 6, 7, 56

World Value Survey, 194

World War I, 4, 30, 47, 49

World War II, 4, 5, 37, 43, 46, 47, 53, 58, 120, 309

xenophobia, 9, 44, 67, 71, 185

Yugoslav Federation, 30

Zaehner, R. C., 115

Zamorin of Calicut, 12, 80

Zionist movement, 51